Harvard Studies in Urban History

Series Editors:
STEPHAN THERNSTROM
CHARLES TILLY

The Making of Urban Europe
1000–1950

PAUL M. HOHENBERG

LYNN HOLLEN LEES

Harvard University Press
Cambridge, Massachusetts, and London, England

Library of Congress Cataloging in Publication Data

Hohenberg, Paul M.
  The making of urban Europe, 1000–1950.
  (Harvard studies in urban history)
  Bibliography: p.
  Includes index.
  1. Urbanization—Europe—History.   2. Cities and
towns—Europe—Growth—History.   3. Urban economics—
History.   I. Lees, Lynn Hollen.   II. Titile.   III. Series.
HT131.H38   1985   307.7'6'094   84-25333
ISBN 0-674-54360-2 (CLOTH)
ISBN 0-674-54361-0 (PAPER)

12.30

69378

I will tell the story as I go along of small cities no less than of great. Most of those which were great once are small today; and those which in my own lifetime have grown to greatness, were small enough in the old days.

HERODOTUS

Preface

URBANIZATION must be approached from a number of disciplinary perspectives. We make no claim to having done them all justice. First and foremost, this is a study in economic and social history. As for other disciplines, we stress two and give lesser emphasis to three more. Demography offers the most reliable and systematic access to the mass of urban dwellers and others on whom urbanization has impinged, particularly in the relatively distant past. Geography allows us to marry a sense of space to the historian's feel for time and adds a nice measure of concreteness to the social scientist's penchant for theorizing. By comparison, we give less attention to the politics, the culture, and the design of European cities, reflecting limitations of knowledge and of space but not, we hope, lack of awareness or appreciation.

A synthesis such as this one tries of necessity to cover too much. The study ranges over ten centuries and surveys the territory from Ireland to Constantinople and from Gibraltar to the Urals. The temporal scope of the work and its periodization will be explained later; our geographic scope demands some notice now. While we claim to analyze an entire continent, the boundaries we use shift over time. The medieval Europe we present virtually lacks those sections of the landmass held by Arabs, Byzantines, and Turks, as well as Slavic areas not yet linked by substantial trade to the West. Only as long-distance trade intensified the interconnections of East, West, North, and South does our Europe grow to meet the surrounding seas and mountains. In a sense, we use a functional definition that rests upon the linkages of Europe's cities, and we hope to show how the continent evolved along with the activities of its urban networks. Nonetheless, in the language of urban geography our Europe remains underbounded, meaning that we fail to give the peripheries their due. Most of our examples and references fall within a thousand-kilometer radius centered upon Strasbourg and passing through Newcastle, Warsaw, Naples, and Barcelona. We include areas beyond it in our analyses, but we do not give their special qualities systematic attention. To exclude them, however, would have meant the loss of important comparisons. Be aware that the particular urban histories of Finland and Macedonia, Andalusia and the Ukraine are largely ignored.

The attentive reader will no doubt discover our interpretations and value judgments. We like and admire cities, notably those of Europe and European inspiration. We wonder at the persistent vitality of the urban enterprise despite its fragility and the perils it has always faced. Time and time again, cities have fended off the Four Horsemen of the Apocalypse or risen from defeat. Trials punctuate urban history, from Viking sacks through Black Deaths and Great Fires to the agonies of Leningrad, Coventry, Guernica, Dresden, and Skopje in our own time. But cities are also prey to more subtle menaces. They must preserve a distinctive quality of life against fiscal exploitation and the corrosive forces of cultural uniformity and mass affluence; they must absorb unexpected floods of refugees and tame or challenge the spectacular follies of builders and civil engineers. The urban environment may often be polluted, violent, tawdry, or callous. Yet here great energies and high consciousness fashion the future while celebrating the past. Nor are the urban masses only toilers and victims in this historic function. Urbanization has brought opportunity to many, stimulation and decent security to most. Finally, we find much good in the urbanizing work of every epoch, including the industrial age and our own.

The more delicate question of an intellectual or methodological position remains. Though we are both American-trained and remain well within the mainstream of Anglo-American social science, we have been greatly influenced by the French historical school, notably by Fernand Braudel and his colleagues at the *Annales*. This is apparent in our emphases on structure and conjuncture and in the diversity of disciplinary perspectives we use. Our concentration upon ordinary people and everyday life, as well as our concern for long-run changes and durable patterns, also owes much to the work of Braudel. Our interpretations are our own, needless to say, and cannot be blamed upon Gallic master craftsmen or anyone else.

Circumstances, tastes, and comparative strengths have guided the shifting division of labor between the two authors. But this is a fully joint effort, as a whole and in its several parts. Each chapter reflects our collaboration. We actively share responsibility and, in general, editorial craftsmanship.

In earlier versions, parts of the book formed the substance of presentations by one or both authors to conferences of the Social Science History Association, Council on European Studies, American Historical Association, International Economic History Association, and European Study Group in Urban History, and of lectures and seminars in Bad Homburg, Germany, and at the University of Pennsylvania, Rensselaer Polytechnic Institute, Temple University, and North Carolina State University. We have benefited from comments by discussants and other participants. We have also discussed our ideas with students at the University of Pennsylvania and at Bennington College. We thank them for their help in the development of the book. The project was undertaken in 1977 in response to an overture by Charles Tilly, who has remained a lively, supportive presence through the long process of study, writing, and revision. His comments have been both provocative and constructive.

Many scholars on both sides of the Atlantic have helped, sometimes by spurring us to reconsider or sharpen arguments or to document them more fully. The following bare and incomplete listing should not be taken to imply perfunctory acknowledgment. We are grateful for the assistance of Maurice Aymard, Al Barr, Dora Crouch, Pierre Deyon, Robert DuPlessis, Martha Howell, Samuel Johnson, David Landes, Andrew Lees, Franklin Mendels, Edward Peters, Charles Rosenberg, Donald Vitaliano, Susan Watkins, and Martin Wolfe. Able and patient secretarial assistance was provided by B. J. Kaufmann and Kathy Keenan at RPI and by Ethel Cooley, Pat Gorman, Joan Plonski, and Valerie Riley at the University of Pennsylvania. The line drawings were done by the Division of Instructional Media at RPI with the participation of Bea Danneger and Hanspeter Kunz. We also appreciate the editorial assistance of Elizabeth Suttell and Janet Marantz.

Contents

Tables

Figures

The Making of Urban Europe, 1000–1950

INTRODUCTION

Urbanization in Perspective

IN A SINGLE MILLENNIUM Europe has become urban. A thousand
years ago the few towns north and west of Muslim and Byzantine
areas were either vestiges of the Roman past or embryos of urbanization to come. Their few inhabitants had a limited place in the
social order of the time. Today, by contrast, perhaps half the European population lives in substantial towns or large agglomerations, while another two or three out of ten lead lives that can only
be called urbanized in fact. In many regions of Europe the proportion is higher still; there urbanization is quite general, regardless
of how administrative distinctions label this or that group of people.
And forecasts call for ever larger conurbations, gargantuan mega-
lopolises that will stretch for hundreds of miles.

This profusion of cities and of city dwellers began centuries ago
in many regions. Indeed, most of the major towns in Europe today
were founded before 1300. Therefore, to study the development
of urban Europe requires a lengthy look backward in time. The
answers to many questions about the nature of contemporary European cities lie in the medieval period, not in the modern industrial
era.

During the past millennium individual cities have had long and
splendid histories. Sited at an important crossing point on the Danube, Vienna had become a fortified town and market by the early
twelfth century. An important trading center for merchants from
southern as well as eastern Europe, the city grew in political importance with its selection as a residence by the Babenberg and
Habsburg families. Crusaders met in Vienna before moving against
the Muslims, and nobles from the many Habsburg lands built urban

palaces there to be near the court. By the eighteenth century it was the capital of a multinational empire, a stunning city of baroque buildings, parks, and suburbs. While the saga of Vienna is particularly dramatic, each of Europe's cities has its own unique history. But studying them all is both impossible and ultimately nonproductive. Urban histories are inseparable from the histories of the economic, social, and political systems of which they are a part. Only a much larger focus than the city itself will reveal the urban role in Europe's past. To find the larger rhythms of urban growth and decline, of influence and independence, requires a different approach, one that traces common functions and structures. Urban development is not just the sum of many urban parts; it is a web of interconnections. To study cities effectively, one has to study urbanization.

Yet deciding just how to study urbanization poses problems. There is no agreement on a definition of the process, and scholars consequently examine vastly different things. Men such as V. Gordon Childe (1936) and Lewis Mumford (1961) have explored the origins of cities in the ancient Near East. Sociologists like Max Weber (1958) and Gideon Sjoberg (1960) reduce an array of urban places to ideal types in order to extract generality from diversity. Others focus on the implications of city life, caring more about what cities do to people than about the structural characteristics of the urban setting. Geographers take a rather dissimilar approach, seeing cities as spaces within which people and activities are located. The study of urbanization leads them to analyze the changing distributions of population, production, and networks of exchange. Taking another road, historians such as Mason Hammond (1972) see urbanization as the spread of cities over time and trace in essentially political terms the development of major cities and their regional importance. The list could go on and on.

But underlying this diversity is a series of rather simple questions. The answers admittedly are more complex, and often imprecise or nonexistent. Scholars studying cities have concentrated on three major topics. One focuses on the beginning. How and why did cities originate, and what characterized their early development? Answers are often speculative in regard to ancient cities because of the lack of written records, and archaeologists' digs uncover only a fraction of the material necessary to reconstruct the evolution of a complex community. A search for urban origins in Europe can,

however, yield much more concrete data because documents marking the foundation of cities are often available. It is not necessary
to speculate about warrior kings or the attracting power of shrines
when it is clear that a particular ruler founded a town, then granted
it a charter and market rights at a given date. Early maps and
drawings sometimes supplement the archaeological record, permitting a detailed reconstruction of urban spaces.

A second major interest guiding the study of urbanization is in
the activities taking place in cities, particularly those economic and
demographic processes that characterize urban populations. Cities
are seen as the sites of specific large-scale actions, as links in the
movement of people and goods. For us as well as for many other
scholars, these topics help to demarcate some of the most distinctive
and widely encountered qualities of European cities in the past,
and we accordingly give them much emphasis.

A third theme of urban scholarship arises from an awareness of
the social consequences of urban life. The recognition that cities
differ from rural communities has produced a vast literature tracing
the psychological and cultural effects of urban living. Do cities
foster crime, alienation, and deviance? Do they encourage independence, diversity, and initiative? Many would answer yes to one
or indeed both questions. Whether they picture cities in positive,
negative, or mixed terms, analysts generally agree on the fundamental importance of cities in shaping the life-styles and mental
life of their inhabitants.

Yet none of these three larger concerns captures precisely the
approach of this book, which is the history of the way Europe
urbanized. In presenting this story, we shall take note of the splendid traditions and terrible crises of individual cities and towns. But
we shall play off these captivating specific cases against an analysis
of the larger processes at work and of the relationships that evolved
between town and country, between city and city, and between
cities and the larger political entities around them.

Processes and Systems

On the most straightforward level, urbanization describes a shift
in the composition of the population. The fraction living in towns
grows in relation to the fraction that remains rural. In practice,
though not as a matter of logical necessity, the shift involves a flow

of people from rural to urban habitats. Even ignoring all the other influences and interactions, it is clear that urbanization is an ongoing activity that affects the country as well as the city. A key step in studying it is to identify important forces that drive the process. We shall focus on three—technology, demography, and markets— thereby linking the modes and factors of production and reproduction to the economic roles of cities. In feudal times cities were the sites of necessary exchanges of goods. Even primarily agricultural economies did not manage autarky. Later, growing long-distance trade and manufacturing gave urban elites added duties as organizers of production and suppliers of capital. In the heyday of merchant capitalism, cities pushed the boundaries of the world economy into new areas. Then, as Europe industrialized, mass production concentrated in the towns, which expanded the ability of cities to supply both goods and sites for exchange. As the European economy evolved, so did the urban role within it. We have tried to make explicit in later pages the connections we see between large economic and social processes and the microcosm of the cities.

Urbanization is more than the result of certain global forces acting on many individual towns and rural areas, however, even with due regard to variations in time and space. As urban places grow, they interact with their rural surroundings, with one another, and with larger sociopolitical units. Indeed, if there is a single defining characteristic of urban life, even in the most fiercely independent and secure city, it is dependence. Not only are the inhabitants interdependent, but the truly isolated city is both unviable and pointless. Unable to sustain itself, it would have no outlets for the fruits of specialization and complex organization. In the words of B. J. L. Berry, "Cities are systems within systems of cities" (1964:147).

We propose two models of such urban systems, and much of our analysis relies on them. The first model is based on the role of the city as a central place, supplying its surroundings with special services—economic, administrative, or cultural—that call for concentration at a point in space. A hierarchy of such centers, the higher-level ones serving as central places for central places, form a *region* around the principal center. The region, key to the relationships of town and country and to the hierarchical links among nearby towns, will receive much attention as we discuss *Central Place Systems* in Europe.

Yet cities are more than the points around which the threads of regional unity are wound. They also link the region with the world beyond, permitting it to reconcile the advantages of specialized activity with the enriching experience of diversity. In economic terms, cities enable the region to pursue its comparative advantage. In this perspective cities also belong to networks of trade, information, and influence that reach far beyond the borders of a country. As an example of the workings of a *Network System*, consider Bordeaux. To understand its activities, the reasons for its growth or stagnation, one cannot look at the city alone or merely at its role as the capital of a region of southwestern France, its influence bounded by that of Toulouse to the east and Nantes and Limoges to the north. Bordeaux has long been an important link in international trading networks along which flowed wine, of course, but also grain, fish, timber, sugar, and oil. To follow the city's fortunes we would need to look to London, to the Antilles or Africa, even to the Levant and the Baltic. Just as in analyzing regions we distinguish hierarchies of centers, so urban networks have their nodes and junctions, their gateways and outposts, their cores and peripheries.

To these largely economic discussions of the Central Place and the Network Systems, we need to add a political dimension. Nation-states and empires came to operate and to mediate between the regional and worldwide linkages of town to town. The relationship of cities to the development of centralized political power has been an ambivalent one, and we shall probe it. Urban elites have been both the allies and the enemies, the agents and the rivals, of monarchs. Urban offices have been a springboard to national power as well as centers of resistance to it. These relationships, to be sure, shift over time and vary among regions. Specifically, cities play a key role in an ongoing struggle that pits centralized nation-states— dynastic or republican, pluralistic or homogeneous, continental or colonial—against an alternative structure that gives greater weight to regional as well as transnational levels of power and loyalty. Until a generation ago the struggle in Europe seemed a very unequal one, but recent developments once again challenge the administrative hierarchy of centers and offer opportunities to regional capitals and world-oriented cities.

Wealth and power are not the only impulses that travel along the conduits linking city with city. Cultural messages pass as well, and cities have always served as centers of cultural transformation and transmission. The two types of urban system correspond fairly closely in this regard to the types postulated by Redfield and Singer (1954). In their scheme, cities are *orthogenetic* or *heterogenetic* according to whether they elaborate and diffuse the prevailing culture or one alien to their surroundings. As is true in the economic and political spheres, cultural leadership of either kind can be viewed as service or exploitation, opportunity or coercion. In the Central Place System, the cities codify local and regional variants of a common language and make possible a high tradition of education, literature, and organized thought expressed as French civilization or Germanic culture. But the diverse folk traditions and values of the regions can easily dissolve in the dominant national culture or come to be viewed as subversive of unity and progress. By contrast, the Network System accommodates continuing pluralism but within a clearly defined structure of dominance and dependence. The good burghers of seventeenth-century Amsterdam could rub elbows daily with Jewish and Genoese merchants, Huguenot and Puritan dissidents, Frisian and Flemish artisans, and slaves from the Indies, West and East. Among the babel of tongues and the kaleidoscope of faces and costumes, it remained, unquestionably, *their* city.

Thus, the two sorts of urban systems model contrasting modes of development, from the rural base upward in one case and from the urban core outward in the other. In one, the nation-state represents the culminating union of a group of regions whose people share a territory and an ethnic heritage. Centralization in network system development, on the other hand, results in the formation of an empire with more diverse components. The experience of most European countries shows both sorts of processes at work, implying that many cities, notably large ones, have a place in both sorts of systems. London is a case in point, as shown by the many entities of which it has been the acknowledged capital: England, Great Britain, the United Kingdom, the British Empire, the— sometimes British—Commonwealth. Think for a minute of the many visitors to London in the eighteenth century. For how many was it an inland voyage as opposed to one abroad? Samuel Johnson of Litchfield certainly felt at home; what of his Edinburgh friend Boswell, or Ben Franklin of Philadelphia? Would an Irishman feel less alien in London than a mulatto Jamaican, or more uprooted for that matter than a Cornishman or a Geordie? To postulate two models of urban systems is to affirm, not deny, the complexity and variety of the urban experience. If our exposition sometimes appears to reify these constructs, it is only a by-product of the search for economy and force of expression.

Major Phases of Urban Growth

The creation of an urban network in Europe has not been a steady, slow progression. Rather, long spurts of growth have alternated with times of stagnation and decline. These rhythms are widely observable, but not everywhere identical. Some regions were dotted with towns by the later eleventh century, while others urbanized only in the nineteenth or twentieth. Partly dependent upon the density of human settlement, city growth began early in the crowded river valleys of the Rhineland and northern Italy but late in the empty forests of Norway and in the Scottish highlands. In general, however, when population increased rapidly in more densely settled areas, so too did the number and size of cities. The long waves of population growth provided the human material for city building. A basic interdependence bound together people, production, and trade; urban activities and urbanites multiplied together.

While figures are few and unreliable for medieval times, demographers estimate that the European population rose from around 1000 to 1350, again less sharply from 1450 to 1650, and then increased explosively after 1750. The centuries from roughly 1350 to 1450 and 1650 to 1750 were times of overall decline or stagnation (Braudel 1979). The demographic engine therefore produced three periods when increasing numbers of people had to be accommodated by social and economic systems. The particular links among city growth, economic change, and population will be explored at length in later chapters, but for now it will be enough to show how urbanization mirrored the large rhythms of population size.

Not enough information is available on the entire range of medieval cities to construct an urbanization rate for Europe as a whole during the years from 1000 to 1500, but hearth tax returns, army recruitment figures, data on mortality, and the changing area inside city walls give clues to the sizes of individual towns. While the margin of error is no doubt high, the pace and magnitude of urban growth can be observed in the estimated sizes of some European provincial capitals. Lyon, Cologne, and Milan grew substantially from the eleventh century until sometime in the late Middle Ages (see Figure I.1). A common pattern of population declines, small increases, and periods of stability, albeit in fluctuating rhythms, marked the period between 1400 and 1800, when long-term growth resumed. Finally, as industrialization accelerated movement into the cities, their populations exploded.

The experience of countless other cities throughout Europe paralleled that of these three major towns. The eleventh, twelfth, and thirteenth centuries were generally times of accelerated city building and of increasing urbanization throughout western and central Europe. This trend reversed, however, with the dearths and plagues of the fourteenth century and then resumed only weakly and in-

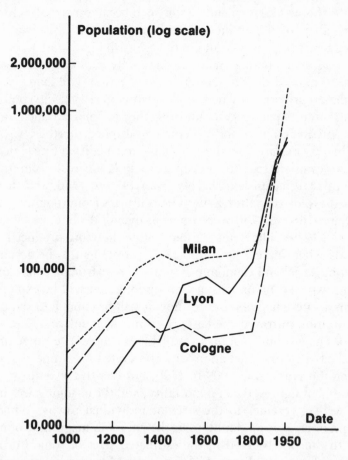

Figure I.1. The growth of provincial capitals, 1000–1950. (Data from Chandler and Fox 1974.)

termittently during the next three centuries. Paul Bairoch (1977) and Charles Tilly (1979) suggest that by 1500, in Europe outside of Russia, the proportion urban had reached 16 percent. After rising more, it then decreased somewhat to reach 13 percent in 1700 before rising slightly during the next century. The years between 1300 and 1800 saw in a variable mixture limited growth and decline. This pattern is echoed in so many sources that it seems a reasonable proxy for the general progress of urbanization in Europe since the later Middle Ages. We therefore picture European urbanization as a three-stage process of growth, trendless fluctuation, and renewed growth, each phase dependent upon the interactions of demography, technology, and markets. Their interwoven patterns of change link human settlements with modes of production and exchange.

Of course, the pattern varied somewhat among regions and types of cities. The epidemics of the fourteenth century affected northern and western Europe more severely than eastern areas. Population growth continued in Poland through the fourteenth and fifteenth centuries, only to retreat around 1550. Although in the northern Netherlands growth and urbanization continued strongly through the seventeenth century, in France population decreases set in after 1630 or 1640 (Pounds 1979). On the other hand, in England many county towns and smaller settlements underwent periods of demographic decline in the early and mid-sixteenth century and then again after 1600. London and other major ports were virtually untouched by economic difficulties at these times and continued to grow, except in times of plague (Clark and Slack 1976).

The forces shaping urbanization prior to the nineteenth century not only changed in intensity over time but were partially reversible in nature. Specific cities grew and then shrank because of wars, plagues, and economic troubles. Regensburg, the largest city in central Europe in the eleventh century and the meeting place for the Diet of the Holy Roman Empire, nonetheless declined by 1700 into a sleepy market town and residence for ambassadors from the various German states. Now a living museum of medieval urban architecture, Bruges was Europe's second or third largest city around 1400 because of its leading role in textile production and commerce. Rome, once the center of urban life in Europe, shrank to a fraction of its maximum size when its empire collapsed. The rhythm of urban population growth and decline mirrors the changing importance of specific cities in the European urban network. Although few towns of any size disappeared after the urban revival of the eleventh century, the relative importance of cities has shifted greatly with the patterns of political and economic development.

Since the year 1000 the location and identities of dominant cities have changed regularly. While not an ideal proxy for political and economic influence, relative population size helps to measure a city's attractiveness to outsiders and the size of its economic base. A list of Europe's largest cities during the past thousand years, along with what we know about general patterns of political and economic development, reveals regular shifts in the hierarchy of major cities both within and among political units (see Table I.1). In A.D. 1000 most cities in western and central Europe were tiny, with the exception of the capitals of the Byzantine Empire and the Umayyad Caliphate in Spain. Virtually all the sizable cities bordered the Mediterranean. The real centers of the European urban world lay to the south and east in the territories of the Muslim and Byzantine rulers. Only Italy had an urban network that included several big towns. By 1400 this pattern had changed decisively. Muslim control of Spain and Byzantine influence in the eastern Mediterranean were virtually ended, leading to the decline of both Constantinople and Cordoba. The major Italian cities had increased in size, Genoa and Milan quickly reaching the top ranks of an urban hierarchy. The growing importance of the Low Countries and their cloth production is reflected in the enormous growth of Bruges and Ghent. Meanwhile, the growing strength of the kingdom of France and the importance of Paris as a university town, national capital, and trading center catapulted that city to the leading position in the urban network of northwestern Europe. No longer was European urbanization wholly centered on the Mediterranean. By 1700 several different places, most of them political capitals, had become major European cities. The growing power of the Ottoman Empire, Portugal's colonial successes, and the commercial triumphs of English and Dutch merchants are reflected in the rapid development of Constantinople, Moscow, Lisbon, London, and Amsterdam. The fast-growing cities in Europe were increasingly located now in the north and west. This dominance of northern areas became even more marked by 1900, when industrial development helped to create conurbations and metropolises whose citizens numbered in the millions. Industrial towns like Manchester, Birmingham, and Glasgow, tiny in 1700, became larger than Rome had been at the height

Table I.1. The largest cities in Europe, 1000–1900 (population in thousands).

1000		1400		1700		1900	
City	Population	City	Population	City	Population	City	Population
Constantinople	450	Paris	275	Constantinople	700	London	6,480
Cordoba	450	Milan	125	London	550	Paris	3,330
Seville	90	Bruges	125	Paris	530	Berlin	2,424
Palermo	75	Venice	110	Naples	207	Vienna	1,662
Kiev	45	Granada	100	Lisbon	188	St. Petersburg	1,439
Venice	45	Genoa	100	Amsterdam	172	Manchester	1,255
Regensburg	40	Prague	95	Rome	149	Birmingham	1,248
Thessalonika	40	Rouen	70	Venice	144	Moscow	1,120
Amalfi	35	Seville	70	Moscow	130	Glasgow	1,072
Rome	35	Ghent	70	Milan	124	Liverpool	940

Source: Chandler and Fox (1974:11–20, 330).

of its empire. Throughout Europe, however, political capitals, especially those that managed to combine industrial development with their political functions, joined the list of urban giants.

A Functional View

The complexity of the European regional pattern of urban population growth and city dominance over time highlights the difficulties of using a purely demographic criterion for urbanization. When all population statistics are of dubious accuracy and when both urban and rural areas undergo mixed and moderate phases of expansion and decline, it becomes particularly difficult to decide whether a region is becoming more urban or less so. It is possible, moreover, for substantial amounts of urban population growth to be occurring in a specific part of an urban network, or indeed in all its cities, while the rural population still increases faster than the urban. Does it make sense in those cases to say that a society or a region is becoming less urban?

In both the mid-sixteenth and early seventeenth centuries in England, urban growth was largely confined to London and a few other cities. Most of the county towns and provincial capitals stagnated in size, even though the sixteenth century was a time of relatively high fertility and population growth (Clark and Slack 1976). In demographic terms cities probably decreased in importance during these two periods, but at the same time the influence of London was clearly increasing. The political dominance of the capital under the Tudor monarchs, the economic influence of the port along with its trading companies and merchants, and regularly high levels of migration to and from London meant that more and more people were experiencing life in the capital city (Wrigley 1969). A series of large-scale activities centered in London and mediated by the network of towns in fact affected the whole country in relatively systematic and intensive ways. At least for the early seventeenth century the scale of these activities was such that it warrants a judgment, based on functional criteria, of increasing urbanization in England, even if by demographic standards only a mixed pattern of urban growth can be discerned. Adding alternative approaches to demographic analyses can help to solve this problem.

Many people, particularly planners and geographers, view cities as parts of a network organized for the exchange of people, goods, and information. The spatial approach to urbanization has also yielded rich results when applied to single cities, for example, in the hands of Kevin Lynch (1960), who has analyzed the changing physical forms of cities and their arrangement in space with an eye toward discovering optimal designs for the cities of the future. Geographers such as Harold Carter (1966) and Alan Pred (1980) have shed new light on urban systems through their maps of the functional hierarchies that link towns in regional networks. Another major focus of the locational approach to cities has been through the historical study of urban economies. Eric Lampard (1954) traces the many connections between economic efficiency and urbanization, which he sees as a way of ordering a population to promote specialization and efficiency. Economic processes become central, therefore, in defining urban functions. Although he gives primary emphasis to the city building of the past two hundred years, Lampard's perspective also applies to medieval and early modern cities. His vision of towns as centers for specialization and differentiation captures a universal property of the city. For centuries European towns have grouped functionally integrated and specialized types of people whose occupations and social roles differed from those of rural dwellers. Following Lampard's lead, we will emphasize the special activities that take place in cities. Tracing the links among cities produced by those activities turns the study of urbanization away from mere population toward the study of process, a richer and more complicated inquiry. The study of cities requires shifts of perspective. Answers to those perennial questions—where, why, when, how, and so what?—will force the seeker to alter his or her point of view to accommodate the varying insights of several disciplines and the multitude of urban experiences that we will seek to order and to illuminate.

PART ONE

The Preindustrial Age:
Eleventh to Fourteenth Centuries

Men, thinly scattered, make a shift, but a bad
shift, without many things . . . It is being
concentrated which produces high
convenience.   BOSWELL, *Life of Johnson*

O UR NOTIONS of the origins of cities are clothed in myth and fantasy. King Lear supposedly founded Leicester, and Athena was said to have watched over the early days of Athens. Tales of divine inspiration and heroic beginnings have given shape to countless urban pasts as cities have sought to strengthen their sense of community and civic pride by finding—or fashioning—a shared tradition. Urban theorists of more recent periods make the same sort of imaginative leaps, even if the cast of mythological characters is more mundane and abstract. Lewis Mumford (1961) sees the ancestors of urban institutions in the graves and caves of paleolithic peoples and in the transformation of the role of hunter into that of king. When the cultures of the Neolithic village and the Paleolithic hunting band fused, he suggests, cities were born. Other institutions of early towns provide pegs for alternative theories of urban origins: Fustel de Coulanges (1864) pointed to the establishment of common centers for tribal religious worship, while others have stressed fortresses or the legal arrangements that produced civic corporations with their own laws and courts.

Clearly, many common needs have encouraged people to band together in towns. Yet an interest in self-defense and in religious ritual can be satisfied without the construction of permanent settlements. Whatever the political and spiritual pressures that foster cities, they can persist only if large communities are economically viable. At the most basic level, cities are sizable settlements of people most of whom do not grow food. They depend, therefore, on the surplus created by food growers elsewhere. At the same basic level, all output beyond what is required to sustain the food growers and furnish seed for the next crop can be defined as surplus. The existence of this surplus, along with a mechanism for transferring it to the city, makes urban life possible. If, in addition, the city provides goods or services in return for the food, urban life has a good chance of lasting. It becomes likely as well as possible.

Cities of the ancient Near East flourished on the economic gains of a technology that increased agricultural productivity and eased the transportation of goods and raw materials. Later, Greeks and

Romans with their more sophisticated tools and ships built towns throughout the Mediterranean basin and supported them with the gains from trade and with taxes. In ancient times, however, intensive urbanization in Europe was limited to lands easily reached by ship from the core of the urban network in the eastern Mediterranean. The Rhine and the Danube marked the effective limits of Roman colonization in central Europe, and both England and northern Gaul (France) had only small urban populations. Even at the height of Roman imperial strength, most towns housed no more than a few hundred people, many of whom farmed nearby land. Although Roman urbanization looked impressively vast and well ordered, the system was deeply flawed by an imbalance between its sophisticated mechanisms for collecting surplus and its relative neglect of production. Whether on rural estates or in urban shops, most of the work was done by slaves. Technology was generally neglected apart from some triumphs of civil engineering. The urban population could not be further expanded or even protected from external shocks without major changes in productivity. But before any such changes could take place, the Roman network of cities unraveled under the pressure of civil strife and Germanic raids. Early losses undermined the surplus-gathering system, making the decline cumulative. People retreated to villas and villages in the countryside, and towns shrank or disappeared. Sites with impressive theaters, aqueducts, baths, and basilicas remained, yet they housed at best a much reduced population. As Edith Ennen argues, "The distinctively urban way of life with its special contributions to civilization had not survived" (1979:33). Towns in ancient times could not outlive the political system that had commandeered the surpluses of the countryside on their behalf.

The next wave of European urbanization rested on a stronger technological and agricultural base. From the sixth to the eighth centuries, another set of discoveries revolutionized northern agriculture, bringing new prosperity to peasants from the Atlantic to the Dnieper. Simple inventions like the heavy plow, the horseshoe, and the horse collar combined with changes in agrarian organization to permit more intensive food production and thus generate sizable and regular surpluses (White 1972). It took at least two further centuries to establish this economic base; outside invaders certainly slowed the process, although they also contributed to diffusion and to early currents of exchange.

Eventually, rising productivity encouraged population growth and a move away from autarky on manorial estates, and tried and true methods of surplus transfer—trade, plunder, and tribute—redistributed output, making it possible to support more nonproducers of food who could relocate to central places. The hierarchical society of kings, warriors, priests, merchants, artisans, and serfs grew in complexity. There was more and more incentive to gather in towns for the purpose of improving production and distribution. Towns could provide links to serve the different orders of the society. Knights in isolated castles wanted armor, war-horses, and harnesses. Nobles sought spices and sumptuous fabrics. Even peasants, all but the most downtrodden, could buy cloth, salt, pots, or tools not locally made. Kings and churchmen had elaborate wishes and requirements that only distant producers could satisfy. The combination of increasing wealth and occupational specialization bred trade and stimulated further growth in output. And the system was extending to newly cleared lands at the inner and outer margins of the settled areas.

All this sounds like the familiar story of economic development; yet the economic order of medieval Europe was not that of the twentieth century on a miniature scale. In contrast to the current market system, even as modified by government intervention, the economy of medieval cities must be called resolutely precapitalistic. The citizens differed in important ways from the model of unrestrained economic man. In the economic sphere the prevailing values, rules, and practices were structured to protect a vulnerable, fledgling system of production at the sacrifice of maximum progress or profit. Conditions of work and trade were regulated by local communities, by temporal and spiritual local lords, and internally by associations of masters. In most places artisans retained control of the means of production within the guild rules; wage work was the exception. With fragmented and limited markets, it was natural that trading profits should be curbed by custom and by restrictions on usury.

Urban communities measured economic and individual goals against a series of social, political, and spiritual yardsticks on which tradition and common needs ranked high. Nonetheless, towns stand out as islands of secular rationality and materialism in medieval society. The urban order remained subordinate to the hierarchical agrarian regimes that stretched across Europe. Despite its limitations, the feudal mode of production generated the surpluses that supported urbanization. Politically, landed elites asserted power in and over the multiplying cities, although they increasingly could not do without these subjects. Cities offered to both the elites and the masses goods and services that were soon found indispensable, and in the process became significant autonomous political actors in the power struggles of the Middle Ages. Although always secondary in the political and social spheres, cities played an integral role even outside the core areas in northern Italy and the Low Countries, in the feudal societies of England, southern Italy, and what would become France and western Germany. Lords founded towns to consolidate their control over a region. Kings used urban wealth and literacy to reinforce the claims of royal authority against rebellious vassals. The church, whose bishops had sustained what urban continuity there was with ancient times, made towns the centers of religious ritual and education. Medieval modes of rule, thought, and production required cities, although spiritual and temporal elites fought to keep the subversive urban orders dependent and under control. Even the pastoral societies at the fringes of the European continent developed central places that filled urban functions, while in the limited core cities actually contested for dominance.

Medieval urbanization flourished in the long period of expansion between roughly 1000 and 1300, and longer in eastern Europe. We will explore the results of this long wave of city building, moving from an analysis of particular cities—their shape, size, and social makeup—to a more theoretical discussion of the linkages between town and countryside and among cities. The generations who lived in towns or produced for them also merit our attention. Urban populations came to constitute a sizable minority; the vital processes by which their numbers evolved help us to capture the human dimension of urbanization on a macroscopic level. In the demographic sphere, too, town and country remained distinct while interacting in substantive ways. The country dweller arriving in town—for a day, a year, or a lifetime—can serve as the microscopic focus and symbol for the still open historical questions that early urbanization raises.

Our primary subjects are the thousands of urban settlements that developed across the vast European landscape, and we will view them and their people from several perspectives. First, the reader will be invited to take an essentially static look at the physical and social organization of towns, along with their economic, political, and social roles. Then, a dynamic picture of urban development will attempt to lay bare the workings of early urban systems. Cities were not autarkic communities and so must be depicted complete with the linkages that ensured their survival and expansion. We will investigate the factors that made some sites evolve into cities while similar ones remained small and without influence. Our hope is to uncover the beginnings of an urban dynamic that has persisted into contemporary times. If we leave population questions, including migration, until last, it is mainly to stress that European urbanization was not simply the result of population growth, let alone a way of relieving human pressure on the supply of land. The concurrent increase of population and its urban share depended on complex processes for which the concept of economic surplus offers the beginnings of an explanation.

CHAPTER 1

The Structures and Functions
of Medieval Towns

BY THE YEAR 1100 thousands of towns dotted the hills and plains of the European landscape. The shores of the Mediterranean sheltered an array of ports: Amalfi, Genoa, Narbonne. Urban revival was marked in France and in Lombardy, where many towns grew on the sites of Roman settlements, and the Moorish cities of southern Spain were large and prosperous. Flanders too was becoming urbanized as craftsmen and traders settled around local castles and monasteries, particularly in areas where the cloth industry was developing. Dozens of fortress cities had been founded in Kievan Russia. Although only a tiny proportion of the European population lived in cities in the eleventh century, recognizably urban places were flourishing out to the Celtic fringes of the northwest and the Slavic lands of the east.

What distinguished towns in the Middle Ages from the villages, estates, and manorial settlements that covered much of the European plain? Mumford (1961) has given us two images of the medieval town: the container and the magnet. Towns attracted and secured their population, drew and held them. A much older symbol for the city is a cross enclosed in a circle. As Lopez points out, the "crossroads within the wall" embodies a paradox: the city closes itself off from the rural environment in order to enlarge the scope and intensity of communication with the wider world (1963:27). The duality of the urban experience, its harmonies and contradictions, will be a persistent theme in our discussion. Economically, towns depended on and contributed to a feudal system of production while developing apart from it. This ambiguity extended also across the political and cultural realms and was central to the town's place in medieval society.

What sorts of settlements could be called towns in the year 1100? Functional definitions of medieval urbanness are more useful than ones formulated merely in terms of size, because the economic and political organization of cities set them apart so markedly from the surrounding countryside. Max Weber (1958), who produced one of the most important typologies of cities, offered two criteria. When seen in economic terms, cities are markets strongly oriented toward the consumption of goods, which they derive from production or trade. This characteristic he applied to non-Western as well as to ancient or medieval towns. But European cities, Weber argued, had a second set of attributes that arose from their particular political institutions. They very early became communities with a territorial base as a result of fraternal organizations, courts, laws, and at least partial autonomy and self-administration. These qualities sharply demarcated Western cities from Asiatic ones, which lacked both autonomy and communal legal arrangements. Following Weber, we view medieval towns as relatively dense settlements having a distinctive economic and political organization. A few scholars, notably Sjoberg (1960), have challenged Weber's assertion of Western uniqueness by pointing out common structural characteristics of preindustrial cities in many places and times. But it seems to us highly misleading to lump together ancient, Middle Eastern, and Asian cities with those of medieval Europe. Although preindustrial cities were usually small, run by elites, and organized into household units dominated by adult males, enormous differences in political orders, technologies, culture, and geography can easily be discerned. Just as there is no one industrial town, there was and is no single preindustrial city. Differences in spatial and social organization, administrative relations to a central government, and urban culture doom the attempt to find the lowest common denominator among Augustan Rome, Uruk, medieval Damascus, Bruges, and Xian. Superficial similarities of economic organization and function do not compensate for widely varying political, social, and cultural arrangements. Finally, cities change over time; history adds another dimension of difference.

An English Provincial Town

Let us look at one medieval city in detail: Leicester in the East Midlands of England.[1] In the first century A.D. a Roman army built a fort at the place where one of their major roads, the Fosse Way, crossed the river Soar. A civilian settlement complete with walls, forum, basilica, and baths was later added when the town was made the administrative capital of the area settled by a tribe called the Coritani. Little is known of the town in the fifth and sixth centuries, but enough survived to permit a Christian bishop to use it as the capital of his diocese in the seventh. Later, when the Anglo-Saxon kingdom of England was divided into counties, Leicester was made the capital of Leicestershire, a position it still holds. After the Norman Conquest, the town's regional importance continued to increase. A castle was ordered built by King William, and by 1086 the town had 6 churches, 378 houses, and a population of probably 2,000.

The map reveals how the medieval town was shaped by its antecedents. Its walls followed the outlines of the Roman settlement, their four gates marking the entry of the major east-west and north-south streets that bisected the central space. Flanked to the west by the river Soar, the town was enclosed by woods on the north and by open fields owned by the bishop of Lincoln and major Norman families on the other sides. Leicester by the mid-thirteenth century was divided into nine parishes and dotted with churches, hospitals, and houses of religious orders that were scarce only in the poorer northern section. Merchants carried on the city's commerce in market areas in the southeast and near the central high cross. Butchers' shambles lay in the west near the Soar and around the Saturday marketplace. Unlike many Italian towns, Leicester had no central square flanked by a town hall and church, and no cathedral spire dominated the skyline. Beautifully crafted public and religious buildings were present but scattered about in a random fashion. The town hall, originally the meeting place of the Corpus Christi Guild, nestled in a back street along Holy Bones Lane near the St. Nicholas Church. Neither religion nor politics, but instead commerce dominated the communal spaces of the city, accurately reflecting local preoccupations.

Medieval Leicester was predominantly a regional marketplace, serving as the commercial center of the county and as a producer of staples, such as bread and beer, for residents. But by the late twelfth century, woolen cloth in substantial amounts was manufactured and sold outside the town. Although this industry soon declined, the town's merchants remained major exporters of wool, and both tanning and leatherwork flourished in the fourteenth and

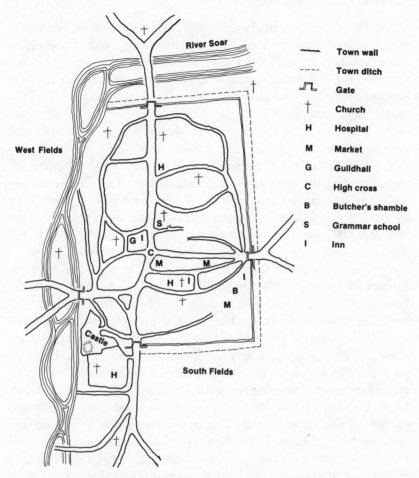

Figure 1.1. Leicester in 1300. (After A. E. Brown 1970:30.)

fifteenth centuries. Early sixteenth-century records of citizens' occupations list butchers, shoemakers, tailors, mercers, weavers, and
bakers as the most common professions. Slightly over half of Leicester's workers at that time were employed in manufacturing. Another
quarter produced food and drink, 10 percent were primarily traders
and merchants, and 5 percent worked in the building trades (McKinley
1958). Noncitizens did the menial work. In order to sell goods in
Leicester, men had to belong to the Guild Merchant, an organization chartered by the first earl of Leicester in recognition of the
guild's control of commerce. The group had its own officers, council, and hall by the thirteenth century. While the Guild Merchant

was not legally the ruling body of the town, much of the borough's business was transacted at its general meeting, and it controlled town finances. Indeed, the Guild Merchant so dominated Leicester's economic life that separate organizations of individual crafts emerged very late and never seriously contested the power of the central organization.

Political power in the town was shared by local officials and representatives of the earl of Leicester, to whose fortunes the national standing of the town was tied. The town court or portman-moot acted as the borough's executive. Twenty-four elders of the town, the jurati, judged minor civil cases and recorded property transactions, aided by a steward and two bailiffs employed by the earl. By 1300 the same group of twenty-four probably controlled both the court and the Guild Merchant. Further steps narrowing the group with political power were taken in the later fifteenth century. By then an elite of wealthy families who worked in the leading trades had consolidated their political prerogatives. Attendance by noncitizens at elections and meetings was prohibited in 1467 because of fears of disorder. Moreover, the multitudes, "being of little substance and no discretion, who . . . have caused great troubles in the elections and in the assessing of lawful charges," could henceforth not even enter the guild hall (McKinley 1958:29). Only a group of forty-eight chosen from among the "wiser and sadder" of the citizens could join in the election of future mayors and elders (McKinley 1958:29). From that time forward, a closed corporation took over the Leicester government. Even the members of Parliament were selected by the corporation. After the earl of Leicester's estates reverted to the crown, the mayor became the most important person in town. He and senior officials were justices of the peace and held court regularly in the name of the king.

Much of the town's cultural life was closely tied to that of the medieval church, which ran the local schools, hospitals, and system of poor relief. Leicester's parish churches sponsored processions, put on plays, and acted as patrons for craftsmen and artists employed to decorate their numerous buildings. There were also religious guilds, which offered members a wide variety of social activities. Leicester had at least eight such guilds by the fifteenth century, each of which had its own feasts, processions, masses for members, and charitable projects. If outward observance is any clue to how important religion was to the residents of Leicester, the sheer volume of public religious activity and the continuing series of bequests by property owners indicate that the church maintained a genuine hold on hearts as well as minds.

A Range of Urban Variations

How typical a town was Leicester? Its Roman origins, walls, castle, riverside site, and regular layout of streets gave it a physical shape not unlike that of Gloucester, Rouen, or Bonn. It offered its hinterland a mixture of economic, administrative, religious, and cultural services common to medium-sized towns. Its role as a market town was perhaps the staple urban function in a time when most people made their living from agriculture. While no two urban economies were identical, the variety of occupations in Leicester closely resembled that of other European provincial towns. The fact that its leading merchants were involved in the wool trade, England's leading export industry until the later Middle Ages, allied Leicester's economic interests closely with those of much of eastern and northern England and created links with cloth towns in northwest Europe. Even if the specific shape of Leicester's government was its own, joint control by a lord and a local elite overseen by royal officials was the most common pattern in a country where the king's authority over both land and central administration had been established early. Leicester's transition from control by a merchant guild, a borough court, a council for elders, and a mayor to that of rule by a closed corporation again paralleled that of many towns elsewhere. Everywhere in Europe rule was increasingly by the few rather than the many, and over time rights de facto were transformed into legal privileges.

Citizens from many medium-sized cities in northern Europe would have recognized much in Leicester that reminded them of their own communities. Yet differences in political and economic functions, as well as architectural styles, produced throughout Europe an array of urban types quite unlike a typical English county town. Who can construct an average from Dutch dike and dam towns, Polish mining settlements, and the pilgrimage cities along the road to Santiago de Compostela? In the south lay terracotta-colored Italian hill towns, many of them city republics in the eleventh through the thirteenth centuries. How many of Leicester's citizens could even imagine Venice's canals and splendid palaces, the mosaics and bronze horses of St. Mark's basilica, the glass factories at Murano? At a time when most English towns had fewer than 5,000 inhabitants, Florence and Milan each had over 50,000 residents, many of whom lived in multistory dwellings or in suburbs outside the walls. The commune of Milan in the late thirteenth century ruled over 50 other towns and 150 villages, whereas Leicester only housed the agents through whom the feudal hierarchy ruled the region. In contrast to Leicester's peaceful acquiescence to domination by one noble family and the king, Milan housed a group of rival magnate families who lived with their retinues, clients, kin, and sworn associates and who constituted a threat to the survival of a republican government ultimately as powerful as an outside sovereign. The nobles' proud towers, strongholds against their rivals, dominated the skyline. The citizens of Italian communes, unlike their English counterparts, were regularly divided and redivided into political groups, and they also participated in the turbulent politics of the Holy Roman Empire. Factions that regularly used violence to solve political disputes eventually gave aggressive magnates and condottieri the chance to seize control from republican regimes. In Italy, as in England, democracy failed to establish a lasting hold. Nevertheless, one preserved a measure of representative government while the other retained more urban autonomy (Martines 1980).

The political heterogeneity of the European urban landscape was paralleled by its physical and functional diversity. Small or not so small English market towns bore little resemblance to the port cities of the Mediterranean culminating in the imperial capital, Constantinople. It is important not to reduce this fascinating array of places to the bland homogeneity of "the medieval town." Scholars have suggested several typologies to order this urban diversity. Edith Ennen (1967) differentiates northwestern European towns from those of the south and from Russian ones on the basis of origins and social and economic structures. Robert Lopez (1963) uses function, rather than geography, to group medieval towns into three types: stockade cities, agrarian cities, and market cities, in order of increasing complexity and date of appearance. These categories can be used to make sweeping distinctions among a wealth of cities. Yet most towns are multifunctional. A label derived from one aspect of a city's many roles oversimplifies. Towns should, at a minimum, be compared on the basis of scale and spatial organization and of their economic, political, and cultural functions. Together these criteria permit more subtle comparisons of cities over space and time. We postpone a discussion of scale until Chapter 2, and turn now to urban geography and urban functions to deepen our analysis of medieval urbanization.

Patterns on the Ground

Cities are artifacts, cultural constructions that order daily life and reveal its contours. Each is a unique design in mass and space marked by geography, human intentions, and historical development. Mass was supplied by heavy walls, gates, and towers, in combination with houses and public buildings. Often, too, a castle or fortified episcopal palace, stronghold of a former lord or his administrator, occupied a hill within or perhaps adjoined the walls. Except for the tower houses of the Italian aristocracy, the castles, and many churches, constructions were small in scale, seldom more than three or four stories high. Their designs and architectural details were meant to impress and perhaps reassure, not to overwhelm strolling citizens. Open space in the cityscape came not only from streets but from public squares, open-air markets, and agricultural land enclosed within the walls. Many of the finest spaces were indoors. The great cathedrals could hold the population of a good-sized town, while hundreds could feast or deliberate in the vaulted cellar of a guild hall. High walls hid peaceful cloisters, busy courtyards, or verdant gardens. Most towns also included land planted in gardens or used for pasture. Indeed, typical burgage plots were long and narrow so that citizens had open space behind their houses to grow vegetables or graze animals. The dark, cramped streets overhung by houses reflected haphazard growth along an old path, not a shortage of intramural space. Population growth was typically accommodated by expanding the area of the city; periodic filling-in of the burgage plots came much later. The combination of solid and void produced by these elements formed a unique, integrated design that took on varied shapes.

The glorious variety of early cities stemmed from differences in terrain, town origins, and local architectural and building traditions. An easy distinction can be made between planned and unplanned towns. The former were more regular and had distinctive street patterns. The bastides of southwestern France, and many central and eastern European cities built for colonization or by a local landlord, typify this tradition. Yet, as the plan of Leipzig shows, the existence of a grid need not imply planning as such. Where towns grew on the land of a Roman camp or settlement, a rectangular shape with major streets laid out in a cross can usually be found at the historical heart of the city. Dutch towns oriented around a canal often grew by the addition of parallel streets and waterways, also producing a grid pattern that followed the design of the engineers. Most frequently, however, less purposefully constructed cities had irregular or radial designs reflecting their slower, more organic development. A round wall enclosed the maximum area for a given length—and expense—of perimeter, which accounts for the fact that there were planned circular towns as well. Unusual sites dictated unusual forms. Venice grew to cover a set of islands in a lagoon; Blois developed a trapezoidal shape at a crossing of the Loire river as it grew around a promontory on which a castle and an abbey were sited. Other towns were located along a river and developed asymmetrically on both banks. Truly irregular plans with mazelike streets haphazard in length and width are

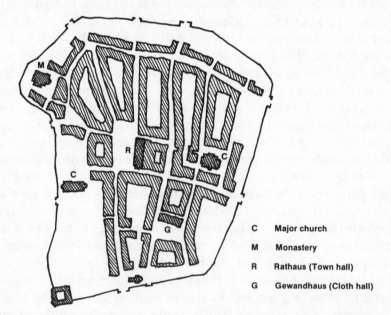

C   Major church

M   Monastery

R   Rathaus (Town hall)

G   Gewandhaus (Cloth hall)

Figure 1.2. A grid city: Leipzig. A town plan in the form of a loose, unplanned grid whose large blocks hide a maze of alleyways and courts. The major squares house the town hall and the cloth hall. (After old plans in Gutkind 1964, I:426–427.)

rare in most of Europe, occurring primarily along the southern periphery in areas influenced by Muslim civilization. The Moorish towns of southern Spain and Balkan towns built during the period of Ottoman rule are the most extreme European cases of irregular building patterns. Far more usual are the limited irregularities of walls and streets that reflect the contours of land, vagaries of ownership, and long-term development.

Some of the diversity and ingenuity displayed in the urban plan resulted from a conflict between a favorable *situation* and a difficult *site*. The town typically arose at a crossroad or a river ford, in a sheltered bay, or at the foot of a pass. Often, topographical difficulties were actually sought out for their defensive value. A marsh (Venice) or a hilltop (Langres) would serve well. Note, too, that a fortified castle often formed the town nucleus, again pointing up the primacy of strategic factors. Once the city gained a secure prosperity, the site often proved awkward, but prodigious feats of civil engineering were performed to accommodate expansion and ceased only with opportunities for growth. The decline of Bruges in the late Middle Ages as a major trading center has been attributed to silting in the channel leading to the sea, but it is far more reasonable to say that regional shifts in trade, which reduced the city's role, discouraged the burghers from regular dredging of the waterway.

Many similarities of medieval town plans arise from two common elements—the marketplace and what Dickinson (1961:325) terms "the cultural dominants." Unplanned towns grew around a single center or multiple nuclei, perhaps a castle, church, monastery, market, or a mix of these. The result was often an oval-shaped city with a radial street pattern that branched out from the public buildings or spaces at the center. Many Flemish towns, like Bruges and Ghent, grew from merchant settlements ensconced around the walls of castles belonging to the count of Flanders. Churches were soon added, as were the town halls, belfries, and cloth halls. Street patterns and allocations of public spaces emphasized the importance of the political and religious institutions housed within. In many towns of southern France, the cathedral served as the dominant building, and the layout of streets and markets was organized around it. In contrast, a marketplace occupied the central space in smaller English towns, where a cathedral or major church was nestled away on a side street, testifying to a different hierarchy of power and

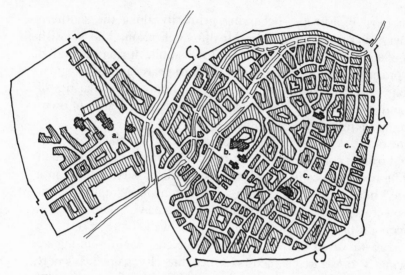

a. Cité
b. Monastery
c. Market squar

Figure 1.3. A concentric city: Arras. An organic town plan with three successive focuses: the Gallo-Roman cité (a), a monastery (b), and two market squares (c). (A plan of Deventer in Lavedan and Hugueney 1974:9.)

perhaps of values in the early days of the settlement. In Italian towns such as Todi, the centrality of the church was balanced against that of the town hall, placed there by an aggressive commune that had wrested political authority away from the medieval churchmen (Bacon 1974). With due regard for diversity, it may be said that if the *cité* or fortress explained the *origin* of many towns, the pole of growth was more likely to be a nearby monastery or the merchant settlement.

One of the most distinctive elements of town design was the perimeter. Most cities had an easily recognizable outline created by their fortifications, gates, and towers. The earliest such constructions of earth and timber were replaced by heavy stone walls, particularly in the period between 1100 and 1500 when methods of warfare became more sophisticated. The walls served many purposes besides defense. They were status symbols, signs of wealth and power. At their gates, tolls were collected and goods checked. They enclosed a separate administrative area within which residents were legally free and usually self-governing. While the walls could limit expansion, they were not permanent barriers. As wealthier towns grew, they incorporated the surrounding land and population by building new fortifications. The citizens and rulers of Paris constructed five such lines of walls between 1180 and 1845 as the city pushed far beyond the Ile de la Cité and the right and left bank bridgeheads. In only a few parts of Europe were there substantial numbers of unwalled towns. For example, many English market towns and about half the settlements in the Spanish Netherlands lacked walls, in some cases because of poverty or a lord's opposition, in others because of relative political stability during periods when fortifications were a practical defense.

How was this enclosed space used by the citizens? Sjoberg (1960) pictures a concentrically ordered town with elites living near the center and the poor pushed to the periphery. Religious and administrative buildings constituted the core of the settlement. This pattern most reasonably fits many Italian towns, as well as Paris and some of the early bishoprics in the north. It is less applicable to Flemish cities and French bastides, which were built around central marketplaces (Dickinson 1961). And many English towns had quite a different pattern of spatial organization. The smallest towns grew around one major street, which widened in one section to permit the holding of a market. Citizens occupied roughly equal burgage plots of land. Social divisions were reflected more by access to the main street than by residence in the center or the periphery. And, as we have suggested, it oversimplifies to assume that towns had only one center. London had two nuclei where elites resided, in the west round Westminster and in the City. The poor lived in between these two places and outside London's wall. There was an almost complete separation of functions between the east and the west, but neither area outranked the other. Many central European towns—for example, Prague, Poznan, and the twin cities of Buda and Pest—also had a dual pattern of organization stemming from the early division of the merchants' settlement from that of political or religious authorities. A continuing residential separation of merchants and craftsmen from clerics and administrators resulted. Elsewhere, residential clustering by occupation was common but not absolute.

The social geography of medieval cities was both simpler and more complicated than Sjoberg indicates. Medieval towns lacked the neat class separations of contemporary American cities with their rings of inner-city slums and middle-class suburbs. In most smaller towns territory was relatively undifferentiated; apart from the few public places and religious buildings, most structures combined shop, workshop, and private residence. Buildings and land use were relatively unspecialized. Vance (1971) argues, in fact, that land assignment did not derive from economic values but from a variety of social and cultural norms that ordered citizens into corporate groups. Social status was a less important determinant of residence than were kinship, occupation, and geographic or ethnic origin. The key distinction is between *congregation*, the voluntary clustering of groups, and *segregation*, the forced separation of certain activities or people (Vance 1977). Although tanners and Jews might be restricted to certain areas, segregation was far from the rule.

Subdivisions were usually based upon the Catholic parish, each of which had its own church and confraternities. Venice was informally organized into neighborhoods, each with its own church, square, quay, and well, defining a territory within which much of the daily life of residents took place. In general, territorial groups served to organize medieval communes. In Genoa, for example, the city's political, military, and judicial structures were ordered around eight *compagne*. Aristocratic families strove to dominate these districts through a combination of property holding and patronage. The common people were co-opted rather than excluded (Hughes 1975). In most northern cities, however, the ties of neighborhood were more informal. And it must be remembered that in all but the few largest cities, the whole of the urban space was easily accessible. Medieval communes were "walking cities" where citizens could have a daily familiarity with a large part of their urban environment. The wall enclosed a single space, a community more concerned with protecting itself against outsiders than with dividing inhabitants among themselves.

Work and the Urban Polity

In societies where wealth is unequally distributed and goods and services are produced by specialized workers, commodities are not uniformly available or desired within a given territory. Supply and demand increase with population density and with the rank of settlers. Under these conditions cities have always served as the centers of exchange, organized in relation to the level and type of production and demand by residents in their regions. While all towns have some functions of exchange, the type and scale of market functions varies in relation to the nature of the local economy. Many bastides in Gascony served a tiny and not very active area. Sicilian towns such as Palermo were centers for the export of grain, while Italian towns in less fertile areas, the Amalfi coast for example, prospered largely in relation to the trading energies of local merchants. Since urban populations did not grow enough food—or directly control enough territorial surplus—to be self-supporting, they had to offer something in exchange, and the choices were usually services or manufactured goods.

Other important branches of urban economic activity were directly linked to trade. These were industrial production, or more accurately, "manufacture," as well as finance and transport, especially shipping. Many cities came to acquire a particular reputation in one or the other of these branches, but seldom in medieval and Renaissance times could such activities be the basis for urban growth apart from commercial needs. Perhaps Genoa as a center of banking and finance came close, as did some textile centers such as Ghent and Florence. Finance developed very early in the medieval period because slow transportation required credit, however disguised, to make merchant ventures possible and also because the tangle of currency units and dubious coinage made exchange a highly specialized and vital component of mercantile activity. Cities also furnished financial backing for the struggles among princes: king against powerful vassal, pope against emperor, pretender against monarch. Public finance promised spectacular profits in the face of daunting political as well as material risks.

To speak of industry in this preindustrial period is mostly, but not exclusively, to speak of textiles. This was never entirely an urban activity, and it became increasingly rural in the postmedieval centuries. But fine woolen draperies were key to the wealth and reputation of Flemish towns, of Florence, and later of certain English ones as well. Like wool, silk and linen assured the renown of certain cities but were worked in a more modest way over wide areas. Metalware was to make important contributions to the development of instruments and machinery for the parallel revolutions in science and technology. There is little need to stress the role of arms and armor, the Middle Ages seeming no less prone than we are to lavishing craftsmanship on the tools of war. Other characteristically urban industries include printing and housebuilding and a variety of processing industries supplying beer, leather, paper, or glass, to mention only major ones. Many of these owed their initial urban location to the presence of a market. Later, in the period of colonial and commercial expansion, others arose that processed such imports as sugar for inland distribution or reexport, and these naturally located in port cities.

We associate cities with the rise of markets, and we too often think that markets work well only when relatively free. So the extent and degree of regulation in early urban commerce may surprise us. But free trade is something of a historical misconception. The premedieval environment was largely anarchic, and contractual relationships, such as those between buyer and seller, first required an orderly framework of security and law. The fairs and towns existed at the beginning to provide a temporary "peace," so that trade might proceed and no violence trouble the crowded assembly. A central purpose of communes and guilds was regulation, largely to protect the good names of the town, its wares, and its people in a time when information was scarce and trust fragile.

A certain amount of regulation was useful, indeed necessary, to reduce the risk (North and Thomas 1973). But the benefits faded with progress in law and economic institutions; they were increasingly offset, and eventually overwhelmed, by the temptation to use powers in furtherance of privilege and by the economic rigidity that regulation imposed on the city. In the words of Henri Pirenne, "Freedom, as the middle-class conceived it, was a monopoly" (1925:153). A key to the declines that dogged cities through the postplague years and periodically for centuries beyond that is their inability to change when the environment did. In modern terms medieval cities were institutionally closed systems poorly attuned to changes in the external environment.

If we make much of the mercantile vigor and economic modernism of medieval towns with somewhat facile references to free trade and capitalism, it is to set off their economic processes from those of the dominant feudal countryside. However hemmed in by regulations or strictures, the urban merchants and craftsmen appear eons removed from the serf tied to his lord's estate. The manorial system, the basis of the feudal mode of production, had emerged in unsettled times to provide local communities with the essentials for survival: security and subsistence. With gradual pacification the manor became less autarkic or self-sufficient. While one can hardly view the lords of the later Middle Ages as rural capitalists, the agrarian economy had room for much more economic rationality and enterprise than the manorial stereotype allows for. Eager to enjoy, display, and increase their wealth, lords marketed the surplus they collected and strove to increase production while adapting to the changing market. As prices shifted, it could pay to collect feudal dues and rents in different forms—perhaps in labor, in kind, or in money. Particular rights were more strictly enforced, commuted, or sold off; leases were lengthened or reduced. The raison d'être of the chivalric nobility, armed conflict, increasingly pitted rival claimants to a growing surplus one against the other: lord and peasant, lord and neighboring lord, liege and vassal. Gradually, however, finance, legal power, and managerial skill became more important; brute force, tradition, and distinctions of birth less so.

Cities and urban elites successfully joined in the struggle for control of rural land and its surpluses. Monasteries had from their earliest days been large and sophisticated landlords. They were joined by merchants, men of law, and royal or church officers, as well as by communes themselves. Nobles who defaulted on mortgage-secured debts unwittingly furthered the process. Urban masters were at least as exacting as traditional lords, perhaps less capricious and short-sighted. In the highly urbanized regions, towns directly controlled the *umland* or *contado* around them, while their trading role gave them influence over wider areas of countryside. Pistoia tried to impose a kind of "protomercantilism" around itself, impeding labor and raw produce from leaving and finished goods from entering (Herlihy 1967).

It would take centuries before rural land became just another form of property and the term *landlord* lost its original meaning. If power and status were the key to feudal lordship in its pure form, material advantage mattered from the start and was pursued with increasing vigor. Had it been otherwise, towns would have lacked most of the basis for their trade as well as the food they needed. To be sure, not all surplus accrued to manorial lords or flowed cityward in the form of rents, tithes, or taxes. Whether serf or free, peasants could produce, trade, and consume on their own account, and their business fed thousands of local town markets. But it is hard to envisage Leicester, to say nothing of Venice or Bruges, except on the basis of large-scale surplus mobilization within the feudal agrarian structure.

At the risk of oversimplification, let us outline the following stages in urban economic development. After the millennium, demand for urban functions was stimulated by population growth, the settlement of new lands, and the spread of the more productive three-field rotation. Fairs were organized and merchants from the Mediterranean and North Sea towns added exotic wares to the mundane staples traded in local markets. The spread of cloth manufacture in northern France, Tuscany, and the Low Countries intensified urban needs for raw materials and food while offering the stimulus of quality wares in exchange for more rural produce. The extent of the market and the scale of production reinforced each other, greater efficiency permitting the city to sell to a larger area, which in turn provided sufficient demand to allow fruitful division of labor.

This picture of building from local to long-distance trade has good logic and some historical evidence behind it, but it is too neat and tidy. As we show in Chapter 2, important cities sprang up on the basis of long-distance trade, and their economy from the beginning involved great specialization, distant markets, and large-scale financial complexity. Craft production might well be organized at the initiative of the merchants, as opposed to having them passively sell the surplus from locally generated production. Finally, close ties with the surrounding countryside could also be a tardy development, owing more to the purchases of land and the forging of aristocratic alliances by the urban oligarchy than to the exchange of goods for food in local markets. This second picture, as it happens, fits the case of Florence rather well. The city's merchants were involved in papal finance as early as the twelfth century, while the city's role as capital of Tuscany was a much later development that would dominate in the less brilliant early modern era (Cochrane 1973).

The exchanges offered by cities to their regions were not merely economic. From classical times cities have been seen as the centers of civilization, producers not only of goods but of cultural models. The diffusion of Christianity throughout the Roman world in the fourth century took place largely through the conversion of the urban lower and middle classes. And the world of the Catholic church became more strongly urban during the Middle Ages. Monastic houses originally "in the fields" were engulfed by expanding cities; Saint-Germain in Paris and St. Martin in London are examples. Canon law provided that bishops had to live in a town, and the newer mendicant orders, such as the Dominicans and the

Franciscans, made religious work in the cities the center of their mission. To quote an English cleric, "The frequency of sermons seems most necessary in cities and great towns, that their inhabitants who . . . see for the most part but the works of men, may daily hear God speaking unto them" (Clark and Slack 1976:15). The many roles played by the medieval clergy—priest, teacher, nurse, judge, landlord, and chaplain—brought a constant stream of people into the towns with a variety of tangible and intangible needs. The sick, the old, lepers, and orphans found refuge in city hospitals and almshouses. Urban church courts, inquisitors, and confessors watched over the doctrinal and moral orthodoxy of their flock. Moreover, the major centers of learning shifted from rural monasteries to the towns, as episcopal academies, urban monastic schools, and universities were organized beginning in the twelfth century. In fact, dozens of cities had a university by 1500. These schools transformed small towns, bringing in as they did hundreds of outsiders with different values and languages and ambiguous legal status.

In addition to the roles exercised through the church, the medieval town had other important cultural functions. Redfield and Singer (1954) note the link between cities and the folk culture around them. Some cities are "orthogenetic"; they carry the local culture forward and help to transform it into a "Great Tradition." For example, printing, book production, and book selling were common urban occupations. Primary schools teaching middle-class children in the vernacular multiplied in Italian and Flemish commercial cities. Other towns had important "heterogenetic" functions because they helped to diffuse throughout a region alien cultures and values. Venetians brought the products, the technology, and the architecture of the East into western Europe. In the south the princely courts of the Italian city-states drew poets, painters, and scholars who looked back to ancient Greece and Rome to develop the Great Tradition of Renaissance humanism. In other areas townsmen acted as cultural innovators and helped to transform local society. The burgesses of the cloth towns used bells, and later, mechanical clocks to announce working hours. By the early fourteenth century, the larger towns of Flanders, northern France, and Italy boasted belfries and clock towers in central squares that brought a new regularity and control to the urban population (Le Goff 1977). A growing bourgeois preoccupation with numbers and precision could extend thereafter from the mechanics of work to the entire framework of daily activity. Urban time became secular, uniform.

In the city new ways of life and ritual expression grew simultaneously. Urban residence freed the serf and fostered technological innovation and literacy. Former peasants learned urban ways in their streets and halls. Le Goff (1972) notes that town folklore shifted in the early Middle Ages from the repetition of forms imported from the countryside to new festivals and symbols. A rampant urban patriotism combined with interest in classical learning to create a "civic humanism" that exalted the commune and its independence in an outpouring of poems and chronicles (Baron 1966). As medieval cities grew in size and in influence, their citizens became more intellectually and culturally aggressive, self-consciously marking themselves off from the illiterate rustics of the countryside.

It is a tempting oversimplification to see cities only as an alien growth in the medieval cultural body, a breeding ground of "modern," secular values and ideas. As we have noted, the medieval church was increasingly urban, and it was in the cities that its major unifying and civilizing missions for the system as a whole were worked out. In other words, cities were integral to the pursuit of medieval social ideals even though they also harbored the practices and reflections that would challenge prevailing values. This cultural dualism of medieval cities extended also to the ways in which they deviated from the norm. The townsman was comparatively free in law and in the range of choices open to him. Yet the urban world—compact, organized, interdependent—could exert a degree of control over his life more exacting and thorough than the villager could imagine. The rules were more liberal in town, but they were observed. In terms of the person's frame of reference, townsmen looked two ways. While ties to the family, the guild, and the neighborhood mattered, a citizen could also think of himself as at once more individual and more cosmopolitan than a member of a village community.

The political role of towns, no less than the cultural, differentiated urban and rural realms. Urban land initially belonged to an overlord who possessed a variety of rights over its inhabitants. But local land law and the restrictions on personal freedom and economic activity that characterized feudal society were unsuited to the needs and governance of commerce and manufacture. Sworn associations of merchants, neighbors, or craftsmen attempted to develop alternatives. By the eleventh century in large parts of western Europe, the result was a socially stratified urban population living under a variety of different laws and sets of obligations (Ennen 1979). Then conflicts between rival rulers, whether they were clerical or lay—remember the Italian struggles of emperor and pope—gave townsmen the chance to trade allegiance and cash for freedoms of various sorts. The exact scenarios of change and their timing varied extensively, but the result was the transformation of corporate groups into territorial communities with their own administratively limited jurisdictions. In Italy associations of urban nobles and rich citizens wrested local power from their bishops and viscounts starting in the late eleventh century. Sworn assemblies of the permanently resident adult males controlled northern French towns, such as Amiens or Soissons, by 1200. While a few royal officials still lived in French towns, executive committees and judges elected by the commune had control of most legal and economic matters, as well as jurisdiction over new citizens. The principle that "town air makes free" was not a gift but a highly prized right won from their lords by litigious burgesses eager to secure their own independence.

One of the most distinctive differences between rural and urban people in medieval Europe lay in this aspect of their political identities. Medieval society was defined in terms of personal allegiance, typically that of lord and vassal, or liege and bondsman. The ties to the soil were a part of this system: one was bound spatially to a manor and personally to a lord. By contrast, the citizen had no lord, even though the city collectively owed something to a bishop, count, or king. The city replaced the idea of fealty with that of association. Ties to the soil were important for the urban dweller, of course, but they were reciprocal. If he was of the city, it was also his city, something that the serf could not say of the manor.

Yet this difference did not completely remove townspeople from the social order of the countryside. Barel (1977) argues that the medieval town was very much a part of feudal society. Its origin was frequently promoted by a lord, spiritual or temporal, as a means of establishing or consolidating a degree of power. Whatever conflicts arose between a ruler and the cities of a domain, participants in these endless struggles remembered that they needed each other beyond the passions of the moment. Common hostility to the feudal nobility often brought kings into alliances with towns. In addition, monarchs found in their cities the liquid wealth and literate officials they needed to forge a state without relying on the Catholic church.

The scope of a town's freedom varied inversely with the power of the territorial authority. Where the overlord was weak, for example in Italy and central Europe, cities developed into city-states and extended their political control over as much of the surrounding land as they could dominate. Towns such as Milan, Florence, and Genoa had their own armies and shamelessly subjugated their weaker neighbors (Martines 1980). The imperial free cities of the German lands, although they carved out only small territories beyond their walls, were essentially independent. They carried out their own foreign policies, formed alliances, and fought wars (Rörig 1967). Elsewhere, princes and kings imposed limits on urban expansion and were in ultimate control of such matters as tax levels, certain types of justice, external affairs, and sometimes even the naming of town officials. The strength of the emerging state kept communal autonomy within bounds. English or French kings found the cities convenient places from which to administer their territories and permitted the burgesses no more than home rule.

Russian princes considered towns their property and retained control of their administration, judiciary, and military forces. As the Muscovite state increased its powers, it asserted central control over the towns, which had no charters of self-government and no separate laws to shield them from princes' powers. Townspeople, who included slaves as well as the omnipresent merchants, clergy, and artisans, owed their lords service, taxes, and rents. Merchants and craftsmen, not organized into guilds, could not control local trades. Unlike the West, Russian urban residence brought no legal privileges or changes in social status. Although a few cities such as Novgorod and Pskov had an urban assembly of free males, it was relatively weak, meeting irregularly during emergencies. Only Novgorod managed to wrest a certain independence from its prince. Russian townsfolk were not citizens of a commune, but people with an official residence in town and the legal obligation to pay taxes there. Moreover, the cities themselves were filled with ecclesiastics and their clients, foreign merchants, peasants, and other special groups, all of whom were tax exempt and outside the civic legal order. The residential community was not a legal unit in any important sense. Only in the seventeenth century did the czars attempt to end the privileged position of outsiders in towns and allow the election of officials to control local fiscal and judicial matters (Hamm 1976).

The political functions of medieval towns must be seen in three different contexts therefore: internal governance, relationship to a territorial authority, and administrative control over a hinterland. All were linked to a precarious balance of autonomy and dependence that constantly shifted according to the identities of other players in the European political game. Weak, distracted rulers and neighbors encouraged urban political freedom and expansion, while royal centralization limited urban power.

The Nature of the Medieval Community

It is important not to idealize medieval cities and allow placid and picturesque remains to efface the harshly competitive, highly stratified society they once sheltered. These were not egalitarian communities. Whatever internal peace and order they achieved came at the cost of systematic repression. Although we associate medieval communes with early advances toward freedom and democracy, they were also citadels of blatant privilege and nit-picking interventionism. Moreover, political inequalities increased over time. Similarly, while the air of the city was held to naturalize the rural stranger, cities were typically xenophobic as well as faction-ridden.

Let us look first at the urban cast of characters and see how they were related. The three orders of medieval society, *oratores, bellatores, lavoratores*—those who prayed, fought, and worked—each had some although not an equal number of representatives in the towns. But our images of contemplative monks, gallant knights, and industrious commoners are far from the medieval reality. For one thing, none of these orders was unified. The church, for example, witnessed conflicts between urban religious orders and the secular priesthood, in addition to the opposition between bishops and the pope or the lay authorities that could wrack local politics. Nonetheless, clerics, who probably made up between 1 percent and 4 percent of the urban population, were a social force to reckon with (Cipolla 1976). The warriors—in this society the king, the nobles, and their henchmen—were represented in the larger towns either directly or by their officials. In Italy, the nobility had early chosen urban residence and directed their lands and dependents from tower houses in the cities. In Russia, too, many landlords had moved into towns by the eleventh and twelfth centuries and formed part of an urban patriciate (Tikhomirov 1959). In most of central and western Europe, nobles and knights stayed in the countryside, although their urban castles and hired administrators were an important element in town society and politics.

The largest part of the town population was composed of the third estate—merchants, craftsmen, and service workers, each with their dependents (journeymen and apprentices, women, children, and servants). While adult male citizens were in theory equal within the community, different occupations held different amounts of prestige, and inequalities of wealth were always highly significant. Among the merchants a wide gulf separated the great wholesale traders and financiers from the small dealers. In the crafts not only did goldsmiths outrank tanners, but a great disparity grew up between the masters and their journeymen, the latter coming to have no realistic chance in most places to accede to the guild short of marriage to a master's daughter or widow. Save for the absence of factories and machines, they essentially came to constitute an industrial proletariat with only their labor to sell. Finally, cities had a permanent population of the poor, whose numbers could swell alarmingly during crises. Tax records indicate that this group made up 12 percent of the Antwerp and 20 percent of the Hamburg population in the late fifteenth century (Cipolla 1976:18).

The relative size of the dependent population in these communities was quite large. Not only were about half the townsfolk female, but children age fourteen and under constituted one third. Servants, who usually lived in their master's house, made up between a tenth and a fifth of the community, particularly in the medium-sized and large towns (Cipolla 1976). In the Iberian peninsula, Italy, and southern France, as well as in Russia, one could add to this group an unknown—though diminishing—number of slaves who worked as domestic servants and craftsmen (Heers 1977). Adult male property owners were therefore only a small proportion of the total urban population. Add to this picture of unequal status the results of an unequal distribution of wealth. While data on income and property holdings for entire urban populations are rare, enough has survived to paint a lurid picture of golden affluence juxtaposed to abject poverty. De Roover (1963b) has divided Florentine families in 1457 into four groups: the rich, 2 percent; the middle class, 16 percent; the poor, 54 percent; and the destitute, 28 percent. While small market towns lacked this sharp stratification, the medium-sized and larger cities were home to the wealthy few, a minority of comfortable position, those who normally managed but were essentially propertyless, and a fluctuating fringe of the indigent.

The most powerful families in the towns, generally the merchants and administrators along with the nobility in Italy, coalesced into a patriciate who intermarried and gained a stranglehold on the town council and other major communal offices. Tensions could splinter this group: note the family feuds that led to miniature civil wars in Italian communes as early as the twelfth century, necessitating the transfer of magisterial power to a neutral outsider in the person of the *podestà* (Waley 1969). Threats from below served to resolidify shaky alliances among the elite. The organized challenges of the guildsmen who wanted to obtain or recover a share of urban power were quite common. Rörig (1967) notes that in most southwestern German towns guilds had secured a share of urban government by the thirteenth and fourteenth centuries, although patricians still dominated most German town councils. In many Italian towns the thirteenth century saw attempts—some successful—by a militarily organized *popolo* to seize power from the nobles, bankers, and long-distance traders. While the *popolo*'s social composition varied, aggressive guildsmen made up a major share of its members (Martines 1980). A few scholars picture these common attacks on privilege as incipient class conflicts. The most famous of the workers' rebellions, that of the Florentine woolcarders *(ciompi)* in 1378, arose at least in part from resentments of the propertyless against the rich. Economic tensions did divide cities at a very early date (Cohn 1980), but workers also acted politically on the basis of kinship ties and personal loyalties. Something akin to class consciousness in medieval cities probably arose only in atypical places and times. For the most part, the loyalties of neighborhood, family, occupation, and clientage overrode the common interests created by economic status. The small scale of most urban communities brought citizens into face-to-face contact with a wide variety of people to whom they had multiple ties. As a result, conflicts were often obscured or muted by cultural and religious allegiances.

Divisions within the urban polity eroded the power of cities in the larger system and called into question their distinctive place in the feudal order. There was a good deal of historical irony and coming-full-circle in all this. Urban communities originally came to strength by profiting from the strains of the feudal world: rigid social stratification, elites dedicated to fighting as a way of life, a crude system of production, and heavy restrictions on circulation and exchange. Their very success engendered sharp social divisions within the city, ambitions for territorial and political dominance, and monopolistic rigidities. Cities were threatened by one another and by the very territorial sovereigns to whom they furnished finance and expertise. Internally, the ruling patriciate had to look to outside help to put down rebellion from below. But the world of landed seigniory and hereditary status also continued to exert a powerful positive attraction on urban oligarchs. Many longed to trade their power and wealth for status in the larger society. Common by birth and enriched by base pursuits, they were aware that landed estates offered the promise of eventual nobility, while exceptional services to the crown could lead to the same end even more quickly. Although we focus on the lure of the city for rural mavericks—skilled artists and artisans, freethinkers and iconoclasts, the restless and ambitious—it is important to remember the persistent power of rural values and modes of life.

CHAPTER 2

Systems of Early Cities

CITIES WITHIN their walls have thus far occupied most of our attention, but what of their important links to the outside? Medieval towns were crossroads as well as separate communities. Indeed, they existed by and for exchange. Goods, information, and influence passed in and through them. Leicester served as the capital of Leicestershire. Located in the center of a county approximately thirty miles in diameter, it was an easy walk for those who needed its economic, political, or cultural services. Weekly and seasonal fairs attracted citizens from a ring of small market towns and villages. Travelers moving from one part of the country to another stopped at Leicester's inns and church hostels, and the presence in Leicester of royal officials and judges brought others into town on administrative errands. Neither Leicester's geography nor its location, which made it the central place in the county, was an accident. Both fitted the city into a hierarchical urban system that was well developed by the eleventh century. Let us take a brief look at the origins of this territorial system and then explore its various properties.

Towns as Central Places

The urbanization of the eleventh and twelfth centuries formed part of a widespread economic revival that involved rural population growth, land clearings, and the gradual assertion of a more centralized political order. As we mentioned before, the development both of towns and of the manorial estates into which land was divided derived from the availability of a surplus and decisions about its distribution. Fundamental to the evolving feudal system was a bargain between warriors and peasants in which support was exchanged for protection. Two aspects of the arrangement deserve special notice. First, the manor could only produce a modest range of mostly plain goods. Second, a part of the surplus could be invested to make the manor more secure and more productive in the future, for instance by strengthening the castle, by supporting and equipping more men-at-arms, by clearing land or building a waterwheel. Therefore, long-term progress depended upon forbearance by the lord in extracting resources. Because the lord enjoyed a monopoly of legitimate force, he was constantly tempted to exploit the serfs for short-term advantage.

These limitations to the progress of the system could be partially overcome by opening up the manor to outside influences, thus allowing the investment process greater scope. Various outsiders held at least a potential interest in manors and their occupants. The arbitrary power of the lord was held in check by the moral influence of the church and by the possibility of appeal to a higher rung in the feudal hierarchy: to the lord's own liege and ultimately to the king. Though they also fought, king and church contributed to gradual improvements in security and law and made possible a great expansion of trade. And it was trade, of course, that overcame the productive limits of the manorial system and so promoted growth and urbanization. We have already noted the interest of nobles in exotic wares: stronger wine, finer cloth, plate, ornaments, and most of all the implements of hunting and fighting. But local trade also had a strategic role to play. One manor might breed fine horses, another specialize in hawks. Serfs traded on their own account in a small way when a market made it possible, selling off a brace of fowl here, a jar of honey or a hide there. Significant as these scattered exchanges might become in the aggregate, some situations generated more systematic stimuli for local markets and regional urbanization. Let us look briefly at two.

The feudal nobility much preferred hunting, jousting, and fighting to business. Although it was common to entrust the management of the domain and the marketing of the estate's produce to a bailiff, an alternative was to let all or most of the land out to serfs and commute the various services and dues to money payments. This advanced form of the manorial economy made for more active local trade and a much higher degree of monetization of that trade.

If a lord controlled several manors, as abbeys often did as a result of bequests, money payments became all the more attractive.

Moreover, some regions and people specialized from earliest times. Their production came from mines, fisheries, grazing lands, or forests. The availability of specialized resources encouraged this development, but it could also result when a people were forced to find refuge in a remote forest, a rugged highland, or a windswept coastal plain. To survive, these people needed to trade their hides, charcoal, or salt for grain on a regular basis. So the zone of contact between natural regions presented a favorable site for early urbanization. Ghent in Flanders, for instance, owed its start to a strategic position between arable and pastoral areas (Nicholas 1978).

As the volume of local trade and the organization of civil society gradually increased, a large number of market and administrative settlements crystallized as *central places* for their surrounding areas. Individual markets needed to be linked to one another to broaden the range of goods traded and to equalize local imbalances in both goods and means of payment. Further, markets had to be duly authorized by charter, protected from violence, and regulated against fraud; this established ties between the administrative framework and the system of markets. Finally, central places were not random in size and placement, but tended to locate at even distances from one another and to form a hierarchy. Each center approximated the center of gravity of its service area in order to minimize transportation costs. And small centers would be arrayed around larger ones, these in turn depending on a city of still higher order.

Such a system of markets is explained by central place theory, first formulated by Walter Christaller in the early 1930s.[1] Fascinated by the problem of apparent regularities in the siting, size, and numbers of towns among regions, Christaller developed a model to predict ideal city distributions and functions. He began by positing a flat plain within which a population of equal wealth was equally distributed. This population produced many services and specialties, thereby generating central places for exchange. But the level of demand necessary to support a baker, jeweler, or canon lawyer, as well as the distance people are willing to travel to buy their products, varies enormously. Because each good has a given *threshold* of minimum demand as well as a fixed *range* beyond which people are unwilling to move to obtain it, only a certain proportion of all towns will offer higher-order goods and services. If the marketing function of the town is made primary, a hierarchy of places can be deduced. Each node in the network has a hexagonal-shaped hinterland, which is the same size as every other town's at the same rank. In this case there are three towns of rank B dependent on city A, three towns of rank C dependent on each B center, and so forth. Urban networks, so conceived, consist of nests of central places, each level having k places of the next lower rank within the hinterland (k being equal to three in this case).

Christaller's model rests upon assumptions not met in the real world. Not only do geography, unequal incomes, and uneven population densities distort settlement patterns, but any values assigned to the thresholds and ranges of goods are arbitrary. Cultural or individual variations in demand are ignored. In any case, the range of urban functions considered is severely limited. Christaller argued that marketing needs were the basic pressure for city building, although he admitted that transportation or administrative networks were secondary reasons for the creation of an urban hierarchy. Yet many factors, including climate, terrain, and historical accident, influence the building of actual urban networks. The power of the central place model rests not with its ability to predict actual city distributions but with its recognition that cities are centers for exchange at varying levels of complexity. Moreover, the notion of urban hierarchy helps describe the wide variation in zones of urban influence.

Central place theory can be used to construct an idealized version of the process of city building and interaction that we call the Central Place System. Over time, economic pressures for urban growth are generated by the existence of a local surplus and by producers eager to exchange their specialized products for a wider range of goods. These pressures give rise to a hierarchy of service centers, centrally located towns whose territorial base is a local agricultural region. In the longer run, as we shall see, administrative functions are grafted onto the economic functions of central places. This process was most fully developed within nation-states, such as England, but could also be observed in medieval times in the *contado*s of the larger Italian towns, the provinces of France, and the constituent units of the Holy Roman Empire. Throughout Europe, kingdoms were made up of provinces and other smaller nested units. In addition, there were the overlapping jurisdictions of military, legal, and ecclesiastical authorities. A hierarchical ordering of territory by those with political power was common in medieval Europe.

Christaller argued that over time seven levels of urban places would be generated by the various needs of a population. We prefer a simpler classification borrowed from Peter Clark and Paul Slack of only four types of towns (Clark and Slack 1976). They have suggested a simple typology on the basis of scale as well as economic and political function, which they use for English towns. It also can be applied to centrally governed areas in the rest of Europe. They classify cities as market towns, county towns, provincial capitals, and national capitals—in order of increasing size, complexity, and political influence. This classification has the merit of combining attention to scale and function with awareness of a hierarchical ordering of urban places.

A look at the actual distribution of towns in the early fourteenth century will illustrate both the distribution of these various sized cities and the links between scale and function that are basic to the construction of the Central Place System.

The most common type of European town was the local marketing center. These tiny places, which had fewer than 2,000 residents, constituted the overwhelming majority of all urban settlements and housed over half the urban population. Pounds (1973) estimated that in 1330 perhaps 75 percent of the French, 90 percent of the German, and 95 percent of the Swiss towns fell into this category. Many such places were little different from farming villages, most of their population working in nearby fields. Yet weekly markets drew regular visitors and itinerant vendors, and there were usually a few craftsmen and service workers in the town. By 1500 even the smallest market towns in East Anglia could boast resident weavers, carpenters, and tailors (Patten 1978). While few such miniature communities had royal charters or complex political institutions, most had been granted the right to a market by the king or manorial lord, eager for a share of the profits that could be earned from local commerce. Hundreds of such places were founded essentially as speculations in England after the Norman Conquest, in southwestern France, and in central Germany. Many failed to attract enough settlers and trade to survive the economic contractions of the later Middle Ages, but others developed more complex economic structures and extended the size of their marketing region over time.

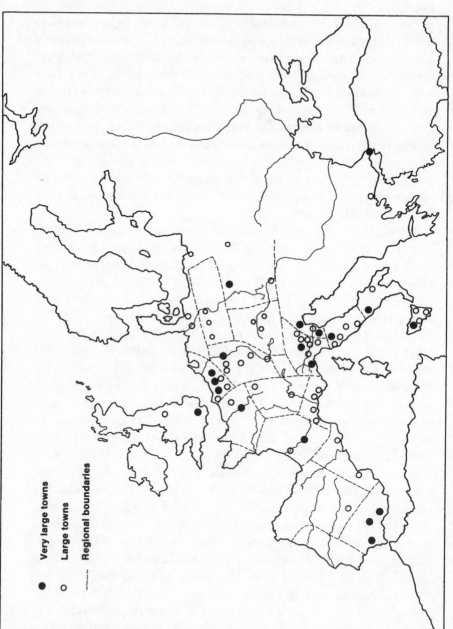

Figure 2.1. Major cities and urban regions of Europe, c. 1350. (After Russell 1972b:27, and

Intermediate-sized towns added local and regional administrative functions to their role as marketing centers. As capitals of districts or counties, these substantial settlements provided a range of economic and political services to people in their hinterland. In England county towns were the sites of parliamentary elections and sessions of royal and county courts. Some had royal castles, county jails, and elaborate religious institutions. In France, the capital cities of governmental units below the level of the province (*élections, bailliages, sénéchaussées*) housed royal officials who watched over various administrative, financial, and military matters. The Italian commune of Pistoia, which had approximately 11,000 residents in 1300 and shrank to 6,000 after 1350, ruled over an area of some 300 square miles within which it levied taxes, labor, and military services. Not only did the town control many hospitals and religious foundations, but it looked after the roads and supervised travelers. Moreover, the city's merchants, bankers, and craftsmen attempted to monopolize the region's commerce, manufacturing, and financial affairs until Pistoia came under the control of Florence in the mid-fourteenth century (Herlihy 1967).

Medium-sized towns were widely distributed in Europe, but they constituted a small minority of urban places. Most numerous in Italy, France, the Rhineland, and Flanders, they were virtually nonexistent in the fourteenth century in areas of limited urbanization on the European periphery, such as Scandinavia, Poland, Russia, Ireland, and Scotland. In the later Middle Ages, their numbers grew in the east hand in hand with the political evolution of their regions. Rozman (1976) estimated that by 1500 there were

Table 2.1. The size of towns in northern Europe, c. 1330.

Size category	Number of towns	Total population
Very large (over 25,000)	9	330,000
Large (10,000–25,000)	38	570,000
Intermediate (2,000–10,000)	220	1,100,000
Small (under 2,000)	3,000	2,250,000
Total	3,267	4,250,000

Source: Pounds (1973:358). Reprinted by permission of Cambridge University Press.

about 100 *uzed* cities in Russia from which czarist officials exercised military and administrative control of their districts.

Cities with more than 10,000 residents stood out in medieval Europe except in northern Italy and Flanders where the spread of cloth production and the growth of trade permitted relatively intense urbanization. Elsewhere, large size was correlated with complex administrative, religious, educational, and economic functions. Many of the big towns—for example, Barcelona, Cologne, or Prague—supported universities as well as a wide variety of religious institutions. Their economies were diversified and included a wide range of artisans and service workers. Provincial capitals, such as Toulouse, housed royal officials of many sorts. Except in the rare case of an international manufacturing town like Bruges, the large cities of 1330 owed their size to the multiplicity of their functions, and even Bruges had once been more of a commercial and financial center than it was then. The same point can be made about the few urban giants of the Middle Ages. Paris, Milan, Venice, and Florence were commercial and manufacturing cities and also political capitals. Oriented more to international than to local trade, they supplied goods and services to distant markets. Moreover, their wealth made them major centers of consumption and attracted large numbers of sophisticated artisans and service workers.

The existence of these medieval metropolises presupposes linkages to smaller, less complex towns of a wide hinterland. In more abstract terms, the relatively spontaneous growth of market centers produces higher-order urban places and culminates in a capital city that has at least economic and usually political dominance over the region that is dependent on it. This implies that the regional capital is more closely tied to the other central places within its hinterland than to any other city or territory outside the system. In theory, therefore, a mapping of the functional interconnections among cities at any date would permit the division of a territory into its constituent regions. Unfortunately, sufficiently detailed information on migration, trade, and the local availability of services cannot be obtained for large enough numbers of towns to make such an exercise practical. The scale of towns, their location, and functions remain the best guide we have to the development of medieval urban regions.

European urban networks grew at various paces and times during the Middle Ages. Northern Italy and the Muslim regions of Spain took the lead and were followed by the Low Countries. Much later, through the thirteenth and fourteenth centuries, towns spread into eastern Germany and Poland; Russian urbanization, which fluctuated in a cycle relatively independent of that of western Europe, constituted an intermediate case. Tikhomirov (1959) estimates that about 100 fortress cities had been founded by the late eleventh century and that almost 300 existed by the time of the Mongol invasions of the thirteenth century. Among them, Novgorod with 20,000 people and Kiev with 50,000 stood out. On the basis of these estimates, Rozman (1976) gives an urbanization rate of between 3 percent and 4 percent for Russia, on a par with northern Europe generally.

The most extensive information on early urbanization is available for England in the pages of the Domesday Book, a survey of land and population taken for the new rulers shortly after the Norman Conquest. The network of settlements on which the urban system would build was virtually complete by 1066. In 1086 England had 111 boroughs ranging from London with 10,000 people to a handful of settlements with fewer than 10 inhabitants. By 1300 the numbers had grown to 480 English boroughs and 70 Welsh ones, while London housed 50,000 residents (Dodgshon and Butlin 1978). The king granted market rights to 1,200 communities between 1227 and 1350 alone (Platt 1976). It goes without saying that most of these centers were and remained very small indeed. Most did not become important links in an urban system. Even in regions of Europe with relatively low rates of urbanization today, a full early network of central places can be documented. For the period 1200–1500 geographers have mapped a total of 1,382 fortified settlements they wish to call towns in the area of present-day Yugoslavia (F. Carter 1977).

Urban Regions: A Critique of Central Place Theory

One implication of central place theory is that the regional hierarchy should be characterized by a predictable size distribution of its cities and towns. This is a complicated subject with a large literature. For instance, one can question whether population size necessarily signifies centrality. If it does, intuition tells us that the cities of a similar rank in a central place system should have similar sizes, clustering in a few size categories. Nevertheless, many geographers accept the idea that within a region the distribution of city sizes will be log-linear, approximating the rank-size rule. Each city's predicted population is given by the formula $P = A/r$, where P = population of the given city, A = population of the largest city in the hierarchy (regional capital), and r = size rank of the given city. Put simply, the rule predicts that a region whose capital has 100,000 inhabitants will have a second-largest city of 50,000, a fourth of 25,000, a tenth of 10,000, and so forth.

The use of the rank-size rule for early regional urban systems has given rise to an ambitious attempt to analyze medieval urban development by J. C. Russell (1972b).[2] His method is somewhere between a test of the rule and an application. He first estimates the population of the major towns, principally in the century 1250–1350, using existing data and constructing new figures. He then defines regions so as to maximize fit with the rank-size rule without doing violence to geographic common sense. In other words, regional boundaries are to be reasonably straight and the regions themselves relatively convex and compact.

Russell has divided western and central Europe into roughly eighteen regions, most considerably smaller than the nation-states of the twentieth century (see Figure 2.1). Only the urban systems in Portugal and the British Isles had a geographic reach in 1300 similar to that of their central governments today. The future France, Germany, and Italy were subdivided into several regional systems only loosely interconnected. Other regions, for example, those of Flanders, eastern Europe, and south Germany, spread over the boundaries of what is currently more than one country. The divisions that would one day produce Switzerland, the Netherlands, Belgium, Czechoslovakia, and Austria were still incipient, and economic ties overrode differences of language and cultural heritage.

Europe thus divided illustrates rather well the workings of the rank-size rule and the creation of central place systems where the sizes of a region's major cities have fixed, proportional relationships. The principal deviations come from the skewed sizes of capitals, which sometimes tended to be either too populous or too small in relation to the next rank of towns. London, Dublin, and Paris, for example, were *primate* capitals, disproportionately large when measured against the rest of their urban systems. On the other hand, Milan, Lübeck, Ghent, and Cordoba did not stand out from the pack as much as the rank-size rule would predict. These deviations occurred in two sorts of areas. Where urbanization was far advanced, an urban pattern of many medium-sized cities was common. In contrast, major cities with political as well as economic functions grew disproportionately large in more lightly urbanized areas. Russell has developed an index of urbanization calculated from the fraction of the total regional population living in larger towns. It shows rates of urbanization ranging between 20 percent and 25 percent in northern Italy and less than 5 percent in northern parts of France, England, and Ireland. In these early times the relative sizes of the higher ranks of urban systems were shaped by overall levels of urbanization.

Some writers have questioned whether medieval towns achieved sufficient integration to form meaningful urban systems (H. Carter 1976). But we reject the implied idea of isolated market centers. As we have already pointed out, the limits to trade among inhabitants of a small district are quickly reached, even if one adds the division of labor between urban craftsmen and peasants. There are also fiscal flows to consider and long-distance trade, which we have deliberately left out of account for the time being. The idea of "distributed" or isolated centers seems to be a fiction of modern geographers trying to situate in the past a starting point for their central place model. It cannot account for the presence of cities with thousands of inhabitants. We do accept the reality of urban regions, certainly in the heyday of medieval economic life (the twelfth and thirteenth centuries for the West). Robson (1973:34) has called the use of city-size distributions as an indicator of city systems "a very blunt-edged tool." And so it is. Nonetheless, differences in scale reflect differences in function and are the best indicator we have of rank in an urban hierarchy. Problems come when systems are delimited purely by criteria of size distributions.

It is instructive to compare the regional capitals of medieval Europe with the major cities of later times. Some have retained their place: London and Paris, of course, but also Prague, Milan, Barcelona, and Lisbon. Some have fallen back: Toledo, Ghent, Augsburg, and Lübeck, for example. And some names are missing from Russell's list: old centers such as Rome and Lyon, and later creations from Madrid to Manchester, Turin, and St. Petersburg (Leningrad). We shall at later points pay considerable attention to the processes by which centers of trade, political capitals, and industrial cities grew and acquired power and influence.

By looking at the regions defined by Russell, we also can get a sense of what the central place approach leaves unexplained in the pattern of early European urbanization. Three points stand out.

(1) The less urbanized regions are larger in area than those with more intensive urban development. This is not due to lower population density in the former; Russell's urbanization index confirms the inverse correlation between region size and the percentage of total population in the principal towns. It can be argued that a small index of urbanization reflects a rudimentary state of economic development, but one must then question whether the large and loosely urbanized areas in question are sufficiently integrated to constitute regions in any meaningful sense. At best, their regional systems will be administrative or political with little economic content, as Rozman (1976) argues was the case in Russia at a comparable stage. However, it is troubling to have to define regions on the basis of political criteria in such clearly feudal areas as thirteenth-century France and central Germany.

The same point can be looked at from the other side, in terms of the potential "underbounding" of heavily urbanized regions. They are drawn small by Russell even though the very intensity of urban development argues for activities linked to a wider area. Russell's regions are in fact designed to enclose the minimum area containing enough cities to constitute a central place hierarchy. They are probably inoperative in intensely urban areas, where the system of cities is larger than the postulated region, as well as in places where the urban fabric is too loose to organize the necessary area effectively.

(2) The Central Place System implies a more or less even spatial distribution of cities around a central capital, with regional boundaries typically falling in zones of weak urban interaction. The analogy with a river basin is appropriate.[3] But Russell's European regions are not primarily of this type. Particularly in the heavily urbanized areas, regional boundaries run squarely through active zones such as Picardy and the Po plain. Moreover, the capitals of large regions often lie near an edge, specifically in the direction of more concentrated urbanization outside the regions: examples include Cologne, Toledo, and Prague, as well as a number of ports such as London and Barcelona. These cities in fact act as gateways or portals into their region, not as distance-minimizing central places.

(3) The Central Place System views urbanization as an outgrowth of rural development. In it, economic activity grows from local exchange and production for local markets to the higher stage of

long-distance trade and a more complex division of labor. In one version of the model, military or religious elites play a determining role by providing conditions of security in exchange for surplus. Yet what we know of their patterns of consumption implies that long-distance trade must have played an earlier and more important role than this model suggests. Moreover, in order to import luxuries, Europe had to export staples. The model is therefore deficient or incomplete in economic as well as in geographic terms.

The Network System

The foregoing observations point to an alternative approach to medieval cities. Let us step back from the attempt to delimit urban regions within Europe and look at the distribution of principal cities over the continent as a whole (see Figure 2.1). The dominant feature is without question the concentration of "large" and "very large" centers in a few areas. Two clusters stand out: northern Italy and the Low Countries. Each has important outriders, Mediterranean ports such as Naples and Marseille in one case, the London-Paris-Cologne triad in the other. Excluding Prague, whose size the map probably overstates, and Toulouse, there were no other major centers in Catholic Europe. Any theory or model of a European system must consider this larger distribution and give due weight to the dual urban core.

Let us go back for a moment to the origins of intensive urbanization near the Mediterranean in the several centuries before the more general urban revival that we have dated at approximately A.D. 1000. First, many of the Roman towns continued to be occupied, although much reduced in scale. Moreover, the kings of the invading Ostrogoths, Visigoths, Lombards, and Vandals called some of the Roman towns capitals and settled in them for a time while attempting to make use there of the administrative procedures of the late Empire (Ewig 1963). Urban continuity was greatest, of course, in the cases of episcopal centers, although the extent of urban activity outside the walls of the bishops' fortified palaces must have varied widely. Between the sixth and eighth centuries the greatest relative concentration of towns was found in Italy. Post-Roman holdovers overlapped with new centers of trade; as Rome, Bologna, and Milan went into eclipse, Amalfi, Pavia, and Venice grew.

Beyond Italy a number of nonagrarian settlements emerged during the period from the seventh through the ninth centuries. Surprisingly perhaps, they tended to be situated along seacoasts and navigable rivers and in other exposed locations. A line of fortified settlements reached north-south from Novgorod to Kiev in Russia. Another set of places bordered on the North and Baltic seas or on rivers flowing into them, from Quentowic on the Somme and Dorestad on the Rhine to Birka in Sweden and Haithabu (Hedeby) in Schleswig. This last is known to have included craftsmen as well as traders, rich and poor. Iron and glass were produced there. Luxuries from the south and slaves were brought in for distribution over a wide area (Ennen 1979). Finally, England seems to have experienced some urban revival in the context of the struggle between Danes and Saxons. The five Danish fortified towns of Nottingham, Leicester, Derby, Lincoln, and Stamford were opposed by royal *burh*s of the Saxon kings. The common characteristic of these various protourban settlements is that they were exposed to the turbulence of war, invasion, and plunder rather than tucked away in a peaceful corner. They testify to the continuing, if precarious, existence of long-distance trade and to the stimulating, if fractious, contacts between rival cultures.

If we accept the idea that neither trade nor the social order completely disappeared and that some urban functions as well as urban places persisted, it is still possible to treat them as marginal vestiges of the past or forerunners of the later urbanization we examined in the previous chapter. In this view the prevailing themes of European life in these so-called Dark Ages remain autarky and anarchy. Only as self-contained manorial estates of warrior lords and serfs could communities hope to survive. But this may be too stark a view. There are reasons to believe that trade, and therefore the economic basis for urban life, fared better than conventional interpretations suggest.

As a means of gathering surplus, plunder is effective but limited. It represents an extreme strategy in the trade-off between encouraging surplus creation and securing a maximum share. This point must be borne in mind in considering the Dark Ages, particularly since we are dealing with extraordinarily long periods of time. If wave after wave of raiders found something to sack and pillage, surely there must have been periods of recovery and reconstruction in between! Moreover, the invaders always settled down somewhere, and a kingdom, even a barbaric one, cannot be managed only by unrestrained exaction. The warriors would receive an estate with slaves or serfs to work it.

In the conventional story of a long European night, the villains were outside invaders, most notably the Saracens and Norsemen. Like others, they began as terrible raiders and later carved out substantial European domains. But these two groups left a lasting mark, becoming assimilated in the case of the Norsemen or Normans, while the Saracens or Moors of Spain were expelled only centuries later. Despite a long and distinguished record, Saracens and Norsemen still bear an image of total and primitive savagery carried over from European accounts of the years of pillage and conquest. To put it bluntly and in modern terms, this record includes a large measure of ideological propaganda. It was compiled by clerics who saw their fledging Christian order threatened with extinction by pagans and who did not hesitate to caricature the enemy. Skilled, daring, and fierce as these attackers were, their accomplishments belie their reputation, as recent examination of indigenous sources make clear. After all, the Saracen pirates belonged to a great empire and a great civilization, whose outpost at Cordoba was a brilliant city of many hundred thousand in which science and the arts, as well as trade, flourished in a climate of tolerance (Arberry 1967). The more rustic Norsemen, for their part, ranged easily from Iceland to Russia, through which they managed to trade with Constantinople (Latouche 1967; Lombard 1972). The mistake is in thinking that trade and war were incompatible, or that cultural and religious clashes precluded mutually profitable exchanges. Scholars now believe that on balance the bold sailors and warriors who controlled the northern and southern seas contributed to the economic activity, if not to the tranquility, of Christian Europe in the High Middle Ages.

If one reflects on the conventional view of the Dark Ages, the conclusion that urban economic activity was negligible then is quite clearly based on the near absence of the structures of civilization necessary to sustain systematic or long-distance trade. Underlying this reasoning is a narrow concentration on Europe as it would become. This cultural parochialism may be unconscious or it may reflect, as in the case of Pirenne (1925), an explicit theory about the barriers raised by cultural hostility. If one broadens one's scope to fit the realities of the period, the picture changes drastically.

Western Europe is seen for what it was: a minor hinterland of two flourishing, though rival, empires in the Near East, centering on Constantinople and Baghdad respectively. Or, if one chooses to give greater weight to the trade of Frisians and Norsemen in the North and Baltic seas, the continent appears as a barrier between two unequal zones of maritime activity.

As has long been known, trade has always shown an amazing ability to permeate remote, desolate, or turbulent areas, even very large ones. All that is needed is a profit incentive and a trading center strong enough to furnish entrepreneurs, finance, and markets. One has only to think of caravan routes through the steppes and deserts of Asia and Africa, or of the sailors taking small ships through uncharted seas. By comparison, the river valleys, plains, and mountain passes of Europe do not seem like formidable obstacles. So it is quite reasonable to accept a certain amount of long-distance trade through and in Europe as part of an Eurasian network reaching out to northern Europe, sub-Saharan Africa, and China from its Near Eastern core. For the period before A.D. 1000 we can reconcile continuing long-distance trade in Europe with very sparse urban activity by noting links to a great network centered to the east.

The idea of trading links provides the basis for a second model of European urbanization, which we call the Network System. Cities form the centers, nodes, junctions, outposts, and relays of the network. We shall consider, in order, the economic, political, and spatial aspects of this system.[4]

Directly or indirectly, a trading network relies on agricultural and other commodity production. Raw materials for traded goods, food to sustain the cities, and potentially large untapped markets are to be found in the countryside. In this light, a primarily agricultural region may develop its urban array in a way almost opposite to the process implied by central place theory. An initial center serves as the gateway, the link to the larger network, and it typically remains the principal city. From this urban base flows the stimulus to production of larger surpluses, drawing on underused reserves of land and labor (Myint 1971). Lesser centers serve primarily to gather and ship the staple or export crop, secondarily to distribute a return flow of goods and provide other central place services. If export-led development is successful, it will in time induce the formation of a central place array based on local trade. How soon

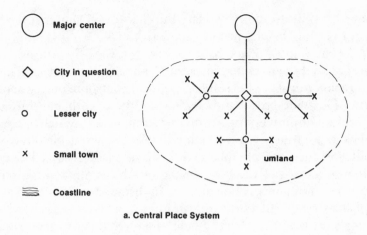

Major center

City in question

Lesser city

Small town

Coastline

a. Central Place System

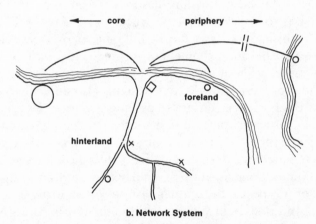

◄—— core   periphery ——►

foreland

hinterland

b. Network System

Figure 2.2. Interurban links for a city in two urban systems. Cities evolve distinctive spheres of interaction. In the Central Place System each city deals with several subordinate towns in its *umland* and with one larger, more complex center. A city in the Network System functions as a gateway for the towns in its regional *hinterland* and is linked to the larger network via its *foreland*.

and how strongly this happens may depend as much on the nature of the export good as on the prosperity of trade. Arable farming probably spreads stronger roots than pastoral pursuits, and fishing is better than hunting, whereas forestry and mining can yield quite varied outcomes.[5] Local processing of export commodities also needs to be considered, but we shall defer it to the discussion of proto-industrialization in Chapters 5 and 7. Although the view of major cities as gateways and originators of regional systems has been applied mainly to the Americas, Burghardt (1971) uses it for Bratislava on the Danube in early modern times.

Like the Central Place System, the Network System has a political as well as an economic variant. The initial urban settlements in a region can serve to establish political control in one or another form. The widespread land clearings of the twelfth and thirteenth centuries within western Europe were anchored by newly created towns and villages with revealing names: Newton, Neuilly, Neustadt. On a larger scale, planned towns or bastides served German colonization east of the Elbe during the thirteenth and fourteenth centuries. They were also common in disputed regions such as the Welsh marches. In Guyenne-Aquitaine, where two centuries of struggle between French and English followed the devastation caused by religious strife and repression, bastides served to resettle territory as well as to secure authority over it (Vance 1977). Finally, cities have furnished the bases for the full range of overseas colonial enterprises, whether for settlement or for trade only, with or without formal assumption of sovereignty by the colonial power.

The spatial properties of the two systems also differ markedly. The key is the Network System's flexibility. Since cities are links in a network, often neither the first source nor the ultimate destination of goods, they are in some measure interchangeable as are the routes themselves. Marketing shifts, political conflicts and policies, even innovations in shipping or banking can lead to the displacement of one center by another. Europe offers many examples in medieval and Renaissance times. Within the Italian core area the earliest ports were Bari and Amalfi. Venice surpassed them before A.D. 1000, while Genoa grew to strength in the succeeding two centuries. From the thirteenth to the fifteenth centuries Florence and Milan disputed the leadership of the two great Italian ports. Pisa, Lucca, Pavia, and others also had days in the sun. Throughout, however, the place of northern Italy as a key center of the European network remained secure. A similar changeable stability characterized the axis connecting Italy with the other urban center in the Netherlands. Until the eleventh century Germany and the Rhine were preferred. Then, with the development of the great fairs of Champagne, the French route prevailed until the troubles of the fourteenth century again caused Germany to come to the fore. By the sixteenth century a variety of routes coexisted. Their relative importance can be gauged by the shifting commercial for-

Table 2.2. Characteristics of Central Place and Network Systems.

Characteristic	Central Place System	Network System
Structure		
Basic unit	Agricultural region and/or local administrative unit	Trading network
Role of city	Central place in a hierarchy of central places	Node in a network of linked cities divided into core and periphery
Shape	Territorial and geometric	Maritime and irregular
Ideal type	Market city (Leicester)	Merchant city (Venice)
Functions		
Economic	Marketing and services	Trade, particularly long distance
Political	Administration with hierarchical, regular links to local units	Informal controls or imperial hegemony
Cultural	Orthogenetic	Heterogenetic
Evolution		
Economic pressures for growth	Supply-push	Demand-pull
Direction of development	Up from the base	Out from the core
Prime movers	Producers: craftsmen and farmers	Traders: merchants and bankers

tunes of the cities—principally Frankfurt, Lyon, Geneva, and Augsburg—that had taken over much of the linkage role from the fairs.

Networks are not bound to linear distance in the way central place regions are. Time and money count for more than geometry: the costs and risks of carriage balanced against the opportunities for profit (Braudel 1966). Routes to forge new interurban links or open up resource-rich plains and ore-laden hills to the world market were constantly being prospected and established. But they could as easily be abandoned. Water transport played a preponderant role throughout, though mountain passes counted also. In particular, the two inland seas, the Mediterranean-Adriatic and the Channel–North Sea–Baltic, served to unite trading centers rather than to separate them. The penumbrae of cities around the cores of European urbanization have already been mentioned. Valencia, Ragusa (Dubrovnik), and Salonika were also effectively close to the southern centers. In the north the member cities and trading posts of the Hanseatic League—Bergen, Danzig, and beyond—sustained easy ties with the core, whereas inland towns away from navigable rivers experienced poorer access and correspondingly more difficult growth even when they were less distant. With the triumph of European maritime expansion, Atlantic ports came to the fore— Cádiz, Bordeaux, Bristol—and new centers displaced or joined the old: in turn Antwerp, Amsterdam, and Hamburg. Also, the northern core eclipsed its senior rival to the south. But the basic articulation of the network showed remarkable staying power. In terms of the Network System the main process underlying early European urbanization was a gradual strengthening of trading centers, originally dependent on an extra-European network, until they became dual cores of the European "world economy" (Wallerstein 1974; Braudel 1979).

Some medieval cities had attractive powers far beyond their agricultural hinterlands. Long before the era of airplanes and railroads, citizens of trading towns overleaped common constraints and forged new links to the far corners of the world. Marco Polo traveled from Italy to Acre, Tabriz, and finally Peking in his search for adventure and profit. A look at his home city, Venice, and its development will help to illustrate the workings of the Network System in preindustrial times.

The city began as a string of small communities on the islands of the Venetian lagoon.[6] Cassiodorus, a Roman official, compared their houses to aquatic birds, who moved from sea to land. Boatmen and salt workers, subjects of the Byzantine emperor, made their living as middlemen, linking the Italian mainland to the eastern empire. Before A.D. 100 they secured their own livelihoods by exchanging salt and fish for food, and then built an expanded trade upon urban demand for slaves and wood. As the Venetians became exporters and organizers of mainland resources, they added a ship-building industry to their economic base. In time they became important intermediaries between Constantinople and northern Italy, and by the tenth century Venetians were the leading merchants of the upper Adriatic. But the city's power stemmed from more than commercial skill. Successes by the Venetian war fleet in the eleventh century brought trading concessions throughout the Byzantine empire, as well as overlordship of Dalmatia. And in the thirteenth century the doge persuaded the knights of the Fourth Crusade to help the city's fleet sack Constantinople and win for Venice control of strategic areas such as Crete and Ragusa. Political control followed on the heels of the Venetian economic presence in the eastern Mediterranean. Unlike service cities whose strength came from their territorial base, Venice used its conquests to reinforce its sea power. Its colonies scattered around the upper Adriatic served as bases for the fleet, information stations, and sources of food, raw materials, and trading contacts. Venice created a maritime empire that served to support the city's far-flung commercial interests.

The core of the empire was the city itself, a magnificent composition of canals, houses, and palaces that in Byron's words "sat in state, throned on her hundred isles." Its center in the area around San Marco comprised the doge's palace, the harbor, a central piazza, and a campanile whose bells rang the hours and whose lights served as a ship's beacon. The city's main "street," the Grand Canal, was kept wide enough for a 200-ton ship to sail through. Traders thronged the area around the Rialto bridge, and eventually the palaces of many noble families lined the banks. Expanded industrial development, which followed Venetian influence in foreign markets, was largely confined to specialized areas where the needed workshops and warehouses could be constructed away from the commercial traffic of the central city.

The close links among government, commerce, and shipping that can be seen in the city's plan were much more than symbolic. The

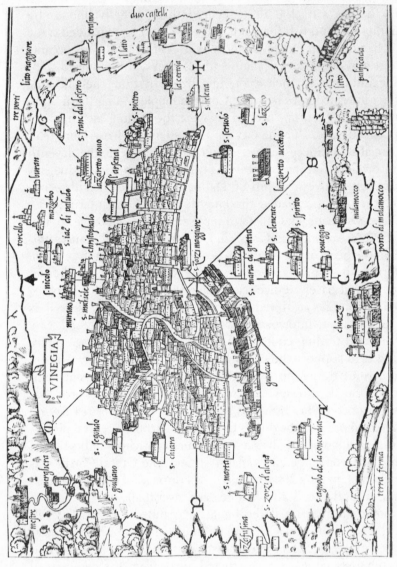

Figure 2.3. Venice. This late-sixteenth-century map by Benedetto Bourdon shows clearly the maritime orientation of the city. Some of the many islands had special functions. The Piazza San Marco was the focal point of the city, while the churches and their squares served as neighborhood centers. (From Molmenti 1927, II:41.)

Venetian commune controlled much of the city's economic life. The state owned the great galleys of the merchant and war fleets and regulated their design, crews, and cargoes, as well as the timing of voyages. Residents of the city owed compulsory military service as oarsmen. Traders' activities were highly regulated, too, in Lane's (1973) judgment in order to improve citizens' chances for commercial profits and to dampen conflicts among sections of the nobility. Since the commune's survival depended upon the unified support of powerful citizens, many of the elaborate rules for economic and political life were designed to ensure evenhandedness among the major families of the oligarchy.

On the basis of their tightly controlled fleet and partnerships of merchants, Venetians built a trading system that provided several centuries of commercial prosperity and political power. The city's domination of the nearby mainland, which was increased by the land purchases of the nobility as well as by coercion and sharp dealing, helped ensure an adequate food supply and made Venice a regional entrepôt. This small territorial base, however, was no more than the pedestal of Venetian power. Navigation laws and the strength of the fleet kept Venice at the center of a vast East-West trade that exchanged the goods of northern Europe for the spices, silks, and other products of the Orient. Venetians brought wool, metals, and raw materials first overland from Champagne fairs and later by direct voyages from Bruges and Baltic towns back to Venice for transshipment throughout the eastern Mediterranean. From Persia, India, and China, caravan routes largely in the hands of Muslim merchants converged on Jiddah, Alexandria, Acre, and Constantinople, where colonies of Venetians bought goods to ship home for resale in the north and sold other products to eastern buyers. Venice, and later its rival Genoa, were the centers of an urban network that bridged the centers of the known world.

Conclusion: A Dual Perspective and a Regional Typology

To summarize, the Central Place System is rooted in the stability of the land and its tillers. A neat geometric mosaic of graduated centers structures the commercial, administrative, and cultural needs of a region and eventually integrates regions into a unified nation. The peril is that the power of the central state and the luster of the court and capital will become too great, draining the land of its material and human riches and imposing the norms of an official culture and a burdensome bureaucracy. The bloated primate capital city in an otherwise torpid array of towns is the visible embodiment of excess in this mode of urban development.

By contrast, the Network System testifies to the mercurial force of movable wealth and universal ideas. If the links among its cities could be described mathematically, it would be with topology rather than Euclidian geometry. At the heart of the system is an "internationale of cities," each determinedly autonomous and more concerned with the world at large than with its own backyard. A single city's culture, like its population and trade, is apt to be cosmopolitan and varied. Typically, a wealthy oligarchy exercises quiet but tough rule over the city-state, tolerating much that territorial societies repress so long as the local order is not threatened. Even though hopelessly outweighed in geopolitical terms, network cities are often able to achieve and retain astonishing power and to control—for themselves, for an alliance of cities, or for a nominal sovereign— vast maritime or colonial empires. On the darker side, their bold quest for profits is no more inhibited by the exploitation of human beings than it is by distance or by traditional values and superstitions. Even before taking readily to capitalism, network cities organized trades built on the unfree workers of galleys, spice plantations, silver mines, and feudal estates. If xenophobic nationalism is the historic sin of one system, that of the other is salt-water imperialism.

How can the dual perspectives be combined? Several possibilities can be suggested. Do they perhaps refer to two separate groups of cities? Van Werveke (1963) in fact suggests that some cities are outgrowths of rural activity and territorial organization, whereas others act as gateways or fit into a network. Certainly, cities differ in their mix of territorial organization, as a comparison of Leicester and Venice suggests. But remember that even Venice had tight links with the mainland and that Leicester had its long-distance traders. Another view, articulated by Berry (1961), is that urbanization passes through stages that approximate successively our Central Place and Network Systems. Other scholars support the notion of alternating historical phases of dominance for one or the other model: the first in much of the medieval period of city creation and the second in the Renaissance and early modern heyday of mercantile trade. Later discussions will show strong central place elements in the onset of industrial urbanization, whereas the generalized urbanization of the twentieth century can perhaps be seen as a take-over by the metropolis with network linkages becoming primary (Friedmann 1953). Finally, Braudel (1967) adopts a dialectical approach in which urbanization results from the synthesis of two sets of forces: rural production and monetary trade.

As must now be clear, our own preference is to retain the two models as complementary ways of looking at interurban relationships and at the complex process that is urbanization. Most larger cities have a place in both sorts of systems. Each model illuminates certain episodes better than others, but they often suggest converging explanations of observed facts. A few brief examples will illustrate this.

Trade can develop to an extent either without towns or beside them. Local markets were far more numerous in medieval and later times than true towns, no matter how modest a population threshold one chooses for an urban place. Also, large fairs were held near small towns, suggesting the existence of a network in which fairs made up for the absence of an adequate urban setting at strategic points. The great twelfth-century fairs were located in Champagne because of the province's situation between Flanders and Italy, not owing to any special local stimulus. By the fourteenth century cities had largely replaced major fairs in the west, although they continued in the east, for example at Frankfurt-an-der-Oder, Breslau, Poznan, and Leipzig. Specialized fairs continued, as they do to this day, and there were many smaller ones (Pounds 1973). A regional fair can make it possible for a weakly urbanized region to enjoy intermittently a high level of central place services. But it can also serve to gather a local staple for export through the larger trading network, particularly when the product is of high value but variable quality, as in the case of truffles or wine.

In addition to the urban cores and the inland sea coastlines, an east-west band in central Germany stands out for early concentration of settlements and towns. A perspective based on our Central Place System would suggest the influence of the region's favorable agricultural situation as a fertile loess belt between the mountains to the south and the cold plain to the north. But awareness of the alternative system forces acknowledgment of the location within the region of an early trade route, the *Hellweg* (Pounds 1973).

The areas of intense urbanization in Europe generally excelled in agriculture. This was certainly the case in northern Italy, in southeastern Spain, and in Flanders. Again, the question is whether large agricultural surpluses hastened the expansion of cities or whether sophisticated commercial farming was stimulated by urban demand, financed by merchant capital, and managed for profit-minded landlords by literate bailiffs or farmers. Both forces, we feel, contributed to growth.

The two models provide a dual framework for looking at the regions formed during the medieval period. One focuses attention on the traditional rural economy and society as the base from which urbanization proceeds. The other suggests the potential of urban stimuli for rural change and points to the importance of a region's position in the European system or network. We have described the dual urbanized core, the coastal extensions and intermediate zones, and the "distant" peripheries. Our framework will make it possible to examine in later chapters regional responses to two developments that powerfully conditioned later European urbanization: centralized states and industrial capitalism.

Hechter and Brustein (1980) offer a typology of medieval regions that helps to give a regional dimension to our systems analysis of medieval urbanization. They distinguish three types of regions, arranged in roughly concentric order around the focuses of urbanization in the Middle Ages. The *Roman-Germanic core* led European urban revival largely on the basis of commercial development. This area was the most strongly urbanized, and it had the most commercial agriculture, clearly influenced by the proximity of urban markets. Here strong central states were slow to consolidate, while commercial and protoindustrial capitalists thrived, from early Italian and south German bankers to Dutch merchants or Belgian iron masters and clothiers. Adjoining the core were strongly *feudal regions* of France, England, central Spain, and some parts of Germany in which, however, commercial towns also grew during the Middle Ages. Clearly, much urban revival here followed central place logic, growth being generated by three-field agriculture with a feudal-monastic order to guide and organize the surplus. Additional growth was derived from proximity to the commercial core. How much is attributable to each is hard to disentangle. Here, however, the central state achieved full power, not least because town and country were well balanced in strength. Finally, the Celtic fringe of western Europe was touched only lightly by the productive energies of long-distance trade and commercial agriculture. It remained pastoral, weakly urbanized, and virtually tribal in sociopolitical terms. These peripheral regions became dominated by external states and in later centuries lagged behind in the development of commercial agriculture and industrial capitalism. Port cities were enclaves with little effect on the interior.

Neither Hechter and Brustein nor we are in a position to give a full account of the genesis of the three regional types. However, their argument has the great merit of pointing out that economics and politics are correlated, and that a regional nexus cannot be understood without reference to culture, social structure, the agrarian system, and urbanization. These relationships, however, are not fixed over time. During the preindustrial period, the economic dominance of the core areas was scarcely challenged. Later, in the age of capitalist industrialization the economic center would shift largely to the earlier intermediate, or feudal, regions. It is premature to pose the question why the shift occurred, except to suggest that the feudal regions had great scope for agricultural improvement and would benefit from the unifying force of a central state. More recently another phase has begun. Europe in the second half of the twentieth century has seen the revenge or renewed flowering of the old core, from the brilliant cities that ring the North and Baltic seas to the several Mediterranean economic miracles.

CHAPTER 3

The Demography
of Preindustrial Cities

THE TUSCAN TOWN of Prato in 1339 held some 10,600 inhabitants, but by 1357 just over 6,000 people remained (Herlihy and Klapisch 1978). This catastrophic loss was, of course, caused by the Black Death or bubonic plague that swept through western and southern Europe in 1348 and 1349, killing perhaps a third of the population (Barraclough 1979). Prato's demographic collapse typified that of many places in the region. Yet this terrible plague was only one episode in the troubled story of late medieval and Renaissance Prato's population. In 1300 the town numbered about 15,000 inhabitants; in 1427 the careful count of the *catasto* showed only 3,533 souls. Epidemics of plague recurred again and again, while hunger, war, and emigration helped other diseases take a quieter but equally relentless toll. Moreover, urban populations could take long to recover, as the nearby Tuscan metropolis demonstrates. Having lost almost as high a percentage of its population as Prato from preplague days to 1427, Florence only began to grow again after about 1460 (Herlihy and Klapisch 1978). The 37,000 inhabitants of 1427 were only about 41,000 in 1480, and the 1552 total of 59,000 represented no more than half the number who had crowded the city in the early fourteenth century. When we think of the artistic glories of Medicean Florence, it is sobering to remember that in human terms the city of Botticelli and Donatello, and even that of Michelangelo, was little more than a shadow of its bustling late medieval self.

Many examples of decline and stagnation interrupt the dominant process of urban growth in early Europe. Recurring catastrophes shook Italy north and south of Florence, too: 100,000 deaths in four major northern cities in 1576–77, with further losses of 25 percent to 70 percent in 1630; half the population of Genoa and Naples gone after the epidemic of 1656 (Mols 1974). While the data are nowhere so rich and precise as for Italy, the sufferings and losses were no less in fourteenth-century France, seventeenth-century Germany and Spain, or even Scandinavia in the early eighteenth century. Demographic data confirm the lurid tales of contemporaries, which we might be tempted to discount as prestatistical hyperbole.

The saga of European urbanization is ultimately one of people who chose to live in cities and were able to settle, maintain, and reproduce themselves there. This implies an urban environment that is comparatively benign as well as attractive. The persistence and resilience of urban life in the midst of catastrophes, such as those we have noted in fourteenth- and fifteenth-century Tuscany, cannot be taken for granted. We need to pose and try to answer a series of questions about urban communities as settings for social life, and the place to start is with a look at town populations.

The vital processes of urban dwellers represent an essential dimension of our examination, letting us gauge not only city size and growth but also the quality of urban life. How many new residents are born, baptized, and raised in a given place? How many die by comparison with rural areas? How many people over time come to settle? How many, natives or immigrants, leave? Demographic patterns in fact supply us with convenient measuring sticks for the relative attraction of the urban community, since changing numbers of people not only influence economic and social trends but strongly reflect them as well. Moreover, looking behind vital statistics to the processes of life and death—marriage, fertility, morbidity, and mortality—brings us closer to the rhythms and occasions of ordinary urban life than almost anything else can.

Research on early population movements has proceeded on an enormous scale in the last few decades, although the key technique of family reconstitution on the basis of parish records has been applied more often to small, relatively closed, rural communities than to cities. Social historians are building on the work of historical demographers by looking closely at family organization, inheritance patterns, and the links between population change and wealth, occupation, and social status.[1] There are still plenty of gaps and uncertainties, of course, and the evidence thins out as one moves away from the urbanized core of Europe.

In this chapter we look at the demographic aspects of urbanization in both medieval and early modern Europe. To be sure, death rates declined and population grew during the later eighteenth century within the period we call "protoindustrial," but the dramatic consequences for urbanization were largely delayed until well into the nineteenth century in most of Europe. As for the implied unity of medieval and early modern Europe, the fact is that we have little hard evidence beyond estimates of town size for the Middle Ages as such. Herlihy and Klapisch's (1978) data for fourteenth-century Tuscan cities and their surroundings are exceptional glimpses of a precociously "modern" corner of the continent.

Malthus Modified

Any analysis of European population in the period before industrialization must begin with the Malthusian model, which was elaborated, as it happens, just when the number of people and the production of goods for their support were beginning a period of unprecedented growth (Malthus 1798). Though far from the whole story, the model retains great intellectual force, and it makes us look closely at developments we might otherwise pass over.

To put the argument as simply as possible, Malthus noted that population growth is inherently a cumulative process, sustaining itself as long as sufficient food can be procured. Food production, on the other hand, is constrained by the finite stock of suitable land. The result is a tendency for productivity and wages to decline until the standard of living falls too low to support further population growth. The only sustainable state is one of general misery, of bare and precarious survival for the maximum number a land can maintain.

Let us focus for a moment on the logic of the model. By its nature, population growth is a positive-feedback process: the output of the system is also an input. In other words, people do not merely produce children; they produce future parents. As with a sum of money placed at compound interest, the greater the number of children today, the greater the potential for even more children tomorrow. Although it is also true that children grow up to work as well as to eat and reproduce, the finite stock of natural resources imposes diminishing returns on their efforts to create more food.

As the number of people working an unchanging amount of land increases, the increments of output get smaller and smaller. In economic terms, the marginal product of labor falls, and with it the market-determined, food-equivalent wage of workers.[2] Malthus focused on the implications of diminishing returns for population growth. To use his terms, unless there are autonomous *preventive* checks on human fertility, which he thought unlikely, the inescapable fall in per capita output and income will lead to increased mortality, a *positive* check to population. The reason is that so long as incomes are higher than the bare subsistence level, fertility remains higher than mortality, and new mouths continue to absorb any surplus.

As a rough first approximation, the Malthusian model explains the population history of Europe at least up to the time of the Reverend Thomas. Long phases of population growth were brought to an end under conditions of widespread misery and increased mortality in the fourteenth and seventeenth centuries. A closer look will suggest that some refinements and modifications are needed, and also that the model leaves some aspects of the record unaccounted for. Different populations may well have relied on different and changing combinations of positive and preventive checks to limit growth. As usual, theory proves too tidy for the historical experience, but it helps focus attention on specific and sometimes new questions by clearing up others and by highlighting paradoxes.

The first point that needs amplification is technological progress as an offset to diminishing returns. From our contemporary vantage point, we tend to believe confidently that human ingenuity can continue to outsmart nature, despite the fact that natural resources are not only finite but actually subject to erosion through pollution and depletion. Even if we look at the apparent victory of the West over resource limitations in the eighteenth to twentieth centuries, much of it actually consists in having gained control over natural resources from an ever wider area in and out of Europe (E. Jones 1981). This appropriation has taken many forms, and began perhaps with the early medieval practice of carrying topsoil to village gardens. In time, grain was brought in from great distances, while coal and mineral fertilizers were dug from the ground. In a sense, however, all this simply made further inroads on the finite stock of natural resources and thus intensified western dependence on nature rather than reducing it. It certainly calls into question whether the western model of development and high urbanization can be generalized or even indefinitely sustained.

To get back to the historical question, if we postulate an underlying acceleration of technological progress in Europe we can explain why, when the medieval wave of population growth ended in a decline, the early modern one merely resulted in stagnation and the nineteenth-century expansion was slowed by preventive rather than positive checks. Figure 3.1 shows population curves and the trend of production. The dashed line indicates the Malthusian population ceiling set by resources and technology, a con-

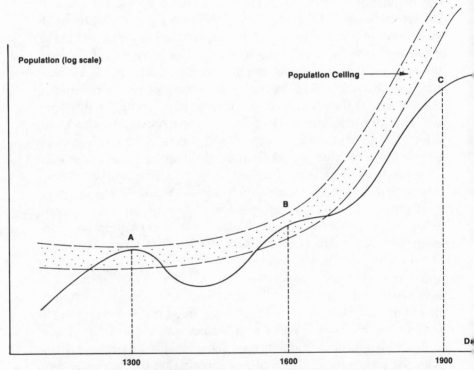

Figure 3.1. A simple Malthusian model of European population in the long run. Resources and technology set a ceiling on the capacity of the land to support people. The length and depth of decline after the crisis at A is not easily explained. The third slowdown in population growth, at C, and in some places even the second at B, resulted from reduced fertility rather than from higher mortality, that is, from preventive as opposed to positive checks.

straint that became less limiting over time. The rough constancy of population in the seventeenth century actually represents a decline relative to the productive capacity of the system. The post-1900 slowdown of population growth—for countries other than France—indicates that affluent, urbanized people can reduce their fertility and so remain comfortably away from any mortality-enhancing ceiling.

A second refinement of the Malthusian model is accomplished by recognizing the stochastic element, the role of "accidents" on the side of mortality. In fact, the principal positive checks to population growth have taken the form of sharp mortality peaks owing to epidemic disease, famine, and sometimes war, peaks that could wipe out decades of normal growth in a year or two. Disease and hunger threaten even sparse preindustrial populations, and mortality surges were characteristic of Europe right up to the middle of the nineteenth century. But the Malthusian view predicts they will be more deadly, and probably more common, when population is pressing on resources. Stocks of grain that can tide people over a bad harvest are likely to be smaller; malnutrition increases the ravages caused by disease; desperate people eat spoiled or indigestible things or take to the roads. In fact, the critical fourteenth and fifteenth centuries saw repeated and sharp mortality peaks in Florence, which had no fewer than sixteen outbreaks of pestilence between 1300 and 1500 (Herlihy and Klapisch 1978). Again in the seventeenth century, one notes eight epidemic years that allegedly wiped out 100,000 people in Amsterdam within half a century, almost as many as lived in the city at that time. Comparable holocausts were reported for Breslau, Danzig, Königsberg, and Leiden (Mols 1974). The point is that population did not grow steadily until it reached the equilibrium of misery or a resource-imposed ceiling. Rather, growth slowed, stopped, or was actually reversed well before, with the growing proportion of the poor particularly vulnerable to recurring catastrophes.

In relation to the simple model, preindustrial western Europe exhibited one striking and aberrant characteristic. While population did tend to grow in the presence of abundant land, the *rate* of increase always remained moderate. The fertility rates, lower than in other societies, indicate the presence of preventive checks to births. These checks were communal rather than individual and amounted to a European system of social control of fertility. The most common mode of control in western Europe was to impose socioeconomic conditions on marriage: a tenancy or guild membership for the groom, an appropriate dowry for the bride. As a result, people were often forced to marry late and many remained single throughout life because they could not achieve an independent situation. When combined with adequate discouragement of childbearing out of wedlock, with long birth intervals associated with prolonged lactation, and with high infant mortality, limitations on marriage reduced the potential for population growth between mortality peaks. In rough numbers, a "normal" couple could expect some five births with perhaps three children surviving to adulthood. Given the proportion of celibates and infertile unions, this meant that the population would not do very much more than reproduce itself. On the other hand, the system retained a strong capacity for demographic recovery. Even the population losses from the most severe plagues and famines could be made up in a very few years (Watkins and Menken 1982). Early marriage and remarriage were encouraged by the property and positions that became available, for instance, after a catastrophic epidemic.

Social control of fertility was not egalitarian. The system operated so as to allow the more prosperous groups to bear and raise a more than proportional share of children. It is true that the clergy were recruited largely from these groups, but this was offset by the advantages of wealth: early marriage—at least a young bride— and better, more secure conditions in which to bear and bring up children. In fifteenth-century Florence there were almost as many children in the city as in the *contado*, simply because Florentines owned most of the region's wealth (Herlihy and Klapisch 1978). A most surprising consequence of this pattern, by the way, is that social mobility in preindustrial Europe must have been predominantly downward! The positive relationship between wealth and population growth sometimes was reversed, however. Elites restricted marriage and limited births in depressed times. But low property incomes could imply relatively high real wages, which encouraged higher fertility among the poor. Marriage ages declined and more children survived during periods when the purchasing power of workers was relatively high.

The idea of social mechanisms for controlling population size has implications beyond the rules for marriage. Indeed, it is familiar even to students of animal populations. Consider the demographic impact of wars, which we earlier included in the list of mortality accidents. As a rule, European wars did not kill enough people to make a real dent in the total population of a region. Yet Europe had its share of long wars—really series of wars—that proved deadly indeed during their hundred-year or even thirty-year courses. The fighting itself was seldom the culprit. Looting and destruction by soldiers living off the land, interference with agricultural tasks in their season, and most notably the spread of disease by soldiers, camp followers, and refugees were more lethal than battles. The question is whether the frequency and deadliness of wars were influenced by the population cycle. Some evidence suggests that periods of slow recovery after population setbacks were somewhat more peaceful than average, for example, the mid-fifteenth century and the second quarter of the eighteenth century. This raises the intriguing possibility that rulers were more reluctant, or financially less able, to fight wars when the human raw material was scarce or found better opportunities than soldiering. In other words, war, like marriage, may have functioned as an element in the social process of population control.

With the inclusion of material progress, random catastrophes, and collective inhibition of rapid growth, the Malthusian model gains further explanatory power. It then helps focus attention on certain features of Europe's population that stubbornly remain unaccounted for. Why did the population continue to decline in many places through the late fourteenth and early fifteenth centuries when everything would suggest that there was ample margin for recovery? And why, even after growth resumed, was it so slow until well into the sixteenth century? Why did growth accelerate so slowly in the eighteenth century, also under apparently favorable conditions? Finally, why did the plague not reappear in the eighteenth and nineteenth centuries even in parts of Europe where population was growing strongly with virtually no improvements in production or living standards (Braudel 1979)?

Since the model does not furnish an endogenous explanation, one approach is to look for an exogenous one, for example, a long-run climatic cycle (Le Roy Ladurie 1967). Although historians do not know very much about the course of climate, they have noted warming trends in the fifteenth and eighteenth centuries and a "little ice age" in the seventeenth. Even minor changes in *average* temperatures can have significant implications for agriculture and therefore for the potential population that can be supported. However, it is unclear that climate fluctuations would work uniformly over areas as wide as the European continent. For example, a warming trend would help lengthen the critical growing season in the north but could aggravate the danger of drought in the south. Similarly, abundant rains improve yields on light soils but worsen the drainage problems that plague heavy ones (Slicher van Bath 1977).

Epidemic diseases, specifically the bubonic plague, pose equally intriguing problems. Why did the plague disappear from Europe, seemingly forever, after the Marseille outbreak of 1720? By a century later, widespread population growth and movements, the social disruptions attendant on early industrialization, and the Napoleonic and other wars would seem to have restored the potential for renewed epidemics. It is true that certain rather mundane measures—the use of brick in construction, better quarantine procedures, and the diffusion of cotton underclothing and soap are examples—helped cities in particular to contain the threat of parasite-borne diseases. But the decline in epidemics and notably the disappearance of plague seem disproportionate effects compared with any improvements in medicine, public health, or living standards that may have occurred.

The last and perhaps most awkward puzzle—awkward in terms of the Malthusian model, that is—derives from the episodes of slow population growth under conditions apparently favorable for more rapid recovery. Herlihy and Klapisch (1978) ascribe retardation in sixteenth-century Florence to slow household formation, but that just focuses the mystery without resolving it. In Chapter 4 we argue that one would expect urban growth to lag behind rural but why they both should have been hesitant during certain periods of favorable ratios between resources and population remains a mystery. Wrigley (1969) calls such departures from Malthusian logic "lurches," and there are positive examples as well in both rural and urban areas, cases of continued high fertility despite widespread misery and poor economic opportunities. For the case of England, Wrigley and Schofield (1981) show that while fertility and real wages changed in a similar pattern, the response of the gross reproduction rate to the movement of real wages was delayed by about forty years! They suggest that marital adjustments to economic conditions were made primarily by the next generation. These and other historical paradoxes and apparent contradictions must, in the end, caution us against putting too much weight on a simple explanatory scheme.

Population change involves more than a simple mechanism of homeostatic balance between numbers and resources. It is now clear that communities have adopted different solutions to the dilemma of adjusting population to the food supply. People can restrict marriage or postpone it until relatively late ages. Alternatively, they can limit marital fertility or force the extra people to leave the territory. All these solutions were tried before 1850 by at least some European communities. Wrigley and Schofield (1981) suggest that the English since the sixteenth century used a low-pressure strategy in which changes in nuptiality and fertility produced equilibrium. They also argue that, in contrast, the French population was at the mercy of a high-pressure adjustment in which mortality fluctuations provided the main mechanism for matching numbers and resources. While their interpretation of the French case is questionable, Wrigley and Schofield have added considerably to the growing mountain of evidence suggesting that European communities successfully limited their own numbers in the interests of maintaining real income. Preindustrial European populations were not at the mercy of demographic forces completely beyond their control.

Long Swings in European Population

By dint of much detective work, scholars have described the normal functioning of demographic processes in preindustrial Europe. Although some social groups and some communities varied from the norm, in general both mortality and fertility were high when measured by modern western standards. Births exceeded deaths in ordinary times while remaining below the biological maximum. Fertility showed nothing like the sharp fluctuations that characterized mortality rates, although births fell during a crisis and then recovered vigorously afterward. Nuptiality behaved as a "leading indicator" for births: marriages postponed during mortality peaks were quickly concluded afterward. In addition, there were more subtle long swings in nuptiality rates matching the secular changes in population growth.

The overall periods of growth and decline or stagnation have been charted, more accurately in fact than the actual numbers of people living in this pre-census age. While regional deviations from the general pattern are significant—parts of central Europe, for example, continued to grow during the fourteenth and early fifteenth centuries but suffered cruel losses in the seventeenth—the uniformity remains noteworthy. When the first peak of population was attained soon after 1300, Europe numbered some 75 million inhabitants (Russell 1972a). By 1450 the number had shrunk to perhaps 50 million by Russell's estimate. Past this time although several recent studies agree on the general trend—more rapid growth in the sixteenth and eighteenth centuries than in the seventeenth— they differ markedly regarding *levels*, as Table 3.1 shows.

The table also shows the urban population at various dates, expressed as a percentage of the total, and allows us to focus on issues surrounding these estimates. Two points may immediately be noted. First, if the town-size threshold of 5,000 inhabitants is used, they leave aside a substantial, if perhaps diminishing, fraction of Europe's urban population. Pound's estimates for 1330 suggest that only 1.25 million or one in four northern town dwellers would be counted as urban using the criterion employed by de Vries and Bairoch (compare Tables 3.1 and 2.1).[3] The second point is the surprising agreement between the two independent sets of estimates for the percentage of urban dwellers in early modern Europe. Bairoch specifically states that the urban population is subject to a smaller error in measurement than the total population and thus than the percentage urban. And indeed, the estimates of total numbers differ sharply between de Vries and Bairoch. Again, the omission of small-town populations from the urban share understates

Table 3.1. Estimates of European population and urbanization, 1500–1800 (population in millions).

	de Vries		Mols	Bairoch	
Year	Population	Percent urban	Population	Population	Percent urban
1500	65	8.6	82	—	—
1600	83	9.9	105	130	9.7
1650	77	10.6	—	—	—
1700	90	—	115	145	10.5
1750	101	11.0	—	167	11.4
1800	129	12.1	190	205	12.3

Sources: de Vries (1976:5, 1981:88); Mols (1974:38–39); Bairoch (1977:7).

Note: Eastern Europe included in all estimates; urban threshold in both sets of percentages is 5,000 inhabitants.

the actual degree of urbanization but probably overstates its progression, as will be made clear in Chapter 5.

Our purpose is not to belabor the point that early population figures are uncertain, much less to throw stones at the brave and diligent scholars who have furnished the only numerical data we have. The particulars of urban growth and of the pattern of urbanization in the quantitative sense—city-size distribution and urban population as a fraction of the total—are addressed later. Here, before retreating to the somewhat more tractable subject of urban vital processes, we merely want to touch on the timing of urban versus total population change. The data suggest two generalizations. First, urban dwellers grew as a share of the total population between 1500 and 1800; in other words, there was an apparent gradual trend toward urbanization. Second, urban growth reflected total growth in somewhat amplified form; the percentage of urban people as well as their numbers rose more in periods of strong growth. The later discussion will amplify and qualify these findings. It is important here to address one possible inference, which is the idea that cities served as catch-basins for "excess" rural population. There is indeed a link to be forged between rural population growth and urbanization, but a far less mechanistic one than just suggested. Urban opportunities and capacities must be considered along with the rural potential for migration to cities.

Natural Change in the Cities

As in other things, the towns of Europe were both a part of and an exception to the prevailing demographic regime. The same broad line of observed behavior—high fertility and mortality—obtained in cities, but there were significant differences as well.

Several factors immediately suggest that urban fertility should have been high relative to rural. First, illegitimacy was not as low in cities as elsewhere, although this may partly reflect the desire of unwed mothers-to-be to give birth in an anonymous town or an urban charitable foundation rather than in the censorious village. Second, towns tended to be wealthy, and we have noted that the European system of social fertility control made early marriage a privilege. Finally, the urban population included a high proportion of young adults, since this group predominated among the recent migrants who made up a significant element of almost every town. We shall see that cities tended to permit only those migrants to remain who had a job or property, and therefore a reasonable prospect of marriage. But other factors pull in the opposite direction, and they may well have been more powerful overall. The first is celibacy. The groups who married late or not at all concentrated in towns. Servants typify the first category and the clergy the second, but long apprenticeships and dowry or other money problems for younger siblings of the propertied classes contributed to the total. In addition, many towns had decided gender imbalances. Feminine preponderance was "normal," but the presence of a garrison, a university, or important port activities, as well as certain kinds of manufacturing, could tip the balance the other way. Also, cities had higher mortality, especially among the insecure laboring population. Finally, although here the picture is particularly uncertain and complex, it may be that urban dwellers were the first in large numbers to restrict family size within marriage, as well as to shape desired family size to economic circumstances.

The use of contraceptive methods was first noted in cities, but this implies no simple argument regarding how family-size limitation spread. At least three points of view have been put forward, notably by historians dealing with England, early modern France, and Hungary.[4] The first sees the techniques and attitudes necessary to effect change diffusing from the modern city to the traditional countryside. In terms of the Redfield-Singer (1954) categories, this typifies heterogenetic processes of urban-rural interaction. Alternatively, there may have been small regions where the "baneful secrets" *(les funestes secrets)* were known and practiced early in both country and town. Hungarian sources mention abortifacient drinks and wooden suppositories that were offered by midwives and older women to females seeking to avoid pregnancy. Here, a town and its region were closely integrated and the cultural pattern was an orthogenetic one. Finally, some writers stress a social or class dimension to the adoption of fertility control, as opposed to a diffusion model or an ecological one. Aristocracies limited their offspring early, and small holders in parts of rural Hungary shifted to a one-child family by the early nineteenth century (Andorka 1978). In terms of our dual urban models, it is difficult to see the Central Place System spreading untraditional values and practices widely, either downward from the national or provincial capitals or from one region to another using high-order centers as relays. It is more plausible to envisage these, along with other new ideas, being transmitted through the "internationale of cities" of the Network System (Bardet et al. 1977). Yet questions remain. To what extent did such cosmopolitan currents touch the urban masses or nearby rural areas? How quickly did new migrants adopt urban values and ways? Ultimately, we can say little more than this: while family-size limitation is associated with urbanization, it was neither the rule in towns nor unknown outside them in the early modern West.

As regards mortality, the city did better at protecting its inhabitants from dearth and less well against epidemics than did the countryside. Urban doctors and hospitals harmed more than they helped, while city food supplies were watched over by aggressive merchants and vigilant administrators. Towns attracted rural produce because of their market function, while their inherent dependence made the food supply an ever-present concern of municipal governments (C. Tilly 1975). Perhaps for this reason, historians have tended to slight the provisioning of towns, despite the fact that it occupied as large a fraction of the urban population as any other sector, and perhaps does so even today. Cities drew on suburban gardens, on pastures in the larger region, on near and distant granaries, and on plantations in exotic and remote climes. Mercantile initiative and public regulation worked, sometimes at cross-purposes it is true, to guard against shortages that threatened the city's survival and even more directly its peace. So food was generally available, but in bad times it would be priced out of the reach of the poor. The effect of market forces was aggravated when high food prices coincided with urban unemployment. Our later study of cycles in the urban economy (Chapter 4) shows that this was quite likely to happen. Then, unless large-scale relief schemes were implemented, hunger could stalk city streets as well as country lanes.

The question of disease is more uncertain. Data regarding the ravages of epidemics usually refer to cities, and it has been assumed that rural areas fared better in the absence of crowding and bad public hygiene. Herlihy (1967) challenges this view for the case of medieval Pistoia, whose *contado* was particularly dense and active, it is true. Goubert (1969a) points out that distressed rural people tended to take to the roads, thus exposing themselves and others to contagion. If it is true that serious epidemics also devastated rural areas, then our earlier argument about a cyclical link between total and urban population growth suggests an important indirect impact of disease on urbanization. The idea that the *potential* for urban growth could be affected is an important one, since we shall soon show that the actual loss of city population could readily be made up by migration even in cases of grave contraction.

The bubonic plague is the most familiar killer, but other infectious diseases were doubtless more deadly when taken together, accounting for the high standard, or normal, rate of mortality. Modern historians identify typhus, dysentery, and malaria among the "fevers" reported by contemporaries, with water contamination, poor drainage, and spoiled food as major culprits. Two other diseases that ravaged urban populations were smallpox and tuberculosis. In time, the first proved readily susceptible to control by vaccination, but the second flourished in dark, crowded urban environments from long before the formation of industrial slums until well into our own century.

It is broadly accurate to associate high urban mortality, plagues and sieges aside, with crowding. But early towns were by no means always crowded. Excessive density typically resulted from rapid growth of population under conditions where the physical extent and housing stock of the town could not be expanded adequately or quickly enough. Thus a walled or fortified town such as Lille or Cologne might have trouble accommodating even moderate increases, whereas the enormous expansion of metropolitan London in the seventeenth century need not be systematically life-threatening.

Infant and child mortality was principally responsible for the high overall death rate. Even in sober, stable, prosperous Geneva, it was not until the eighteenth century that death was statistically more likely to strike an old person than a very young one (Perrenoud 1979). And for some large French cities, at least, the registered burials seriously understate the true picture. A veritable system of social infanticide operated in Lyon and Paris under the guise of massive baby farming. Wet-nursing was a common practice in an age when only human milk gave infants a realistic chance of survival. But only the affluent could afford to import peasant women into the household. Others sent the babies out to the villages, thus providing significant by-employment for rural women. The burial records of villages along the roads leading from a town record the sad progress of convoys of newborn infants, whose chances of survival improved only marginally if they reached their destination. Individual arrangements were supplemented by institutional ones for dealing with abandoned babies and foundlings. These charitable institutions, by the way, received not only illegitimate babies but many legitimate ones as well. Since the payment scheme gave the rural wet nurses little incentive to preserve the lives of their little charges, the whole system amounted, as we have said, to social infanticide. No participant was guilty of any specific moral or legal crime; yet the whole achieved a de facto slaughter of innocents that served to depress the urban natural balance (Garden 1970).

The conclusion of this checklist of life-supporting and life-threatening aspects of European towns must be a mixed one. Such as they are, the data understate the tendency for a natural urban deficit except where rural refugees from war or dearth or illegitimate babies from the country came to die in town. Yet towns, particularly smaller central places (as opposed to ports, protoindustrial centers, or great capitals), were by no means always death traps. Mols (1974) estimates infant mortality, the key component in normal times, as equal for rural areas and smaller market towns: 25 percent to 33 percent of the children up to five years, as opposed to 40 percent to 50 percent in larger cities. As the discussion of early modern urban growth will show (Chapter 6), there is a direct correlation between mortality and growth, highlighting the importance of migration. But even before turning to that topic, it is clear that urban demography in the medieval and early modern periods cannot be approached except by considering towns in relation to their surroundings. A systemic perspective is crucial in the demographic, as well as in the economic and political, spheres.

The Lure of the City: Wanderers and Migrants

The move of an individual or family from farm to town or from village to city is part of what urbanization is all about. This human experience or adventure brings to life a process that otherwise risks becoming bogged down in verbal or statistical abstraction. Yet pulling up stakes here and settling there represents only the tip of the iceberg, the visible trace of a wider phenomenon of population movement whose magnitude and complexity in preindustrial Europe have only recently become clear. We need to discard the image of a traditional rural society, immobile and unchanging, from which an enterprising few could escape to the dynamic city. Our task here is to sort out the population flows that affected towns: magnitudes, determinants, and consequences. We begin with a numerical look at two early modern German communities.

In the year 1700 the city of Frankfurt-am-Main boasted some 27,500 legal residents, of whom 9,000–10,000 were noncitizens, including 3,000 Jews (Soliday 1974). In fact, more than this number lived within the walls, but the aliens were too lowly and perhaps too transient to be counted. Frankfurt, which in 1500 had approximately 11,500 residents, had experienced strong population growth from 1550 on, broken only by the setback of the Thirty Years War (1618–1648), which cost the city a relatively modest 16 percent of the 20,000 people who lived there in 1602. Yet between 1500 and 1700 births exceeded deaths in only two decades and then by small numbers. During the rapid recovery of the years 1655–1700, for example, the natural deficit amounted to about 1,000, while a total of 10,500 were added to the population. Net immigration both compensated for the deficit and produced the increase. New inhabitants, notably Dutch refugees from religious strife, also accounted for the vigorous growth before 1620 and the resistance to decline afterward. It is understandable that two thirds of the *Beisassen* or nonburghers counted in 1700 were from outside the city, but so were half the citizens. Indeed, immigrants made up more than half the persons admitted to citizenship over the period from 1600 to 1735, the preferred route being marriage into a burgher family. To appreciate these numbers, one must know that the burghers of Frankfurt put up stiff resistance against the extension of citizenship to nonnatives. Candidates had to be Lutherans of legitimate birth and upright character, but mainly they needed enough wealth to reassure the authorities and to pay the discriminatory and increasing fees. And still they came.

In the panoply of German cities, Frankfurt occupies a median position. It seems a careful, not to say parochial, community in comparison with the booming *Residenzstädte*, the capitals such as Mannheim, Dresden, Hannover, and of course Berlin, which almost sprang up out of the ground (François 1978). Yet among the group of *Reichsstädte*—the free imperial cities—Frankfurt's controlled growth stands out as daring and headlong. One hundred miles to the southeast lies Nördlingen, which probably had two thirds as many people as Frankfurt in 1620 but not much more than one quarter the number in 1700.[5] After a century of growth, the number of households stabilized from 1580 to 1620, dropped by half in the next twenty years, and made up only about half the loss by the 1720s. The population curve looks rather like that of Frankfurt with the growth trend taken out. The proportion of noncitizen households—9 percent in 1579—also indicates a much less open community than Frankfurt, and Jews were excluded from residence in Nördlingen. The city applied equally strict criteria for admission to citizenship and adjusted the financial threshold to the need for people, notably raising it after the losses of the 1630s had been recouped.

Can we conclude that migration was unimportant for static Nördlingen? Apparently not. Even within the group of newly admitted citizens, one in six was born outside the walls. Moreover, the more selective the process of integration became, the wider the area of recruitment. By the seventeenth century the migrants represented the whole of German-speaking Europe, and only a minority came from nearby places. Finally, household counts and naturalization records significantly underestimate mobility in Nördlingen, as in Frankfurt. A fifteenth-century tally shows four dependent serving persons for every seven households in the former, which extrapolates to 950 persons in 1579. For their part, the "beggars, vagrants, travelers and other transients" have left no record (Friedrichs 1979:41). Also, a comparison of recorded births and enumerated households suggests that substantial numbers of people may have lived on the margin of the organized community. Add the naturalized citizens, and it may be that a quarter of the population at a given time was foreign-born or lived with parents who were. Nördlingen was healthier than Frankfurt, judging from the recorded burials and baptisms, and it never outgrew its late-medieval form or size. Yet even here population mobility played an important part. Apart from townspeople who left, immigrants were needed during recovery from crisis and were cautiously valued at other times as well.

What can we learn from these examples? Clearly, European cities were open to outsiders; just as clearly, that openness was limited by communal control. Immigrants were needed for recovery or growth and often merely to sustain the urban population. Emigration had to be made up, along with any natural deficit, and there was dirty or menial work that townspeople shunned. But the need for immigrants does not imply that they were always welcome. Towns were concerned about the quality as well as the quantity of potential immigrants, and they placed restrictions on residence and on integration into the urban community. The controls varied according to the degree of urban autonomy.[6] Standards were also relaxed for a time when population losses had to be made up or when the urban economy was expanding. Crowding, political strife, or cultural biases could harden urban attitudes. In general, however, most cities could draw on an ample supply of potential migrants except, perhaps, on the fringes of the European urban system. Thus, they were more often engaged in keeping out unmanageable numbers than in recruiting. Even when admitted, newcomers faced continuing discrimination that affected not only their social and economic prospects but even their chances for remaining in the chosen city of residence. As we shall see, recent migrants were more likely to leave again or to die young than were established burghers.

We associate mobility with modernity. Certainly, population flows have shown an upward secular trend. Moreover, within preindustrial Europe the more feudal societies were relatively restrictive in regard to the movement of people. But it is a mistake to infer that in the "world we have lost," migration normally represented a positive step for those involved. If one compares time periods, regions, or social groups in a less macroscopic perspective, it may be nearer the mark to view a fixed domicile as a privilege and migration as a perilous response to difficulties. The "choice" to migrate often resulted from lack of local opportunity, when it was not in fact forced by war, death, or persecution. We must thus distinguish between migration for "improvement," and "subsistence" or "distress" migration (P. Clark 1979).

How much mobility was there in preindustrial Europe and how much of it represented migration as opposed to simple travel? Both questions are hard to answer, even approximately. Population reconstitutions do not do justice to mobile people, and we have seen that towns tended to exclude transients from their population counts. Our mental image of the past encompasses the immobile village but also the bustling road as reflected in countless folk tales, songs, journals, and travel accounts. It sometimes seems as if at least articulate people were always on the move: touring journeymen, pilgrims, soldiers, piepowder (*pieds poudreux* or dusty feet) mer-

chants, rogues, clerics, peddlers, and players. The scholarly estimates of mobility do not converge. Goubert (1969a), who attaches
importance to rural mobility particularly for the years leading up
to the French Revolution, believes that no more than 5 percent of
rural Frenchmen moved before the last years of the ancien régime
(see also Guillaume and Poussou 1970). P. Clark (1979), on the
other hand, argues that rather more than half the people in England
moved at one point or another in their lives during the troubled
first half of the seventeenth century. Elsewhere, Spanish emigrants
went by the thousands to the colonies and large numbers of Germans settled in eastern Europe, including 300,000 whom Frederick
II sent to his dominions from overpopulated western areas (Guillaume and Poussou 1970).

The definition of migration also poses problems. One dimension
is distance. The parish is too small a basic unit, since it is clear that
moving to a neighboring parish, as a spouse or servant did, for
instance, involved no sense of separation. Similarly, going to a
provincial town from the immediate *umland* or the suburbs implied
no great change in the life of the person concerned unless other
things, such as profession or social status, also changed. A variety
of other criteria can be used, for example, a specific distance that
must be covered or the crossing of county borders, but they are
necessarily arbitrary. Scholars also distinguish short-range from
distant migration. Note, too, that migration represents a permanent
move, whereas a simple journey ends with a return to the point of
origin. But in times of short lives, slow and perilous travel, and
poor information, the planned journey may prove definitive while
the intended move can be reversed. Moreover, the term *temporary
migration* suggests that intermediate cases need to be considered.
In early Europe many people moved seasonally or for longer periods
in search of work. Harvesting called for the most extra hands, but
the list of the occupations of wanderers is endless. And some jobs
were by their nature mobile, for instance, long-distance carriage.
Chatelain's (1976) study of temporary migration in France draws
mostly on nineteenth-century data, but it is clear that the early
decades of this period continued much older patterns. The growing
numbers involved—around 200,000 in 1800 and 500,000 in 1850—
still fall within the 5 percent of the rural work force suggested by
Goubert. Mountains and rugged hills furnished many emigrants,
while major cities were favored destinations. Given the precarious

situation of new urban settlers, it can be argued that rural migrants, at least, should have viewed their move as temporary. It would become permanent if they managed to establish themselves in town or, more probably, if death overtook them before they left again. For a move to count as migration, therefore, distance, intention, and even chance have to be considered.

How much migration was there in early modern Europe? Our view is that mobility, like urbanization itself, occupied a dual place in the social system: an exception that yet played an integral part. From a theoretical point of view we must realize that while many considerations retarded mobility, others favored it. The difficulties of transportation were more of a barrier to merchandise than to people, who could and did walk. Travel was costly and slow. But time is a subjective thing, and many found the time and money to go, or did without money not lacking for time. Travel was dangerous, to be sure, but so sometimes was staying put. And there is a more fundamental reason not to underestimate mobility. The movement of persons is only an aspect of greater mobility in general; there are also trade-offs between the movement of goods and information on the one hand and persons on the other. This is clear in the case of early medieval merchants, who were able to stay home as opposed to accompanying their goods once security was adequate and trading networks—fairs, factors, and so forth—were in place. It applies also to the case of an overpopulated countryside. With poor communications, there is no alternative to flight. With improvements, food or raw materials for cottage industry can be brought in. The best indication of the force of this point is the long-standing predominance of rugged, relatively isolated upland regions as sources of emigrants, for example, the French Massif Central and Brittany, the highlands of Scotland, and the central Alps and Pyrenees. On the other hand, the more accessible uplands proved especially hospitable to protoindustrial development.

The idea that mobility was often the consequence of misery or despair and was forced rather than voluntary is an important one for understanding early migration. To begin with, it helps overcome the entrenched idea that poor transportation and other hardships would reinforce the sedentary nature of traditional society. Second, it integrates many well-known episodes associated with wars, religious persecutions, and other historical dramas. It is worth noting that refugees tended to move to urban locations whether they themselves were urban or not. Antwerp's exiles fled to Amsterdam and Flemish artisans to Leiden, Frankfurt, or London; French Huguenots went to Geneva, Amsterdam, London, and Berlin, which they practically founded as a city. On a more local level, famines drove peasants and cottage workers to the roads, again with a tendency to seek help in towns rather than in other, more fortunate rural areas.

Although poverty or trouble may have forced many to move, this does not imply that the better-off did not leave home. There were positive incentives to migrate or engage in extended travel and residence elsewhere. Migration for professional reasons was important. Apprentices were recruited for major towns according to stable geographic patterns. Indeed, strong occupational links were capable of overcoming considerable distance, even though most immigrants continued to arrive from relatively nearby. Patten (1976) and Perrenoud (1979) have charted the spatial distribution of migrants for East Anglian towns and Geneva, respectively. The more skilled and specialized workers might come from far away, whereas servants and laborers tended to be recruited in the region. Thus, female migrants traveled less far, on average, than men. However, foreign merchants or aristocrats might bring their numerous domestics from much farther away, as Garden (1970) shows in the case of eighteenth-century Lyon. And these elites were highly mobile themselves.

To complete the picture, it is important to mention interurban migration, which has tended to be underestimated (Perrenoud 1979). Attention has tended to focus only on the net contribution of immigration to urban numbers, but urban populations were fairly mobile in general. Rural migrants often left again after some years: servants to marry and put their savings to work, elderly workers to retire, the unemployed or unsuccessful to resign themselves or to try elsewhere. Urban natives also left for other cities, more often than not the larger ones. This stepwise migration probably affected middle-class persons most—shopkeepers, professionals, or artists. Finally, many who could afford to travel for pleasure would reside for extended periods in this city and that.

Despite the rich complexity of migratory movements involving urban areas, it remains true that great mobility was characteristic of a limited proportion of the urban population: those concentrated at the lower end of the social spectrum. Recent migrants and temporary residents were predominantly employed as laborers, servants, and in other menial and unpleasant occupations, and they often dominated these categories. On the other hand, the more affluent and "established" were predominantly native and less likely to leave. This pattern prevailed despite efforts to recruit respectable migrants and limit the presence of others.

In light of the foregoing, it is clear that neither migration nor relatively high fertility and mortality led necessarily to social instability and rapid change. European cities had almost a dual structure: a permanent cadre of inhabitants and a substantial floating group of recent immigrants, temporary residents, and transients. Although native and permanent residents could be poor and newcomers wealthy, the former dominated the latter in every way: socially, economically, politically. And their control ensured the stability— sometimes the immobility—of the city.

In the next chapter, we argue that the European economic system of the fifteenth through the eighteenth centuries had built into it major long-term fluctuations in urban activity. Cities therefore needed a way of responding to positive as well as negative stimuli, but also of limiting their effects. Otherwise, they would come to the end of an economic boom facing costly unfinished investments in housing and infrastructure and large numbers of distressed people who needed to be fed at a time of diminished resources. Another threat was the loss of cohesion if during extended depressions native sons yielded influential or protected positions to the ever-present and perhaps more able "strangers." As in insect colonies, the security and continuity of the collective unit were preserved at the expense of individuals. Unlike the analogous case, however, urban communities often managed to make marginal groups, notably recent migrants, bear the burden of adjustment.

Urban dualism has important demographic implications as well. It has been commonplace to see persistent urban immigration as the consequence of a regular natural deficit, itself the result of high mortality induced by urban crowding and other horrors. Sharlin (1978) has turned this argument around, advancing the view that the natural deficit of urban populations resulted from the presence of immigrants and temporary workers. He argues that the "permanent" fraction of the urban population would usually have been able to sustain, perhaps increase, its numbers, whereas the migrants and temporary residents experienced a chronic excess in deaths over births. Sharlin's argument relies principally on the high proportion of unmarried persons among the migrants. Servants, journeymen, and clergy are examples. Others, however, have pointed to the social incidence of mortality, suggesting that marginal groups were more subject to disease and experienced greater infant mortality in particular. Garden (1970) details the Lyon case of immigrant silk-workers, many of them women. Like later industrial workers they could marry easily, but living conditions and the demands of work gave rise to very high rates of infant and child mortality. A principal factor was baby farming, since these women entrusted their new-borns to wet nurses, but the high death rates for those two to four years old make it clear that conditions were bad for the survival even of children who lived to return home.

On the other hand, evidence from Geneva, at least, confirms that the native bourgeoisie took the lead in limiting family size, which meant that migration served to sustain the permanent fraction as well as to renew the floating population (Perrenoud 1979). Even though cities could restrict access to citizenship, they retained mechanisms for naturalizing newcomers. Burghers did not maintain native purity at the cost of demographic suicide.

BY WAY OF CONCLUSION, we can sketch out briefly the demographic conditions in which Europe confronted the "Great Transformation" that we call the Industrial Revolution (Polanyi 1944). Into the eighteenth century the pattern was the familiar one: a short life for most, death a familiar companion, infants and children the preferred victims. Marriage was a sober and deliberate affair, for most a sensible if not a calculated choice made no earlier than the mid-twenties. And many married later or not at all.

The banality of death did not lessen the impact of crises of mortality, which resulted from epidemics or famines. These diminished in frequency and virulence in the eighteenth century, particularly in western Europe. So population increased. Nonetheless, Europe retained a reservoir of potential fertility that would be tapped by the economic changes of the century after 1750. This is important because the early phases of development of industrial urbanism would surely do little to protect the vulnerable masses from the fragility of life. Indeed, new dangers would arise from urban crowding, mass migration, cyclical industrial unemployment, proletarianization, and technological or economic displacement of employments. Even though destitution would continue to be the lot of many, in fact of more people than before, it would largely be true that no positive checks, no massive triumphs of death, would blunt the unprecedented growth of European population and its rapid urbanization.

PART TWO

A Protoindustrial Age:
Fourteenth to Eighteenth Centuries

The foundation of every division of labor that is well-developed, and brought about by the exchange of commodities, is the separation between town and country. It may be said, that the whole economic history of society is summed up in the movement of this antithesis.   KARL MARX, *Das Kapital*

BETWEEN roughly 1300 and 1800 the map of urban Europe persisted in quite recognizable form. Few new cities were founded and overall rates of urban growth slowed. Indeed, in some regions and in some periods, particularly the mid-fourteenth and late seventeenth centuries, the urban population decreased in size. The tidal wave of medieval urbanization receded from west to east to be replaced by more cyclical, as well as geographically and functionally specific, curves. While the total urban population rose, at least after 1500, its increases were less dramatic than redistributions among regions and among cities of different sizes and types. Parts of central and southern Europe were hit so hard by the effects of war, plague, and economic competition that their cities, especially the smaller ones, lost their medieval vitality and resilience. At the same time, urban culture, politics, and architecture were transformed. It was a time of great brilliance for many cities, one in which they greatly increased their influence within the society as a whole. All in all, qualitative rather than quantitative changes were the order of the day. Medieval towns faded beside the new mercantile metropolises and baroque capitals. Major cities looked different in 1800 than they did four centuries earlier and interacted differently, too. The urban systems we associate with central places and trading networks responded to altered economic and political conditions.

In the political sphere cities both lost and gained. The growth of the centralized state, notably in its absolutist form, reduced urban autonomy. Yet the administrative functions of that state were increasingly exercised through cities and the Central Place System, while imperial ambitions and mercantilist policies harnessed the activity of Network System ports. Market cities, particularly the larger ones, expanded their political influence over the countryside. The commercial centers, on the other hand, stimulated production for the market in sheltered villages and remote overseas plantations. Enhanced administrative and economic roles contributed to a new conception of what made a city. Earlier definitions resting on juridical status or on a long and glorious past gave way gradually to a functional identity in which size and influence came to be of primary importance. The new vision of the city also had a spatial aspect. Whether the nearly ubiquitous walls were taken down or not, the sharp distinction between inside and outside faded in favor of a developing sense of center and periphery. Ultimately, the city as a clearly defined entity gave way to the more flexible statistical concept of the urban agglomeration.

While the political fortunes of the city were mixed, no such reservation is necessary in the cultural sphere. The superiority and leadership of the city were openly acknowledged and vigorously exercised. However many nymphs and shepherds might be painted or put on stage, the creator and his patron or patroness were both urban. Even in the moral sphere, where the city had long represented evil as well as some good, the great movements of Reformation, Counterreformation, and Enlightenment spread from the cities. And the urban location of prime movers in education, science, belles-lettres, and publishing was even more absolute. When Romantics, Physiocrats, and Methodists came to question the superiority of urban civilization after the middle of the eighteenth century, they did so within a resolutely urban framework.

In terms of a demographic measure of urbanization, the period may well have experienced a slow upward trend in the proportion of total population living in cities, urban growth exceeding the overall increase somewhat. However, exceptions, reversals, and gaps in knowledge threaten to obscure the trend. At the same time, Europe experienced something never before seen outside the Mediterranean basin—the growth of very large urban entities. From a medieval peak of some 200,000 inhabitants, the summits of the urban hierarchy grew to 500,000 by 1700 and to more than 1,000,000 by 1800. Yet there was no clear link between the economic vigor of a city and its size. Some of the largest towns were more parasites than producers. As in the Roman Empire, urban growth could result from no more than an improved capacity to capture rural surplus. The forms as well as the amounts of extraction evolved. While many of the feudal instruments were retained de jure, cities also relied on newer property relationships, closely enforced, to exact maximum advantage. Although the ability to collect the various types of rents fluctuated with economic conditions, the share of land under urban control, aristocratic or common, tended to increase, as did the role of cities in collecting the growing share of the state. It may be added that surplus tended more and more to be transformed and monetized under the control of the city.

Cities had always been centers of trade as well as of consumption. These functions induced increased activity in direct production: handicrafts, manufactures, building. We shall see that the numbers so engaged formed a remarkable fraction of total urban employment despite the importance of service occupations and the growing pace of nonagricultural commodity production carried on in the countryside. One characteristic of urban economies in early modern Europe that sets them apart from later patterns of development is that economic activity was dominated by cyclical changes: periods of growth were likely to be halted, if not canceled out, by times of decline. Self-sustained growth awaited industrial times, although the conditions for it were already being prepared in northwest Europe. While not all cities experienced sharp, regular economic contraction, even the most brilliant position did not insure against it. There was no protection against the acute terrors of siege or plague; in addition, spatial shifts and economic cycles threatened setbacks in trade, production, and employment. Even privileged places, drawing their wealth from high finance, long-distance trade, or the exploitation of a teeming countryside, could not insulate themselves securely from difficulties. Urban fortunes were so deeply intertwined with those of rural areas that the inexorable rhythms of population growth interacting with the size of the harvest and the levels of surplus-absorbing rents ultimately pushed urban economies in the direction of regional economic fortunes. The demographic and economic collapse of the fourteenth century and the bad times of the seventeenth show these connections at work. Cities fought for survival in an economic order whose fortunes still depended on precarious foundations.

Renaissance and baroque urbanism deserve separate attention in our long-run survey of European cities. Unfortunately, social theorists have tended to divide western development in our millennium into only two periods: a preindustrial age with a "feudal" mode of production and an industrial age corresponding to the capitalist mode. This division is reductionist with respect to change in the first period, and it introduces ambiguity regarding the threshold of capitalism. It is common to trace capitalism much further back than the age of factory industry into the centuries of extra-European exploration, colonization, and exploding mercantile trade (Wallerstein 1974). The Marxist device of "transition" does little to solve the problem. Every period is in some sense one of transition. The term is vague, and it telescopes five eventful centuries into an interlude. Moreover, it suggests an analysis determined by what was to follow. A system must be approached in its own terms, not reshaped with a teleological end in mind. We refuse to accept an approach that views half a millennium of urban evolution through the lenses of two models, one obsolete and one premature.

The alternative framework we propose links early modern modes of production to the cyclical rhythms of growth in population and economic activity, resulting in a third subdivision of Europe's long-term urban experience. Medieval urbanization was followed by a qualitatively different phase that we choose to link to the political economy of protoindustrial production. Economic historians have in recent years identified a widespread surge in manufacturing that antedates factory industrialization by several centuries (Mendels 1972; Deyon 1979). Although the technology and the size of individual units of production underwent little change, the rise in production involved major social and economic reorganization. Industrial employment became an alternative to the occupancy of land as a minimal condition for family formation. Social controls on fertility were subverted, permitting more rapid population growth. One consequence was enhanced subsistence migration to cities, posing the problem of viability in acute form. Many rural regions shifted their economic base from food production to manufacturing for export. By so doing, they became closely tied to the urban groups supplying capital, raw materials, and marketing services. There was also increased demand for urban-made goods as a result of entrepreneurial profits and increased rural surpluses. Despite these stimuli, demand was unstable and the momentum of growth subject to reversal. As with the city-supporting agrarian surpluses of earlier times, there was a gap between the sophisticated financial economy—embracing long-distance trade, banking, and markets—and the real economy supporting it. Little technological change accompanied the vast expansion of marketing networks. Commercial and financial capitalists invested little in the development of productive forces, while soil exhaustion silently undermined the means of subsistence. Finally, power struggles among the traditional elites diverted large amounts of surplus. Royal hegemony was won by outdoing the church and the nobility in war, lavish consumption, and grandiose display. Under these circumstances, the intertwined fortunes of city and countryside were constrained as well as unstable.

CHAPTER 4

Cities in the Early Modern European Economy

THE FORTUNES of European cities as a whole were to a large extent cyclical between 1300 and 1800, periods of stagnation or contraction balancing those of expansion. A squeeze on demand for manufactured goods, linked to high food prices, regularly depressed first rural then urban industries and thus the economic base of urban activity. More directly, periodic famines, plagues, and sieges could decimate city populations. While a few places of extraordinary economic buoyancy bucked the trend or recovered quickly from bad times, most were not so lucky. The combined effects of war and plague, accentuating an "antiurban" phase in the long-term economic cycle, produced major population declines in Cologne, Siena, Palermo, and Pisa between 1300 and 1500. Around 1650, when the wheel had come full circle, stagnation and decline were again widespread, for instance in the protoindustrial towns of northern France. In Amiens the number of apprentices taken into the textile trade dropped markedly between 1630 and 1655, and both baptisms and marriages were especially sensitive to the negative effects of high food prices (Deyon 1967). Goubert (1968) stresses the generally difficult conditions in seventeenth-century Beauvais; regular failures and recurring catastrophes mark the period all the way from the 1630s to 1720. And even when recovery came, structural change in the urban system meant that some urban settlements could be by-passed. The number of market towns in England declined by two thirds between 1350 and 1550 (Everitt 1976). In Germany and southwestern France, too, many medieval settlements disappeared.

Also remember that political decisions engineered drastic changes, declines as well as expansions. The desertion of Brussels by the Habsburgs in the mid-sixteenth century paralleled the economic misfortunes of other Flemish towns, all culminating in the double disasters of war and the closing of the Scheldt waterway. When the Spanish capital shifted to Madrid in 1561, that hitherto insignificant place received a stimulus matched only by the negative shock to Valladolid. There, within a few years recently built suburbs beyond the walls were largely abandoned (Bennassar 1967). Three centuries later, Valladolid's population was still smaller than during the days of Habsburg residence.

If we accentuate negative episodes at the outset, it is to fix in the reader's mind the limits to urbanization and urban development in Europe of the early modern period. As important as it was, the urban population we follow remained a minority, even in the most highly urbanized regions. Citizens' activities and fortunes, even their very lives, were still dependent on a rural order beyond their control. Conversely, the rural transformation critical to mass urbanization unfolded sometimes under strong urban influence, sometimes independently, sometimes despite the towns.

Decline and Recovery

Our immediate task is to discern amid the fluctuations a few steadier trends in urban development linked on the one hand to the shift in regional power, on the other to the rise of more differentiated and specialized cities. The marked difficulties and declines of Italian city populations were a reflection of the peninsula's loss of economic hegemony as the north of Europe overtook the south. Florence bucked general trends by losing population after 1500 when most European cities were growing; decline in Venice and Genoa preceded the difficult mid to late seventeenth century (Chandler and Fox 1974). Meanwhile, northern centers such as Amsterdam, Rotterdam, London, and Hamburg pursued their steady growth regardless of reverses elsewhere. As a result, the Mediterranean lands and their cities were evicted from the position of economic and social primacy they had enjoyed since the time of the Greeks. In Immanuel Wallerstein's (1974) terms, they changed from being the core of Europe to being a semiperiphery. Yet amid the loss of political and economic dynamism, aristocratic and bourgeois urban elites kept up their incomes by intensifying the extraction of surplus from sharecropping peasants. Mediterranean towns remained centers of consumption, culture, and elite residence, even though the associated costs perpetuated and confirmed economic weakness. These areas also sustained a high proportion of urban population, since the development of the countryside was held back by loss of surplus. Up to the middle of the nineteenth century, for instance, the Mediterranean areas of France were urbanized out of all proportion to their degree of economic development, although the relationship held well for other parts of the country (Aydalot, Bergeron, and Roncayolo 1981). Thus, the interaction between urban growth and regional economic success was a complex one. Cities grew in the rising north and stagnated in the fading south. But a high *level* of urbanization relative to the health of the regional economy constituted a continuing handicap to the south, not an asset.

If the relationship of north to south within Europe was one of rivalry and displacement, that of west to east can be characterized in terms of dominance and dependence. Eastern Europe remained less urban than more western portions, apart from the Atlantic fringe, but echoed the latter's cyclical experience with a substantial time lag. Like other factors affecting the growth of certain cities relative to others, the regional specifics are best tackled in a systems framework, and we return to them in that context in the next chapter.

The second relatively steady trend conditioning urban growth was functional differentiation. Specialization increased in the early modern period with the result that towns tended to become sensitive to specific growth-affecting influences. We can mention capitals and court cities, fortresses, and naval ports and will deal below with protoindustrial cities. We can also add spas or resorts to the list. All these urban functions were capable of generating very high rates of population growth for the town concerned, to say nothing of the mathematically extreme case of development ex nihilo. The political function, alone or in combination with others, could also result in unprecedented absolute size. These points illustrate why it is natural to assume that the trend toward European urbanization must have been continuing, however veiled by random or systematic fluctuations and regional differences.

Certainly, the list of major cities gives the impression that urbanization proceeded steadily between 1500 and 1800 (Table 4.1). With recovery from the late-medieval decline presumably well along,

Table 4.1. Growth of the European urban network, 1500–1800 (population in thousands).

Size category	Number of cities[a]				
	1500	1600	1700	1750	1800
20–50	76	87	105	131	154
50–100	21	24	24	27	43
100–200	3	10	9	12	16
200–300	1	2	1	2	5
300–500	—	—	—	1	1
500–750	—	—	2	2	1
Over 750	—	—	—	—	1
Total	101	123	141	175	221

Source: Bairoch (1977:41). Reprinted by permission of Université de Lyon II.
a. Russia included.

there were only four cities larger than 100,000 inhabitants in 1500, but by the beginning of the nineteenth century, twenty-four had reached this total. Moreover, the numbers of towns with 20,000 to 50,000 and 50,000 to 100,000 people doubled. Finally, the sustained pace of growth in at least some cities was unprecedented. Madrid realized the equivalent of 1.25 percent annual (compound) growth over 260 years in going from 6,000 in 1520 to over 150,000 in 1780, while Moscow rose from 36,000 to 238,000 over roughly the same period. Since Spain and Russia were by no means at the forefront of economic change, is not the progress of their major cities strong evidence of general urbanization?

This conclusion must be resisted, however. Small market towns with or without significant administrative functions remained dominant in number and in total population. Changes in their overall size are impossible to quantify for the centuries before national censuses, but it seems likely that they stagnated in many areas and decreased in size during periods of contraction. Note that ports gained at the expense of other markets, maritime ones even more than those on inland waterways. Second, the degree of specialization in trade increased: by 1600 one third of English and Welsh market towns concentrated on a particular product (Everitt 1976). While this could spur growth, it also increased vulnerability. Finally, the smallest centers faded at the expense of larger ones. At the least, the former would not be revived during recovery from a crisis that had emptied them. Small settlements could also fall prey to changes in agriculture; consider the abandoned villages during the too-famous enclosures in sixteenth-century England, when sheep were said to eat people.

In the absence of data for the entire array of cities, the answer to whether urban growth between 1500 and 1800 managed a positive trend must be based on casual, if informed, empiricism that balances growth in new towns and the upper ranks of the urban hierarchy against stagnation and even shrinkage in small settlements. In general, declines are easily overlooked, particularly lasting or fatal ones. Historical research has in any case devoted more attention to the developing northwest of Europe than to the more negative experience of south and east. All in all, it seems reasonable to accept C. Tilly's (1979) view that Europe may well have become slightly *less* urban between 1500 and 1800 if small as well as large towns are included in percentages. When urbanization is measured in terms of towns over 10,000, a modest increase results (see Table 4.2).

Our account of early modern urban Europe must thus recognize vastly different growth patterns. In Poland and other parts of eastern Europe, towns declined as the rural nobility's power over people and exports increased. Stability is typified by the many small towns of Germany and France, away from the zones of great expansion as well as those of decline. Whatever gains rural development—agricultural or protoindustrial—may have brought them were offset by the loss of trade and population to larger cities and by the shift of activity to the new Atlantic-centered world economy. So they were preserved in quaint semi-isolation, often until late into the nineteenth century (Walker 1971). On the other hand, there is

Table 4.2 Percentage of European population by region in cities over 10,000, 1500–1800.

Region	1500	1600	1650	1700	1750	1800
North and west	6.0	8.1	10.7	13.0	13.8	14.7
Central	3.8	4.8	6.6	6.7	7.1	7.1
Mediterranean	9.7	13.2	12.5	11.7	11.7	12.9
Total[a]	6.1	8.0	9.3	9.5	9.9	10.6

Source: de Vries (1981:88). Reprinted by permission of Croom Helm.
a. Austria, Poland, Bohemia, and Balkan areas excluded.

England. According to Clark and Slack (1976), the proportion of the population living in the larger towns (over 4,000 inhabitants in 1520, over 5,000 in 1700) rose from 6 percent to 15 percent between 1500 and 1700. Several types of settlements accounted for this drastic rise, which probably includes a measure of recovery from earlier troubles. Larger centers and county towns gained at the expense of small ones, notably in the half century after 1570. Specialized towns, for example, ports such as Newcastle, Chester, Exeter, and Colchester that serviced protoindustrial hinterlands, profited from a thriving export trade. Finally, and most important, London multiplied throughout the sixteenth and seventeenth centuries, accumulating influence along with size, and size with influence, as the center of British political, cultural, and economic life (Wrigley 1978b). But neither the clear expansion of larger towns, particularly in the north and west, nor the stability and contraction of settlements under 5,000 typifies the range of urban experiences in this protoindustrial age. Cyclicality and balance were the order of the day. Self-sustained growth for the entire spectrum of cities arrived only with industrial urbanization.

Urban Industry in a Fragile Economy

The relative weakness of pressures for urbanization from the late Middle Ages until the economic booms of the late eighteenth century was a function of technological stagnation. An inability to increase productivity, particularly in the agricultural sector, placed a ceiling on expansion. The interplay of population growth and limited resources regularly put pressure on wages, decreased income, and triggered a downturn in local economic fortunes.[1] Expansion in the system—new lands brought under cultivation, colonial conquests, a series of good harvests—produced only temporary respite. Over time, cyclical relationships reasserted themselves. A conjunctural rhythm of growth and decline dominated economic interrelationships in the long run.[2]

The rural sector dominated the economic fortunes of early modern Europe. Here most clearly fell the weight of the Malthusian trap of diminishing returns. Population growth was restrained through squeezes on workers' incomes, since marginal productivity declined with increases in population. Remember, however, the link between an agricultural surplus and city growth. Much of the surplus was siphoned off by urban landlords to feed themselves and urban workers. It was an economy based upon individual property holdings, and those with a claim on the surplus controlled access to the land. Competition among the landless allowed landlords to hire workers or tenants for a total wage less than the total product of the land. Over the long run, laborers were only as badly off as they would have been in the pure Malthusian case, but there were fewer of them, and they had an identifiable exploiter. The urban population clearly benefited from this diversion of the rural surplus in the form of rents. They thrived during periods when the rural population grew and rents were bid higher, but eventually this relationship shifted. Diminishing returns triggered a decline in population and, later, in rents. Cities eventually felt the effects of rural contraction, and good times were replaced by hard ones. The changing availability of food, based upon changes in population levels, was reflected in prices, and it exerted a profound effect on urban economies. Over the long run, economic fluctuations generated a regular alternation of rural and urban prosperity that cut across short-run expansions and contractions. Urban areas had the upper hand during booms and retained it during the early phases of decline. The rural economy withstood depression better and profited during times of recovery.

A second sort of production, manufacturing for export, linked countryside and city between 1500 and 1800. In recent years, economic historians have looked with heightened interest at protoindustrialization. In probing the roots of modern economic growth, they have found that the seventeenth and eighteenth centuries witnessed more manufacturing than was previously realized, and they argue that it played an important role in maintaining the economy and triggering change (Mendels 1972; Deyon 1979). Although the technology and scale of production remained largely traditional, industrial employment offered an alternative to occupancy of land as a condition for family formation. This subverted the social mechanism for control of fertility and could stimulate and support rapid population growth. Most research to date has focused on rural protoindustrial activity as the key to eventual industrial development, suggesting that urban production remained, on the whole, limited in scope and stagnant in volume. We wish to challenge this assumption and also to extend the notion of protoindustrial production backward in time.

Cities have for centuries been major sites of manufacturing. The

bulk of urban workers have always transformed materials into products. Stone, sand, and clay were metamorphosed into the fabric of
the city. Flesh and grain were turned into hearty stews or elaborate
pastries. Wood took a thousand shapes from a lofty roof frame to
a fragile violin. Just to dress and ornament the citizens and visitors
took dozens of materials and scores of trades. Human work took
on endless variety and nuances of specialization. In 1400 a town of
moderate size such as Nuremberg registered 141 separate crafts
(Strauss 1966). In most towns, industry was organized in the traditional pattern of small masters, usually retail sellers as well as
makers, grouped into guilds. But as we shall see, many cities manufactured goods for export under much freer conditions. Other
towns developed larger establishments to fill special needs: arsenals,
shipyards, mines, and "manufactories" for luxuries such as porcelain and tapestries. Historians have amply documented the great
variety of these urban arts.[3]

Urban industry was not a duplicate of rural production. For one
thing, Braudel (1979) claims that urban industry flourished in a
reciprocal relationship with rural manufacturing. Moreover, cities
specialize in luxury goods, which are consumed mainly by urban
and rural rentiers—that is, landlords and other recipients of surplus. In contrast, rural manufacturing areas produce plain goods,
which are bought by ordinary folk when wages are high enough to
allow it, at times when labor has enough scarcity value to share in
the surplus. If we turn from production to the returns to labor, we
see that prices fluctuate directly with population but that money
wages change little. Therefore, labor's purchasing power is greatest
during periods of low prices. Rural industry thrives especially on
conditions of low prices and high real wages. Urban manufactures,
on the other hand, prosper when grain prices and property income
are high because the products are bought mostly by recipients of
rent. The relative prosperity of urban and rural worlds shifts, therefore, according to the allocation of shares of agricultural surplus.
Overall, demand conditions were at least as important as costs in
stimulating or retarding production.

A Cyclical Model

In order to clarify the interactions between the rural and urban
economies, we have developed a simple model whose structure is
outlined in Appendix A. In the fashion of models, this one neglects

local specifics and regional variations in the timing and amplitude of expansion and contraction (or stagnation). It links the fortunes of the rural and urban sectors to long-term cycles in population and prices. These two variables generally moved together, and the movements affected wide areas of Europe similarly. Their trends are also much better documented than are shifts in urban and rural production or wage and property incomes. We therefore use the theoretical relationships embedded in the model to infer what can-

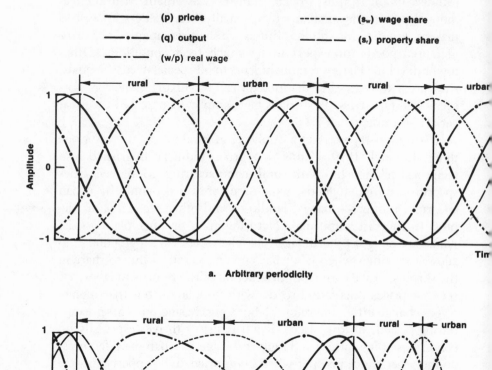

——————— (p) prices   - - - - - - - - (s_w) wage share

——•—— (q) output   — — — (s_r) property share

——··— (w/p) real wage

a.   Arbitrary periodicity

b.   Historic cycles for Europe, 1300 - 1800

Figure 4.1. A cyclical model of a two-sector economy.

not generally be measured. Examples from particular cities and regions serve to illustrate the model or to reinforce the cautions and qualifications that accompany it. They do not constitute a formal test.

The results of the model are set out in Figures 4.1a and 4.1b. The five time series offer a stylized description of the early modern European economy in terms of two movements: expansions and contractions in economic activity on the one hand—a long-run trade cycle—and alternating rural and urban phases on the other. Since the "output" series best tracks the business cycle, it can be seen that the rural phase corresponds to the depression and recovery periods, whereas urban areas enjoyed the economic advantage in boom and downturn. It is also nearly true that rising prices favored cities and falling ones the country. However, it must be noted that noble landlords and other elites form part of our "urban" world even when living in their manor houses.

Let us look now at the model in action. Begin on Figure 4.1a at the trough of the output series (q), when prices and property incomes are still declining. The purchasing power of wages (w/p) is still high, although employment is secure only for those who have guaranteed access to land. Recovery comes to the countryside first, triggered by favorable harvests on plentiful land and by the demand for wage goods from cottage industry. Prices (p) recover, which further stimulates activity, and population begins to grow again spurred by the effect of improving economic conditions on family formation. As the expansion proceeds, urban capitalists and merchants share in profits, while rents (s_r) begin to recover once the contractual terms of claims on surplus are renegotiated. This is a phase of balanced development in which the advantage gradually shifts to the urban sector. After a time, rural production (q) begins to suffer the effects of diminishing returns. Higher grain prices reduce the discretionary incomes on which the demand for wage goods depends, hurting rural manufacturers. Real wages (w/p) fall in both town and country, but urban employment is high with buoyant property incomes paying for lavish consumption and monumental investment. Eventually, the crisis of the overpopulated countryside makes it difficult to collect the high rents and taxes, particularly in the increasingly frequent poor crop years. Distress triggers increased mortality, and eventually the landlords find their incomes declining. The feverish urban boom breaks, and prices start to fall amid the aftershocks of mortality peaks. Urban economic activity declines, pressured by high labor costs (w/p) and falling rent (s_r) incomes. In the countryside, on the other hand, competition for the services of a diminished population allows labor to assure itself some discretionary income with which to buy goods once more.

Figure 4.1b fits this scenario to the historical record. A sharp decline in prices and population lasted through the fourteenth century, after which a long "century of the common man" arrived with the fifteenth. The recovery was fueled by the output of German mines and rural workshops until increasing overseas trade began shifting prosperity to urban centers after about 1500. Output growth continued for a time with urban industry making up for diminishing returns in agriculture. The long price rise of the sixteenth century, fed by imports of American silver, culminated in hard times. But urban prosperity, resting successively on trading profits, industrial production, and receipts of rent, lasted well into the seventeenth century. The decline in prices from their 1620–1650 peaks announced the end of a feverish boom increasingly based on rents. After the famous "crisis of the seventeenth century" (Hobsbawm 1967), recovery again centered on agriculture and cottage industry. It must be said that rural progress in such places as England, Holland, and northern sections of France and Italy helped make the late seventeenth-century contraction far less severe overall than that of the fourteenth century. Like the fifteenth century, the early eighteenth again belonged to common folk. Balanced development in the middle of the century gave way to inflation and renewed pressure on real wages. The French Revolution came at a time when high prices threatened the subsistence of a dense population and the employment prospects of a large generation of young adults. The "aristocratic reaction" in the immediate prerevolutionary period can be interpreted as an attempt to refurbish claims to surplus, neglected during the time of low population pressure, which had again become enforceable. The turn of the century was marked by widespread war, but the model suggests that labor would have had a difficult time in any case.

This scenario of development unfortunately treats the whole of Europe as a unit. But clearly, all areas did not march together in unified rhythms of growth and decline. Our discussion later in this chapter and the next will specify some important exceptions. In the meantime, two important geographic distinctions should be kept in mind. The European core, whose location changed over time, can be viewed as urban relative to the periphery, and in general, southern Europe is urban when compared with the north. The spirit of the model is preserved if the urban-rural dichotomy is translated into regional terms.

The system depicted by the model passes through alternating rural and urban phases. Within this rhythm, the economic basis of urban life evolves in a series of four stages. Begin on Figure 4.1a during the early recovery of output (q). Increased rural activity leads to more trade and protoindustrial production, and cities participate in the recovery through their role as central places. Urban markets grow in scale and volume. As the recovery extends and property incomes revive, long-distance trade increases, stimulating urban participation in trading networks. International connections expand. In a third stage, that of maximum prosperity in terms of peak output for the system as a whole, urban manufactures grow and join commerce and finance to increase urban incomes. The final stage of urban prosperity, which coincides with growing economic distress, can be called "parasitic" rather than productive or "generative" (Hoselitz 1954). Property incomes take an increasing share of a no-longer-rising surplus. Even in the city, the contrast between rich rentiers and the inflation-wracked poor is heightened. Recipients of rent, including church and state, not only consume ostentatiously but take advantage of the flood tide to commend themselves to posterity in stone. Monumental construction and public works also provide a form of outdoor relief, an active fiscal policy long before Keynes to counter depression.

Within this system, towns can prosper in a number of ways. They can concentrate on trade, on what geographers call central place or gateway functions. They can also be centers of direct production, protoindustrial cities in a sense. Finally, they may administer the collection of surplus and organize its consumption. The model suggests that these options will be successively favored as the cycle moves from the recovery of output through the price paroxysm and beyond. Such a progression can indeed be observed in the sixteenth century. Around 1550 or somewhat later, many cities embraced protoindustrial activities to offset flagging trade. In the seventeenth century, on the other hand, political capitals nearly monopolized urban growth from Stockholm to Madrid. It is striking that these "cities of surplus," built when property incomes were taking the maximum share from a no-longer-growing pie, were more magnificent than the towns of trade and enterprise in their heyday. Absolutism, Counterreformation, and landed opulence fostered stylistic departures and monumental creations for which commerce and industry had little time.

Despite the length of the period under review, only one urban phase is included in its entirety. Data on urban populations, trade, and urban industry leave no doubt that the extended period economic historians call the "long" sixteenth century saw widespread urban prosperity.[4] Yet during this phase of expansion, urban industry flourished at a relatively late stage, most notably between 1570 and 1620, with an uneasy plateau lasting until about 1660 when decline became general (Deyon 1978). The wool and silk industries of Milan contracted somewhat earlier, declining by the 1630s and 1640s (Sella 1979). Specific textile centers for which production data exist show the following peaks: Venice 1600, Hondschoote 1640, and Leiden 1660 (Braudel and Spooner 1967). Since urban industrial booms result from increases in property incomes, this timing of expansion and collapse is just what our model predicts. Demographic and production data also testify to widespread urban difficulties from mid to late seventeenth century.[5] War, plague, and famine compounded the pressures of cyclical decline. Even in England the bulk of the small and medium-sized towns underwent general downturns in the second half of the seventeenth century (Clark and Slack 1976).

Paradoxically, the phase of urban decline was often a time of architectural brilliance when baroque extravagances were added to the cityscape. Perhaps merchants were too busy making money in the sixteenth century to bother with excessive architectural display. In the busiest centers of trade and industry, for example, Nuremberg, Amsterdam, and Hamburg, rebuilding remained restrained and in a functional style. In economic terms merchants preferred to reinvest their profits. In sociocultural terms, their values and place in the civic order dictated some sobriety. Gascon (1977) argues that seventeenth-century building was a delayed response to sixteenth-century urban growth. But fine town houses, huge churches, and wide promenades often required land to be cleared, and they therefore tended to aggravate crowding rather than to relieve it. We prefer to note that heavy investment in urban architecture in early modern Europe depended largely on passive property incomes, rather than on savings drawn from wages or profits. As the model shows, rents increase past the peaks of production. Rentiers, therefore, are at their most affluent during times of declining output and low wage incomes, for example, in the late seventeenth century rather than the sixteenth.

Focusing on urban demand and changing income distribution in the long run helps resolve a paradox regarding commercial agriculture and Europe's cities in the sixteenth century. Agriculture in many regions turned away from arable farming and toward specialties after 1500. Dutch tulips and cheese, English and Spanish sheep, and Italian silkworms are cases in point.[6] Why? One key to the puzzle is that rising grain prices meant rising property incomes and urban demand for luxuries, including delicacies from the land. Yet if the nearby countryside turned away from producing basic foodstuffs, how could the thriving cities feed their growing mass of workers, servants, and even paupers? The answer is that they drew on more distant breadbaskets. The grain trade expanded greatly in the sixteenth century, and the demand from west European cities stimulated a transformation of agriculture and society to the east, notably in Poland (Wallerstein 1974). The effect of this development on the European periphery was far different, however, from the urban boom that attracted the grain. In the fourteenth and fifteenth centuries eastern Europe had experienced expansion of its central places based on local trade and crafts. This fledging system of regions was quashed when the rural nobility reinstituted full control over rural surplus by means of the "second serfdom." They managed to generate considerable grain exports without improving the productivity of land or labor, but the result of this exploitation was a great simplification of economic life marked by an urban regression. Only the Baltic ports through which grain flowed out and urban luxuries returned withstood the decline as part of the burgeoning network of long-distance trading connections linked to the Hanseatic cities.

The grain trade leveled off in the seventeenth century. In addition to the cyclical reversal in urban fortunes, special factors intervened. The weakening of the Mediterranean region and the Thirty Years War affected the demand for, as well as the production of, grain even in the first half of the century. By the second half England's progressive agriculture was beginning to generate significant surpluses (Ormrod 1975). Then the return of higher prices in the eighteenth century stimulated domestic production rather than imports in western Europe, a significant sign of change as we shall see. Not until the second half of the nineteenth century, in the full flush of industrial urbanization, would massive imports of basic foodstuffs again be important to Europe.

Country and City: Flanders and Brabant from 1300 to 1750

Let us now use the model to analyze the economic development of Flanders, Hainault, and Brabant from the fourteenth to the eighteenth centuries.[7] This group of regions makes up the populous northern part of modern-day Belgium with extensions into France and the Netherlands. It was and remained a heartland of urban Europe, one pole of the dual core in the Network System. Relatively rich data allow us to investigate the interrelations among population, prices, output, and incomes. In terms of the model the natural periodization breaks the four centuries into three subperiods: 1300–1500, 1500–1650, and 1650–1780. The first and last periods are predicted to be ones of decline followed by rural recovery, the middle period one of urban prosperity—along with rising prices, population, and rents—closing with a worsening rural crisis. Two cautions are in order. One is that political events will strongly inflect the course of economic life in this battleground of cultures, religions, and empires. The second is that the entire region is in a certain sense urban relative to the much more rural mass of Europe.

As was true elsewhere, the region suffered a decline in population beginning early in the fourteenth century. Although plague was a factor, the first epidemics were associated with harvest failures, notably in 1315. The Black Death appears to have missed parts of Brabant, but recurring episodes caused the population to decline until late into the fifteenth century. Household censuses of Brabant recorded a drop of 20 percent between 1437 and 1496 (van Houtte 1977). Interestingly, the province's rural areas suffered more severe losses than at least the major cities. Our model predicts severe losses in rural areas at first, and it is also true that the many paupers may have been counted more completely when they sought refuge in towns. The comparative health of urban Brabant, which contrasts with the decline in the Flemish cloth cities, was due to the rise of Antwerp as the dominant port in northwestern Europe. Towns such as Bergen op Zoom and Bois le Duc (s'Hertogenbosch) with close ties to Antwerp did better than others, such as Brussels and Louvain.

During the rural crisis lands were left fallow or planted to trees, yet grain supplies were ample enough for prices to fall.[8] Whether landlords exacted feudal dues and rent in kind, as the nobles did, or commuted them to money payments, as did many bourgeois, they were forced to lower their demands to attract or hold tenants, and leases renegotiated in the later fourteenth century reflected the lower rents (Nicholas 1971). The counts of Flanders and other territorial authorities also tried to increase or sustain tax revenues, notably in time of war. But the fifteenth century saw real wages rising with the bargaining power of laborers, and there was increased production of food and industrial goods for the market. In the later fourteenth and early fifteenth centuries a new cloth trade emerged in the countryside and the lesser towns, particularly in the Lys and Dendre valleys and in Hondschoote. This partly replaced the hard-hit woolen industry of the great medieval Flemish cities. Clearly, the latter were hurt by the fact that the English now made cloth instead of exporting wool, but the decline in demand for the fine, heavy "old draperies" of Flanders was perhaps aided by the shift in income distribution.

As the population data indicate, recovery came late to the region. Indeed, the entire "urban" phase from 1500 to the middle of the seventeenth century was punctuated by war. Brabant in particular was the locus of struggles among French, English, Spanish, and Dutch power, struggles involving religion and mercantile empires as well as continental supremacy. In this context the performance of the regional economy and its cities, though checkered, gives support to the urban label. Population grew from 1500 to the 1540s and again from 1600 to 1660, and urban fortunes were relatively bright except when cities were under direct military attack. The great exception is Antwerp, which, having survived a twelve-day sack by the duke of Alba's troops in 1576, soon lost its leading role as a port and financial center to Amsterdam.

During this time of mixed expansion and turmoil prices rose almost steadily, pushed by the torrent of American silver and the rise in population and demand for commodities. Agricultural prices, trading profits, and rents all rose, encouraging investment all over Europe. Indeed, the fortunes of the towns in the southern Low

Countries depended on their ability to satisfy the growing European market for specialized and luxury products. Tapestries, paintings, church ornaments, and armor were turned out in profusion, while new trades such as printing became important urban industries. The major cloth towns shifted to the fashionable light fabrics and so fought back in textiles. Workers in Ypres, Courtrai, Bruges, Malines, and Lille turned out growing numbers of says, serges, and mixed cloths (van Houtte 1977). On the other hand, heavy rural taxes and the growing competition for local wool contributed to declines in the rural woolen sector by the 1580s, for instance, around Ypres and Hondschoote (Craeybeckx 1976). Some compensation was afforded the rural areas and small towns by growth in the linen industry, including lace. Two observations help reconcile this development with the model. One is that lace is a partial exception to the generalization that rural goods are plain. The other is that the expanding colonial trade no doubt favored linen production over wool and cheap products over finer grades. Even in its decline, the Flanders-Brabant region had easy access to the mercantile networks.

War continued to haunt the region during the second half of the seventeenth and first half of the eighteenth centuries. This time the principal protagonists were the French and Austrians, although England and the United Provinces also took part. While there is no doubt that the marauding armies brought famine, epidemics, and destruction with them, it must be noted that the more intense earlier fighting had not prevented substantial urban growth and economic development. Van Houtte (1977) points out that agricultural depression had a lot to do with the stagnation. Despite much rural poverty, encouraging signs appeared in agriculture and industry by the late seventeenth century. The spread of potato cultivation made it possible to market more grain and/or feed a larger population, and the cultivation of hops, flax, and tobacco progressed. While the health of rural industry was mixed, such goods as nails, iron, brick, paper, and coal were made or mined in the countryside. And Verviers developed as a major protoindustrial textile center in the later eighteenth century (van Houtte 1977).

For urban areas the picture is more clearly negative, in both demographic and economic terms. Most towns throughout Brabant and Flanders decreased in size until roughly the mid-eighteenth century.[9] The cloth industry declined also, despite efforts to change the product mix, reduce high labor costs, and loosen corporate control. The case of Lille makes clear that the crisis was specifically urban. As the production of says and other light woolen cloths fell after the 1630s, rural output remained high (Deyon and Lottin 1967; Craeybeckx 1976). Even brewing and distilling tended to move to the countryside. Without elaborate production series, it is impossible to balance growth industries—printing in Antwerp and machine making in Liège, for instance—against contracting ones, but the weight of the evidence and the dominance of the stagnating cloth trade argue for a negative trend.

Faced with stiff foreign and growing rural competition, the cities of the southern Low Countries could not sustain prosperity by relying on the internal market. The agricultural rents on which urban incomes depended declined substantially. The fall amounted to 80 percent southwest of Ghent and 30 percent to 40 percent in the area of Bruges between the middle and end of the seventeenth century. As late as 1750 rents were a third to a half lower in the Austrian Netherlands than they had been in 1650 (van Houtte 1977).[10] Most likely, the decline in rents actually paid preceded their renegotiation.

How well does the model hold up in the case just reviewed? Alternatively, does it help clarify and give coherence to a complicated story? We have noted the catastrophes of war and civil conflict along with exogenous economic events specific to the region. The invisible hand of supply and demand had many all-too-visible helpers in its direction of the regional economy. The cyclical forces of early modern economic development interacted with complex political and cultural currents. At the same time, we must note that the producers of Flanders and Brabant were unusually involved in the surge of international trade that marked the expansion of Europe overseas. They were also in the forefront of developments in agricultural and industrial technology that eventually broke down, for a long time at least, the Malthusian limits to population and urban growth. But more of this later. In the meantime, we would argue that the predictions of our model, while they clearly do not explain everything, stand up reasonably well. They also help to suggest new questions by freeing the account from overreliance on ad hoc causes. Why, for instance, were the violent conflicts of the

Figure 4.2. Stocking-frame weavers in their home. Protoindustrial workers commonly worked at home. The French silk weaver's assistant, probably his wife, is winding thread onto bobbins. Invented in England during the late sixteenth century, the stocking frame was often too costly for the domestic worker to purchase. Therefore, merchant entrepreneurs might own the fixed means of production in addition to controlling the raw materials and markets. (From Diderot, *L'Encyclopédie*.)

sixteenth century less harmful to the cities than those of the period after 1660? Certainly not because the armies of Spain were more gentle than those of Louis XIV and Louis XV.

The Protoindustrial City

The role of citizens as large-scale producers of industrial goods between 1500 and 1800 has been largely ignored by scholars of protoindustrial development. Yet manufacturing was an important activity in virtually all early modern cities, and industry for export proved a vigorous engine for growth in a large number of them. Workshops were not so glamorous as wharves or palaces, but many more towns could support manufactures than could fill a role as leading port, financial center, or major capital. In many cases this activity was significant enough that one can properly refer to the place in question as an industrial—or protoindustrial—city. In France, Lyon became a major producer of silk, Amiens and Beauvais of woolen cloth. Nuremberg artisans crafted hundreds of items for export, from clocks to bells to armor. In the Low Countries, Leiden and Verviers made textiles, while Liège became a metalworking and glassblowing city. A number of English towns were noted for their textile industries in the seventeenth century, Norwich and Leeds among them, and the metal trades of Birmingham and Sheffield were also well established by that time. To the south, Genoese silks were preeminent in Europe until the seventeenth century, while Bologna's prosperity rested on its output of silk veils. Other town names throughout Europe were virtually synonymous with lace, cutlery, ceramics, fine leather, violins, or soap.

Theorists of protoindustrialization have focused too exclusively on rural production in examining the growth of home and workshop manufacturing, reserving to cities mainly the roles of distribution and control. Kriedte, Medick, and Schlumbohm (1977) set out the conditions under which substantial domestic production for export could flourish: rising demand for the product, a supply of underemployed labor, an available food surplus, and capitalists to furnish raw materials, finance the period of production, and handle marketing. In themselves, these conditions did not require a rural site. Urban labor was typically more organized and costly than rural, to be sure, and guild regulations raised costs and hampered entrepreneurial response to the calls and vagaries of the market. Urban

Figure 4.3. Porcelain manufacture in the Limousin. Fine china, much of it for export, was produced in a number of European cities, including Limoges in France. This eighteenth-century engraving shows workers breaking up (a) and grinding (b) clay, then sifting (c) and roasting (d) it. Potters shape the vessels (e), which are finally fired in the kiln (f). (From Diderot, *L'Encyclopédie.*)

workers could not generally complement their wages with seasonal agricultural work or share two pursuits among members of a household. It is on this basis that historians posit a progressive division of labor in which direct production moves to the countryside while cities concentrate on shipping, markets, and finance.

Though fruitful and largely valid, this reasoning leaves out a great deal on both the empirical and theoretical levels. The busy centers we enumerated above were not holdovers from the days of medieval crafts. They and others like them rose, maintained themselves, or revived through the fluctuations of the fifteenth through the eighteenth centuries, and some have retained the same specialties into our time. We return below to the important advantages cities enjoyed in lines demanding skilled labor and also to the crucial complementarities between town and countryside. But there is a fundamental argument involved concerning the supply of labor. What makes protoindustrial development important is not that domestic production could mop up temporary, seasonal, or local reserves of underemployed labor. Why should entrepreneurs go to the trouble of finding a market and organizing production if success led only to the quick exhaustion of the pool of available workers? Low wages and a free hand were useful in the short run; what really mattered was an *elastic* supply of labor in the long run. One had to be able to expand production without running up against sharply higher labor costs owing to shortages either of workers or of their food.

The model of rural protoindustrialization works through this process very clearly. Food came from nearby regions or subregions whose farmers, like those around cities or in highly urbanized areas, responded to the stimulus of demand by growing and selling more. As for the supply of labor itself, cottage workers could marry sooner and bear more children than people who needed to establish themselves on a farm (Levine 1977). In Marxist terms, rural protoindustry could grow because it *reproduced* its labor force.

What of towns? Finding additional food supplies posed no special problems since cities had long been attuned to external food sources near and distant. On the demographic side much remains shadowy if not totally unknown. Ready access to urban jobs for adults together with "opportunities" for child labor in many trades no doubt encouraged early marriage and childbearing. Households could retain or exchange children and adolescents since they participated in production (Laslett 1965; Deyon 1981). In France, at least, households were further enlarged by the hiring of (presumably rural) female servants (Hufton 1974). Against these positive factors must be set living conditions generally conducive to the spread of disease and high rates of infant and child mortality. Yet the proletarian population of Lyon, for example, had higher birth than death rates in the eighteenth century despite the ravages of baby farming (Garden 1970).

However the balance between births and deaths may have worked out, the key to expanding urban manufacture certainly lay in immigration. Natural increase cannot account for a reported eightfold increase in the number of urban wage laborers in Saxony between

1550 and 1750 (Blaschke 1967; C. Tilly 1979). Moreover, the addition of young adults gave the age structure of urban populations a favorable shape with respect to birth and death rates. At any rate, early cities seem never to have wanted for newcomers despite ongoing discrimination on the part of urban establishments against "strangers." Immigration provided the "unlimited supplies of labor" on which protoindustrial growth depended in cities (W. A. Lewis 1954). The major difference between rural and urban labor, that one was homegrown and the other not, was of little consequence for protoindustrial growth. Where it did matter, as we shall see, was in periods of difficulty or decline.

A regional perspective is important in analyzing all protoindustrial development, and this leads us to focus on the relations between cities and the surrounding countryside. Political dominion by the city extending to basic labor processes of the local peasantry made it possible to block or control the spread of craft industry to the *contado*, as in Spain and Italy (Pounds 1979). Peasants in the Bologna hinterland raised the raw silk on which the export trade in silk veils depended. From the city's point of view, a strict division of labor enforced by urban landlords guarded against rural competition in spinning and weaving while ensuring supplies of the precious raw material (Poni 1980). The agrarian system could also restrict labor supplies if it was thriving and well organized around urban markets, just as it could where feudal bonds remained strong. The farms of Holland used and paid their labor well, while the estates of eastern Europe clung to their serfs.

In northwestern Europe conditions were often favorable to urban protoindustrial development. Guilds and restrictions on labor movements were frequently weak. There were areas of advanced agriculture to furnish food but also poorer ones to provide urban labor or to house complementary rural production. Norwich in East Anglia is a good example. Wool weavers there regularly evaded the supervision of the weaver's guild which by the early eighteenth century was effectively dead. The hinterland was densely populated and labor free to move. Moreover, weavers came from other towns as well as from France and Flanders. Newcomers who practiced a trade were obliged to purchase citizenship; a ready mechanism existed therefore to integrate them into the social and political life of the city (Corfield 1976b).

Flexibility for growth was important but insufficient: cities also needed a way of coping with contraction. New goods could push aside a town's proudest exports, as Norfolk's light draperies had ruined the fine, heavy cloths of Exeter and Ypres in their time. Cyclical changes dampened demand for industrial products. While newcomers to the city might become integrated into a community if they had skill or capital, most immigrants had only precarious status and could be forced out. This preserved the chances of native sons and daughters in times of decline and so helped to maintain the continuity of the city. We saw in Chapter 3 that migrants were probably subject to greater risk of death; they were also more likely than the native-born to emigrate. The skilled core of urban artisans left only in case of disasters, such as the religious wars visited on French and Flemish cities in the sixteenth century. Otherwise, the last in were usually the first out. Then as now the Swiss showed the way. Although Geneva innovated vigorously to renew its protoindustrial base, access to permanent residence, not to mention citizenship, was closely controlled (Perrenoud 1979).

Without question, the long-term trend was for manufacturing to shift from urban to rural locations, or at least to expand more in the latter, although cyclical changes in the economy could affect the trend. But in some cases, an urban location was always desirable, for example, where industries involved relatively heavy use of capital—fixed, circulating, or human—or the need for close entrepreneurial control. Less abstractly, the need to respond quickly to fashion or to other market changes, as well as the use of skilled labor, valuable raw materials, or expensive equipment argued for an urban location. The armor and clocks of Nuremberg and the fine damask of Lisburn, Ireland, exemplify the importance of craft skills. Urban artisans were better trained than cottage workers. However restrictive and retrograde guilds may have been at times, they preserved standards of craft pride and quality control. In the more specialized branches of textile production, the demands of fashion made particular products obsolete quickly and rewarded clever designers. Roubaix weavers competed successfully with their rivals in Lille next door, continually inventing patterns and new mixtures of fibers (Deyon 1981). Roubaix also shows that there were urban as well as rural refuges from burdensome regulations. Finally, towns continued to house the complex equipment needed for certain auxiliary stages of textile production: fulling mills, dyeing vats, and printing blocks or rolls.

The silk trade illustrated many of the ongoing strengths of urban location. Much of Lyon's prosperity rested on the ability of skilled weavers to execute the subtle creations of a respected elite of designers. Coordinating these efforts was one function of urban merchants; finance was another. Backed by urban bankers, they scoured the Italian and Levantine countryside to buy the precious raw silk for processing in throwing and spinning mills. These "protofactories," found in English and French as well as northern Italian towns, represented substantial fixed investment. Bologna in 1683 had 113 silk mills powered by water, and most stages of silk processing were mechanized (Poni 1980). Even when the factories left the city in the eighteenth century, some shifted to smaller towns in the area. Weaving, however, remained in the cities, in Bologna but also in Genoa. Lyon anchored another regional division of labor in silk. Raw silk brought in by the merchants was sent to Saint-Chamond to be spun and thrown and the processed material distributed among various towns and villages. Saint-Chamond's own weavers made brocaded ribbon. Those of Saint-Étienne, then a lesser center, produced plainer sorts, while part-time rural or village workers made the simplest goods (Latreille 1975).

The last example makes an important point about protoindustrialization. It flourished best not as town *or* country, but as a complementary system involving both rural and urban places and the various elements of a regional urban hierarchy. Textiles, metalware, and other products passed through several stages of processing between the raw material and the finished article. The more rudimentary tasks, which in earlier times might have been done by women and children in the artisan household, could easily be shifted into nearby villages. Big-city entrepreneurs took advantage of lower rural wages and of heightened divisions of labor in decentralizing parts of their production while reserving the more delicate operations to city artisans. Regional integration added flexibility and so helped business remain stable overall in a changeable market. In Picardy urban and rural production of textiles coexisted, each sector having its own rhythm of expansion and decline. The weaving of light woolen fabric spread out from Amiens and Abbeville, whereas cruder, heavier cloth was produced farther south near Beauvais and hosiery and linen elsewhere in the region. The patterns of regional specialization in the seventeenth and eighteenth centuries were complex as well as changing, involving both complementarity and competition (Engrand 1979). Throughout, however, the structural framework for these export-oriented activities—embodied in markets, merchants, and sources of credit—remained urban. Wherever physical production might take place, the intangible processes of information flow, decision making, and exchange concentrated firmly in cities.

Over time, these regional complementarities evolved, showing that the rural-urban symbiosis could survive even mechanization. Technological change often helped artisan production to adapt and so endure. It created new divisions of labor as it swept away old ones. Our account of urban industrialization in Chapter 6 will focus on the evolution of protoindustrial regions and on continuing small-scale urban production, as well as on the more familiar story of the modern factory.

The consequences of mass production for the life of early cities have been little investigated, and much remains unknown. Conjectures about the demographic impact have been offered, but what of social and spatial effects? If it had ever been true that the bulk of a city's population was made up of a homogeneous body of independent burghers, such rough equality had vanished before the sixteenth century. Protoindustrial development accentuated the divisions between men of property and proletarians lacking both economic and political privileges, as well as the disparities of wealth and power among burghers. As early as the fourteenth century, journeymen had often lost any realistic chance of acceding to mastery and guild membership. Many artisans, in turn, become little more than hirelings of merchant entrepreneurs, perhaps owning their tools but not the raw materials representing most of the capital. Their guilds came increasingly under the control of the town councils, themselves more and more dominated by wealthy export merchants who thus solidified their hold over both trade and town (Clark and Slack 1976).

Under the pressure of changing patterns of production and marketing, urban communities were thus becoming more stratified. A widening gap—cultural and political as well as material—divided rich and poor, attested to in many places by outbreaks of violent protest and more violent suppression: food riots, carnival attacks, or disorders by journeymen. Yet one should neither rush to apply modern ideas of social class and class consciousness to varying resentments and fears, nor paint the picture in too highly contrasted tones. Between the great families of urban patricians and the marginal population of laborers and paupers, often born elsewhere, a sturdy middle group of shopkeepers and artisans enjoyed a modicum of property, skills, and claims on the town and its government. In the larger towns of sixteenth- and seventeenth-century Germany, the development of the *Verlag* system of domestic industry proved favorable to this class (Friedrichs 1978). In Leiden and Lille the merchants in control of the urban economy seem to have taken pains to preserve small, independent textile producers, tempering immediate greed with concern for the long-term health of the urban community (DuPlessis and Howell 1982). Easy access to citizenship and social mobility within the guilds made Elizabethan London a relatively open, stable city (Rappaport 1982).

It is easy to take for granted the remarkable persistence of cities throughout centuries of political strife, social upheaval, and economic booms and slumps. This underlying constancy implies both a strong capacity to adapt or recover and forbearance by those with the power to break traditional patterns. Perhaps one additional reason for transferring production to the countryside was a sense that the new activity might well prove transitory and that fluctuations were best absorbed outside the city. Protoindustrial cities managed to strive for prosperity while limiting the risks to their labor force.

The horrors of factory-town life are so well known that it is hard to credit the idea that conditions were worse in many early modern cities, notably in protoindustrial centers. Yet they undoubtedly were. The crowding, filth, and absence of basic amenities could reach epic proportions, although before the age of reform and mass politics there is mostly the mute testimony of high mortality rates for evidence. Urban workers suffered from lack of space and often of adequate food. But the biggest problem was water: too much in cellars, swamps, and drains, too little to drink and wash with and that little usually polluted. Crises of mortality in eighteenth-century Bordeaux clearly demonstrate this pattern (Poussou 1980). Epidemic "fever" habitually spread from the industrial suburbs during the hot months. When food prices were high—as a major port, Bordeaux did not need to fear actual dearth—disease took a major toll in lives.

Most urban functions have left their visual mark on European cities: market halls, cathedrals, fortifications, docks, palaces, even streets named for a traditional craft. Yet except for privileged establishments such as royal manufactories or arsenals, neither rural nor urban protoindustry has left a strong visual legacy. Even when cities hummed with activity and profits soared, investments in building and urban design were kept to a minimum. Most of the installations have long since been swept away by waves of expansion and transformation. In general, production and workers were either crowded into existing spaces or allowed to spread beyond the town limits in anarchic, slapdash suburbs.

Among the few good case studies, three deal with cities in Flanders and one in Provence. As a major border fortress, Lille remained painfully corseted within its walls, although this did not prevent vigorous protoindustrial development. One major addition was enclosed in the seventeenth century, but free extension awaited the late 1850s. The result was extraordinary crowding, squalor, and misery. Workers—who nonetheless kept arriving, let us remember —paid painfully high rents for tiny houses or cellar rooms, with densities equaling those of central Paris despite the presence of a loom in most dwellings. This congestion allowed Roubaix, a couple of miles away, to grow into perhaps the first purely protoindustrial town (Aydalot, Bergeron, and Roncayolo 1981). As put together by speculative builders, the city "plan" had all the simplicity of checkerboard towns on the American prairie without their regularity. Two houses were built on the narrow facade of each lot, with a narrow alley reaching back down the middle as much as 500 feet. The alley was lined with tiny two-story, two-room houses. A store or cabaret on the street, a nearby water tap, and a common latrine at the back of the dead-end lot were all the services available to some 50 to 300 inhabitants of a *courée*. This style of settlement remained dominant through the period of mechanization and through the growth of Roubaix to over 100,000 inhabitants in the nineteenth century. Basic services at the municipal level lagged badly: a post office in 1820, adequate drinking water in 1863, a hospital only in 1899. Undoubtedly, part of the problem was that Roubaix lacked any regional role and, unlike mining and metallurgical settlements, had no dominant employer.

Nîmes offers an interesting comparison with Lille and Roubaix. Midway through the seventeenth century a successful conversion from wool to silk took place, and growth was rapid in the eighteenth century with a near tripling of the population to 50,000 in 1780

(Teisseyre-Sallmann 1980). The small space within the old walls was soon full, as in Lille, but the city was burdened neither with a strategic role nor with a powerful establishment of merchants, administrators, or landed proprietors. The silk merchants had a free hand in locating production, but, unlike their counterparts in Roubaix, saw to the layout of new, relatively well-planned suburbs, which were eventually integrated into the city. Still it is noteworthy that these rich and influential men declined to participate in the eighteenth-century architectural renewal of the inner city, even though they lived there. Such profits as were not reinvested went into the purchase of shares in trading companies or of rural estates, not great town houses.

A final example, that of Ghent in the period of French domination, shows how cities were able to accommodate transitory booms. During the Revolution and Empire, roughly 1790 to 1830 for the full episode, the old textile center was able to profit from the absence of English competition (Gerneke and Siravo 1980). As many as 13,000 people were employed at the peak, and a variety of products, techniques of production, scale, and forms of organization were involved. Nonetheless, total population never grew by more than 10 percent—from 55,000 to 60,000—and the built-up area was not expanded. Apparently, the marginal population was sufficiently numerous to staff the expanded textile sector, no doubt with some transfers from other activities. Workers and production were housed in empty or converted structures, notably convents, and in sheds put up in backyards or vacant lots. No doubt, considerable crowding into existing houses also took place. But all these changes were readily reversible when the region was freed both from Napoleon's army and from his trade blockades.

Toward Self-sustained Growth

The inability of the European economy between the fourteenth and the eighteenth centuries to break through the barriers that limited it to cyclical growth and decline stemmed from the combined pressures of limited resources, technological weakness, and institutional barriers. Diminishing returns to labor on the land, combined with the siphoning off of surplus for the benefit of consumption by rentiers and urban elites, placed a ceiling on the economic potential of the system. Moreover, shortages of specie (metallic money) regularly threatened to choke off trade and economic activity. Over time, however, changes in agricultural techniques, investment patterns, trade, and finance lifted the system to new heights of productivity, overleaping the centuries-old obstacles to growth and mass urbanization. These crucial changes were not confined to England or to the eighteenth century, but it is easiest to summarize them in that context. Three are of special note: convertible husbandry in agriculture, rural investment by landlords, and the full implementation of an imperial mercantile system dominated by Europe.

The Malthusian limits on productivity were substantially pushed back by combining arable and stock farming. Agriculture became more intensive while soil fertility was preserved or enhanced. As a result, the progressive agricultural regions provided an increased and more elastic supply of food, as well as more farming employment. They lost rather than gained industrial jobs, but their demand for wage goods, tools, and modest luxuries such as books rose substantially. Agricultural improvement, combined with good prices and fairly low real wages, added greatly to the wealth of landlords, and provincial towns flourished as a result of expanding local trade. Although aristocrats and gentry lived on a lavish scale, they were still able to put large amounts of surplus to more productive uses than had been typical earlier. The new agriculture called for substantial investments, both on the process of enclosure and on the newly consolidated farms. Moreover, great sums were spent on turnpikes and canals and for the extraction and processing of raw materials. England had fortunately rid itself after 1688 of the threat of an absolute monarchy and a militant church, together with their "edifice complexes." Its eighteenth-century urbanism was limited in scope and solid rather than grandiose.

Europe gained many things from its maritime expansion, and among the most important was a great improvement in the terms of trade, the price received for exports relative to the price paid for imports. Specifically, the tempting exotic goods, from pepper to tea and sugar, became much cheaper. Europeans captured the trade and often gained control of production itself. This meant they could buy for less, produce more if demand warranted it, and retain or reduce the huge markup between producers' cost and landed price. The Dutch were the first to grasp the possibilities of demand elasticity and to seek profit from volume rather than high markup.

Eventually, the English took the leading role in a lucrative reexport trade.

More favorable access to imports helped conserve specie and allowed more Europeans to indulge their taste for products that were formerly luxuries, but changes on the export side may have been of greater strategic importance. We can distinguish three classes of overseas demand. Cheap trinkets and coarse cloth served for trade with tribal peoples and for outfitting field hands in plantation colonies. The planters, merchants, and administrators imported the urban goods needed to approximate the life-style of European elites. And the colonists who settled the towns and farms of North America bought a mix of wage goods, implements, and modest luxuries not unlike those purchased in the prosperous agricultural regions at home. These exports promoted a set of industries that made relatively cheap or rural goods, which were England's forte, despite the unfavorable movement of the macroeconomic system. Demand continued strong enough not only to keep protoindustry going but also to stimulate the search for fuel- and labor-saving technology.

In summary, the phase of price increase in eighteenth-century England departed in significant ways from the pattern described in our model. Agricultural progress sustained population growth despite rising rents. Together with the opening of new lands for settlement, it kept some labor incomes high enough to sustain demand for rural protoindustrial goods. Tariff protection of agricultural goods added yet more to buoyant property incomes, but the effect was to increase investment rather than to subsidize conspicuous consumption. While the real dimensions of the economy—population and output—grew steadily, prices and wages stayed nearly constant. No bottlenecks arose to derail the expanding machine sector or to slow its attendant urbanization. By the early nineteenth century, the old pattern of alternate urban and rural dominance was substantially destroyed in favor of more balanced development. New urban centers grew up around the initially rural mines and mills. At the same time, the increase in trade expanded the older manufacturing cities. A protoindustrial economy gave way to an industrial one.

CHAPTER 5

Beyond Baroque Urbanism

THE CYCLICAL FORTUNES of many cities coupled with the restricted growth of Europe's urban sector from the fourteenth through the eighteenth centuries give a false impression of urban stability during turbulent times. Statistical averages homogenize dramatic growth and catastrophic decline, robbing the specific case of its power and interest. During these centuries ports and court cities burgeoned. Rome, in 1450 a "wilderness among crumbling ruins," reemerged as the rapidly growing capital of Christendom (Partner 1976:5). Meanwhile, Valladolid sank into oblivion when abandoned by the Spanish court. Remember, too, that numbers can be a poor guide to political and cultural influence. Urban printers helped to spread far beyond a city's boundaries the revolutionary ideas of humanists, scientists, and philosophers. At the same time, growing bureaucracies made capitals and towns the administrative centers of royal absolutism. Outside a central band stretching from the Netherlands south through the Rhineland, Switzerland, and Italy, urban autonomy weakened greatly, and monarchs exercised on their own behalf the haughty dominance of the city. Thus baroque urbanism, while it had a firm economic and demographic base, also embodied a story of social, political, and cultural influences. Wealth often served only as a means to more rarified forms of power and glory. In this chapter we focus on the social, political, and spatial organization of cities, looking first at a dynamic example of urban power in France.

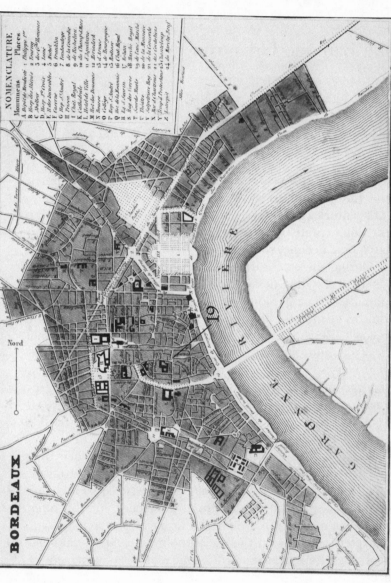

NOMENCLATURE.

Monumens	Places
A Ste Ste Bénédict	1 Philippe Ier
B Hosp. des Malades	2 Tourny
C Abattoir	3 des Quinconces
D Hosp. St Crois	4 Louis
E Hôtel Invalides	5 Richel
F Caserne	6 Franklin
G Hosp. St André	7 Boulangerie
H Prisons	8 de la Croselle
I Chat. Royal	9 de Richelieu
K Cathédrale	10 du Champ d'Aulneau
L Hostelle Ville	11 d'Aquitaine
M Hot. des Douanes	12 Bernadrot
N Bourse	13 d'Armes
O Collège	14 de Bourgogne
P Roy. St André	15 Boulbon
Q Bal. de la Saumur	16 Chat. Royal
R La Corderie	17 Roban
S Bat. des Vivres	18 Saint le Royal
T Grande Marte	19 de l'anc. Marché
V Théâtre	20 de la Monnaie
X Salpetrière Roy.	21 de la Concorde
N Bar et Boutique	22 des Cordeliers
Y Tempid Protestant	23 Sauvetage
Z Entrepôt	24 du Mar du Neuf

BORDEAUX

Nord

RIVIÈRE

GARONNE

Figure 5.1. Bordeaux. This map from the early nineteenth century shows both the medieval street plan and later additions. Long, straight avenues have been cut through older parts of the city in the south and west. The newer sections are located to the north and include the major squares, the Place Philippe I and the Place Tourny. (Drawn by Monin and engraved by Laguillermie and

A French Port and Regional Capital

Bordeaux lies along the west bank of the Garonne at the crossing of ancient trade routes between the Rhineland and the Pyrenees, the Atlantic and the Mediterranean.[1] The territory of the city proper was defined, up to the period that concerns us, by the line of fourteenth-century walls with their massive gates and towers, culminating in the bastion of the Château Trompette that guarded the downstream entrance to the town.

Our map shows the major changes that took from Bordeaux much of its medieval character in the eighteenth century. Until then, it offered the typical picture of narrow and winding streets overhung with gabled houses. As the port grew, open space was gobbled up except for the convent and monastery gardens near the walls. The town centered on the old marketplace (19 on the map) and the adjoining town hall, while merchants, carpenters, and even vineyard workers shared the limited intramural space, rich and poor residing in close proximity. Although a 1630 engraving shows gardens right up to the walls, mean houses undoubtedly straggled along the roads leading out from the main gates (Duby 1981, III).

The great mercantile activity of the eighteenth century justified a great deal of building and rebuilding. The walls and fortress vanished, partly replaced by a boulevard and a monumental square facing the water. Docks, warehouses, and shipyards spread far up and down the bank. In the old city, stone replaced wood, and royal officials as well as merchants built elegant *hôtels*. But the symmetrical squares and parks, the noble theaters and government buildings, and the straight, wide streets lay in what had been the outskirts. Here also, though less visible, lived concentrations of humble folk, most of them recent immigrants. Here as well were the large institutions—jails, hospitals, almshouses—in which the city tried desperately to contain and assuage the dependent poor.

Where the traveler nearing the city had once seen only crenellated walls and churches, emblems of the higher functions of war and prayer in the medieval order, there was now a true townscape. The merchant, the jurist, the burgher of taste and leisure now had visible settings. But even though the mansard roofs, the balconies, and the decorative classical flourishes resembled the best and latest in Paris, medieval Bordeaux had not disappeared. At the heart of the baroque city the tangle of crooked streets remained.

Figure 5.2. The port of Bordeaux in the eighteenth century. A focal point for the city was its riverfront, lined with impressive buildings. The ships loading and unloading along the Garonne quays would have come from the Caribbean, the Baltic, and the Mediterranean seas. (Engraved by Mignon from a painting by Vernet; Musées Nationaux, Chalcographie du Louvre.)

Between 1300 and 1600 the population of Bordeaux fluctuated around 30,000, making it one of the half dozen largest provincial cities of France. From some 45,000 in 1715 it grew by means of migration to 110,000 at the onset of the Revolution, when it was tied with Marseille as the country's third city and its first seaport. As one might expect, a majority of the migrants came from perhaps 150 kilometers or less, but many, notably adult males, traveled from the Pyrenees, the Massif Central, Brittany, or even Alsace to work in Bordeaux. The city recruited servants and laborers, shipwrights and masons, sailors and civil servants.

The social structure of Bordeaux resembled a pyramid with a very wide base and little room indeed at the very top. Ennobled office holders—the members of the *parlement* and the chief royal administrators—occupied the peak of status and, usually, fortune. Their only rivals for local influence were the richest of the native merchants. Although these groups constituted only about 5 percent of the population in the 1780s, they held a major share of the city's wealth, including many of the best *châteaux* in the nearby vineyards. The middle ranks of the society comprised members of the liberal professions, lesser merchants, and rentiers whose wealth was in bonds or rural rents (see Table 5.1). The privilege of citizenship

Table 5.1. Occupational distribution of the employed population of selected European cities, 1500–1750 (percent).

Occupation	Monza (1541)	Venice (1660)	Geneva[a] (1625–1650)[c]	Geneva[a] (1745–1749)[c]	Bordeaux[b] (1740)
Food distribution and agriculture	39	17	13	7	6[d]
Textiles and clothing	25	43	29	14	15
Building	1	4	6	4	4
Metalwork	10	5	9	28	3
Woodwork	2	8	1	5	17
Leatherwork	—	7	9	6	—
Professional	0.5	5	6	5	6
Transportation	1	9	—	—	17
Miscellaneous	21.5	2	27	31	32

Sources: Cipolla (1976:76); Poussou (1978:90); Perrenoud (1979:156).
a. Married males only.
b. Males only.
c. Year of marriage of households sampled.
d. Food industry only.

could be claimed by anyone who owned a substantial house and had lived in Bordeaux for five years. Ranking below the men of property and making up almost half the population were the artisans and journeymen, less well-off and less well-considered although benefiting from corporate organizations that allowed them to control production. In fact, the poorer artisans and the journeymen merged into the ranks of the urban proletariat: sailors, laborers, gardeners, and vineyard workers whose incomes barely bought food and shelter. Service workers—servants, lodginghouse keepers, cooks, purveyors of food and drink—were another large category typically with little if any property. Females made up a large proportion of the labor force, more in services than in direct production. But there were seamstresses and spinners as well as street sellers, wet nurses, and laundresses among married as well as single women. How many beggars, thieves, and prostitutes the thriving port supported we do not know. Much of the city's labor market was shaped by Bordeaux's dual role as a port and as a center of consumption. The large artisanal population built ships and wine casks, processed sugar and tobacco, made ropes and bottles. In fact, more males were reported in material production than in services, despite the heavy representation of trade and transportation. Woodworking, textiles, and building led the list of "industrial" occupations.

Political power in the town was technically in the hands of a mayor and six *jurades*, a town clerk, and a treasurer. By a royal charter of the early thirteenth century they were given control of local industry, commerce, and police, and they also exercised the city's seigneurial powers over suburban lands. These officials embodied only the illusion of local autonomy, however. From the time the city returned to the control of the French crown in the mid-fifteenth century, the king intervened regularly to choose the town government. In any case, the authority of the military *gouverneur* and of the royal *intendant* regularly infringed on that of the municipality. After a tax revolt in 1548, royal power proceeded unchecked except that local loyalties always threatened to subvert the principal agents of that power. The history of Bordeaux's judicial assembly illustrates the ambivalence that resulted because the monarchy relied so greatly on urban elites for control over the provinces and their cities.

When he reestablished French control, Charles VII revived the provincial *parlement* of Guyenne at Bordeaux, although he appointed its members from his supporters in other provinces. Acting as an appeals court, the *parlement* was supposed to advance royal interests throughout western and southwestern France. Its president meddled in local elections, challenged the archbishop on church matters, and chastised the inefficient town government. In the longer run, however, its aristocratic officials, their charge handed down from father to son, formed the core of the Bordeaux elite and took on the role of provincial spokesmen against royal centralization. The king countered by adding new officials: the *intendant*, responsible to the king through his council of state, gained effective control of Guyenne in the later seventeenth and eighteenth centuries. In fact, *intendants* and royal architects took leading roles in the remodeling of the city.

As the capital of the region, Bordeaux became the residence of military and fiscal officials, along with a variety of assessors and secretaries responsible for overseeing financial and police matters. They and their assistants fanned out to the lesser towns in Guyenne and Gascony: Agen, Perigueux, Sarlat, and a score of others. A complex administrative hierarchy, ultimately centered on Paris and Versailles, reached full development. It extended through Bordeaux via the centers of *subdélégations, élections, capitaineries, maîtrises,* and other units down to the communes, hamlets, and dwellings of the countryside. Bordeaux occupied the central place in the region's political hierarchy. Orders flowed down the administrative chain, while taxes and information worked their way back up.

How well was this centralization tolerated? The urban conflicts of the early modern period in France are particularly difficult to sort out. The previous chapter suggested that conflict during the seventeenth century could be explained in terms of the changing balance of economic advantage, and it is certain that there was more protest during the reign of Louis XIV and just before than in either the preceding or succeeding centuries. Yet during the mid-seventeenth-century civil wars of the Fronde, royal officials were expelled. At one point, a "popular" government, its members drawn from the petite bourgeoisie, took over the city. Hence, resistance to the expansion of monarchical control was at least an aspect of protest against high taxes and hardship.

The regional hierarchy dominated by Bordeaux typifies what we have called a Central Place System. Goods and services flowed up and down the hierarchy of towns and villages linked politically and economically to Bordeaux. In addition to the administrative ties we have already described, the region supplied wine, grain, brandy, and cloth for export, as well as workers for city jobs, and it absorbed a modest quantity of exotic imports from the plantations in the French Antilles. Yet this role as the center of a territorial system cannot account for Bordeaux's eighteenth-century expansion and brilliance. The French southwest, although prosperous, underwent no great development at this time. The population growth rates of its major centers were in fact dwarfed by that of Bordeaux. To the southeast, the territorial influence of the Atlantic port was checked by that of Toulouse, a long-standing bastion of royal power as well as the center of a major grain- and woad-producing area. Bordeaux's regional hinterland was therefore limited in size and dynamism.

On the other hand, Toulouse offered little competition in the realm of foreign commerce. By sea, Bordeaux joined the exploding network of oceanic trade that reached from the Baltic to the East and West Indies. The value of goods passing through the port multiplied tenfold from 1720 to 1779. Most of the major shipments from the city, with the exception of wine, were reexports— colonial products to and staples from northern Europe. The city's docks spread downstream from the town, illustrating their dependence on the Atlantic trade. The vitality of overseas connections penetrated the social life of the town, too. Foreigners controlled much of the port's wholesale trade and credit. Especially important were Sephardic Jews originally from Portugal, as well as Dutch, Germans, Irish, and Scandinavians. Meanwhile, the wealthy Bordelais continued to make and ship their famous wines and tend the town's and the king's business. Crouzet suggests that the native elite was too conservative to commit itself totally to the risks of overseas trade (Higounet 1968,V). But note that the urban connections we call the Network System fostered international linkages and migration. Bordeaux was a major junction in a system of cities that stretched from a core in northwest Europe to peripheries in the New World. People as well as goods moved along its paths.

The city's wealth and expanding size supported a rich cultural life. In the milieu provided by the university, the *collège*, and several printing firms, the humanism originally brought into the city by Italian priests and lawyers could flourish. Michel de Montaigne exemplifies the parlementarians who, themselves writers and book collectors, helped spread new ideas. By the mid-seventeenth century, modern studies and high French culture held sway. An academy of sciences, founded in 1664, encouraged literature and history as well as scientific subjects. With the acquisition of a museum, an opera, a ballet, an orchestra, and a theater, the city could offer culture to the public, while the salons of literary women testified to the health of private efforts. Bordeaux's cultural preeminence matched its economic and political dominance over Guyenne, Gascony, and part of Languedoc. In contrast, the city's international links apparently had little cultural impact.

Social Contrasts in Early Modern Cities

How typical was Bordeaux? Its closest analogues were coastal regional capitals such as Barcelona, Bristol, and Königsberg. Other major ports—Venice or Danzig, for example—were less bound up in a regional-national system. Bordeaux's occupational distribution exhibited the diversity characteristic of a city with important functions in both types of urban systems, with many professionals and a good balance between manufacture and services. Earlier data for regional centers in Italy and Switzerland reveal a high proto-industrial concentration in Venice and Geneva but similar proportions of professionals. Monza, a manufacturing center lower down in the urban hierarchy, lacked large numbers of professionals and transport workers but included many agricultural workers (see Table 5.1).

Occupational data for the period are scattered, uncertain, and difficult to compare. But the substantial share of artisans in early modern cities stands out as a common trait, one that blunts the conventional image of trade and administration as urban dominants. Food and textiles occupied more than half the employed population in both Venice and Monza and over 40 percent in early seventeenth-century Geneva. Bordeaux's figures would be higher if available statistics counted the females in these sectors and the specialized vineyard workers. Metal- and woodwork were often locally important, while building and public works could mobilize virtual armies, skilled as well as unskilled. Many workers were needed to meet the consumption needs of the city. Larger centers not only housed more affluent consumers but also served as a source of supply for the elite customers scattered throughout the region. The larger the city, the more diverse and sophisticated the crafts represented there, in general; but even the smallest market towns had their tailors and bakers to supply local residents (Patten 1978). In principle, the diversity of secondary occupations and the balance of employment among them should allow us to draw functional distinctions between cities in terms of their systemic roles, although practical questions of data and of definition or classification cannot be underestimated. A high degree of diversity and balance among occupations in a given city indicates a strong role as a central place. In contrast, unusual concentration on a few trades suggests specialized production for an external market, the mark of a true protoindustrial city. Cities with important positions in a trading network had large transport and commercial sectors.

More visible than artisans, if not always more numerous, service workers were a universal feature of towns. Cabarets or alehouses could thrive in even the smallest settlements on the business of market visitors, rural workers, and passing travelers. In addition to dispensing cheer, such places served as social and informational centers. Larger towns had barbers, innkeepers, lawyers, and tax agents, to name only a few of hundreds of specialties. Court cities, with their swarms of servants and government clerks, their officers, clerics, and artists, represented a polar case of dominance by tertiary occupations, although it is easy to forget how many wigmakers, tailors, confectioners, apothecaries, and harnessmakers it took to put and keep the show together. Centers of power also drew more than their share of those with no profession— at any rate none that fit into official categories. Besides respectable pensioners, widows, and rentiers, as well as beggars, vagrants, and the institutionalized marginal population, one met with all manner of lobbyists, hangers-on, intriguers, and go-betweens.[2] In Valladolid, for a time capital in Spain's Golden Century, the combined rentier, service, and unemployed groups made up 80 percent of the households (*vecinos*) surveyed (Bennassar 1967; data from 1570).

In Valladolid, as elsewhere, the carriages of the rich and great clattered past numerous beggars on the street. Harsh contrasts between a privileged minority and a deprived majority were neither new nor specifically urban, of course. But larger, more complex baroque cities embodied sharper extremes than the typical medieval towns, and the loss of urban autonomy added a degree of anonymity. In the biggest places it was even harder for town fathers to take care of "their" poor and keep strangers out. Charitable institutions tried hard to control the situation with a mix of confinement, relief, and dissuasion, but the human results seldom lived up to the grand scale of eleemosynary architecture.

In societies with low wages, only wealth could secure a decent living, to say nothing of ease or luxury. Skilled artisans and professionals could perhaps achieve comfort from the product of their labor alone, but they were often dependent on the fickle favor of rich and powerful patrons. The independence and prosperity of urban artisans were threatened from many sides. Most common was a gradual takeover of control by a merchant manufacturer, which could happen in response to increasing competition from rural sources or from imports. The mercantilist/cameralist state, though loudly proclaiming its support for manufacturers, increasingly taxed and regulated the guilds and set up its own establishments to make tapestries, porcelain, or arms.

Wealth, of course, was highly concentrated. In Lyon in 1545 over half the wealth belonged to a mere 10 percent of the population, while the least-favored 60 percent owned just a fifth (Gascon 1971; Cipolla 1976).[3] Land and rights tied to land—mortgages, forest leases, seigneurial dues—remained the primary form in which wealth was held, and city dwellers increased their control of rural land at the same time as noble landholders were tending to identify more with the city and to spend more time there. But movable forms of wealth were growing in importance. The more active "capitalists" (in the original sense of holders of capital) were merchants, entrepreneurs, or holders of income-producing offices. The French crown, in particular, resorted to tax farming and the sale of offices on a grand scale. Passive opportunities—not always free of risk—included shares in trading companies, public and private debt, and the relatively new idea of urban rental property (Vance 1976).

We have seen that the poor were a constant presence and an endless concern, if only on grounds of public order. Reports and estimates of their number are plentiful, but it is wise to treat these with more than the usual reserve and to stress changeability. Migration in and out and variations in mortality could quickly escalate a city's contingent of paupers or provide apparent relief. Moreover, the problem was not so much the destitute fringe—whatever its size—as the larger group who just scraped by in good or "normal" times. If two thirds of the urban population of England lived below or very near the poverty line in the early sixteenth century (Hoskins

1976), what of poorer regions of Europe? What, also, of the sharp, disorganizing crises periodically occasioned by crop failures, plagues, or wars? More fundamentally, the problem of urban poverty was closely tied to the vagaries of economic life both in the cities and in the countryside. Hoskins estimated that the early sixteenth century represented a relatively favorable time for urban wage earners. What then must urban poverty have been in the hard times of the seventeenth century? As our model in Chapter 4 made explicit, cyclical changes led not only to periodic increases in food prices relative to wages but at the same time to unemployment, as the markets for urban goods dried up or the rural rents on which cities depended fell in arrears. To compound the problem, the poor from the countryside would flood in to seek work or relief.

At all times supplying the cities with food was an absorbing task for local and state authorities. Nothing was more certain to set off violent protest than a threat to the secure supply of bread (L. Tilly 1972a). The large cities were a special concern. Not only did they house, and therefore potentially threaten, the higher political authority, but they could not be fully supplied from the lands immediately surrounding. We have previously examined the long-distance grain trade that developed in the phases of urban growth of the sixteenth and eighteenth centuries, mobilizing the surpluses of great estates in Prussia, Poland, and Sicily. Within countries the urgent task of feeding both major cities and armies illustrated the failings of early markets, although it contributed to their development. In addition to the perils of weather and war, contemporaries greatly feared and resented attempts to corner the grain market or withhold supplies, and bread riots invariably focused on middlemen as the culprits. Yet as economists have often pointed out, demands that prices be controlled and bureaucratic efforts to regulate them often aggravated shortages by interfering with supply and demand. If the authorities stocked grain, for example, it became nearly impossible to enforce a higher price that would stretch the provision until the next harvest. However, the need to ensure supplies also caused governments to strengthen and liberalize interregional trade. The wider scale of food marketing forged closer ties between the producing areas and the summit of the national urban hierarchy (C. Tilly 1975).

The degree of social and economic inequality in early modern cities can be judged in a variety of ways. Certainly the elite was small, often immensely rich, and relatively closed, while many were desperately poor and many more perilously vulnerable. On the other hand, compared with the wider society of the time cities can be seen as "islands of *relative* social mobility, democracy, and literacy" (P. Burke 1975:15). A substantial middle group had some voice in local politics, possessed a little property, and enjoyed the respectable status of citizens or burghers. In particular, their lot was probably better on balance than that of middling peasants, yeomen, or substantial tenant farmers. Few rural regions of Europe were really free from feudal exactions or from the inequities and vexations of arbitrary authority and aristocratic disdain. And while it is true that many town dwellers, even though not destitute, were proletarians in the full sense of being dependent on their labor for survival, students of protoindustrialization point out that the creation of a proletariat was well under way in rural areas by the seventeenth century and perhaps before (C. Tilly 1979).

The distinction between rich, middle-rank, and poor was well established in early modern Florence, Amsterdam, or Lyon (P. Burke 1975). Regardless of how each society might precisely define these groups, they were often more real than the older ordering of civil society into noble and commoner. Yet horizontal economic divisions were softened by vertical links based on occupation, religion, kinship, nativity, or place of external origin as well as by the chance for social mobility. Popular culture also served to bind together people of diverse statuses. Until the mid-sixteenth century, citizens in English boroughs participated in a rich ceremonial life led by craft and religious guilds (Phythian-Adams 1979). All over Europe local communities united in annual celebrations of a patron saint as well as in universal festivals such as Christmas, Carnival, and midsummer. On these occasions all work stopped in time to let people prepare for the parading and feasting to come. While the Reformation ended the more elaborate ceremonial displays where it displaced the Roman church, holidays linked to the calendar year, such as May Day and Halloween, survived, as did many periodic fairs. In any case, Lutherans, Huguenots, and Puritans soon developed their own cultural life, with books, prayer meetings, and hymns providing substitute rituals and pastimes. Popular culture was capable of retaining its hold on a large clientele while undergoing major change. Looking at France, Natalie Davis (1975) sees urban-based printing and the spread of literacy as orthogenetic, enriching and confirming the beliefs and traditions of city dwellers in the sixteenth century.

Popular culture, like other unifying vertical ties, tended to weaken after the Reformation, however. Although in 1500 the elite may already have had a loyalty to the ideas and customs of the high tradition, we can say with Peter Burke (1978) that at that time popular culture was everyone's culture. Then, as the intellectual currents we group under the labels humanism, Counterreformation, and Enlightenment diffused, the elite began to reject what it saw as vulgar or superstitious popular culture. The affirmation of civilized values over folk culture was not a simple matter of city versus country. While urban elites decried local folkways, they partially adopted those of the rural gentry. Horse races and indoor balls for the rich joined the theater as substitutes for civic pageants (Clark and Slack 1976). Although increasingly urban in taste as well as residence, the aristocracy retained its commitment to virile pursuits, above all hunting. Within the city, the upper classes first contracted out of popular celebrations and then moved to suppress rowdy and licentious spontaneity. The people were offered instead sanitized and passive festivities, generally for the greater glory of the sovereign (Chartier and Neveux 1981).

The split came earliest to England and France; towns ceased their elaborate public celebrations in England before 1600 (Burke 1978). Change was long delayed in eastern Europe, where elite culture was in any case largely imported. But the split was all the deeper there for the fact that elite and folk, town and country, often spoke entirely different languages: French in the manor house, German in the shop, a Slavic language in the fields.

Even in the eighteenth century the process of communal disaggregation was not complete where it was the furthest along, in the major cities of France and England. The very forces that promoted it in the name of order were also by nature sensitive to tradition. Meanwhile, reaching outward from the same major cities, a new egalitarianism was developing around shared tastes and pursuits in literature. Though not quite constituting a "republic of letters," the world of academies and salons played down distinctions of rank and fortune, even of gender, and preferred to select its participants on the basis of talent, manners, and wit. By the end of the century the new vertical bond of nationalism was already at work, ironically spurred by the same revolutionary wave that exacerbated horizontal divisions. Meanwhile, communal traditions lived on in the old urban core of Europe. In any case, cultural loyalties can combine hosts of inconsistencies and syncretisms, and in doing so they soften or obstruct the divisions and solidarities among social strata.

So far we have stressed the larger cities, in part because they led the way and in part because social distinctions and cultural manifestations tended to be more dramatic there. What of the hundreds of smaller cities and towns, the lower rungs of the urban hierarchy? In the early modern period they gradually acquired a rather balanced social structure in which local property ties, longer-distance trade relations, and links to the higher sovereign power all had a place. High and folk culture coexisted, both typically in somewhat tamed or watered-down form. This was a world neither of sharp social distinctions nor of democratic community. Rather, it was a society led by *notables* in which several paths to high status competed. Alongside the ranking government and church officials, the major landlord, the banker, even the doctor or solicitor/notary could occupy a leading position of influence, for example, representing the city and its region in a legislative assembly or state council. This structure easily made room for factory masters when industry gravitated toward urban locations in the nineteenth century. Provincial society might be closed, petty, and hidebound; it was also remarkably durable and adaptable, taking economic and political convulsions in its stride (Walker 1971; Perrot 1975). Though slowly increasing their ties with the larger urban system at the expense of purely local concerns, the medium-sized cities provide a strong element of continuity in urban Europe between the early modern and industrial periods.

The Architecture of Absolutism

The political centralization of the early modern period had its visual counterpart in the ordering and focusing of the city upon its dominant elements. While the shapes of most medieval towns show the results of centuries of slow, irregular growth, city plans after 1400 testify to the conscious manipulation of urban space. The dream of an ideal city, given geometric form in the later fifteenth and sixteenth centuries in Italian and German essays on town planning, tempted architects, artists, and engineers to work out new urban designs. Their plans exalted symmetry and order. All eyes must be led down broad, straight streets to monumental squares and, ultimately, to the seat of power. Palaces and other public buildings dominated open areas, becoming the endpoints of long perspectives. Ancient glories and grandeurs were reworked in an aesthetic that served absolute power. The designs had and still have undoubted visual appeal, but they shifted the scale of the city from the human to the grandiose. Moreover, if implemented they absorbed huge sums. Although the impetus for change included the need to accommodate more people and to solve problems of circulation and congestion, the results were shaped most strongly by the political and military needs of the sovereign. Little was done, for example, if the impetus for adding to the city came only from an increase in craft production or even trade. Altogether, while the medieval town tended to obscure the true weight of inequality and authority, urban design now flaunted the priorities of the powerful.

The new architectural treatises and town plans reflected and promoted the idea that existing cities were outmoded in form. The call of fashion was answered by that of military security and traffic: cannon and carriages made medieval city walls and narrow streets obsolete. While small market towns and provincial centers lacked the means as well as the incentive to change, elites in the larger cities were prepared for the effort needed to gratify their comfort as well as their security. Rulers were the greatest builders of all, seeing in the new architecture and urban design the means of symbolizing and thus affirming their political dominance as well as their cultural refinement. Together with architects and engineers, they set out to create rational cities. If the ideal city embodied perfect social and political arrangements in a perfect urban form, could not the real-world town planner effect improvement through building or rebuilding? From the time of Alberti, this elusive dream has animated the architects of cities.

Changes in the cityscape between 1500 and 1800 took several forms. Lewis Mumford (1961:367) has called the avenue "the most important symbol and main fact about the baroque city." Its rigid geometry could control urban space. In Rome the Piazza del Popolo and three new radiating streets made a triumphal entrance into the heart of the city. The Champs Elysées was laid out in the 1660s to give the French king a fitting processional route when he traveled from the Louvre to one or another summer palace or hunting field.

The idea of the city as a theatrical stage was accepted. All over

Europe enlarged urban palaces, public buildings, and churches—
think of the great domes on the new St. Peter's in Rome and St.
Paul's in London—were made the focus of monumental compo-
sitions of streets and squares. The Venetian government transformed a medieval market by stages into the elegant Piazza de San
Marco and Piazetta, linking the Grand Canal, the doge's palace,
and the cathedral of San Marco into one majestic public space.
The construction of residential squares such as the Place Royale
(now the Place des Vosges) in Paris and London's Leicester and
Bloomsbury squares fashioned suitable environments for the elite
in the turbulent town.

Other cities made massive changes in their perimeters. In the
interests of self-defense, cities such as Vienna, Geneva, and Antwerp rebuilt their fortifications to include elaborate salients and
star-shaped redoubts. Where major growth was in progress or anticipated, as in Nancy or Lille, entirely new areas were developed
and enveloped in the much-imitated style of the great French engineer Vauban. A few new towns were actually built—remarkably
few, perhaps, in view of the utopian drive behind the movement.
Most were naval ports or enlarged forts near exposed or strategic
borders. Places such as Palma Nova (1593), Coewarden (1597), and
Philippeville (1555) gave Italian, Dutch, and French engineers a
chance to put into physical form the fanciful geometries of Renaissance city planners.

The pièce de résistance of the new style was unquestionably
Versailles, begun in the 1660s but far from finished at the end of
Louis XIV's reign in 1715. The best French architects and landscape gardeners worked there under the close supervision of the
monarch himself. Park and town, streets and *allées* were linked in
one symmetrical composition whose focal point was the grandiose
chateau of the Sun King. All the tricks of perspective and relative
scale were employed to glorify one man, whose residence dwarfed
its surroundings. A town was needed to house courtiers, officials
of the military and civilian administrations, and support services—
perhaps 30,000 people in all. It was designed in a grid pattern and
awkwardly fitted into the spaces between and around the major
avenues sweeping up to the palace. Building heights, public spaces,
even construction materials were regulated in the interests of assuring an ensemble worthy of, yet totally subservient to, the royal
residence (G. Burke 1971; Chartier and Neveux 1981). After all,

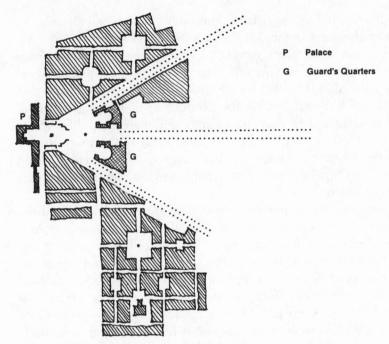

P   Palace

G   Guard's Quarters

Figure 5.3. A prince's city: Versailles. The town grew up in the shadow of
Louis XIV's palace and on lower ground, most of it tucked away on either side
of the central axis. The great avenues radiating eastward from the palace
balance the gardens but bear no relation to the rest of the town plan. (After a
plan of Le Pautre in Duby 1981, III:119.)

the king had not forced his nobles from their provinces only to have
them form a rival urban community in the shadow of his court.

In fact, the relationship of dominance and dependence conflicted
with the intended harmony of town and palace in Versailles. Today's tourist who comes upon one of the great radial avenues in his
progress through the quiet town is struck by its disproportionate
width and lack of relevance to the urban plan. From the palace, on
the other hand, nothing in the townscape arrests the eye, just as
the symmetrical view from the terrace over the gardens gives the
illusion of open space to the horizon. Ultimately, the town itself
was built more slowly and with much less control than had been
intended.

The extravagant geometric symbolism of Versailles immediately
stimulated imitators. *Residenzstädte* for minor German princes sprouted
during the recovery from wartime devastation—Karlsruhe and

Mannheim are good examples—while more imposing versions appeared at Charlottenburg (Berlin) and later in New Delhi, Washington, D.C., and Canberra. The colonial versions also drew on the bastide tradition of planned settlements, with formal guidance embodied in the *Leyes de las Indias* that guided Spanish organization of the vast American empire (Vance 1977; Crouch, Garr, and Mundigo 1982). Peter the Great of Russia hired a French architect to create a plan for his new capital on the Baltic. The specific plan was not followed, as it happened, but the development of the city during the eighteenth century was guided by a Commission for the Orderly Development of St. Petersburg, which prepared new plans, issued zoning regulations, and enforced building codes. The capital was graced by a series of monumental constructions, the work of many European architects hired by successive emperors and empresses, periodic fires adding to the opportunities for new projects (Bater 1976). Like Versailles, St. Petersburg sprang from an act of royal will with a clear political purpose (in this case the modernization of Russia), but in both instances the development of the town mixed public and private sources of energy. The forced residence of nobles at court was a major stimulus to urban growth, the obligation being more explicit in the Russian example. St. Petersburg outgrew its function as a court city: it was soon the largest city and port in the country with privately owned buildings and with industry in the outlying areas. Ironically, the city's success meant that growth swamped the planning process (Konvitz 1978). Still, its visual image was dominated by the artifacts of the Russian court and government—palaces, administrative buildings, and fortresses—which lined the riverfront. The style fed the vanity of the monarch while affirming claims to a monopoly of power and wealth.

Throughout the continent it was usually the will of the prince that instituted the reign of geometric order and symmetry in the larger towns. Yet the new ideas of urban form and the role of elites extended also to communities where control was informal, as typically in England, or where it was exercised by the civic community, as in Scotland and the Netherlands. For better or worse, it was the spirit of the age. Lesser cities, when they could, also tried to refurbish and expand, opening the space beyond the old town boundaries to development (Perrot 1975). Baroque visions also guided the smaller-scale projects of the bourgeoisie. Grandiose designs for urban space have proved long lived and easily exportable.

The energy and cash available for massive urban projects ebbed and flowed, but the increases in central taxing power, the revenues of overseas empires and maritime trade, and the extractive abilities of landlords meant that cities could prosper even when, and at times because, their hinterlands did not. Of course, entrepreneurs appeared to translate the demand for urban building into reality, indeed to speculate by developing new areas in the expectation of demand to come. Gilbert van Schoonbeke, the illegitimate son of an Antwerp burgher, parlayed some family capital and the profits of town customs duties into a lucrative career as a developer. He then took over the construction of new fortifications and public buildings. For a brief period in the sixteenth century van Schoonbeke dominated the Antwerp building trade, while at the same time managing to reorganize the city's brewing industry and contracting to provision Dutch troops. For good measure, he served on the Netherlands *Conseil des Finances* (Soly 1977). His meteoric rise was financed by capital he raised in the form of *renten* or mortgages on his acquisitions in a time of rising property values. We find similar speculative builders at work in sixteenth-century Seville and in Amsterdam and London in the next century. Paris's exclusive Faubourg Saint-Germain was planned and financed by a syndicate of wealthy men headed by Louis Le Barbier (L. Bernard 1970). Urban land and construction offered tempting profits well before the industrial era.

The eagerness of the prince to express his power over the civic commune in visual symbols contributed to a process of spatial differentiation, again most advanced in the major cities (Argan 1969). Zones of governance, of commerce, and of manufacturing became more distinct. In autocratic St. Petersburg or in republican Venice, as in Bordeaux, industry was relegated to outlying districts. Residential areas, particularly new ones, acquired a clear and often contrasting social personality. The distinction between a fashionable west side and a popular east side, still evident today, became established in London and Paris. Rich merchants in Amsterdam chose to live near the town hall along the major canals, the Herengracht and the Keisergracht, whereas immigrants and proletarians settled into the southwestern section (P. Burke 1974). Sheer scale had something to do with these changes, as did fashion. But an important element was the growth of a market in urban land that allowed high bidders to preempt choice locations and made it profitable to develop large, homogeneous residential areas.

Thus, the impetus for change came from both the private and the public sector. Most of the capital for actual construction was private. Government contributed plans and regulations, provided street improvements, and strategically sited public buildings. Its decisions then molded the elite's choices among urban locations. We began by noting the sharp contrast between grandee and beggar that might be seen on a city street. Together, the centralized state and nascent capitalism worked to rub out such too-vivid images— not by leveling inequalities but by ordering urban space so that squalor would not intrude on splendor.

Whatever their social or moral shortcomings, the achievements of these city designers and builders are impressive, even more so when we consider the limited technical means at their disposal and the need—almost unchanged over a long period—to rely on raw human and animal power. Yet in many ways their reach exceeded their grasp. Only in a very few cases were they able to indulge the urge to start afresh and to conceive the city as a symmetrical whole. For the most part it was necessary to deal with existing cities. As we saw in the case of Bordeaux, planned change affected mainly the zone just beyond the old urban limits. The core was little changed, while large areas in the fast-spreading outer districts lacked order as well as amenity. Even in the most ambitious townscapes the glorious facades and perspectives hid a great deal of filth and squalor. The baroque city was indeed in some ways a stage set. Most attention was devoted to visible and decorative improvements: fountains, squares, arcades, as well as to peripheral facilities such as bridges and embankments (Chartier and Neveux 1981). Waterworks supplied the royal park rather than street taps in popular neighborhoods. Broad avenues brought traffic to the edge of the city core but did not ease congestion within it. The visual record of the baroque city has something of a chamber of commerce quality: it notably lacks the dimensions of smell and hearing.

Overall, then, the physical transformation of the city was partial except when disaster intervened—one thinks of the earthquakes at Dubrovnik in 1667 and Lisbon in 1755. Yet it is noteworthy that London was rebuilt conservatively and not along the monumental lines projected by Wren after the Great Fire of 1666 (Vance 1977).

Building also responded tardily to increases in population and economic activity. As in other times the first response was to fill in empty spaces within the urban fabric, adding stores to houses and crowding people into existing structures. But the model of Chapter 4 also shows how fluctuations in the economic system could systematically produce a lag between the wave of prosperity and the peak fortunes of the elites who decided and financed building. Of course, this meant that big projects were often undertaken under conditions of severe physical congestion as well as fiscal pressure, and that they were quite likely to be overtaken by economic disturbances associated with the cyclical downturn. Finally, we cannot fail to recall what a burden the vast, costly undertakings represented, one that not only bore down on the poor but also materially limited the productive force of most European societies in the longer run.

If capitals show baroque urban planning and design at their most impressive, port cities illustrate well the limits and paradoxes we have also noted. Of course, maritime activity, commercial as well as military, underwent enormous development during the early modern period, with the Atlantic and North Sea coasts taking the lead. Ships and cargoes also increased in size, requiring larger docks, yards, and warehouses. In many port cities, however, little if anything was done to integrate the city with its growing port area (Konvitz 1978). Although the trade of the Spanish empire was forcibly funneled through Seville, this resulted only in a straggling expansion of wharves down the Guadalquivir river to the sea. With variants, this absence of spatial reorganization of cities to reflect their maritime vocation holds for Bordeaux, Naples, Genoa, or Liverpool. On the other hand, a number of monarchs set out to build new port cities or extensions in the seventeenth century as part of a quest for naval power. France and Sweden took the lead, imitated by Peter the Great of Russia. But whereas St. Petersburg became much more than a naval base, the French and Swedish efforts fared less well. Louis XIV, a territorial monarch par excellence, would not entrust his fleet to the cosmopolitan trading ports of the west coast, but even his more successful creations at Lorient and Brest had great trouble achieving any economic autonomy. Although politics and corruption contributed to less-than-ideal locations for these arsenals, their principal weakness was simply that they remained outside any urban system. As for Sweden, the plans perhaps owed too much to the ideal-city tradition; at any rate, few were implemented before the country abandoned its imperial ambitions around 1720.

Paradoxically, it seems that port-city planning and maritime activity were antagonistic rather than complementary. This holds true in terms of time as well as of space. The heyday of planning was the difficult seventeenth century, not the more active periods before and after. Why so little planned growth? A part of the answer is suggested by the model of Chapter 4. Since planning was typically carried out by the sovereign, it flourished during times of high "rents" rather than during phases of strong growth and investment. Although active merchant cities may have needed rational expansion most, their capitalists begrudged the sums involved and were seldom prepared to act together. When the waterfronts of London and Bordeaux were developed in the eighteenth century, the impulse came from each city's role as a capital rather than from its commercial success, and the new buildings and avenues were unrelated to the port. The river offered a pleasing site, not a challenge for commercial architects.

Only in Amsterdam was port planning truly functional, although the enlargement of Antwerp in the mid-sixteenth century offered a precedent. With its half circles of canals enveloping new districts as they were developed, Amsterdam's plan was also a unique case of allowing for future growth. The fact that Amsterdam did not so much occupy land as create it made planning necessary, and also favored the close integration of land and water and thus of port and city. But it is also worth noting, first, that Amsterdam enjoyed almost unique prosperity during a period of active planning when much of the European maritime economy was in difficulty; and second, that it was run by capitalist interests who cared more for profit and comfort than for glory and spectacle.

Mercantile Networks and Dynastic Centralism

The easy spread of baroque styles testifies to the interconnectedness of the early modern urban world. Patrons imported artists and architects from foreign capitals. Travelers made pilgrimages to ancient and modern buildings, while books and engravings of urban wonders fueled the imaginations of the stay-at-home. Ambassadors and bureaucrats circulated among court cities and administrative centers. Exotic goods and ordinary staples moved from port to port and then inland, bringing people in their train. City dwellers were part of a large network of cultural, political, and economic connections that stretched from the Atlantic to the Urals and from Portugal to the Ottoman territories. Overall, between the fifteenth and the eighteenth centuries the links among trading cities, which we have called the Network System, stretched and gained importance relative to territorial urban hierarchies. Yet the Central Place System changed, too, as larger towns increased their dominance over smaller market towns and villages.

Before amplifying and illustrating, let us look first at the boundaries of the dual system that was urban Europe. In a territorial sense, the effective limits of Christian Europe shifted in significant ways over the period. By 1500 the elimination of the Moors from Spain had added the rest of the Iberian peninsula. English invasions of Ireland brought more of Celtic lands into political and trading relationships with Britain, while increased migration revivified Irish urban life, particularly in the north and east. Scandinavia too was the home of conquering monarchs who founded towns in their quest for greater, more secure dominion. Christian IV of Denmark founded several settlements in his country and Norway. In addition, Gustavus Adolphus of Sweden established ports and mining centers as well as market towns (Gutkind 1965, II). Urban Europe thus expanded to meet its maritime boundaries.

In the east the situation was less straightforward. Until perhaps the mid-seventeenth century the effective limits of the European trading system contracted. Polish urban life regressed, except in the grain ports, while Russia remained quite isolated from the European economy. The expansion of the Ottoman Turks into the Balkans and central Europe removed most of Hungary and present-day Bulgaria and Yugoslavia from the European orbit. The rearrangement of trade routes away from the eastern Mediterranean toward the Atlantic successfully neutralized the impact of the Turkish advance, but it contributed to isolating the lost lands (Wallerstein 1974).

In a sense, however, these territorial adjustments are beside the point. When measured in terms of influence, the European urban system came to extend far beyond the limits of the continent itself. Spain and Portugal claimed the whole Western hemisphere and effectively controlled much of it, while a slower process of exploration and colonization established the British and French presence in North America. The not-so-hidden hands of European traders —among whom the Dutch occupied an envied place—took hold of Caribbean islands, set up enclaves on the African and Indian coasts, and established control of the valuable trades in slaves, precious metals, spices, and plantation crops from source to market. In return for these riches, Europe exported manufactures and intangibles: while a few soldiers, merchants, and administrators traveled the East, a whole civilization went to dominate the New World.

Although the conquerors, traders, and settlers planted the flag of their sovereign, a limited number of ports actually directed the expansion. These cities developed ties to overseas settlements and to one another that were stronger than their links with the territory at their back. As a group, they constituted the core of a powerful, Europe-centered trading network whose outposts spanned the world and through which, via overseas gateways, were funneled the plunder and produce of vast regions. The shores of the great oceans made up the "foreland" of the port cities; their "hinterland" embraced most of Europe (see Figure 2.2). However, the nature of overseas trade was such that the ties of these ports with their immediate region were often of limited importance, since commodity exports played a minor role. We saw that with the exception of the wine trade, Bordeaux relied on the Garonne basin mostly for labor and as a minor market for imported goods. Nor were the areas around Seville, Nantes, Saint-Malo, Bristol, or Hamburg notable for their involvement in trade.

How did the Network System of the mercantile era compare with the corresponding medieval network we examined in Chapter 2? Then, recall, Europe was moving from the periphery to the center of a long-distance trading system. A dual core developed whose major pole lay in northern Italy, the minor one in the Low Countries. Soon, a series of ports in the Mediterranean and Atlantic–North Sea–Baltic areas formed a kind of corona around each urban cluster. The two centers were linked mostly over land, despite the early importance of waterborne traffic. Finally, absolute leadership among core cities was changeable. Genoa struggled with Venice, while Milan and Florence remained handicapped by want of direct access to the sea. In the north, the fading of Bruges left a vacuum, but this posed little problem so long as financial leadership remained in the Mediterranean.[4]

Figure 5.4. A merchants' city: Alkmaar in 1675. This view of a Dutch town, drawn by Romeyn de Hooghe, shows the busy cheese market and weighing hall. The market buildings are elaborately decorated but echo the citizens' houses in shape and style. (From Brugmans and Peters 1909, I:188.)

In the mercantile period, the center of gravity shifted strongly toward the northwest. Indeed, the north Italian urban concentration, though it persisted, lost much of its systemic role. Not only did Marseille and Barcelona overtake Genoa as ports, but they did so as elements in the Atlantic, not the Mediterranean, network. A location on the Atlantic coastline favored the growth of the western ports, but the major urban centers remained within the northwestern core throughout the century-by-century shifts from Antwerp to Amsterdam to London. These changes were correlated with the cyclical shifts outlined in Chapter 4. Braudel (1979) argues that expansions decentralize a system, attenuating disparities among regions, while contractions accentuate contrasts. Times of retrenchment were, therefore, the most likely period for the replacement of dominant cities by others. During the difficult decades of the fifteenth and the late seventeenth centuries, major shifts took place in the location of the European core, from south to north and along an axis in the northwest.

The above view of the early modern period is quite close to the European "world economy" of Immanuel Wallerstein (1974) and to Braudel's (1979) interpretation of it. Wallerstein postulates the development in the sixteenth century of a Europe-centered capitalist system involving dual processes of (1) competition between unequal states and (2) economic differentiation among interdependent regions. Political struggle was crucial to the location of the core, victory bringing the attendant privilege of exploiting the periphery through direction of the interregional division of labor. Of course, material factors also influenced the outcome, particularly during the periodic crises that called into question the existing order and permitted changes to take place.

Cities play an important part in Wallerstein's model. Their elites organized commercial production in the agriculture hinterland, as well as linking the state as a whole into the world market. Thus, the trading core had a highly developed commercial agriculture, while much of the trade of the far-flung Habsburg empire—it encompassed both Austria and Spain—was coordinated in Antwerp during the sixteenth century. Moreover, the city as well as its financiers regularly lent money to Charles V, so that most of the silver from Mexico and Peru quickly found its way there from Seville. Economic domination and political expansion reinforced each other.

Figure 5.5. Persistence of the medieval world: Bologna in the seventeenth century. While many Italian towns were extensively rebuilt during the Renaissance, medieval street patterns and buildings remained very much in evidence. This view by Mattaeus Merian shows the dozens of towers that turned the homes of Bologna's noble families into fortresses. (From Merian 1638.)

Wallerstein's model has the virtue of linking several types of historical processes and of emphasizing structural links among regions. Its systemic vision nicely combines a unified framework of analysis with scope for change. Within the limits of the theme of urbanization, our own approach is similar, but our analysis differs from Wallerstein's on two central points. We argue that the network model of urban relations can be applied also to medieval Europe. It was modified by the emergence of a capitalistic world economy, not created by it, as Wallerstein contends.[5] Moreover, we limit the scope of the network model, preferring to analyze processes of state building and regional development in terms of a territorial hierarchy of central places. Relationships among settlements of various sizes and among regions cannot be reduced to the simplistic trichotomy of dominance, dependence, and semiperiphery that Wallerstein uses. Towns and cities have a variety of roles, depending upon the framework within which they are placed. Regional linkages deserve as much attention as international ones.

To understand developments in the Central Place System across the regions of Europe, it is necessary to recall the bases on which such links arise. In brief, two sets of primary forces are at work: trade in rural-based surpluses and territorial administration. In the long period that concerns us here, the process of establishing or consolidating centralized state power often overshadowed rural economic development and sometimes actually hampered it. Dynastic government tended to function as a surplus-gathering operation, continually scrambling and squeezing for funds with which to affirm power through costly wars and grand displays.[6] In consequence, large cities—notably regional and royal capitals—did not typically build on a base of thriving lesser ones but benefited directly from rents. Judicial and fiscal administration, display, and consumption tended to outweigh directly productive functions.

The use of population figures or building activity as indexes of urbanization reinforces and perhaps exaggerates the trend toward primacy—the disproportionate development of the largest cities or city. As we have noted, active centers of trade or protoindustry were streamlined places that had little beyond the necessary people and facilities. Scale, magnificence, and idleness characterized the rentier city, whether it was living off wealth accumulated in more active days or commanding the ongoing surplus from a substantial territory. But some cities combined significant roles in both systems, and these had exaggerated potential for growth. Recall the example of Bordeaux, although London and St. Petersburg illustrate the point more spectacularly.

From this general base we can survey the varieties of central place development in protoindustrial times. In the old urban core, although it would be a long time before modern nation-states became established, city-states were weakening. Where they did not surrender autonomy to aggressive powers such as Prussia or France, they expanded into territorial entities themselves. The Venetian and Dutch republics are examples of such defensive extension, as is the grand duchy of Tuscany. Yet for Florence as for other cities, the formal assumption of regional sovereignty was poor compensation for the loss of influence in the wider world.

The long-established territorial systems of French and English cities offer an interesting comparison during this period. During the seventeenth century the team of Louis XIV and Colbert gave great impetus to a secular process of centralization with specific implications for regional capitals such as Toulouse and Rennes and for naval ports. But with a sluggish rural economy, trade was slow to develop in these royal favorites. For natural as well as institutional reasons, the process of integration into a national market failed to keep pace with administrative and fiscal centralization. The linkages among regional systems remained spotty, as did the joining of maritime and internal commerce. The overall result was not so much primacy as a degree of retardation in overall urbanization and development. Despite the advances of the eighteenth century, Paris housed only about 15 percent of French town dwellers and under 3 percent of the total population.

In Britain mercantilism remained a weak force inside the country, so that economic functions closely conditioned urban growth. Only Edinburgh and Bath among major towns could rightly be called rentier cities. The rural economy progressed, while internal and external trade were closely interwoven. Was this because English liberalization contrasted with French *dirigisme*? Or is the answer to be sought in the easier access most of the island enjoyed via river and coastal navigation? At any rate, as urbanization proceeded in Britain, the regional centers, though dwarfed by London, progressed hand in hand with rural development.

Germany shows clearly why numerical growth can fail to give a true picture of change. By the end of the eighteenth century, expansion had enabled the German hierarchy of cities to more than make up late medieval losses. From twenty-four cities of 10,000 or more in the year 1500—the top seven with 20,000 to 40,000 people —the list grew by 1800 to some sixty places, of which the seven largest ranged up from 50,000 to 238,000 (François 1978). Numbers aside, however, the striking change is that cities with a primary political function almost completely displaced the once dominant free trading cities. Even if one leaves aside the great capitals and new *Residenzstädte*, there is the telling example of southern Germany. With the transfer there of the elector's court from Mannheim, Munich surpassed all other southern cities, notably Nuremberg, Augsburg, and Ulm. In fact, these once illustrious centers of trade and crafts could not even regain their population levels of 1500.

Thus when economic growth is considered, the German urban flowering between 1650 and 1800 is at least in part an illusion. Big-city development was not the natural outgrowth of heightened market activity in local central places, the visible tip of a generalized urbanization process. Instead, the drain of surplus by large and small sovereigns stimulated a series of "minimetropolises" while tending to depress or hold back rural areas and their service centers. Only a few merchant cities prospered—Frankfurt, Leipzig, and most of all Hamburg—because they handled state finances and/or served as links with the supranational trading network. Only during the nineteenth-century phase of economic development and national unification would these German towns integrate into a true, well-balanced urban system. Then, even Berlin's headlong expansion did not drain the rest. Eventually, some of the smaller German capitals of the eighteenth century grew along with the older trading cities to be among the most vital and livable of Europe's cities in the industrial and postindustrial ages.

In Germany and Poland the early modern period was in part a time of rebuilding urban networks. Farther east, city creation contributed to the initial development of an urban system. New fortress towns and administrative centers arose in Rumania and in areas annexed to the Russian empire, notably in Siberia and beyond the Volga. Private cities within the empire were annexed as state property and assigned various military and fiscal-bureaucratic chores as part of the process of administrative centralization. At the same time, increasing internal trade produced new marketing centers (Rozman 1976).

Because the land over which the czars extended and intensified their control was vast, often primitive, Russian urbanization was partly colonization. Our Network System model in which cities serve as gateways or outposts that tie a region to an outside center and organize its production in view of trade, helps to explain this development. A good deal of debate about early Russian urbanization turns on the question whether the town stimulated rural development or proceeded from it. Certainly, city building was a spur to development in the annexed territories; the fortress towns in southern Russia served as gateways there, fostering the rather fitful development of smaller places in the region (Shaw 1977). In contrast, Morris (1971) stresses the role of agricultural surpluses on good soils around Moscow as the driving force for local trade and the building of market settlements. In the core of the Russian territory the marketing variant of our Central Place model applies.

In an elaborate analysis of urban systems, Rozman (1976) charts a seven-level structure on the basis of both population size and function. Networks of cities reach down from a national administrative center (level 1) through regional and district administrative cities or ports (levels 2, 3, 4) down to local administrative centers and intermediate and local marketing settlements (levels 5, 6, 7). Rozman situates the establishment of the full Russian system in the century between 1650 and 1750, emphasizing the role of political centralization over commercial factors in the process. The dynamic is noteworthy: the system neither builds uniformly up from the bottom nor down from the top but rather fills in the intermediate levels last. Thus, the presence of major size gaps in an urban hierarchy would serve as a rough indicator of primitive, incomplete urban system formation.[7]

Rozman's attempt to trace equivalent patterns in England and France with no more than a century or so of lead over Russia does not fit in easily with widely shared views about the timing of basic urbanization in the West. In any case, early modern Russia cannot be looked at as simply another western Europe a few centuries behind. Unlike the medieval West, Russia urbanized in the presence of a European "world economy" whose trading network reached into Russia and influenced the modernization efforts of Peter the Great and his successors. Russian urbanization had a certain urgency, even if most towns were unlike the artificial "Potemkin villages" put up along Catherine the Great's travel route in 1787.

Nonetheless, when Hittle (1979) calls the Russian city a "service city," the implied master is the crown, not the surrounding countryside as in the geographers' central place model.

City and State

In trying to bring together the diversity of urban growth and decay during the long period that overlaps the early modern era, one unavoidably returns to the phenomenon of primacy. The growth of some cities, such as London, Naples, or Constantinople, seems to run counter to most accepted economic and demographic trends. They dwarfed other towns around them. They filled no economic function remotely consistent with their size. Whether in terms of the general level of wealth or of cyclical fluctuations, that size seemed almost impervious to material distress. One constant is that the very large cities were associated with areas of large-scale agriculture and a strong feudal/manorial tradition. Yet by the early modern period the estates might be worked by unfree labor using age-old techniques or entrusted to capitalist farmers by landlords bent on improvement. If London was the economic center of a fast developing country, Naples managed a figure of 275,000 inhabitants by 1600, and 443,000 in 1770, largely by collecting subsistence migrants from an impoverished countryside. Although primacy derived from quite different circumstances in southern England and southern Italy, it was hard to find another town much over 10,000 in either.

Ultimately then, primacy has less to do with economic strength than with political development. Recall that it was in the "feudal" regions outside the urban core of medieval Europe that nation-states developed (Hechter and Brustein 1980). If one compares the big capitals with Bruges or Augsburg, Norwich or Bologna, the former seem almost like a throwback to an older, Asian form: a minimum of autonomy, more consumption than production, shocking contrasts of grandeur and misery. Yet they and the governments and elites they housed came to exert powerful political control and intellectual dominion over the plains of Europe. Only along the central trade routes from the North Sea to the Mediterranean were the free cities strong enough to block for centuries the attempt of princes to master them. The split between a central belt of city-states and the peripheral kingdoms helped produce tangled conflicts and shifting alliances as the different units struggled to secure their borders and extend or defend their power (Rokkan 1975). Cities resisted by playing off rival states or by forming alliances among themselves. Neither pure urban leagues, such as the German Hansa and the unsuccessful attempts at union in Languedoc and Flanders, nor takeover of territory by a single city, Florence and Venice, for example, proved as effective as combining the two strategies. Witness the United Provinces, led by the merchant cities of Holland, and the less urban Swiss confederation. But these, too, were defensive actions. By the eighteenth century the lead actors on the political stage were all kingdoms or empires.

Cities, then, played a dual role in the early modern European political system, depending upon their geographic location and the regional intensity of urbanization. Clustered and armed with the resources of active trade, protoindustrial production, or sophisticated finance, cities retarded the development of nation-states until well after 1800. To the west and east of the core, where postfeudal monarchs and their armies could dominate them, cities were turned into agents of centralization by princes intent on binding the territories of the realm ever more tightly to the crown. By borrowing their money and selling them royal offices with perquisites of status attached, French kings co-opted the urban middle classes almost as effectively as they did the courtiers at Versailles. Barel (1977) uses the term *feudal bourgeoisie* to bring out how frequently this class turned away from enterprise toward bureaucracy and passive landholding.

The shift in power away from the old urban core, and the centralizing trend that allowed capitals and courts to dominate large realms were nicely replicated in the area of high culture. Spain, France, England, and Austria gradually took over intellectual and artistic leadership of Europe, even though their models and many creators were drawn from earlier core areas, notably from Italy. In the eighteenth century, German composers found their greatest recognition in London, while aesthetic quarrels among Italians and Germans were already dividing Paris opera audiences. In Germany itself, it was a real setback for J. S. Bach not to find employment at the Saxon court, even though Leipzig was a busy city and still larger than the *Residenzstadt* of Dresden. For writers, mobility was somewhat limited by language, but Italian poets found welcome in Vienna, while the ideas of French philosophes, deemed subversive at home, provided enlightenment at the even more autocratic courts of Prussia and Russia. As for cultural centralization within countries, we can take Dr. Johnson's word for it that London was the only place to be. Or we can listen to Molière's *Précieuses*, a century earlier, proclaiming that outside Paris there could be no salvation for persons of culture.

Yet the major cities were not passive or inward-looking in the cultural sphere. Despite the importance there of the plastic arts for purposes of display, they stimulated an even greater boom in the "reproducible" pursuits of music, theater, and letters. The courts and capitals acted as poles in which this culture developed and from which it spread. They drew talented and ambitious people from everywhere, defined standards and set styles, and distributed the products of culture to growing audiences in what was becoming known as "the provinces," even more tellingly singular in French! In turn, books and plays contributed to a sense of national identity that gradually became stronger than allegiance to the sovereign, political division, or "foreign" domination. Cities therefore helped to provide the cultural cement that molded urban residents into citizens and that lifted regional notables into a national aristocracy.

PART THREE

The Industrial Age:
Eighteenth to Twentieth Centuries

It was thus that through the greater part of
Europe, the commerce and manufactures of
cities, instead of being the effect, have been
the cause and occasion of the improvement
and cultivation of the country.

ADAM SMITH, *The Wealth of Nations*

Two events that marked the turbulent year of 1848 were the publication of *The Communist Manifesto* and the passage of the first public health act in England. Only one is generally remembered, but both were landmarks. The manifesto summed up in one dramatic statement the great process of economic change we call industrialization. Speaking of urbanization, it was as much prophetic as descriptive: "The bourgeoisie has subjected the country to the rule of the towns. It has created enormous cities [and] has greatly increased the urban population as compared with the rural" (Marx and Engels 1848:18–19). If we substitute the later term *capitalism* for *bourgeoisie*, we identify the economic driving force for industrial urbanization.

Nineteenth-century urbanization was also shaped by political change. To Marx and Engels the nation-state was a natural outgrowth of the centralizing power of capitalist accumulation. "The bourgeoisie . . . has agglomerated population, centralized means of production, and has concentrated property in a few hands. The necessary consequence of this was political centralisation . . . Loosely connected provinces . . . became lumped together into one nation, with one government [and] . . . one class interest" (1848:19). Yet the passage of a public health act in the same year, however circumscribed in scope and timid in enforcement it may have been, suggests that national governments would play a far more complex role than that of mere handmaiden to "free competition, accompanied by a social and political constitution adapted to it" (1848:20). We shall find it useful to look at government—in both its political and its bureaucratic aspects—as an autonomous influence on urbanization in the modern period.

Using the term *capitalism* to characterize the dominant mode of production in nineteenth-century Europe invites us to look at the role of capital in urbanization. We can subsume the many forms of capital under a dual definition: (1) produced means of production, and (2) the use of resources over time. Cities embody large amounts of fixed capital in the form of the infrastructure—roads, wharves, bridges—as well as the structures necessary to urban exchange and production. Remember market halls, workshops, and warehouses along with the dwellings. Cities are also privileged centers for mobilizing and allocating financial capital: circulating or working capital in the form of credit to finance production and more speculative venture capital to launch innovations. Most important of all, perhaps, is the urban location of human or intellectual capital, defined as the skills, knowledge, and information that allow human effort to be more productive than raw labor power. For centuries, cities have housed skilled craftsmen, knowledgeable middlemen, and well-connected financiers.

During the protoindustrial period fixed capital was relatively unimportant. As we have seen, urban construction did little to enhance—and could in fact retard—the cities' economic contribution. Nonetheless, urban commerce, finance, and enterprise mobilized nearby rural as well as international resources and eventually stimulated fixed investment in the countryside in the form of canals, roads, improved farms, and mines. Still, the circulating capital controlled by urban merchants remained so important that artisanal workers could effectively lose control of the means of production even while retaining ownership of modest tools.

The first phase of modern industrialization continued the emphasis on rural investment with the building of railroads and the progressive mechanization of manufactures. As the workers concentrated around mills and workshops, industrial capital simply became urban. In later phases factories and their machinery were predominantly sited in already urban places. At the same time, a substantial amount of new capital began to be devoted to the city itself, to the stock of housing and to the infrastructure required for the city to function as a human environment, from sewers to libraries. By contrast, in the early stages of industrial concentration and urban growth the absolute minimum of new capital had been allotted to what development economists call social overhead, with predictable consequences in terms of squalor, crowding, and suffering.

Capital accumulation is one facet of capitalism. Another is the market: private ownership of productive resources and their free exchange on the basis of income-determining prices. Markets and money values had long been at home in cities, although the quest for individual profits was always hedged about with regulations and social constraints. Laissez-faire flourished in the nineteenth-century urban marketplace. Yet we shall see that the communal tradition of intervention, of concern with collective interests as opposed to individual ones, reasserted itself strongly as the century progressed. Cities were at the forefront in the struggle over capitalism and on both sides. They had once housed the guilds and churchmen, the royal inspectors and tax collectors whom early entrepreneurs went to the country to escape. Now they would lead the way in attempts to reform the worst excesses of market capitalism—inequality, pollution, instability—as well as in more global attacks on the capitalist system.

Human labor and land stand out among the "resources" uprooted by the market whirlwind and turned into free-floating commodities. An important dimension of capitalism is the overriding place of wage labor, with a corresponding separation of the worker from the employer-controlled means of production. The shift from a protoindustrial to an industrial mode of production involved a concentration of workers into workshops and factories, first for purposes of control, later to serve the needs of power-using technology. The connection between scale of production and agglomeration of population is an obvious one, noted by Marx and Engels, although sizable workshops could be rural while domestic production continued in cities. It is important to stress, however, that much of the "Great Transformation" of labor into a commodity took place in rural areas (Polanyi 1944). The wage proletariat recruited for industrial towns was created in the countryside. The separation of labor from capital and land not only changed the social relations of rural Europe but also loosened the system of constraints on human reproduction. As for land, the relaxation of extraeconomic constraints on the use and transfer of agricultural land was an important element in transforming the rural economy, for example, in the case of enclosures. Land was also critical to urban growth, and urban land values reflected capitalist competition for space. As we shall see, treating urban land as an ordinary market good has posed theoretical challenges, practical problems, and policy issues that rival in complexity those raised by the system of wage labor.

The economic history of European urban capitalism is not merely that of industry. It took increases of agricultural productivity to feed the urban masses, even allowing for the contribution of overseas territories. As the exchange of urban goods and services for primary commodities expanded to the remote corners of the earth, shipping, trade in all its forms, banking, and other services developed apace. Leisure pursuits also evolved into a massive economic sector. All these activities generated urban employment and animated interurban ties. Thus, the relative growth and occupational structure of towns relate capitalist development to the workings of urban systems. Government bureaucracies and nonprofit institutions also distributed their activity and employment in towns according to size, function, and systemic role. Cities formed a hierarchy of administrative centers, along with specialized university and garrison towns and the preferred urban locations of early transnational institutions. All testify to the systemic logic of political urbanization as well as to the urbanizing force of political organization even in the age of laissez-faire.

While our study of industrial urbanization takes account of capitalism and the nation-state, many writers subsume these influences under the more general term *modernization*. This term is perhaps less polemical than *capitalism*, but it is even more resistant to definition. As commonly used, it embraces centuries-long processes of technological and demographic change, increasing literacy and mobility, economic growth, secular rationalism, democratization—in short, a shopping list of traits identified with the industrialized West in the twentieth century. With so much implied, it is difficult to disentangle the component parts or relate them to one another. Unanswered questions abound. Do all these changes proceed together? If not, which are primary and why? It is usually noted that industrialization is a central aspect of the shift to modernity (Landes 1969); yet many changes that are supposedly a part of modernization long predate the English Industrial Revolution. As the cases of Italy and the Netherlands show, there is no necessary link between modern and industrial in history (Wrigley 1972; Krantz and Hohenberg 1975). The links between modern and urban are also too easily made. While the industrial city and the metropolis are widely used symbols of modernity, their interconnection has more intuitive and aesthetic appeal than logical substance, since both great cities and large-scale urban production have existed for centuries. We have therefore avoided the term modernization, preferring to discuss population growth or industrialization in their own terms without reference to an illusory standard.

CHAPTER 6

Industrialization and the Cities

WHEN WILLIAM COBBETT wrote in the 1820s of his tours of England, he called his journey "rural rides" (Cobbett 1830). Most of the settlements he passed through were sleepy market centers or older county and cathedral towns, where farm houses and pastureland were an easy walk from the central square. Even though he was quite ready, and indeed eager, to denounce the results of the new technology, only in a few places, like "black Sheffield," did he encounter the results of industrial urbanization. And Sheffield, of course, had a long protoindustrial manufacturing tradition. Travelers from town to town in continental Europe at about that time would have had even fewer glimpses of the impact of economic transformation. The new industrial order began in the countryside and only slowly worked its way into the established urban networks that spanned the Continent.

An analysis of industrial urbanization must therefore begin in the countryside. For it was there, notably in regions of rural protoindustry, that the force of economic growth together with demography—migration and heightened fertility—brought new industrial towns into being. Only in a second phase of industrial development did scores of factories appear along the streets and on the fringes of older cities. But even then, many towns were bypassed by the new army of smoke-belching, coal-consuming mills. Despite the rapid growth of urban industry in England, Belgium, France, Germany, and northern Italy after 1840 or so, economic development was a spatially selective process. Some regions deindustrialized while others were transformed by the new technology. Here a new urban network was quickly built around production sites; there adaptation meant taking on the newer modes of production at a measured pace. Within regions some towns could mushroom while others stagnated. While industrialization and urbanization are certainly intertwined in the history of modern Europe, the links between them cannot be reduced to the dual phenomena of factories springing up in towns and towns growing up around factories.

In this chapter we explore the relationship of the new technology to urban networks from roughly 1800 to 1920. Three phases of development can be distinguished: (1) protoindustrial growth, (2) early, coal-based industrialization, and (3) a second industrial revolution, when new sources of power made raw material supplies less important in locational decisions. These phases affected a region's cities in different ways. Both central place and network hierarchies had to adapt to the vast increases in goods, to changes in the way they were produced or distributed, and to the associated shifting of people and occupations. Note, however, that these phases were not simply stages through which regions moved in a lockstep rhythm. Continuing overall change was compatible with stagnation, stability, or incomplete transformation in particular towns or urban groups. Because of the heavy investment in fixed capital within cities, there is always much persistence of technology and division of labor, as well as of physical and institutional structures. Human capital also shows the imprint of the past. Even when technology, markets, and consumer preference have shifted, inertia and short-run fixed costs produce continuities. Handloom weavers could still be found in home workshops in the 1890s. Obsolete low-pressure steam engines still pumped out English mines and ran antiquated spinning machines in smaller Italian towns after 1900. Cities are palimpsests upon which earlier modes of production remain imprinted.

Protoindustry in Country and Town

Around 1800 rural manufacturing was widespread in Europe. Every major country had its protoindustrial regions, often near streams or in upland areas, where textiles, metal products, and other small wares were produced. Peasant women in northern and western Ireland wove linen. Thread was spun in the uplands around Zurich. Knives and other metal products came from the region of Solingen in the Siegerland. What can be said about the locations of these productive areas? First, protoindustrial zones were concentrated outside—though often near—the best agricultural zones, where commercial food production gave steady employment. Second, protoindustrial textile regions tended to adjoin but not overlap with areas of metal production, and both were often found in areas with coal deposits. This geography, however, was not static. Both Léon (1970) and C. T. Smith (1967) argue that during the eighteenth century, rural production became more concentrated. Not all regions were able to sustain their production even before machines entered the competitive race. In England, for example, clothmaking centers in the West Country declined long before the triumph of factory production in Lancashire and the West Riding.

What prompted the concentration of rural protoindustry? One partial explanation hinges on local social factors. Certain institutional systems of inheritance and certain agrarian structures were more favorable to protoindustry than others; equal inheritance, fixed land rents, and tenancy seem to have encouraged rural industry more than did primogeniture, sharecropping, or direct working of farms by landowners. It can also be argued that success in a given region was cumulative because human capital was amassed there. Entrepreneurial, commercial, and technical skills were "learned by doing." Natural resources also had a part to play, notably the presence of streams that could be harnessed or good access to food and markets. Finally, the choice of staple proved important. Cotton and light wool draperies (worsteds) had a bright future, linen a somber one. Primary metallurgy based on charcoal smelting would not only become obsolete, but it also tended to migrate ever deeper into the forests after fresh timber. Metalworking, on the other hand, nurtured skills that withstood shifts in process and product.

The rise and eventual transformation of protoindustrial regions was highly dependent upon one important factor: the availability of entrepreneurs. They could come from two different sources, each of which is compatible with one of our models of urban systems. First, the energy for change could arise in the countryside or in a village from a local producer. Industrial enterprises often originated with a craftsman who devised machinery to improve productivity and eventually expanded his operations to become an industrialist. His efforts would require the markets of nearby towns to supply raw materials, customers, and possibly capital for expansion. The business would expand to larger centers and through

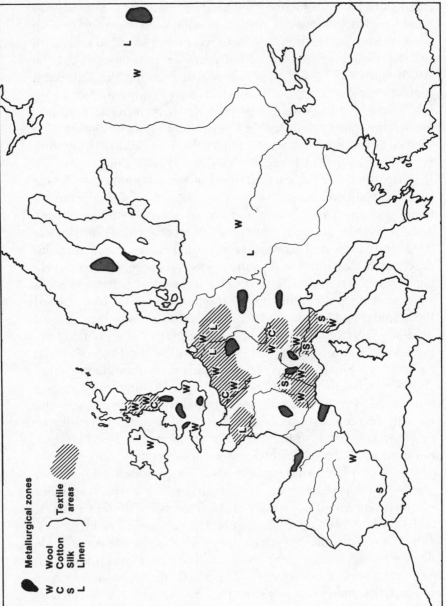

Figure 6.1 Textile and metallurgical regions in protoindustrial Europe. (After Léon 1970:285.

them to other regions along the links of the Central Place System. Development proceeded from the base up with supply leading the way.

As we have seen in our expositions of the Network System, urban elites in trading centers could also take the initiative to expand production. Similarly, landlords and territorial authorities often took leading roles in developing natural resources, such as mineral deposits and waterways. Merchant or gentry capitalists, whether traders, financiers, clothiers, or ironmasters, were driven to innovate. They also could muster the resources to overcome the technical, organizational, and spatial limits of protoindustry. One common strategy was, of course, to concentrate the work force in a single indoor location. This familiar scenario of factory development paved the way for new divisions of labor and for the introduction of expensive or large-scale equipment. Development from the top in this manner depended, however, on access to markets, ideas, and finance via an urban center or gateway to the region. Towns, then, performed several economic roles in the protoindustrial era. Even where rural industry was much more dynamic than urban, city elites helped to direct and to finance manufacturing in the countryside. Cities provided markets, transportation facilities, and skilled workmen to finish goods. Town dwellers and country workers both contributed to the complex divisions of labor that underlay production and distribution.

Over time, protoindustry reshaped urban networks in two ways. Under the spur of economic growth, hamlets swelled into villages and villages became towns. By 1800 in the West Riding of Yorkshire, Dewsbury and Barnsley, which would not become incorporated towns until after 1860, had turned into sizable settlements. The populations of Halifax, Wakefield, and Bradford had passed the 10,000 mark. A wide scattering of settlements along the valleys of Yorkshire had become by 1800 a partly urban manufacturing network of woolens and worsteds centered on Leeds, which served as a gateway city to the region. Protoindustry had provided the impetus for substantial urbanization. The outposts of the network expanded and revised to fit the changing geography of production. In general, protoindustrial urbanization bypassed the regularly spaced market towns in favor of more concentrated growth, where the combination of entrepreneurs, work force, and raw materials permitted expansion.

A second sort of protoindustrial urbanization affected the upper ranks of urban hierarchies. Regional capitals such as Leeds, Leipzig, and Lille, which already had substantial marketing and service functions, gained new importance with the growth of manufacturing in both town and hinterland. Cities that combined major central place functions with an expanding role in manufacturing and trading networks grew particularly rapidly. In fact, national capitals and major ports, where economic influence kept pace with political dominance, consolidated their position as primate cities. Manufacturing supported their growth and profited from it. Note that protoindustry did not produce major new cities but worked through the upper ranks of existing urban systems. The urban legacy of protoindustry, therefore, combined new growth in some areas with substantial amounts of continuity.

The Rise of Industrial Regions

Well before the end of the protoindustrial era, technological change made it profitable to begin replacing hand labor with machines and tiny workshops with factories. The combined impact of steam engines, spinning mules, and open-hearth furnaces triggered new modes and geographies of production, particularly in the textile and metallurgical trades. Even as West Riding weavers continued in the early nineteenth century to produce woolen cloth at home, entrepreneurs in Lancashire towns enlarged their cotton spinning factories and began to introduce power looms. Mines and engineering works expanded, attracting migrants to the new jobs. A new era was fast approaching.

In the longer run, the shift in technology reshaped economic regions in three major ways: thorough transformation, gradual adaptation, deindustrialization (the disappearance of industrial production). Each change affected the type of urban network found within or near the regions.

Thorough transformation. The best examples of the transforming power of rapid industrial growth are to be found in the coal-mining regions. There the explosive concentrated effects of the first, or paleotechnic phase, of modern economic change can be seen in pure form. Since coal was needed to run the engines and smelt the ores, factories and furnaces tended to locate very near coal supplies or in places where they had good access to transportation. As demand skyrocketed, mining areas with their expanding numbers of pits, workshops, and new firms attracted workers. Many of the larger coal fields, moreover, were found under or near areas of active protoindustrialization. Lured by relatively good wages, many protoindustrial workers simply changed the form of their employment, and newcomers flocked into the area. Both high fertility and migration bred an extreme density of settlement, which soon surpassed anything that the protoindustrial era had known. These coal basins grew by a kind of regional implosion, whereby a rural milieu crystallized into a densely urban one. Later in this chapter and in succeeding ones, we shall look closely at these core areas of paleotechnic industrialization, at the economic organization and evolution of the regional system, and at the new communities that grew around the factories, mines, and railyards. Yet these regions—the Ruhr, the Borinage, the Black Country—are familiar by comparison with the other successors of active protoindustrialization.

Gradual adaptation. Some regions managed to adapt to the new technology without abandoning their ties to craft production. Foremost among these is an "Alpine" type of industrial region, marked by small firms in scattered clusters. Whether one looks at Swiss cottons and watches, at textiles in Piedmont and the Vosges, or at metalwares in central Germany, the picture is similar: upland valleys fashioning an enduring industrial position without ever turning their backs on the protoindustrial heritage. A wide range of power sources, techniques, establishment sizes, and organizational forms coexisted for long periods, ebbing and flowing in response to market conditions rather than succeeding each other as linear stages. Small towns rather than cities remained the predominant urban form of these areas in the longer run.

Gradual change also characterized many protoindustrial urban regions. Here, too, the division of labor between town and country persisted while changing its specifics. Production could concentrate in the central city or scatter to the country and to lesser centers within the region. The world at large identified products with the principal city, where the major exporters and trade associations were located, regardless of the configuration of production proper. Thus, people spoke of Nottingham hosiery, of Lyon silk, and of woolens from Verviers, Mönchen-Gladbach, or Bradford as a kind of shorthand. Old metalworking centers also sustained their activity while allowing locations and processes to evolve, as, for example, the cutlery industries of Sheffield, Thiers, and Solingen.

Deindustrialization. Other regions lost their industrial base during the later eighteenth and nineteenth centuries. In a sense, the process of concentration begun during the protoindustrial period merely continued. In western France and southwestern England, for example, rural industry was in decline long before factories made any significant impact. However, mechanization and new materials could change a slow retreat into a full-fledged crisis. The classic case is the linen industry in the mid-nineteenth century, particularly in Ireland and Flanders. The debacle was delayed but ultimately aggravated by special circumstances. The nutritive power of the potato had long helped contain labor costs, allowing the industry to hang on in the face of competition from machine-spun cotton. The potato famine of 1845–1847 struck at economies that had no reserves and poor prospects. Emigration became for many the only hope of survival.

However, deindustrialization could occur in more gradual and even benign ways, with the loss of employment offset by agricultural progress, slow emigration, or falling human fertility. In some mountainous areas the tradition of outmigration to find work antedated protoindustry and easily reestablished itself when local employment faded. This kind of deindustrialization occurred in the French Pyrenees, in part because the appropriate urban centers, principally Toulouse, failed to establish a strong place in the commercial network of the industrial age. A common pattern in rural areas was two-stage deindustrialization: extinction of protoindustrial exports followed by loss of the local market for craft goods. One result of the economic simplification of rural regions was a further strengthening of the upper ranks of the Central Place System. As local domestic production faded, services also became concentrated in the larger central places at the expense of villages and small towns. Manufactured goods were supplied from the city by shops, itinerant traders, and periodic markets, and later by mail-order houses via the post and railroads. For instance, despite its limited role as an industrial gateway, Toulouse grew much faster than the lesser towns of the Garonne basin.

Let us look at the process of economic change in two sorts of areas in order to clarify the relationship of towns to the exploding numbers of factories. Two regions of intensive, coal-based industrialization and one with more diffuse, adaptive development will serve as examples. Our first case is the Ruhr.

Around 1800 what was to become the center of German heavy industry was an impoverished region of backward agriculture bordering on the protoindustrial areas of the Siegerland, Sauerland, and the Wupper valley.[1] Its few small towns, by origin medieval commercial centers, were evenly spaced along the line of an east-west trade route. The largest, Soest, had only 5,000 inhabitants. Around 1850 came the exploitation of the Ruhr coal deposits. As deep mineshafts bored into the hillsides and fields, cottages sprang up along the roadsides. Nearby nucleated villages housed the local population of farmers and small-holding miners. Entrepreneurs in the iron industry rushed into the local towns. Friedrich Krupp began his works in Essen, and Jacob Mayer moved into Bochum. Exponential rates of growth soon lifted those towns, along with Duisburg and Dortmund, into the ranks of the urban giants and turned groups of villages into sprawling cities like Gelsenkirchen,

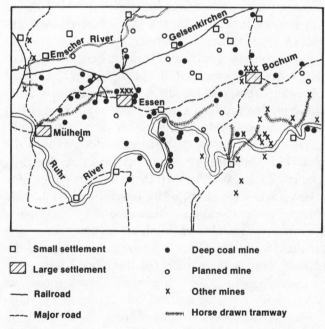

□	Small settlement	●	Deep coal mine
▨	Large settlement	○	Planned mine
——	Railroad	x	Other mines
----	Major road	⊬⊬⊬	Horse drawn tramway

Figure 6.2. The Ruhr region in 1857. (After Steinberg 1967:map 2.)

Wattenscheid, and Castrop. By 1900 almost half the Ruhr's two million people lived in its five largest towns. Two sorts of settlements grew in profusion: mining villages scattered over the coalfields and cities based on iron and steel production, often dominated by a single firm. The need to bring in iron ore and to market the flood of metal products pouring from the furnaces of Thyssen, Hoesch, and Krupp produced a spiderweb of railroads and canals that linked these cities via the Rhine to Rotterdam and other major European towns. The products of mine and forge were whisked out of the region to the markets of the world. These new networks brought the Ruhr into an international city system. Meanwhile, local central place hierarchies were hesitantly readjusted. Soest remained a sleepy market center dwarfed by its neighbors to the west, and a host of new cities rearranged local marketing patterns. Political hierarchies, moving to their own dynamics, remained separate from economic ones. Split among several rulers in 1800, the region fell under the authority of the Prussian state in 1815, becoming part of the province of Westphalia. But it was divided among several county units (*Regierungsbezirke*) whose administrative centers were Münster, Arnsberg, and Düsseldorf. Even after they rose to dominate the region, the newer industrial superstars were not given administrative functions by the state. Growth brought no automatic gift of local political influence.

Relatively similar economic functions characterized the towns of the Ruhr, which formed a complex but not highly differentiated urban system. In other areas, coal resources combined with a richer protoindustrial heritage to produce a much more specialized urban network. In Lancashire, coal-fired steam power drew cotton mills away from the fast streams of the Yorkshire border and into the ring of towns around Manchester.[2] They stayed even after fuel costs ceased to be critical because by then there were no compelling reasons for change. Over time, Lancashire developed into a finely articulated industrial system, more sophisticated than the popular image of endless cotton mills and workers' slums suggests. Liverpool and Manchester divided the functions of a regional capital, and the composition of their employment reflected the shared leadership roles. By 1851 only 24 percent of Manchester's work force was actually in textiles, and much of that outside the basic spinning and weaving branches (Sharpless 1978). Machine building and other auxiliary industries were important, but Manchester's principal role was that of commercial and service center to the circle of cotton towns around it: Bolton, Bury, and Stockport nearby, Preston, Blackburn, and Burnley further north. Liverpool was even less industrial in the narrow sense, and then mainly in support of trade and shipping. In brief, Manchester was the summit of the array of central places, whereas Liverpool served as the gateway city linking the region to European and trans-Atlantic urban networks.

A zone devoted to processing industries—glassworks, metal smelters, and chemical plants—stretched from Saint Helens south to the Cheshire coal fields, between the two regional centers. Even in those undemanding times, it was deemed prudent to segregate the worse nuisances; good transportation and deposits of salt and coal added positive locational attractions (Warren 1980). It was transportation, in fact, that sealed the unity of the whole region. In 1835 one George Head entertained himself by exploring the various ways of going from Manchester to Liverpool. He found three quite distinct routes without subjecting himself to the inconvenience of a road journey (Head 1835). The date is noteworthy because it marks the precise changeover point between canals and railroads for passenger traffic in England. By mid-century the regional system was finely tuned and of unequaled efficiency and technical as well as economic sophistication.

While Lancashire and the Ruhr illustrate the transforming effects of coal-based industrialization, the Lyon region provides an example of gradual adaptation to the new technology.[3] The legacy of protoindustrialization lingered long there, and mid-nineteenth-century efforts to expand the Lyon economic base to banking, chemicals, and heavy metallurgy had rather checkered careers. Because of problems in the silk industry, the future of the region looked dim by the 1870s. Yet by 1914 the picture had once again changed greatly. New industries were flourishing in and near the city, the Loire coal basin and the rest of the periphery were holding their own, and the venerable silk industry was again demonstrating its staying power. Many smaller cities, such as Givors or Chalons-sur-Saône owed their industrial strength—well above average for France—to Lyon's impetus. To simplify somewhat, the attempt to leave protoindustry behind in a "great leap forward" had failed, but the old industrial heritage, suitably transformed, was supporting a successfully diversified regional economy.

The Lyon region is difficult to define geographically because rivers serve to define boundaries as well as to join one region with another. Lyon virtually touches Burgundy and the Dauphiné, with the Auvergne and Languedoc (Vivarais) less than fifty miles away. The traditional Lyonnais itself consists mainly of rough uplands west of the Rhône-Saône, whose population very early outgrew the meager land and so set the stage for protoindustrialization. Thus, we can define the region either in terms of Lyon's links to central places or by the city's zone of dominant network ties. In addition to the Lyonnais proper, the region certainly includes the foothills of the Alps across the Rhône, the valley itself, and perhaps the nonvineyard areas of southern Burgundy as far north as the coal basin around Le Creusot and Montceau-les-Mines.

The city of Lyon itself had long been an important center of trade and finance, an outpost of Italian commerce and banking integral to the network of the Middle Ages. During a troubled sixteenth century, Lyon bore the brunt of a number of major developments—consolidation of royal and Catholic power in France and a northward shift of economic dominance—and concentrated thereafter on a single industry, silk. As was pointed out earlier, silk proved a remarkably durable staple for the long run, though quite fickle over short periods. The need to maintain quality and respond quickly to the vagaries of the market favored small enterprises and control by merchants, who soon came to appreciate the flexibility and cheapness afforded by rural labor. They drew workers, chiefly young women, from the countryside, and also conducted certain steps in production in rural locations.

Let us look at the region around 1850. Fully half the work force in silk was located outside the city of Lyon and its immediate suburbs. At the same time, Lyon merchants controlled a variety of other protoindustrial lines whose locations easily shifted from town to country or from the capital to lesser centers and back. Just then, it happened that wool, paper, and glass were becoming more urban, while hardware, millinery, and glove making were tending to scatter. Away from the Rhône, the most active concentration lay in the Loire basin—actually the valley of the Gier from Saint-Étienne down to the Rhône—where mining and heavy metallurgy were growing rapidly alongside the traditional ribbon and metal-working industries. The first railway in the country had been built between Lyon and Saint-Étienne. Overall, females predominated in industrial employment, textiles over heavy industry in other words, one reason being that so many men were needed in transportation and construction.

All seemed to augur well for Lyon in the coming boom (1850s to 1870s). Yet the promise went partly unfulfilled. Lyon capitalism remained commercial in an age when production mattered more than these capitalists were prepared to recognize. Each new technology was treated as an *affaire* (a deal) rather than as a long-term enterprise (Bouvier 1961). Moreover, in the very sphere of financial control, Lyon proved unable to withstand the centralizing pull of Paris. In 1883 the famed Crédit Lyonnais made a mockery of its name by shifting its headquarters to the capital. At the same time, the silk industry suffered a double blow: silkworm disease followed by an export-inhibiting turn away from free trade. In Lyon itself, chemicals and engineering were sputtering, while regional coal production, though growing, could not keep pace with the rival northern region of France, to say nothing of the Ruhr. The principal urban centers, Lyon and the Saint-Étienne and Le Creusot complexes, were growing rapidly by French standards, but they induced very little urban development elsewhere in the region.

After the 1880s Lyon and its region regained the industrial initiative by drawing once more on the old protoindustrial virtues of flexibility and human capital. Once the dreams of financial killings and monopoly control were abandoned, the urban region proved receptive to creative ventures. Saint-Étienne shifted to steel and shipped cycles and firearms—via mail order—all over France, while Le Creusot's Schneider works, farther north, formed part of what some saw as a sinister international cartel of great arms merchants. Lyon and the Rhône valley downstream acquired vigorous new industries from photography and artificial fibers to electrical equipment and vehicles, belatedly fulfilling the city's promise as a chemical and engineering center. Meanwhile, the old textile industries, all except for silk now fully scattered to the periphery, gradually transformed. They went from domestic to factory operation while remaining largely rural or small-town in location, following the "Alpine" model.

The Lyon region is a dramatic example of the limitations of rapid, concentrated industrialization on the basis of natural resources, as well as of what can be achieved when an active urban center supports creative human efforts of innovation and adaptation on a regional scale. The center linked the regional system of production

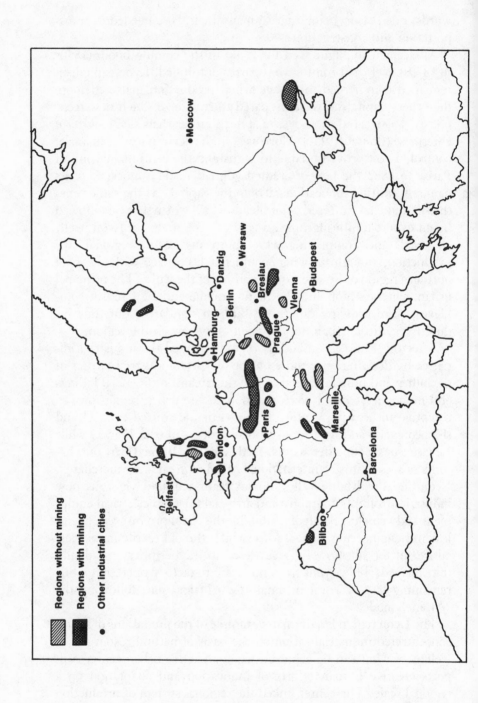

Regions without mining

Regions with mining

• Other industrial cities

to larger networks of markets. While it is right to focus on the growth of urban centers such as Lyon and Saint-Étienne—or Turin, Stuttgart, and Sankt Gallen—the gradual transformation of protoindustrial uplands, which we are calling Alpine development, was also notable for its ability to retain people in populous rural areas with no real agricultural prospects. Dispersed industrialization did, of course, imply a degree of urbanization. Market centers, mill towns, and industrial villages dotted the hills and valleys. But as rail and road transportation reached beyond the principal corridors, much of the industrial labor force was able to retain its rural domicile with other household members continuing in agricultural occupations.

The comparison of three industrial regions just sketched brings out certain lessons relevant to our effort at disentangling the connection between economic transformation and urban growth. First, industrialization involves a number of factors: the natural resources that promised explosive growth are only one. Creativity, adaptability, and diversity also matter, and these human advantages are apparently best nurtured within well-articulated urban systems. Second, the development of industry in one place is scarcely intelligible except in the context of its relations to other places, once again highlighting the significance of regions and their urban hierarchies.

Industrial Europe in 1880

Over the longer run the combined effects of regional change, ranging from deindustrialization to explosive growth, altered the economic landscape of Europe as well as the shape of its national urban systems. Since new hierarchies of urban power were based on the outcomes, let us inspect some of these changes as they looked around 1880, or at the end of the mid-Victorian economic boom.

However one chose to measure industrial power, all statistics confirmed the story the traveler's eye told. Britain spun the most bales of cotton, dug the most tons of coal, smelted more iron, commanded more mechanical horsepower, and exported more than any other country. Behind the "workshop of the world," France ran second, although little Belgium displayed a more intensive commitment to industry, while Germany's headlong rush had brought it to the brink of surpassing France overall. Elsewhere, the larger countries of southern and eastern Europe could point to promising regional developments and other isolated accomplishments, but these had little statistical impact on what remained backward economies. The small nations of the north and west, on the other hand, were going through a much quieter but more thorough transformation, preparing an industrial maturity that would attract little notice until the second half of the twentieth century.

Modern industry meant principally iron, cotton textiles, and steam-driven machinery. The crowning glory of this revolution in technology was the railway, and this was its greatest hour. Not before or since has one mode of transportation so dominated all others on land. Inner Europe—north and west of a line from Madrid through Naples, Budapest, and Danzig to Stockholm—had pretty well completed its primary network linking major cities and industrial sites. Secondary and suburban lines were being filled in, while electric urban rail transportation was only a decade or two away. Meanwhile, the engineers, bankers, and equipment manufacturers of the advanced countries more than made up for any slackening of domestic construction by extending railroads to Iberia, the Balkans, and Russia, as well as to overseas markets. The sprawling railroad typified the age in another sense, too. If any single quality represented modern industry in people's perceptions, it was size: huge machines, vast establishments, great concentrations of people, wealth, activity, and power. Forecasts of the future hoped for "better" but confidently predicted "more."

With the advantage of hindsight, it is easy to see what contemporaries may have missed by extrapolating the most dramatic changes in their recent experience. For one thing, industrial strength could not be accurately assessed in quantitative terms alone. New scientific industries were developing, and the degree to which a nation paid attention to them proved a good indicator of future performance. It is true that the earliest of these, industrial chemicals, never caught up with the basic sectors in terms of employment (Hohenberg 1967). Light engineering and electricity, on the other hand, had an enormous future. Focusing only on the early "leading sectors" of the Industrial Revolution would prove misleading in another way, too (Rostow 1960). The less spectacular group of industries directly supplying consumers with food, clothing, and shelter were then, and were destined to remain, larger than either the old or new leaders. Even without counting the many employed in the transportation and distribution of goods, more people were at work in the clothing trades, in food-processing, and in construction than in all the cotton mills and iron works combined. Moreover, these unspectacular sectors, where small-scale production remained important, maintained a staunchly urban identity. Labor productivity was growing in small-scale production as well as in large, but increasing disposable income sustained the share of consumption-good industries in employment as well as in output. In England, for example, the clothing, building, food, and woodworking sectors held exactly to a combined 21 percent of total national employment between 1851 and 1911 (Musson 1978). Without attempting to catalogue all the significant industries, we need to emphasize just how diversified and sizable in the aggregate "small" industry was. In France alone, a sampling of wares would disclose pipes, cutlery, watches, porcelain, musical instruments, fashion articles, lace, and spirits. Although technology superseded some articles and forms of organization, product innovation kept pace, while technological change could take the form of small electrical motors as well as assembly lines, alternatively threatening small business and giving it a new lease on life.

The geography of industrial Europe in 1880 is not easy to sum up, although the leading centers and concentrations are clear enough. A map tends to understate the spatial concentration of activity by showing the extent rather than the intensity of an industrial zone. It does, however, make it clear that the region, not the nation, is the natural unit for a descriptive account, which must begin with the principal "basins" or industrial regions associated with coal fields. The fastest growing of these extended from the Ruhr westward through the Belgian Borinage to the French Pas-de-Calais. Much of industrial Britain conformed to this type of industrial region as well; Lancashire (with Liverpool and Manchester as principal cities), the West Riding (Leeds and Bradford), the Black Country (Birmingham), and the river "sides" such as Tyne (Newcastle), Tees (Middlesborough), and Clyde (Glasgow). So did South Wales (Cardiff), the East Midlands (Nottingham, Leicester), and the Potteries (Five Towns). In France the textile region around Lille fused with the coal fields to the south, engulfing such medieval centers of trade as Douai and Arras. Of the scattered concentrations in south-central France, only the Lyon–Saint-Étienne group was growing, and it was in the process of losing its rank to the north and northeast. In Germany, too, the early lead of Silesia could not withstand the onrush of the Ruhr. Elsewhere, we may cite the Moravian portion of the Silesian field and the Donets basin in southern Russia, while some others awaited development in the coming decades (Urals, Saar-Lorraine, Asturias).

Industrial concentrations could arise away from coalfields. Indeed, in many upland regions, quite vigorous growth proceeded without the development of major mines or industrial settlement. Production and settlement, though widely diffused, tended to cluster ribbonlike along the narrow valleys. Such groupings, typically with strong protoindustrial roots, were found from Catalonia to Thuringia (Guichonnet 1972). Their capacity to adapt and compete lasted into our own century when the benefits of cheap electricity were added to other strengths.

Among urban centers of industry, ports and other transport junctions on canals, rail lines, and rivers, stood out. Along with earlier protoindustrial towns that were successful in making the transition to newer modes of production, some of the very largest cities were also becoming notable industrial centers. Still conspicuous by their relative weakness, but soon to embark on a frequently successful course of industrialization, were regional capitals and some other larger central places.

Urbanization and Industrial Regions

We have looked at the creation and evolution of industrial regions, noting that the pace and style of their urbanization was largely determined by their type of industrial development. Yet urban settlement was more than a passive consequence of the need to house large concentrations of workers. Cities played many roles: organizing the intraregional division of labor, anchoring the flows of people, goods, and information thereby entailed, and linking the region to its outside markets and sources of inputs—tangible raw materials and equipment, intangible capital and ideas. Sheer numbers of new urban dwellers indeed reflected rapid industrial growth. As we noted earlier, the quality of the regional urban system also mattered, exerting an influence on the capacity to innovate and adapt and thus on the long-term economic health of the region and its cities.

The two types of industrial region on which we have concentrated

Figure 6.4. A metallurgical city: Sheffield in 1880. Industrialization eventually brought factories into the larger towns. By the late nineteenth century this long-time center of file making and cutlery, among others, had acquired many new firms. The large steel mill is sited on the river. Note the continued presence of livestock in the city. (From *Illustrated London News*, August 23, 1879.)

gave rise to two new and contrasting forms of urbanization. The gradual adaptation of the Alpine type produced a kind of hidden urbanization with minimal transformation of the rural landscape and the rural life-style. In some cases, indeed, only the place and type of work justify the urban designation. Factories, workshops, and some dwellings clustered in small-to-medium-sized towns or straggled along the bottoms of valleys. Scattered though it was, the settlement pattern may be called urban by its overall regional mass and by the degree of labor specialization, market involvement, and sophistication of industrial production.

In the coal basins urbanization also took over the countryside, but this time with brutal visual and environmental impact. Particularly where the ground was reasonably level, mining centers, mills, and metallurgical complexes sprang up with little regard for the preexisting patterns of land use. Growth was rapid, unplanned, and largely unregulated. Calculation was applied only to the logistics of transporting bulky products. Otherwise, the settlements had little form, less amenity, and no systematic relationship to one another. Each tried to provide for its own minimal service needs. As they spread, devouring the countryside and its central places, they gradually merged into an entirely new type of major urban concentration. This bore no name and appeared hard put to find one. Some areas were simply called the Black Country or the Five Towns; others were awkwardly hyphenated. They might use the name of a natural feature quickly being smothered by the growth, such as the Ruhr river, or be called after the work done there, as in the Borinage, whch means coal extraction. Today, the generic term that best fits these dense but weakly centralized regions is one coined by Patrick Geddes (1915) to denote any very large urban area, *conurbation*.

Up to the 1880s economic growth changed urban systems in

Figure 6.5. Miners' settlement near Carmaux, France. Carmaux's coal miners lived in their own neighborhoods, generally apart from the glassblowers. This small village, Bruyères, was built to house the many who arrived to work underground as the mines developed. The houses are small and uniform, but not notably crowded or dilapidated. (Personal collection of P. Hohenberg.)

three major ways. As we have shown, mining, especially when combined with other industries, gave rise to heavily urbanized regions. The explosive expansion forcibly rearranged the network, which channeled international trade. Aggressive entrepreneurs in these rising areas soon charted new geographies of production and distribution. But few of the industrial settlements that resulted joined the ranks of the urban superstars. At the same time, local central place hierarchies withered at the lower levels as marketing needs and transportation routes changed. Only at the upper ranks of urban hierarchies, where cities combined functions in the two urban systems, did the new technology substantially aid the growth of older city systems.

Elsewhere, in regions slowly adapting to economic change, existing cities played a larger role in the complex divisions of labor that linked villages and towns. Roads and waterways channeled entrepreneurs into urban centers, where a resident labor supply and many services could be found. On the other hand, in regions where manufacturing declined—Flanders and southern or western Ireland, for example—arrested growth was the fate of towns. A relative eclipse of urban life followed the collapse of protoindustry. Largely excluded from the trading network, the local urban hierarchies retained their roles as marketing or service centers, but offered little to attract or retain migrants or entrepreneurs.

The Modern Urban Economy

So far we have slighted what would seem to be the central topic of this chapter, the growth of factory industry in cities. It was important to begin with a broader view of cities in the changing process of production and to consider urbanization outside the established urban system. In fact, industry made its major direct contribution to the growth of existing cities rather late. During the century when the Industrial Revolution took hold in England and began to spread to the Continent, up to about 1850, urban manufacturing continued largely in a protoindustrial tradition. After that time, the industrialization of cities accelerated markedly. The combined effects of railroads, electricity, internal combustion engines, and new information-based technologies broke the chains linking production to the pit head. Nonetheless, other kinds of work remained very important both in terms of the numbers employed and of the economic functions of cities in the new economic system.

Textbooks in economics generally list the inputs to a production process as land, labor, and capital. Yet at a more fundamental level, production involves the organization of natural resources—materials and energy—by information.[4] Human labor applies some of the energy and furnishes essentially all the information. For any given process, the relative importance of these two factors of production gives an important clue to whether that activity will be carried out in a rural or an urban setting: the more resources, the more rural the location. The development of power-driven machinery and coal-based metallurgy opened the way to using vast amounts of additional resources, and so seemed to favor rural production. But as labor gathered around the mines, the waterways, and the large, machine-filled factories, new urban places were carved out of the countryside.

Soon, however, the forces of change began to favor production in older cities as well. The new technology fashioned means of transportation, notably the railroad, that were powerful and also surprisingly flexible. They allowed resources from widely separated sites to be brought together and also made it possible to bring materials to labor. In addition, technological change soon allowed resources to be used more economically by the application of information. For example, closer tolerances and better design increased the power and efficiency of steam engines, thus saving fuel, metal, and space. As labor-saving devices progressively displaced the heavy physical component of work, people dealt more and more directly with information: reading, meeting, dealing, explaining, designing, and supervising.

Now we come to two paradoxes. A single human being or piece of information is seemingly far more mobile than inert material and easier to control than energy. Why, then, the tendency to agglomerate people and bring materials to them? The answer is a double one. First, although one person can readily move, in nonnomadic societies the community and habitat cannot. Second, information, like electricity, manifests itself as it flows in the form of communication. Its productive use generally requires encounters and collaboration among many people, as well as large, organized collections of data. Information-intensive production naturally takes place in permanent, structured concentrations of people, that is, in cities.

The second paradox is that the neotechnic, information-rich mode of production is most often associated with smaller firms and large urban units. We noted earlier that the resource-intensive phase gave rise to new types, as well as new locations, of urban settlement. In the later phase, however, activity increasingly concentrated in older existing cities, in particular in the largest among them. On one level, this resurgence of venerable preindustrial capitals is surprising. On another level, it merely highlights the functional raison d'être of cities in any age. Whether involved in central place or network linkages, cities were, after all, nothing more than centers for the flow and exchange of information, and the more important ones were the more involved in this process. So they attracted markets, centers of business decision making, and the rapidly growing information industries such as publishing, education, research, and entertainment. The heart of the city—the City of London— came to be occupied by banks and other financial services which, even though they apparently deal with money, credit, and capital, in fact traffic in timely information. It is not by chance that the most famous name in insurance belongs not to a company but to a onetime coffee house—Lloyds—where brokers met to pool very large risks by forming consortia. In every city, cafes served as the real place of business for journalists, stock jobbers, *litterateurs*, impresarios, and politicians.

Most production, certainly in its modern, capital-using form, gains in efficiency from being carried out on a large scale. Plant A, twice the size of plant B, will yield more than twice as much product. Economists call this important truth *economies of scale*. In the days before highly automated facilities, efficiencies of size implied concentrations of people, that is, urbanization. Many urban areas were dominated by enormous establishments, notably in Germany where size was highly regarded. However, the economic life of modern cities, and especially the dynamic growth of large centers, has depended on a quite different link between efficiency and size. For a firm of given scale, productivity may depend on the scale of the economic environment in which it operates. In other words, a good-sized city can be a productive asset in and of itself. Economists use the name *economies of agglomeration* to designate the benefits of scale external to the firm. They come from the fact that the firm can find in the large city all manner of clients, services, suppliers, and employees no matter how specialized its product; this in turn promotes increased specialization. Surprisingly, however, economies of agglomeration encourage firms in the same line to locate close to one another, which is why names such as Harley, Fleet, and Lombard streets and Saville Row—to stick with London—call to mind professions rather than place. Besides the non-negligible profit and pleasure of shop talk, all can share access to services that none could support alone. Buyers from out of town, free-lance specialized workers, repair and consulting services all congregate in a particular neighborhood to do business, if not with one firm then with another. The urban geography of medieval guilds lives on.

A key point about economies of agglomeration is that small businesses depend on them much more than do large ones. The latter can internalize these "external economies" by providing their own services and gain locational freedom as a result. But the city provides a fertile environment for the development of small firms, from the humblest sweatshop to the most prestigious partnership. Some have been in business, father and son—or son-in-law—for generations. Most do not last long, but the principals of failing firms soon crop up in the trade in another capacity or under a different business name. The relationship between large cities and small business is in fact a symbiotic one beneficial to both. The reason is that small firms are the major carriers of innovation, including creative adaptation to change. This was even more true in the days before systematic scientific research contributed much to new technology. Jane Jacobs (1969) calls cities the source of "new work." In the American context, Chinitz (1961) argues that a city with many small firms in a variety of sectors is apt to prove more vital and globally stable than one dominated by a few giants and a limited range of products.

One deceptively simple way of categorizing urban production and employment is to identify the share destined for export and therefore available to pay for the food, fuel, and other goods the city needs to obtain from outside. This *basic* sector is often identified with manufacturing, implying that services are *nonbasic* or auxiliary, a kind of "taking in each others' laundry." Economic growth is frequently said to be dependent on basic employment, the rule of thumb being that a basic job will support one additional worker and both families.[5] In view of economies of scale and specialization, it is normal for many cities to produce large quantities of few goods and to engage in exchange. In nineteenth-century European cities, the share of employment in manufacturing ranged from very low values up to the 80 percent recorded for Bochum in the Ruhr in 1882 (Crew 1979). At the high end of the spectrum, we find single-industry and "company" towns. Often associated with secret military technology in our time, the latter go back at least to the naval ports, such as Brest and Toulon, founded by Louis XIV. In the nineteenth century, single enterprises developed sizable towns or came to dominate an urban area. Port Sunlight (Lever) in England, Leverkusen (Bayer) in Germany, and Sochaux (Peugeot) in France are examples. Entrepreneurs were motivated by the determination to exercise total control over the human as well as the technical environment. Nonbasic employment was kept to a minimum because the paternalistic employer discouraged competition and "frivolity" in the provision of services.

As a general rule, the basic-to-nonbasic ratio is lower in large cities, a fact attributed to the greater diversity—and therefore self-sufficiency—possible in a large market. But the relationship points to some of the larger issues and difficulties raised by the "basic" concept. To begin with, the distinction is fuzzy. A cook in the plant canteen is presumably "basic," but if the workers lunch around the corner they are fed by a "nonbasic" restaurateur. Furthermore, we have seen how misleading it is to draw an economic boundary narrowly around the city. If the notion of an urban balance of trade means anything, it probably should apply to the urban region in its dealings with other areas, and it should include traffic in services as well as commodities. It is a mistake to downplay the extent to which cities pay their way by providing services. Central places process information needed for production around them; gateway and network cities earn commissions as brokers and distribution centers. Tourists, business travelers, and rentiers buy urban services with money from elsewere. All in all, a city with a very high proportion of basic employment is probably functionally underdeveloped, of little significance as a regional center, and limited in its range of industries. It typically has few of the diverse, creative small firms on which long-run economic health depends, since these tend to rely on outside services that large enterprises furnish for themselves. If there is an optimum, it involves a balanced mix of activities either within a single city or distributed over a regional urban system.

Cities house markets in two senses of the term: places for exchange and concentrations of buyers. For many reasons, industrial production frequently locates near the market. Transport considerations may be determining and so may informational factors. In industries such as brewing, processing adds weight, so that it pays to ship the raw materials rather than the product. But weight is not the only factor in transportation costs; perishable or dangerous goods—meat or corrosive chemicals—were long processed near the point of use. Especially when water transportation is used, distance matters little compared with transshipment or "breaking bulk." Therefore ports proved to be natural locations for markets in imported commodities and also for the related industries (Kindleberger 1978). The great maritime harbors of Europe, from Danzig around to Genoa, added important industrial concentrations to the commercial functions derived from links to trading networks. Sugar refining, flour milling, spice grinding, and soap boiling were traditional examples, later joined by ferrous metallurgy and petroleum refining. Shipbuilding was also common. As important network junctions, ports dealt largely with other ports, reselling imports in smaller lots and in processed form and gathering small export shipments into full shiploads. But the activity of the hinterland could make a real difference. The mouth of a major navigable river proved a potent stimulus, as the fortunes of Hamburg, Rotterdam, and Le Havre make clear. By contrast, the ruralization of southern and western France held back Nantes and Bordeaux, situated at the heads of lesser arteries of commerce, in the nineteenth century. Only London, combining the functions of a central place capital and a network center of international finance, needed no industrial hinterland to sustain the port. Transport-related industries also flourished in river ports, rail junctions, and other centers of inland transport. Paris, Rouen, and Lyon outranked most French seaports in the volume of waterborne traffic; towns such as Crewe and Vierzon owed their very place on the economic map to the railroad. Berlin and Milan generated their own man-made transport spokes.

Construction and urban transportation, nominally a part of the nonbasic sector, fixed a variety of industrial activities in towns:

making, assembling, and repairing. In many cases, however, the real impetus to an urban location came not from transportation costs but from informational considerations. The early uses of new construction technology were often in public buildings in major cities. The Crystal Palace in London, Les Halles, and the Eiffel Tower in Paris were really industrial products, pioneering structural uses for iron and glass. The new components were first produced in the cities; Paris became a leader in shaping structural iron, which potential clients came from afar to inspect and to buy. When such methods became routine, manufacturing was transferred to the more conventional centers of heavy industry (Gaillard 1977). The electrical industry is even more telling. Large cities were the first to be outfitted with the plants, equipment, and conduits needed to generate and distribute electric current. However, this major industry was sufficiently labor-using to remain urban. Berlin's exceptional growth toward the end of the century owed much to the great Siemens and AEG establishments. In turn, of course, electric trams, street lighting, and small motors made it possible to increase the scale and activity of cities while actually reducing pollution, congestion, and street crime. Finally, information dictated a market orientation for manufacturing even in well-established industries when the product needed to conform to precise, changeable, or subtle buyer needs. Fashion goods, printing, and musical and scientific instruments are cases in point. Only in a later stage of mass-produced precision goods, such as cameras, motor bikes, and domestic appliances, could the spatial link between maker and buyer be loosened, and then the need to employ large numbers of technicians and skilled workers might still dictate a major urban site.

The lesson of our excursus into the economics of industrial location is that urban development is a dynamic process whose driving force is the ability to put information to work. After 1850 the large cities became the nurseries as well as the chief beneficiaries of an explosion in knowledge-centered economic growth—a second industrial revolution (Landes 1969). New industries were spawned and established ones transformed. The effects were felt in all urban areas, of course. The replacement of iron by steel, in particular, sustained the growth of urban areas associated with resource-based concentrations. But these industrial basins now represented the passive end of a transmission belt whose power came from elsewhere.

Concentration and Decentralization

Broadly speaking, industrialization after 1850—note again how rough and arbitrary such a date must be—can be seen as a process of concentration or condensation followed by a countermovement of spreading and scattering lasting until our own time. We summarize the evolution of urban industrial Europe by looking successively at the centripetal and centrifugal forces at work.

As we have already noted, the growing role of information in production gave prominence to economies of agglomeration. Recall that Lyon grew best after the region lost its predominance in coal and ferrous metallurgy. All over Europe the largest cities kept on growing, undeterred by the absence of a nearby natural resource base or even, in many cases, of good water transportation. Berlin caught up with Paris. Breslau, Vienna, Moscow, Turin, Madrid, Bucharest—the list of large, active cities without a coal mine anywhere near them is a long one. It is noteworthy that the biggest often grew fastest, suggesting that agglomeration had strong elements of positive feedback. The more activity gathered in a single city, the better the access to information and therefore the more impetus to locate the next new enterprise there as well. What applied to firms also held for the specialists and professionals whose human capital constituted the critical informational input. Transfer to the capital meant success, whereas a provincial assignment amounted to exile. The movement of industry into the major cities of the less developed southern and eastern periphery of Europe can be explained by the fact that the critical mass of human capital could be assembled there in only a very few places. Centripetal forces not only favored urban activity, and large cities as compared with small ones, but also the center of the urban area over its periphery. The railroad seems to have played a key role here: although trains can, indeed must, go both ways, they exerted an asymmetrical effect on the location of enterprise for a time, both within and between urban areas. A city strongly affected by this positive feedback process of growth came to be known as a metropolis.

Physicists tell us that the universe contains concentrations of matter so dense that they exert an irresistible gravitational pull and so suck in other matter anywhere near them. In the late nineteenth century the major urban centers threatened to act somewhat like these "black holes." How could concentration be limited and eventually reversed? As people and activity piled up in large cities, notably in and around the central business district, they generated serious congestion and pollution. This was nothing new, of course, but the numbers and effluents reached new heights, while the standards of comfort and safety demanded were beginning to rise. In addition to regulation by political authority, the capitalist city of the nineteenth century evolved two control mechanisms of its own: infrastructure capital and price. We have noted that technology, embodied in the appropriate capital investments, could alleviate the problems and we shall return to these solutions in later chapters. Less visibly, the market system rationed the fixed amount of available land by allowing its rental to be bid up to fantastic levels. Eventually, it was cost that compelled many enterprises to give up the advantages of the center and choose a location on the periphery of the large city or in a lesser center. Rents were not the only problem of doing business in town, of course. Taxes were high, workers had to be compensated for their journey and/or living costs, and everything was cramped, complicated, and subject to delay. In time, technology showed its dual nature. Trams could bring customers out to the suburbs as well as into town. The mails and even more the telephone almost abolished distance as a consideration. Interurban train service tightened the links in the Central Place System: businessmen could go up to the capital for periodic or unforeseen occasions. Trade fairs regained some of their importance of centuries past, providing provincials with concentrated doses of informational encounters. Catalogues and traveling salesmen supplemented these intermittent face-to-face contacts.

Even without the new incentives to decentralize, urban innovation was always spinning off activities. The nature of information as an input to production is that it ceases to be important once a given process becomes routine. At that point other costs—for materials, basic labor, and space—take over, and central cities are at a serious disadvantage. Moreover, economies of scale become critical, and we have already noted the paradox that very large cities are not especially favored locations for the largest enterprises. The role of large cities as centers of innovations that would be applied elsewhere is an old one. Take as an example the birth of industrial chemicals in France. Around 1800 the first plants concentrated around Paris and Marseille, only later gravitating to the principal industrial markets of Rouen, Lyon, and Lille (J. Smith 1979). Gaillard (1977) notes a similar pattern for Parisian industries during the creative push of the Second Empire (1850s and 1860s). Toward the end of the century the largest cities were still growing, but their industry chose peripheral locations such as the emerging "red belt" around Paris. Engineering industries predominated, and a pattern could be discerned. Small workshops occupied the outer districts of the city proper, apparently staying as close to the center as they could afford, while the large enterprises sought out large suburban expanses with minimal prior constraints (Daumas 1976). In Berlin, Siemens even got to name its "company suburb" after itself.[6] The interurban transfer of industry is typified by the move out of London of mature, cost-sensitive industries such as footwear and ready-made clothing once they achieved some mechanization and economies of scale. They gravitated to textile centers with surplus labor (Leeds, Leicester) and to cities somewhat bypassed by industrialization (Bristol, Northampton, Norwich) (Musson 1978).

It is instructive to follow locational decisions by profit-seeking capitalist industry. The danger is that one will overlook the gradual weakening of binding constraints, occurring because various cost factors came to balance one another and because technology offered increasing possibilities of choice and substitution. Industries became "footloose," in practice locationally responsive to secondary or discretionary factors. The entrepreneur could indulge a desire to stay "home" even if the firm outgrew its original base. Sometimes, public policy was able to achieve transfers of industry, for example, from the exposed northeast to the secure southwest of France during and after World War I. One result of this greater flexibility in industrial locations has been a growing convergence between the structures of manufacturing towns and those of old cities at the top ranks of regional urban hierarchies. While the big cities acquired more industry, as well as the shapeless expanse of slums typical of industrial conurbations, manufacturing towns evolved a higher degree of internal differentiation and occupational diversity (Jäger 1978). To return to the example of Bochum in the Ruhr, the share of industry in total employment fell from 80 percent in 1882 to 70 percent by 1895, although it had climbed again to 75 percent by 1907 (Crew 1979). These shifts reveal two trends in the growing structural maturity of the city: a doubling of employment in trade and services, partly offset in the longer run by the rapid growth of engineering industries that built on the strong base of iron and steel production. A first industrial phase based primarily on the processing of natural resources was reinforced by the development of much more labor-intensive and information-using lines of work.

In more recent times, the calculus of locational decisions has shifted somewhat to include a concern for the total environment, especially for the quality of life provided for technical and managerial employees. We look in the Epilogue at changes in Europe's regional balance to which this concern has contributed but will note here the implications for central places left behind in the push to industrialize. In the longer run such spots came to look doubly attractive, combining as they did the facilities and connections of the Central Place System with the charms of neglect. The cultural and aesthetic riches of the past were preserved from air pollution, speculative development, and extreme congestion. As a result, hundreds of small towns as well as cities ranging up to the magnitude of Munich, Lausanne, Florence, and Copenhagen developed or revived an industrial base, combining the structures of an older urban world with the dynamic economic energies of the new.

A Cornucopia of Urban Occupations

Just as industrialization did not automatically submerge cities in a sea of factories, modern economic growth did not turn most citizens into factory workers. Urban labor markets, which translated industrial demand into specific jobs, retained the complexity of earlier centuries. Look at Milan in the later nineteenth century (see Table 6.1). Despite the great importance of industry, only about half the workers had industrial jobs. The rest labored in a variety of trades that ranged from banker to beggar. Such cities were crowded with doctors, domestic servants, clergymen, and peddlers. Their back streets teemed with a floating population that mixed thieves with vagrants, casual laborers, and prostitutes. Remember, too, the processors and distributors of food. Cities were provisioned from outside and required thousands to unload, pack, move, and sell, as well as bake their daily bread. Also note the enormous number of shopkeepers. Retail merchants are as old as the city itself. But higher incomes multiplied their numbers, perhaps even faster than urban populations as a whole. Also, retail commerce became far more

Table 6.1. Occupational distribution of the urban labor force in selected towns, 1871–1891 (percent).

Occupation	Bochum (1871)		Milan (1881)		London (1891)	
	M	F	M	F	M	F
Agriculture	0.3	0.3	5.7	5.5	1.0	0.2
Mining	12.3	10.5	—	—	—	—
Industry	55.6	34.8	44.9	52.7	38.3	32.5
Transportation	1.8	1.8	5.0	—	17.3	0.5
Service	18.6	34.0	17.8	33.5	6.5	54.1
General labor	—	—	—	—	7.3	0.1
Commerce, finance	5.3	6.4	12.3	3.6	21.7	6.4
Administration, professions	2.5	3.6	13.7	4.5	6.6	6.2
Miscellaneous, unknown	3.7	7.8	0.7	0.2	1.2	—

Sources: G. S. Jones (1971:359); Crew (1979:14); L. Tilly (1973:114).

specialized, increasingly separated from wholesaling and direct production. Finally, it gave rise to a major new occupational classification, that of shop clerk or assistant. Where apprentices or family members had helped wait on customers in the past, the shop assistant became one of a growing urban army of the genteel poor, required to cultivate appearance and speech however pinched and sordid his or her private life had to be.

In the larger cities, a wide range of office and administrative jobs were available as well. The mountain of paper generated by the increasing need for information required people to write, sort, copy, and file. The male clerk of the counting house was joined by the female clerk, later a typist or secretary. This, too, was a category of persons who were subject to strict standards of hierarchy and propriety, yet who were paid modestly in salary and in prospects. Their work served another growing group, the bureaucrats themselves. These men—for almost none were women—were predominantly, one might say aggressively, middle class. They might work for a ministry, an insurance company, or an import-export house. It made little difference.

This potpourri is only the surface of the occupational mix. In large cities especially, we would need to add the raffish or showy population of artists and entertainers, as well as the many who worked behind the scenes in the arts; also students, teachers, and intellectuals of every stripe. Finally, remember the many foreigners who resided or passed through, and those who catered to travelers from near and far. For cities continued their age-old function of helping those with money to spend it. From foreign nabobs to gawky rustics, from insecure tourists to provincial businessmen, all found the risky pleasures they sought and a large population waiting to cater to every taste.

This rich occupational mix varied considerably among sizes and types of towns. In general, capital cities had far more varied and complex labor markets than did manufacturing towns, and larger places housed a greater number of trades than did smaller ones. Compare London and Bochum (see Table 6.1). Far more administrators, traders, and professionals worked in the English metropolis, and its port and transportation system, moreover, required thousands of workers to load and unload goods and people. The capital's great wealth and resident aristocracy attracted fine craftsmen and supported a rich array of shops and specialty stores. London's theaters, schools, and newspapers made the city a mecca for aspiring actresses, musicians, and writers of all sorts. Their German counterparts lived in Berlin or Munich, not Bochum. In contrast, metallurgical towns like Bochum had relatively few administrators, professionals, or entertainers. Not only did they lack a complex service sector, but commerce and retail trade were comparatively limited. Opportunity in Bochum lay primarily in industrial work, in the mines and foundries of its metallurgical firms. Cities with different functions had different employment patterns.

Urban labor markets also varied over time. The industrial economy constantly eliminated certain tasks. Motors and piped utilities decreased the need for laborers to lift and to carry. Other machines supplanted certain handicrafts at the same time as they created new specialties. Each of the major phases of urban industry we have discussed in this chapter shaped a city's employment pattern. Although a certain number of clothing and food shops were always needed, the proportion of more complex trades changed along with regional patterns of production and urban functions.

Until the middle of the nineteenth century, women were employed in domestic industries, in household service, and in petty commerce. By the late decades of the century, they were losing their role in direct commodity production, although they still figured strongly in textiles, clothing, and a variety of largely urban small-scale trades. The rough data for Milan and Bochum show the effect of the industrial mix on female employment even at a comparatively early stage (Table 6.1). Moreover, the German coal and metal center had comparatively few women workers overall. On the other hand, the contrast between up-to-date London and Milan makes clear that women were asserting their presence in both old and new service sectors. Manservants became rare outside the largest domestic establishments, while the "typewriter," the telephone operator, and the sales girl appeared in ever larger numbers.

The durability of urban protoindustrial manufactures meant that older patterns of employment persisted. Many towns even housed a few agricultural workers who labored in the nearby fields or gardens. Workers classified as "industrial" were often really artisans, some of whom worked independently and had employees of their own. The number of true factory employees before 1850 or so was quite small. Although the service sector was apparently large, a sizable number of urban workers had only part-time jobs as street sellers or day laborers, betraying the large amount of underemployment to be found among the poor. Of the rest, the bulk was accounted for by an army of women who ran households and an almost equal horde of male laborers who dug, hauled, and fetched. While the middle and upper classes employed most of the servants, life was so inconvenient and raw labor so cheap that even quite modest households struggled to maintain domestic help. Overall, working for wages characterized a growing share of the labor force, but regular cash wages for fixed hours remained the exception.

This pattern shifted markedly in the middle and late nineteenth century under the pressure of advancing industrialization. Employment figures for Bochum illustrate common changes (see Table 6.2). As the Ruhr became Germany's foremost mining region, the proportion of industrial workers, particularly those employed in mines and foundries, skyrocketed. Artisans abandoned their trades or took up skilled jobs with the large firms in the area. Simultaneously, the number of domestic servants and day laborers dropped sharply. In the first phase of industrial expansion, Bochum's work force became strongly proletarianized. Wage work in industry became the most common way of earning a living. At the same time, older elites of merchants and professionals were supplanted by industrial capitalists. The town became polarized between the extremes of owner and employee.

Table 6.2. Changes in occupational distribution for males in Bochum between 1858 and 1907 (percent).

Occupation	1858 (n = 3,778)	1882 (n = 12,914)	1907 (n = 45,993)
Agriculture	—	0.7	1.2
Industry	30.7	76.5	74.5
Mines and foundries	9.5	48.4	34.2
Crafts	21.2	3.1	—
Trade and transportation	7.1	13.0	15.9
Domestic service and day labor	35.4	2.3	2.8
Civil service and professions	4.7	4.3	5.6
Miscellaneous	1.0	—	—

Source: Crew (1979:13–16).

The social effects of this shift are discussed in Chapter 8. However, European towns were not destined fully to trade their diverse social mix for Marx's stark division between subservient labor and dominant capital. The split into proletariat and bourgeoisie became less extreme as the century progressed. By 1907 a growing service sector in Bochum itself indicated a trend toward renewed occupational complexity. Not only did commerce and transport increase in size, but the number of professionals and administrators also rose. Mining and metal production occupied a substantially smaller share of the work force, while white collar jobs multiplied. In the long run the labor force diversified, as information-rich technologies and new forms of power became more important. The second industrial revolution eventually led even Bochum away from the absolute dominance of mining and metallurgy.

Industrial urbanization in all its phases was far more than the agglomeration of dwellings around factories or the rise of factories in and around cities. It reflected a transformation in which cities and urban systems forged new economic links. The integration of this economic system played as great a part as did growth and concentration. With rapid technological change and large-scale production triumphant, it was urgently necessary to coordinate, inform, and stimulate efforts that were ever more interdependent as they grew. It was also imperative to prod and guide the transformation of the countryside, without whose food, labor, and increasing custom the whole enterprise must grind to a halt. This became the quintessentially urban role, the truly "basic" productive function of the urban system, which extended from quiet market centers and manufacturing towns like Bochum to great nerve centers like London and Milan, whose administrators, financiers, and entrepreneurs masterminded the flow of information and goods.

CHAPTER 7

Urban Growth and Urban Systems

THE COMBINED FORCES of industry and government exerted transforming power, turning small settlements into urban giants. A modest town could become a metropolis within a few generations if
multiple attractions drew outsiders from a wide territory. Berlin
offers a spectacular example.[1] About 30,000 people lived in Berlin
in 1701, most within the elaborate walls and water fortifications
that enclosed the medieval core of the city. Then as the Prussian
court and army expanded, so did the capital. State funds and privileges brought new industry into the town, which soon outgrew its
limited space. Planned suburbs were added, and new administrative
buildings and wide boulevards were built in central areas. By 1800
the thick defensive walls were replaced by a more distant set of
customs barriers, doubling the territory of the city—a necessary
expansion because the Berlin population now numbered over 170,000.
Despite the town's distance from sources of raw materials, its ex-
cellent transportation network and government market regularly
attracted new industries and workers. Metal, chemical, machine-
making, textile, and clothing firms multiplied through the nineteenth century. Outside the gates, suburban settlements grew up
along the major roads and canals that linked the capital to the towns
of the Brandenburg region. Entrepreneurs and their workers, particularly in the engineering sector, moved into northern parishes,
while land near the Tiergarten in the southwest housed the burgeoning numbers of commuting officials and wealthier middle-class
families. Over 400,000 people lived in the capital by 1850; then the
pace of growth accelerated. Indeed, the city doubled in size during
the next twenty years and doubled again to reach 1,600,000 by

1890. Density was sustained as block after block of barracks-style apartments were built to contain the newcomers. Large industrial suburbs of factories surrounded with such *Mietskasernen* spread out in the northwest, some of which were annexed as the city government progressively extended its administrative and planning authority over the region. Meanwhile, the core of the city was transformed by the acres of government offices, banks, and shops of the central business district. Thanks to trams and the railway, people abandoned the old city and flocked into suburbs such as Wedding, Moabit, and Schoeneberg. Still the influx of heavy industry continued, fed by the seemingly insatiable demand for machinery, track rails, engines, and munitions. A new ring of industrial settlements was born farther out from the city center. By the time of World War I, Berlin had grown to meet a network of satellite communities, themselves large towns in their own right. Greater Berlin housed over 4 million people by 1925 and had engulfed 352 square miles.

When pictured in terms of a single city like Berlin, urban growth seems a matter of simple superlatives: more people, more streets and houses. For much of Europe in recent times, abundant statistical records and town plans allow us to trace urban expansion. Yet when the question of growth is examined in terms of a region or a large array of towns, the matter becomes less straightforward. Most cities or only a fraction of them may contribute to overall growth; the rapid growers may be the established centers or newly created ones. Moreover, size and activity matter as well as age. Did large and small towns grow at similar or different rates? And what of ports, resorts, administrative centers, and market towns? Perhaps places with different functions had entirely different patterns of expansion. It is also true that statistics are not so clear-cut or precise as the neat numbers imply.

Despite the rapid progress of urbanization during the past two hundred years, the rush into Europe's cities was neither indiscriminate nor universal. Cases of spectacular expansion need to be weighed against those of long-term stagnation. The constraints of a medieval wall posed no problems for sleepy towns such as Avila, Urbino, or Dinkelsbuehl. People chose to migrate to some cities, but not to others. As a wave of accelerated urbanization swept across Europe from the northwest to the southeast, some regions and places were left largely untouched. The selectivity of growth is an issue that few researchers have considered in detail.

Much of the explosive urban growth of the last two hundred years has been channeled into regional and national capitals. A long-established core of dominant cities has widened and lengthened to cover a broad zone from London to Milan, while a series of central and eastern European towns have joined the top ranks of the Continent's urban hierarchy. Although political divisions between east and west now block long-distance population flows, both halves of Europe have developed strong urban networks, linked by bureaucracies, banks, and distributors who use cities to tie together the vast territories in which they operate.

Urban Population Growth

Between 1800 and 1910 the urban population of Europe grew about sixfold (Bairoch 1977). This can be broken down into two components: a doubling of the total population and a tripling of the percentage classified as urban. The shift in proportion contributed more to urban growth than did overall population increase, but both were important.[2] However, it must be noted that Europe remained more rural than urban at the outbreak of World War I, indeed until after World War II if one includes the Soviet Union. The reason is that countries whose urbanization lagged still participated in the wider growth of population and so weighed appreciably in the European total.

What about the time path of urbanization? Figure 7.1 shows acceleration in rates for both total and urban population during the second half of the century, with a leveling off after 1910. As a result, the urban proportion grew quite steadily. This is brought out in Figure 7.2. The record of individual countries shows the amount of variability underlying the smooth evolution of the whole. Some parts urbanized rapidly, others slowly. For France and Italy the curves are almost straight lines, for the Netherlands and Russia sharply angled. Overall, the differences among countries widened during the course of the century and only began to converge after World War I. Throughout, one nation or another was experiencing a strong rural-to-urban shift, but never all or even most of them at one time.

The foregoing takes census data and official statistics at face value. But major problems of comparability and reliability must be noted. Some early figures are frankly estimates, antedating census counts of the urban population. Moreover, definitions of what constituted a town differed somewhat by country and changed over time. Some places retained urban status backed by no reality; many more concentrations were urban in fact long before they received official recognition as such. New agglomerations and conurbations were acknowledged late or in artificial pieces; suburbs were ignored or separately enumerated after they had become integral parts of a metropolitan whole. The differing size thresholds for towns can create spurious anomalies or hide real ones. The apparent jump in the Danish urban proportion after 1910 is due in large measure to

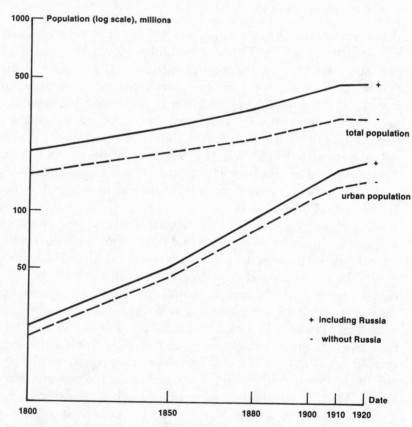

Figure 7.1. Total and urban population of Europe, 1800–1920 (millions), with and without Russia. (Data from Bairoch 1977:7.)

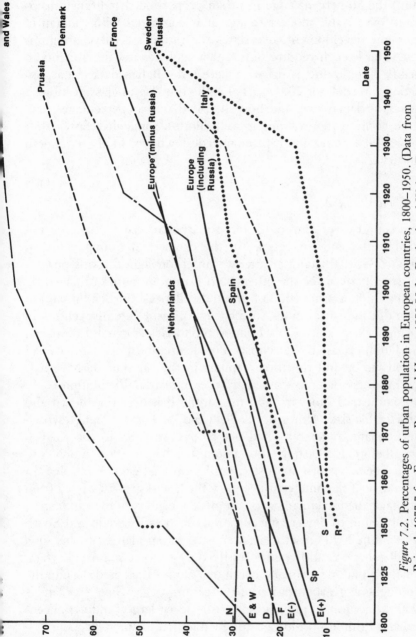

Figure 7.2. Percentages of urban population in European countries, 1800–1950. (Data from Bairoch 1977:7 for Europe; Berry and Horton 1970:75 for England and Wales, France, Sweden, and Russia; W. Lee 1979:120, 231, for Denmark and Italy; Schmal 1981:173–174 for Prussia; and A. Weber 1899:115,119 for the Netherlands and Spain.)

a lowering of the urban threshold to 250 inhabitants. On the other hand, the 50 percent edge in urban proportion that France maintained over Italy, modest though it is compared with the gap in economic development, overstates the former's relative urbanization. The French require only 2,000 agglomerated inhabitants to qualify a commune as urban, whereas the Italian data use a population threshold of 20,000. As for the time lag in classification, it causes the data to overstate how sharply the urban percentage grew. More accurate figures might well show a somewhat faster shift before 1880 and a more pronounced slowdown in the twentieth century.

National Variations

The countries of Europe differed in the pattern of their overall urbanization and, of course, in the extent and timing of urban growth. Great Britain led the way in chronological terms but did not set a pattern for the others. No European nation achieved by 1950 as high a proportion of urban dwellers as did Britain, and in none did industrial cities so thoroughly displace older centers in the higher size ranks. Only London and to a lesser extent Edinburgh and Dublin resisted the eclipse. To be sure, most other towns had trailed far behind the three capitals in the early modern period. Among those later bypassed by the Industrial Revolution, only protoindustrial Norwich and mercantile Bristol had achieved any considerable size. Although Sheffield and the East Midland towns— Nottingham, Leicester—had not figured strongly in the English array before 1750, they were among the few to show much continuity between protoindustrial and industrial economic roles. In the course of the nineteenth century the fastest growth passed from the major manufacturing and commercial centers to their industrial satellites and to newer concentrations such as Teesside and South Wales. The high growth rates reported for specialized towns such as rail junctions and resorts testify only to their minuscule start. Finally, London's primacy continued almost unabated despite the thoroughgoing urbanization of the country as a whole. As late as 1900 the combined populations of the seven largest industrial centers and Edinburgh did not quite equal that of the metropolis.[3]

French urbanization was much more gradual than British, in line with that nation's moderate industrialization and slow population growth. Whereas the earliest statistics available, for the middle of the nineteenth century, show that one Briton in two lived in a town, it took until the 1930s for the same proportion to be attained south of the Channel. Yet the northeastern half of France underwent urbanization along what one might call modified English lines. Paris continued to dominate and, like London, to inhibit other urban growth for quite a distance around itself. Outside the capital, growth in the northeast concentrated in industrial towns and largely by-passed established regional centers such as Dijon and Orléans. Lille, Lyon, Reims, and Nancy were among the few cities that combined industrial strength with a significant regional role. To the south and west, on the other hand, only regional capitals and major ports grew rapidly. Nice, Marseille, and Bordeaux did relatively well by combining these two growth-promoting factors (*Le Peuplement urbain français* 1973).

The steadiness of urbanization in France contrasts with lags and spurts observed in many other countries. One reason is that French urbanization accelerated ahead of economic change in the 1815–1840 period. The urban system recovered from twenty-five years of revolution and war, while rural overpopulation drove people out of the countryside (Aydalot, Bergeron, and Roncayolo 1981). One factor was that the French were much less likely than other Europeans to emigrate overseas. At the other end of the century, urbanization remained gradual even in the boom of the *Belle Epoque* (1890–1914). The failure of most major provincial towns and industrial centers to grow at the pace typical in other European regions increased the primacy of Paris. In 1911 the capital with its suburbs still numbered more inhabitants than all other French cities of more than 50,000 put together. Nonetheless, Table 7.1 shows that some concentration was taking place within the urban population even if one excludes Paris. In the course of 110 years, the towns over 50,000 (including Paris) increased their share of the urban population from a bit more than one fourth to well over a half, and to two and one half times their early share without the capital. Yet in 1911 fewer than one Frenchman in ten lived in a sizable provincial town. If one recalls that the French size thresholds are lower than those for other countries, the pace of urbanization seems tame indeed. This is true in overall terms, and also because

Table 7.1. Distribution of the French urban population, 1811–1911.

| Size category | Number of cities and share of the urban population | | | | | |
| | 1811 | | 1851 | | 1911 | |
	No.	Percent	No.	Percent	No.	Percent
Paris	1	15.0	1	19.5	1	28.7
Other cities over 50,000	6	11.9	10	16.0	32	26.9
20,000–50,000	24	16.9	31	15.3	55	11.3
10,000–20,000	48	16.0	66	14.6	119	12.1
5,000–10,000	143	23.4	155	17.0	222	11.0
3,000–5,000	187	16.7	304	17.5	365	10.0
Total urban population (thousands)		4,190		6,388		13,800

Source: Dupeux (1981: Tables II-b, V-a).

in so few places outside the metropolis—Saint-Étienne, Le Havre, Nice—was urban growth both rapid and sustained to considerable size.

The contrast is sharpest if one looks across the Rhine to Germany. Population growth, production, and urbanization all followed a much stronger dynamic there, admittedly beginning from lower levels in the early nineteenth century. The German pattern of urban growth is also distinctive. It was marked by good regional balance and by very rapid growth of the major centers in each region. Yet this growth, and the spectacular expansion of Berlin that we noted earlier, did not make for a high degree of regional primacy except in the east (J. Lee 1978). Finally, the fast-growing large cities, the Ruhr conurbation aside, were themselves functionally balanced. This was the result of attracting industry into centers of commerce, administration, and service. Germany was no more able than other nations to diversify industrial towns.

It has been argued that Germany developed as it did because rapid urbanization preceded political centralization but came after the start of railroad building. Certainly, the rail grid sustained weakly hierarchical relationships among cities, by contrast with the Paris-centered star of French rail lines. In this respect, German urbanization resembles that of the United States west of the Appalachians in developing a number of relatively independent large regional centers. We need to use 1925 data to capture the strength of urban growth in German regional centers, even though this was a period of economic depression. Behind the three largest concentrations—Berlin, the Ruhr, and Hamburg—came no fewer than six cities bunched around 600,000 inhabitants. And there were six more with between one third and one half million people, all larger than Bordeaux, then France's fifth largest city (Chandler and Fox 1974).

As regards other countries, the rush into the cities began earlier in western regions than in northern or eastern lands. Indeed, before 1850 only Belgium joined England as a setting for rapid urbanization. Then by mid-century, every part of Europe with the exception of Portugal saw an intensified transfer of population into the cities. Between 1850 and 1900 the most rapid gains outside Germany could be found in Austria, Switzerland, and Sweden. But even Spain, Rumania, or Serbia, where industrialization made little progress, showed a shift in the urban and rural balance at this time (Bairoch 1977). Regions with a large initial urban population, particularly Holland and northern Italy, exhibited relatively low rates of increase during the later nineteenth century. In addition, their growth leveled off earlier than that of territories with an initially weak urban network, allowing countries on the European periphery to become almost as urbanized as those of the older core area by the mid-twentieth century. Since World War II the countries of eastern Europe have combined economic transformation and high mobility, bringing them closer to the western pattern of earlier decades.

A comparison of city growth in northern Italy and in European Russia during the nineteenth century will illustrate differences in regional patterns of urbanization among the second wave of industrializing countries.[4] In 1800 the northern Italian city system was composed of many medium- and small-sized towns, most founded in medieval and ancient times and many of which had shown little or no growth for centuries. In the country as a whole, approximately 30 percent of the population already lived in cities, and the proportion was much higher in Lombardy and in coastal districts. While Venice and Milan housed more than 100,000 people, there were six other cities with at least 50,000 inhabitants and over a dozen that numbered between 20,000 and 50,000. Tuscany, Lombardy, Venetia, and Piedmont had well-developed Central Place Systems of market towns and administrative centers serving the surrounding territory. In addition, many of the largest cities—Genoa, Venice, Milan, and Florence, for example—had strong network linkages to places north of the Alps. When the pace of urbanization accelerated after 1820, the number of larger towns increased with every census. Moreover, by 1860 over 70 percent of the Lombard and 60 percent of the Ligurian population were already living in centers of 5,000 or more inhabitants. Urban growth was spread over a wide array of towns from small to large. Northern Italy was not a unified urban region, however. Political fragmentation was paralleled by economic disunity.

After unification, sharp increases in rural-to-urban migration diversified the northern Italian urban network. Along the roads and railways linking Florence and Milan to the sea, relatively dense lines of cities developed, and the corridor of places between Milan and Venice grew. The older centers of the Via Emilia from Milan through Bologna and Ravenna thrived as they drew in industry and intensified the marketing of agricultural produce from adjacent areas, thanks to the stimulus of the railroad. Similarly, there was expansion in a line of older cities between Florence and its port, Livorno—for example, Pisa and Lucca. Already existing cities became the nodes in developing economic networks, as industry, trade, and agriculture grew in tandem. The emerging supercenter of this developing economic system was Milan, which became the core of a manufacturing region spread over the Lombard plain. Not only did the town engulf nearby communes, but manufacturing and commercial activities moved into a wide network of other Lombard towns when machine-made textiles and heavy industry settled into the territory. As Milan became the economic capital of Italy, the settlements in its region grew and functioned as parts of a metropolitan system unique in Italy.

The relative balance of northern Italian urban development was lacking in the European areas of the Russian Empire, where two large cities dominated the urban hierarchy. Both Moscow and St. Petersburg, which together housed 19 percent of the empire's urban population in 1811, deserve to be called primate cities. Their only Italian analogues were southern cities such as Naples, Palermo, and Rome, disproportionately large when measured against other towns in their regions. Most of the rest of the Russian city network early in the nineteenth century consisted of small provincial centers, sleepy places whose populations were dominated by the resident nobles, clergy, and military. At that time (1811) only 6.4 percent of the empire's people were recorded as living in cities. Urbanization in the first half of the nineteenth century served to expand the size, and fill in the middle ranks, of the Russian urban hierarchy. Towns having between 10,000 and 100,000 people leaped in number from 34 to 130 and doubled their share of the urban population by 1861. During the second half of the century the total number of towns grew, while the number of large cities multiplied even faster. By 1911 thirty cities of over 100,000 housed about 40 percent of the Russian urban population. This extraordinarily rapid urbanization was strongly concentrated regionally in the northwestern and southern gubernia: Poland, the Baltic seacoast, the developing areas north of the Black Sea; and, of course, in the Moscow region. The end of serfdom and the start of railway building and factory industry gave a particular boost to larger towns in commercially active districts after 1860. Dispersed industry moved into the towns. Port cities gave easy access to water transportation of raw materials and products, and railways reinforced the interconnections of major trading cities. Network System stimuli far outweighed those of the Central Place System in the Russian case. Despite the well-articulated urban hierarchy that had existed in Russia by the mid-eighteenth century, it took the extra impetus of long-distance trade and quick transportation to accelerate and shape Russian urban growth. Where these stimuli were absent, urbanization languished, as in large parts of European Russia between Poland, Moscow, and the Black Sea. Indeed, vast areas became less urban during the second half of the century. As a result, no more than 15 percent of the Russian population was counted as urban on the eve of World War I. The true urbanization of Russia, notably the development of a full array of major centers, came about only as the result of deliberate Soviet planning. Yet even Stalin and his successors could not stop the continuing growth of Moscow or diminish its functional dominance. Ironically, the authoritarian methods with which they pursued balance in fact accentuated the centralization of the system by enlarging the bureaucracy.

Both in style and in pace of urbanization, Russia stands diametrically opposed to northern Italy. Nevertheless, the heavy weight of earlier urban networks can be seen in both places. Where relatively dense urban systems existed, growth was channeled into older centers whose services offered advantages over rural sites. Expanded industrial and commercial functions were taken over by well-located settlements. In particular, higher-ranking central places and cities along major transportation routes drew disproportionate amounts of industry and immigration. Only in newly developing and formerly rural areas, such as the Donbas and the southwestern Caspian, did urbanization produce a reworking and major expansion of city systems.

The Urban Hierarchy, 1750–1950

Another way of measuring urban growth is to trace over time the changes in size of individual towns. By looking at the very largest European cities, we can illustrate both the changing intensity of urbanization and shifts in the nature of urban systems. Table 7.2 lists the "top forty" European cities in 1750, 1850, and 1950.[5]

First, how big did a city need to be to accede to the list? In 1750 the threshold was just 50,000. It rose to 108,000 a century later and to 675,000 in 1950, exactly the size of the biggest city in 1750. Two centuries of urbanization gave Europe forty Georgian Londons, at least in terms of numbers. London itself grew thirteenfold over two centuries, and it took a bit more than that pace to maintain position in the hierarchy. In other words, the city occupying a given rank in 1950 was 13.8 times as populous, on average, as the equivalent city two hundred years earlier, and this ratio held quite well throughout the hierarchy.[6] Although the hierarchy grew rather evenly over the period as a whole, there were distortions over shorter intervals. Table 7.3 shows the increase in each of the fifty-year subperiods.

Save in the case of the perennial leader, London, these percentages do not represent the growth of actual cities. They do tell us that any city rising in rank had to grow more quickly than the number shown. The highest ranks grew faster between 1800 and 1850, whereas the lower ranks were catching up in the second half of both the eighteenth and nineteenth centuries. The real acceleration in growth came only after 1800, and after 1850 for many middling towns. On the other hand, Europe's major cities were still growing as fast in the first half of our own century as a hundred years earlier, despite two world wars. Overall, a representative large European city occupying a rank around twentieth had 80,000 inhabitants in 1750, 100,000 by 1800, and twice as many in 1850.

Table 7.2. Leading cities of the European urban hierarchy, 1750–1950 (population in thousands).

	1750		1850		1950	
Rank	City	Population	City	Population	City	Population
1	London	676	London	2,320	London	8,860
2	Paris	560	Paris	1,314	Paris	5,900
3	Naples	324	St. Petersburg	502	Moscow	5,100
4	Amsterdam	219	Berlin	446	Ruhr	4,900
5	Lisbon	213	Vienna	426	Berlin	3,707
6	Vienna	169	Liverpool	422	Leningrad	2,700
7	Moscow	161	Naples	416	Manchester	2,382
8	Venice	158	Manchester	412	Birmingham	2,196
9	Rome	157	Moscow	373	Vienna	1,755
10	St. Petersburg	138	Glasgow	346	Rome	1,665
11	Dublin	125	Birmingham	294	Hamburg	1,580
12	Palermo	124	Dublin	263	Madrid	1,527
13	Madrid	123	Madrid	263	Budapest	1,500
14	Milan	123	Lisbon	257	Barcelona	1,425
15	Lyon	115	Lyon	254	Milan	1,400
16	Berlin	113	Amsterdam	225	Glasgow	1,320
17	Hamburg	90	Brussels	208	Liverpool	1,260
18	Marseille	88	Edinburgh	194	Naples	1,210
19	Rouen	88	Hamburg	193	Leeds	1,164
20	Copenhagen	79	Marseille	193	Copenhagen	1,150
21	Florence	74	Milan	193	Athens	1,140
22	Genoa	72	Leeds	184	Bucharest	1,100
23	Granada	70	Palermo	182	Katowice	977
24	Barcelona	70	Rome	170	Brussels	964
25	Seville	68	Barcelona	167	Amsterdam	940
26	Bologna	66	Warsaw	163	Prague	938
27	Bordeaux	64	Budapest	156	Stockholm	889
28	Turin	60	Bristol	150	Lisbon	885
29	Valencia	60	Sheffield	143	Munich	870
30	Cádiz	60	Bordeaux	142	Newcastle	830
31	Stockholm	60	Venice	141	Rotterdam	803
32	Dresden	60	Turin	138	Warsaw	803
33	Prague	58	Copenhagen	135	Kiev	800
34	Brussels	55	Munich	125	Kharkov	730
35	Edinburgh	55	Prague	117	Sheffield	730
36	Lille	54	Breslau	114	Turin	725
37	Cork	53	Wolverhampton	112	Cologne	692
38	Breslau	52	Newcastle	111	Frankfurt	680
39	Koenigsberg	52	Valencia	110	Genoa	676
40	Leiden	50	Ghent	108	Lodz	675

Source: Chandler and Fox (1974:322–328, 337–339).

Table 7.3. Population growth of steps in the European urban hierarchy, 1750–1950.

Rank	Percentage growth over 50-year intervals			
	1750–1800	1800–1850	1850–1900	1900–1950
1	27	169	179	37
5	11	80	238	158
10	22	105	172	77
15	17	90	142	128
20	26	93	176	116
25	25	96	192	93
30	32	80	208	90
35	31	63	228	90
40	32	64	234	87
Mean	25	93	197	97
Standard deviation	7	32	33	34

Source: Calculated from Chandler and Fox (1974:322-330, 337-338).

By 1900 it numbered half a million, and it reached one million in 1950. The growth of Copenhagen approximates this stylized pace.

How stable was membership in the urban hierarchy? Copenhagen occupied the twentieth rank at both end points, but was it an exception? One way to judge is to look at the cities making up the first and second groups of twenty in 1750 and 1950. We can see what happened to the leaders of the pre- or protoindustrial hierarchy and also look at the "recruitment" of the twentieth-century leaders.

If we compare the largest twenty cities in 1750 and in 1950, we see that about two thirds of the original list remained in the top group, while most of the rest disappeared from the list entirely. The very largest cities therefore showed much stability in their overall rank in the European urban hierarchy. Matching the second twenty cities on our 1750 list with their equivalents two centuries later reveals a much higher rate of change: about two thirds of these towns were displaced by newcomers. And only Barcelona managed to grow fast enough to climb into the ranks of the twenty largest cities. Mobility for these lesser and regional centers was most often downward. The corollary is that the 1950 hierarchy consisted either of long-time leading cities or of places too small in 1750 to figure at all in the ranking. Of course, these endpoint comparisons can pass over intervening periods of eclipse or glory. Brussels dropped from the list in 1800 and rose as high as the seventeenth rank in both 1850 and 1900; yet it ended as it began in the second group of twenty. Stockholm, Turin, and Genoa also left the hierarchy and rejoined it, whereas Rome languished in the second twenty before recovering exactly its 1750 place as Europe's ninth largest city.

While each of these cities has its own history, some regularities emerge regarding "winners" and "losers" in the pecking order of urban size. The eclipse of Mediterranean Europe shows up clearly in the disappearance from the top ranks of Venice (eighth), Palermo (twelfth), and Granada (twenty-third). More unexpected is the modest performance of western outposts from Cádiz to Cork and Rouen. French cities generally grew too slowly to hold their place, Paris always excepted. As for the climbers, or urban supernovas, they certainly include industrial towns and conurbations, from Manchester to Katowice in Poland. But these should not obscure the strong general showing of cities in the later-developing center and east of Europe. Even in 1750 eight of forty lay east of the Elbe river, and the thirteen in the 1950 hierarchy would have been more had not World War II so damaged such cities as Dresden and Breslau (Wroclaw).

Also note that there was a substantial shift in the functional character of Europe's largest cities between 1750 and 1950. At the earlier date political capitals and ports each comprised about one third of the list, whereas industrial towns accounted for fewer than one tenth. By the 1950s port cities such as Leningrad, Cork, and Genoa had failed to keep pace numerically. On the other hand, many more industrial towns and conurbations—for example, Sheffield, Newcastle, and the Ruhr—joined the ranks of the urban giants.[7] Major capitals and multifunctional cities still dominated the top ranks of the urban hierarchy, however. It was the combination of political, service, and industrial activities that produced Europe's metropolises.

The Role of Size and Function

In looking at the top ranks of the European urban hierarchy we were able to note a variety of growth rates for individual cities, along with occasional stagnation or even decline. The very fastest growth rates, however, belong to much smaller places, for the simple arithmetic reason that the larger the size in 1750, the larger the denominator of the fraction from which percentage changes are calculated. But one can still inquire whether growth, on average, tends to be stronger among the smaller or the larger towns, and so whether the spread of city sizes tends to expand or contract over time. It should be recalled that growth here means relative growth, the implication being that large places will normally add more absolute numbers to their population than lesser ones.

Why concentrate so strongly on numbers of inhabitants? Population size is certainly a convenient and natural variable to use in classifying and comparing urban experiences. Beyond this, investigating the relationship of size to growth allows us to set in motion the study of interurban relations, to look at urban arrays and hierarchies in a dynamic perspective. It is a first step in capturing as historians the concept of urban systems, now used largely by geographers in a static way.[8]

If a relationship between growth and size exists, it can be derived from theory or looked for empirically. An abundant literature deals with the question from the point of view of statistical theory, examining the effect of the growth process on the shape of any size distribution over time. The so-called law of proportional effect implies that cities attract population in proportion to their size. A variety of circumstances can bias this result, however. For example, annexation of suburbs or industrial centers by a metropolis or a conurbation, the "birth" of new towns, stochastic or chance disturbances in growth, or a bias in interurban migration in favor of movement from small to large places will all tend to increase concentration. On the other hand, a reversion to the mean, or inverse relationship between size and rate of growth, is also theoretically plausible and is observed in many distributions.

If theory does not settle the issue, what of actual measures? Urban growth in England and France has been investigated in some detail. Robson (1973) plotted decennial growth rates of English towns against size in the initial year of the decade for the nineteenth century. His principal finding was that the variation in growth rates declines markedly from small to large towns. While lesser places can grow enormously or decline, large ones almost always grow by relatively moderate percentages. Moreover, it is striking how rarely they decline. Figure 7.3 shows the central tendency and the band within which most cases are found. Figure 7.3a is characteristic of the early nineteenth century, when growth correlated positively with size. After 1860 average rates became almost uniform for cities of different sizes (Figure 7.3b).

Our examination of the European hierarchy also showed how rarely very large towns declined. If we look at the cities of the 1750 hierarchy in terms of their 1900 population, only eight failed to double their population in a century and a half, and all experienced at least some growth. Only Granada, Venice, and Leiden, each with a total gain of under 10 percent, can really be called stagnant over the period.

Robson's approach has been applied to nineteenth-century France (Tugault 1975; Pumain 1982). The findings are similar to Robson's, except that the positive relationship of growth to size is clear-cut only when the smallest towns—those with fewer than 5,000 inhabitants—are compared with the rest. At least for the medium and larger towns, the law of proportional effect describes nineteenth-century growth quite well. Put another way, the French case shows that there is a size threshold, perhaps 20,000 people in the early nineteenth century, above which no city fails to grow or at least to maintain its size. Among smaller towns, however, many declined (*Le Peuplement* 1973; Lepetit and Royer 1980).

What are we to conclude? There is certainly no evidence that city sizes reverted to the mean during the nineteenth century, with growth working to compress the size distribution. Among small

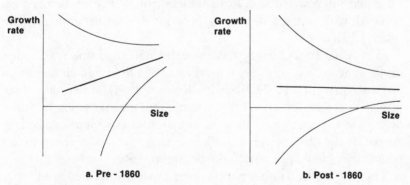

Figure 7.3. Growth and size in nineteenth-century English towns. (After Robson 1973:88.)

places the opposite seems to have happened: a process of selection caused some to grow vigorously while others fell ever further behind and perhaps dropped out of the urban array altogether. If we focus on large towns, the salient result is their staying power, their near-universal propensity to grow. On the other hand, the fact that a large number of lesser places did not share in the overall urbanization process has a wider implication. It suggests that we can easily underestimate the urban character of Europe before the time of industrialization. Relative to our own time, towns were more closely spaced, size contrasts were less blatant, and small towns perhaps less dependent on big ones. As a result, most Europeans could readily experience true urban life even outside the highly urbanized core or the few major towns. This observation should correct the frequently heard point that the line between urban and rural was once very sharp and has only become blurred in our own time by generalized "urbanization."

Urban function is less clear-cut than population size as a way of typing cities or accounting for differences in their growth. Towns house many activities that are not always easy to categorize, for instance, as "productive" or "unproductive." Also, the direction of causation may run from population to employment as well as the reverse: businesses take advantage of a labor force and a market, whereas the promise of jobs draws new migrants. Despite these problems, it is worthwhile asking whether function has systematically affected urban growth, as our focus on the links between urbanization and the evolution of modes of production would imply. Of equal interest is the way in which growth may have been associated with a high degree of functional specialization or with relative balance.

Fairly clear functional types can be distinguished among Europe's urban centers, for example, with the use of a threefold classification proposed by Bird (1977; see also Robson 1981). There are three principal sectors: manufacturing and mining, transportation by water or rail, and services including administration as well as marketing. Actual cities fall somewhere inside the triangular space whose apexes denote complete specialization (see Figure 7.4).

The first point to note is that large cities are located well away from the points; they support a whole range of functions within as well as among the three main sectors. Stereotypes make us forget,

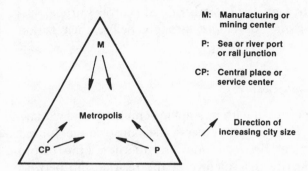

Figure 7.4. The relationship of urban size and functions. (After Bird 1977 and Robson 1981.)

for example, how much industry the capitals of Europe, even Naples in the eighteenth and nineteenth century, supported (de Seta 1982). A corollary is that at least some diversification is a natural concomitant of urban growth. Even Bochum in the Ruhr increased the share of service employment as it grew (Crew 1979). More typical is the grafting of substantial industry onto maritime activity, as in Barcelona, Marseille, or Hamburg. Regional capitals doubled as industrial centers, Manchester and Lille, for instance, and more rarely as major ports. In general, we can discern two functional patterns associated with rapid growth. One is characteristic of industrial settlements, where the very high degree of employment concentration relaxed only slowly. Even though growth was very rapid, sometimes explosive, it tended to reach a ceiling. Moreover, there was relatively little chance of renewing growth once the original industrial base played itself out, as we can see in the cases of Lancashire textile towns and Lorraine mining communities. In the second pattern, growth was favored by functional balance. This is clearly true of the largest cities, those that acquired the designation of metropolis. Especially noteworthy are primate capitals of smaller countries, such as Greece, Portugal, and the successor states of the Habsburg Empire. Like Athens and Lisbon, Prague and Budapest combine administrative, cultural, and financial leadership. But the positive effect of a mix of roles also shows in what we can call the submetropolis, as it developed in central and eastern Europe. Munich, Breslau (Wroclaw), and Lemberg (Lwow) are examples of regional capitals with strong industry and a concentration of transportation routes. In fact, the capitals of east-central Europe, such as Warsaw and Prague, developed strongly before their nations achieved political sovereignty.

The Impact of Economic Change

Too often the factory town with its smoking chimneys and workers' slums has been used to typify the cities of the industrial age. Indeed, the visible connections between cities and the new units of production have given rise to a picture of the relationship between industrialization and urbanization that is more neat and simple than it is faithful to the realities of history. These two phenomena should be seen as related, but distinct, changes. Their interaction cannot be reduced to a two-way accretion of towns around factories and spread of factories in towns. Remember that in the early and mid-nineteenth centuries, Italy and the Netherlands were sustaining and even increasing their high proportions of urban dwellers with little help from an industrial revolution in the usual sense. Moreover, in Switzerland and in parts of northern France, manufacturing was thriving with only slow urbanization. Even where urban and industrial growth were more nearly congruent, as in Germany and England, regional patterns of change show much variation.

While hundreds of new towns had mushroomed early in the West Midlands, west Yorkshire, and Lancashire, urban growth in the industrializing East Midlands was largely confined to the county capitals and market towns, which had been in existence since at least the eleventh century. Economic development in the Ruhr area produced new settlements; yet in central Germany older cities remained the major sites for economic development. Finally, industrialization could displace employment elsewhere, leading to a restructuring of settlement patterns if not to actual deurbanization in regions of economic decline. No simple, direct relationship between urban and industrial growth can explain the diversity to be found across the European landscape.

At a minimum, understanding the impact of industrialization upon urban networks requires us to examine the settlement patterns produced by the three different phases of economic growth in the nineteenth century. By looking first at protoindustrial development, then at coal-based expansion, and finally at the era of the second industrial revolution, we can trace how the linkage of urban and industrial growth changed over time and show that the appearance of new towns was a limited phenomenon closely linked to the exploitation of particular natural resources. The reader will note that this discussion complements Chapter 6's brief look at urban effects of the formation of industrial regions.

As we have stressed in Chapters 4 and 6, much industrial production in Europe before 1850 took place in the countryside as part of a complex division of labor with urban production sites and market centers. This interdependence of town and country before the era of the factory often produced a penumbra pattern of new settlement. The need to distribute materials and to collect finished goods in the absence of mechanized transportation limited the radius of development. Villages near a country town or commercial center grew along with protoindustry. In the environs of Ghent, Leicester, and Berlin, urban merchants put out raw materials into the hands of domestic workers. The hinterlands of Abbeville, Saint-Quentin, Amiens, and Nottingham became more densely settled with rural industrial workers; yet burgeoning villages did not turn into cities. They remained dependent upon older central places, as investments in services and administration lagged behind the needs of growing populations.

Despite the amount of growth in production and employment under protoindustrialization, the impact on existing settlement patterns was therefore minor in many regions. In fact, this was a major economic strength of the system. In Marxist terms, the early capitalists were spared the costs of reproducing labor and its living environment. The weavers of western Ireland usually lived in scattered cottages and small villages; cloth production was a common by-occupation of rural women (Freeman 1957). The early combination of farming with rural spinning and weaving encouraged dispersed settlement, as did the need for wood as fuel for early forges. When the silk industry expanded from the center of Lyon in the early nineteenth century, two sorts of sites were favored. First, suburban weavers' areas were created. Then factories at a greater distance from the city were built along rural streams. But new towns did not result. Units of production were small enough so that factory dormitories could provide housing. Services and supplies came from nearby market towns (Cayez 1981). Growth of the silk trade in the area was accomplished through existing settlement patterns. Even cities closely involved with protoindustry did not always increase their population, let alone their physical size. Rouen, the center of a thriving cotton region, grew only slightly between 1750 and 1850. Ghent's strong, even if short-lived, textile boom during the Napoleonic period required adding neither people nor buildings (Gerneke and Siravo 1980). Only high and sustained growth actively modified the settlement pattern, for instance, in the West Riding of Yorkshire and in the Lille region, where Roubaix and Tourcoing became major towns and textile producers.

The dominant influence upon location became physical power, whether available from an adjoining mine, a waterfall, or an accessible transportation artery. Mill villages multiplied along the upland streams of west Yorkshire (Wild and Shaw 1975). Intensified urbanization outside the confines of an older central place array took place primarily where the combination of technology and coal gave rural sites strong production advantages. There, migration and high fertility rates turned hamlets into villages and finally into towns.

Despite the increasing importance of large-scale producing units, the new industry did not quickly seek out existing concentrations of potential workers. There were good reasons why early factories and older cities remained wary of each other. Urban location raised production costs, from land rents to wages reflecting the expense of urban living. Early engines were too inefficient to operate far from cheap coal. Moreover, political fears of large concentrations of workers settling into the urban community made elites reluctant to welcome modern industry. From the point of view of the entrepreneur, a rural or village location was efficient and cheap. The older towns of a region could easily provide marketing, finance, and other services at a distance. As long as employers were willing to build housing, coal-based settlements were able to grow enormously without massive, early investment in urban services. In newly industrialized regions such as South Wales or the Borinage, specialized settlements were grafted onto older urban hierarchies but did not displace them. Eighty percent of the towns in Wales in 1800 dated from medieval times; the economic development of the nineteenth century then doubled the size of the Welsh urban network (Dodgshon and Butlin 1978).

The geographic limits of this paleotechnic expansion can easily be seen with the aid of a French example. In the department of Pas de Calais new towns arose primarily between 1850 and 1900 along the coal fields. Growth of the mines brought an influx of migrants, who settled in villages and hamlets such as Hénin-Liétard, Bailin, or Bruay-en-Artois. Yet in nearby districts, expansion was largely limited to older centers and their suburbs, around Boulogne, Calais, Saint-Omer, and Arras. Away from the coal fields, migrants drifted into existing towns (*Paroisses* 1975).

Thus, industrial development did not automatically produce an array of new towns. Outside the Alpine regions of adaptable protoindustrial heritage, older towns with their resident labor supplies, markets, and service sectors provided entrepreneurs with decisive advantages. In northern Italy industrial expansion in the later nineteenth and early twentieth century centered upon Milan and two lines of older towns along the railway lines east to Venice and southeast through Bologna to the coast. In the economically dynamic parts of Italy the mid-nineteenth century urban networks constituted a "favorable condition for modern industrialization" (Caracciolo 1981:140). In Sweden, too, where economic development in the later nineteenth century did not depend upon coal, 80 percent of the urban growth between 1840 and 1920 took place in existing cities. Only twenty-five new towns were created during this period, and they accounted for less than 10 percent of the increase in urban population (Ohngren 1981). Even where new towns and mill villages had expanded urban networks, development in the longer run concentrated in the larger places, where railway and business services eased both production and distribution. Growth in the Calder valley after 1850 centered in the towns along the railway—Halifax, Elland, and Sowerby Bridge. While outlying mills closed, housing was built and new firms were founded in and near the towns (Wild and Shaw 1975).

The true merger of industrial with urban growth took place during the later part of the nineteenth century in western and central Europe. The second industrial revolution became established in and near major cities. As new industries moved into southeastern England, London and its hinterland leapt ahead of the north in growth rates (Mitchell and Deane 1962). Other national capitals such as Vienna, Berlin, and Paris attracted a great deal of industry and consequently exploded in size (Thienel 1973; Gaillard 1977). In central and eastern Europe, where capital of all kinds was scarce and the rail network more centralized, the concentration of industry in larger cities was particularly strong. There were large, thriving firms not only in St. Petersburg and Budapest, but also in regional capitals such as Leipzig, Prague, and Breslau (Bater 1977; J. Lee 1978).

If there is one constant in the complex and changing story, it is that the factory town has never adequately represented the urban dimension of the industrialization process. Rather than seeing nineteenth-century urban growth from the vantage point of Bochum or Le Creusot, we should recognize its true habitat: the teeming streets and spreading suburbs of Berlin, Milan, Lodz, and Leeds.

Dual Systems in the Industrial Era

In earlier chapters we presented a dual model of urban systems that served to analyze the origins of European urbanization, as well as the variations in city density and in intensity of urbanization over the Continent in medieval and Renaissance times. The two systems helped account for the uneven growth of cities in the early modern period, when ports, capitals, and some protoindustrial towns expanded during a time of limited general urbanization. We were also able to offer an explanation for disparities in timing between urban activity and visible urban brilliance on the basis of the roles and relationships of cities. It is useful to recall briefly the salient properties of the Central Place System and the Network System, with the reminder that large cities, in particular, tend to participate in both.

Beginning with the notion of a town as the market for a small farming area, one can build up a system of central places or service centers in which large towns function in turn as central places for lesser ones. This nested hierarchy culminates in a regional or provincial capital, itself subordinate to the seat of a sovereign power. As developed by Christaller (1933), the Central Place System has a number of variants corresponding to different urban service functions, which in turn imply particular spatial configurations. Central places house markets, transmit goods and messages, and administer the population of the land around them. All three functions call for a hierarchy of towns, but the fact that each suggests a separate spatial arrangement of subordinate centers around the higher-order one poses obstacles to congruence.[9]

In Europe, central places above the very smallest participated in all three types of service activity, so that actual configurations had to compromise somewhat, and one could not expect, even on theoretical grounds, a pure Christaller model to develop. Moreover, the importance of the several functions could shift over time (Parr 1980). As activity and communications evolve in the course of economic development, one expects contrasting forces to work on the system. A more intensive rural economy should support more market centers of a given size, but the range of goods, and perhaps their minimum market area or threshold, will favor a looser set of central places. Administrative and cultural functions are subject to the same conflicting forces. Rural people come to have closer dealings with the town, as agriculture becomes more commercial and children go more regularly to school, but railroads allow them to bypass the local and county town and deal directly with the regional or provincial capital when the occasion warrants. Still, the basic pattern of smaller and larger towns in regular spacing is likely to remain stable, given the rigidities of geometry and land occupation. Moreover, the central place pattern of interurban relationships is durable: each town communicates with one or two larger places and with a proportional number of smaller ones.

The limitations of the Central Place System leap to the eye if one looks at any map showing the distribution of towns and urban population over larger parts of Europe. Even Christaller's stylized depiction of southern Germany shows departures from the model. Two are most striking: the lineup of major towns along two northwest-southeast corridors (Whebbell 1969), and the clustering of cities near the Rhine. The major towns running in two parallel lines from Frankfurt to Linz (Austria) and from Karlsruhe to Salzburg are much larger and more complex than towns with similar central place ranking located between the corridors. If the urban system were isotropic, as the Christaller model implies, places such as Landshut, Ingolstadt, and Dinkelsbuehl would show far greater centrality than they in fact do.[10] As for the Rhine corridor, it lacks any semblance of geometric order in the sense of widely spaced large towns separated by more numerous small ones. And if one turns away from the agrarian plains of Europe to the regions of concentrated industrial growth, the central place model loses all relevance. Yet these regions accounted for a large fraction of total nineteenth-century urbanization.

Once again, it is necessary to juxtapose a different model of urban development and interaction. Note that we do not, as Vance (1970, 1975) does, suggest discarding a central place model. While both its structure and evolution raise unresolved issues, the model still embodies much that is useful regarding spatial relationships and processes. It simply leaves too much out. The Network System, with quite different properties, complements the Central Place System. Instead of a hierarchical nesting of similar centers, distinguished mainly by the number and rarity of services offered, it presents an ordering of functionally complementary cities and urban settlements. The key systemic property of a city is nodality rather than centrality, whereas hierarchical differences derive only partly from size and more from the nature of the dominant urban function. Control and innovation confer the most power and status, followed by transmission of goods and messages, and finally by execution of routine production tasks. Since network cities easily exercise control at a distance, the influence of a town has little to do with propinquity and even less with formal command over territory. The spatial features of the Network System are largely invisible on a conventional map: trade routes, junctions, gateways, outposts. Finally, the lines of activity, and thus the importance of particular places, shift more readily over time in the Network System. Interurban links are fashioned by the thrust of new ideas and the quest for profits, restless forces compared with the "eternal order of the fields" from which the Central Place System derives.

Long-term changes in the European urban core of the Network System attest to this fluidity. Although the core remained in west-central Europe through the centuries, its focal point shifted: first among Italian cities, then from northern Italy to the shores of the North Sea, and within this restricted space from Antwerp to Amsterdam and to London. Atlantic ports rose and partially fell back, as did Hanseatic towns. The system underwent further change during the industrial period. The juxtaposition of a financial center with the seat of political power proved a potent combination for urban dominance. Close links to industrial concentrations also helped promote the activity of particular cities such as Düsseldorf and Liège. In time, the system core became Atlantic just as it had once located along the Mediterranean and later the North Sea. Cities that were far apart in miles but in direct contact over water shared in and competed for dominance.

Nineteenth-century urbanization, so different in scale and circumstance from what preceded it, poses a strong test for the dual model. We would argue that the Network System concept readily incorporates the vast new industrial and mining settlements, which have no place in the Central Place System. They typically grew without reference to their rural surroundings and failed to acquire functional diversity commensurate with their population. Specialized activity in an isolated location implies strong ties with more distant places, since the industrial settlements remained dependent for all essentials: food, finance, markets, and even people. The cotton towns of Lancashire demonstrate this character, which we can call parochial cosmopolitanism. In the nineteenth century they were more closely linked with the pampas of the River Plate than with the downs of Suffolk. The American Civil War had a greater impact on Oldham and Bolton than the revolutions that swept the nearby Continent in 1848. The English cotton trade began by excluding the products of nimble-fingered Indians and faded in the face of aggressive Japanese imitation. In between, increasing European competition came from people and from towns remote to the Lancastrians: Rhinelanders, Catalans, Bohemians, and Piedmontese; Liberec, Mulhouse, and Sankt Gallen. At the same time, financial and political decisions with serious implications for the region were being reached in the City and in Whitehall: despite their economic strength and sophistication, Manchester and Liverpool grew more, rather than less, subordinate to London. Similarly, the steel furnaces of the Ruhr were fed by iron from Lorraine and Asturias; yet they also drew on Polish workers, Russian wheat, and Hungarian cattle. Meanwhile, the region's larger banks were moving to Berlin. Proximity could not preserve the influence of the old Rhenish financial centers over the region's industry.

Specialization in the Network System was not confined to gritty factory towns. Rail junctions such as Crewe and Vierzon joined river and canal ports and towns at the mouth of valleys as commercially strategic places. The growth of spas and resorts such as Bad Homburg, Cannes, and Ostend added a note of elegance missing from much of the period's urbanization. Favored by the rich and elderly, these cities today attract conferences and festivals.[11]

The stress on urban systems brings out what is perhaps an underrated aspect of recent advances in transportation, namely, increased flexibility. The Network System in the nineteenth and twentieth centuries broke free of the constraints heretofore imposed on it by ports and strategic crossroads. Although many traditional nodes and gateways continued to flourish, the pull of territorial capitals on trade, finance, and enterprise could grow unchecked. With their concentration of power and wealth, these cities commanded the design of the rail networks and later of the motorways, and so secured the links on which future nodality depended. Where once the trade routes and waterways had determined urban locations and roles in the urban network, rail transportation now accommodated the expansion needs of the great cities for both local traffic and distant connections.

To see the Network System in relatively pure form we can turn to Holland. Through the nineteenth century the Netherlands gradually lost special status as a mercantile oligarchy and evolved into a centralized nation on the European model. At the same time, the country was slow to develop factory industry, relying on sophisticated commercial agriculture and the substantial remains of a colonial empire, as well as on traditional financial and commercial expertise. Amsterdam and nearby cities remained the urban heart of the country. The principal new economic stimulus came from rapid industrial development along the Rhine and its tributaries in Belgium, France, and Switzerland as well as in Germany. Two cities rose to challenge Amsterdam's primacy: The Hague as residence of the court and the rentier class and Rotterdam as the port commanding the mouth of the Rhine river system (van Engelsdorp Gastelaars and Wagenaar 1981). They grew from 27 percent and 24 percent of Amsterdam's size, respectively, in 1795 to 58 percent and 77 percent in 1930. That the political capital and the link with the industrial heartland should have grown faster than a city whose international functions and influence were waning is not surprising. But the three Dutch cities did more than achieve balance in size. They gradually joined into an articulated whole that has come to be known as Randstad (Hall 1966). Because Holland is small and because its land has long been actively managed, the network connections assume clear physical shape there. Randstad incorporates a number of other towns—Leiden, Haarlem, and Utrecht, in particular—while limiting the inroads of urban settlement on the scarce stock of fertile land. Given the prevalence of urban sprawl in the twentieth century, Randstad's spatial discipline and well-defined, closely linked cities stand as a bracing contrast to other conurbations such as the French Riviera or Greater London. On the level of function, if not of amenity, the industrial conurbations of Lancashire and the Ruhr were also effectively articulated, as we saw earlier. But in the Network System close links develop between places of complementary function rather than on the basis of distance and demand thresholds, as in the Central Place System.

How do the dual systems fit in with the earlier discussion of urban growth? The Central Place System generally has tended toward primacy, or a positive correlation of growth rate with town size and centrality. On the lower levels small market centers often lost their urban role, administration became more centralized, and the "rare" urban services that concentrate in higher-order centers expanded more rapidly than the small-scale, ubiquitous functions. Rail connections also favored large centers over most small ones (Morrill 1964). To an extent, the simplification of the rural economy and the commercialization of agriculture involved a takeover of some central place functions by the Network System: large-scale agriculture producing for export could bypass local merchants. This further weakened the lower-level central places.

There were exceptions, of course. We have noted that certain rural areas intensified their industrial production while others developed labor-intensive, high-value crops and animal products. In either case, activity in the central places of the region profited. Cottage hosiery production coalesced into larger workshops in the minor East Midland towns. Market centers on the fertile plains of Picardy or Pomerania acquired a beet-sugar refinery, an agricultural

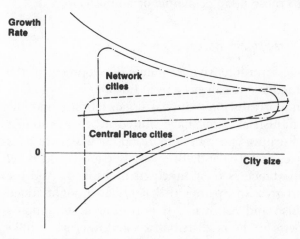

Figure 7.5. The relationship of growth and size in two urban systems.

cooperative, or an experimental station. Yet the trend toward faster growth for larger places extended beyond the region to the national hierarchy. Overall, regions were losing their definition and individuality to the cultural power of the nation, and the disparity in capital sizes reflected this. Bloated primate cities threatened to drain labor, savings, and leadership from the lands they were supposed to serve (Gravier 1972).

In contrast, urbanization along the lines of the Network System accounted for most of the additions to the urban array, notably the fast-growing industrial newcomers. Along with other burgeoning specialized places, they counteracted the central place trend toward primacy and helped achieve the rough size-neutrality of urban growth rates that we noted earlier. Furthermore, even key cities in the Network System did not grow excessively. The argument is summed up in Figure 7.5, a simple schema that builds on the findings of Robson (1973). Growth is proportional to size in one system and inversely related in the other. The largest centers participate in both systems.

City growth is related, therefore, to many things, particularly to function, size, geographic location, and roles in urban systems. While the timing and type of industrialization in an area, as well as the evolution of a centralized state, set the stage for growth in the nineteenth century, the scenario in a given locale depended also on factors more specific to cities than to technological or institutional change. Urbanization has its own dynamics and parameters; they are not reducible to those of an economic or political process.

Urban Systems in Contemporary Europe

The political changes and intensive economic development of the past century have modified urban systems in Europe. New political capitals, public and private international organizations, and the further spread of industrialization have shifted urban hierarchies and integrated the European periphery more closely with core areas of Germany, France, and England. Brussels, Budapest, and Basel have gained in importance as their functions multiplied. And the recent industrial progress of Spain and Poland has brought added prominence to Bilbao and Katowice. It is reasonable to suppose that quite a new pattern of city distributions and interurban links would be emerging as a result of so much change. Yet the new is in some ways very old.

The French geographers E. Juillard and H. Nonn (1976) have proposed a typology of West European regions in the 1970s. Although the specifics of the model do not concern us here, the authors emphasize the spatial distribution of towns by size and activity as well as by the quality and intensity of transportation and communication links. What strikes the historically minded reader is how nearly their results recreate the regional typology that Hechter and Brustein (1980) applied to medieval Europe (see Chapter 2). The contemporary schema also distinguishes three classes of regions, called Rhenish, Parisian, and peripheral, with some gradations and transitional types (see Figure 7.6). Like the old Roman-Germanic core, the "Rhenish" areas are densely urbanized and tightly bound together by transportation networks. A number of medium-sized cities share organizing functions with no one place dominating. This model holds sway from the English Midlands to Switzerland, and it also applies to much of eastern France and parts of northern Italy. The "Parisian" regions, strongly organized by a dominant city but more rural overall than the Rhenish, are recognizable descendants of their "feudal" counterparts. While Paris and London remain archetypes, cities from Vienna to Lisbon fit this model. It is interesting to note that the retardation of northern Italy has displaced it toward the Parisian model. Today Milan dominates the once-proud oligarchy of north Italian cities.

Although far more developed than in the Middle Ages, the European periphery retains its weak urban structure. The industrial concentrations in Scotland, Wales, and northwest Spain have only limited effects beyond a short radius. Agricultural work occupies a larger share of the work force here than elsewhere, and the urban networks tend to be anemic or incomplete. In this context, the Iron Curtain acts as a sort of seacoast, limiting the development of border areas, notably in West Germany.

Even more than in the Middle Ages, the Europe of Juillard and Nonn is defined by its cities. Their size, their activities, and the axes of communication radiating from them imprint the surrounding region. At the same time, the location of a city-region in the larger whole powerfully conditions its development. Through centuries of change, the nature of the urban core has persisted, as has the effect of greater or lesser distance from it.

The weight of history has affected the European Community, or Common Market, designed by dreamers of European unity to break down national barriers to place and prosperity. Since the

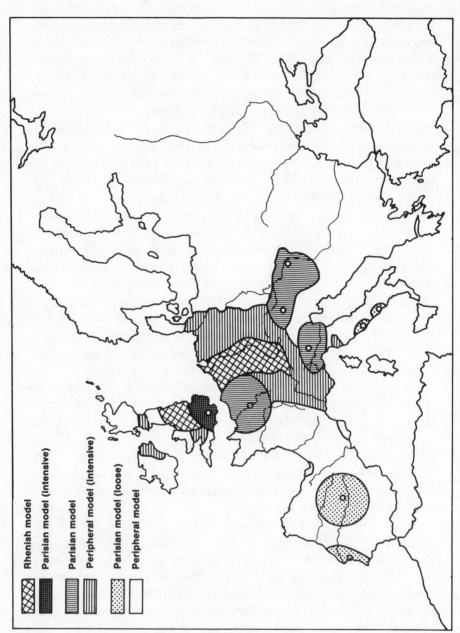

Rhenish model

Parisian model (intensive)

Parisian model

Peripheral model (intensive)

Parisian model (loose)

Peripheral model

state borders run right through the old urban core, lowering them has revitalized the heartland while accentuating the lag of peripheral regions. The Mezzogiorno, the Massif Central, and the Highlands of Scotland have shared only partly in the European economic miracle despite generous economic assistance and well-intentioned planning. Their cities—Reggio Calabria, Le Puy, and Inverness—do not fully receive the stimuli to growth found in the Europe core. Meanwhile, the eurocrats have promoted the influence of older regional centers. Strasbourg with its parliament and Brussels with its international civil service have become focuses of a new urban network that ignores national and even Common Market boundaries. The two cities have close ties to the member capitals, of course, but also to the seats of supranational organizations, such as Basel, Geneva, and Vienna, and to centers of finance and power from Zurich to Tokyo. In the case of urban Europe, change has not overcome the legacy of social and economic differences inherited from the past. Indeed, recent technological and institutional innovations have breathed new life into deep-rooted geographic and cultural forces that have shaped regional and urban processes for centuries.

CHAPTER 8

The Human Consequences
of Industrial Urbanization

IT IS EASY to caricature industrial towns. Their sprawling jumble of factories, railroads, and mines conjures up images of visual and social pollution. Charles Dickens's description of Coketown, a place of "unnatural red and black, like the painted face of a savage" gives a common indictment of the structures of industrial urbanism (1854:30). Patrick Geddes (1915) and Lewis Mumford (1961) argued that the new technology, largely unrestrained by communal planning or government regulation, turned cities into slums and superslums. Moreover, Coketown stands condemned for its psychological and cultural effects, as well as for its degraded environment. Friedrich Engels, who constructed one of the most powerful critiques of urban life in the nineteenth century, saw in the new cities a suicidal style of social relations: "On the one hand the most barbarous indifference and selfish egotism and on the other, the most distressing scenes of misery and poverty. Signs of social conflict are to be found everywhere" (1845:31). Indeed, Engels anticipated that class warfare would break out after a large proletariat was created and then confined in squalid city housing. Both Engels and Dickens, however, looked at atypical places during the early decades of industrial expansion. The textile towns that sprang up like mushrooms in the English north represented only one facet of industrial urbanization. Much more common in the European setting was the vast array of older cities, linked by their central place functions, into which industry moved slowly as economic development shifted from the countryside to urban settings. In any case, protoindustrial towns like Nuremberg, Geneva, Bologna, and Leiden had long been the sites of extensive manufacturing and the home of a large propertyless worker population. How did advanced technology affect these older settlements? To see industrial urbanization only in terms of Coketown is not only simplistic but misleading.

The biggest changes wrought by the nineteenth-century burst of urban growth can be grouped under two headings: increases in scale and heightened density. Each affected the social as well as the physical shape of the city. Ever greater numbers living in ever closer proximity altered the ways people related to one another: rising density necessitated shifts in housing patterns, and increases in scale altered lines of distribution and circulation. Even more importantly, scale and density changed the nature of personal relationships. Size and social complexity are closely correlated. In larger places people become embedded in more intricate networks. They are more vulnerable to forces beyond their control as they need remote groups and institutions to supply food and other services. At the same time, individuals become more anonymous and are freer to move both geographically and socially from the place and the status in which they were born. In this perspective, many of the excesses and much of the suffering can be ascribed to instances in which urban settlements were too dense and/or too large to manage, particularly when an overly rapid pace of local urbanization overloaded the system.

While scale and density are the dimensions on which we focus, their effects were compounded by technological and political shifts that also triggered astonishing transformations of social life. The impact of technological change is the easiest to picture. Steam engines, spinning machines, locomotives, and rotary printing presses rearranged work processes and the allocation of urban space, at the same time as they polluted the air. Work rhythms and groups, travel patterns, and access to information all changed under the pressure of the new machinery. The shift toward production for the market, affecting food and services as well as manufactures, swelled the ranks both of the proletariat—those who did manual labor for wages and had no control over the means of production—and of the middle class of owners, managers, and professionals. At the same time, political changes brought large-scale social repercussions. The "Age of the Democratic Revolution" spread new patterns of political participation and expectations (Palmer 1964). As the right to vote was extended in most European states from

England east through Russia, liberal political parties formed and drew larger and larger numbers of citizens into contests over both power and principle on the local, as well as the national, level. Meanwhile, the development of nation-states throughout most of Europe led to a corresponding growth in institutions and in the numbers of bureaucrats who counted, taxed, permitted, and inspected. The extension of state services required more civil servants who moved out from the capital into the administrative centers of the polity. Cities were therefore the settings where the leaden abstractions of proletarianization, liberalization, and bureaucratization spring to life. In rushing from countryside to town, citizens brought themselves closer not only to the effects of urban growth but also to the workings of both industrial capitalism and the nation-state. Social processes in the city, therefore, are often multiply determined, and care must be taken not to overburden urbanization, or industrial capitalism for that matter, with consequences whose origins are much wider.

Another caveat is that the city is not the only or even the main focus of social action in the nineteenth and twentieth centuries. Nations, regions, and also neighborhoods have been arenas of contention and compromise, with groups and individuals interacting on many levels. For example, a socialist might organize a club in his or her neighborhood, vote for like-minded candidates in a town election, join a countywide demonstration, belong to a national political party. Any or all of these actions might involve working with other socialists in a particular city, but the town's role as a focus for activity would vary widely. Urban structures of all sorts shape individual actions, most clearly at the level of city and neighborhood, but disentangling the effects of urbanization requires that sufficient attention be paid also to a wider web of social change. The trick is to relate urbanization and urban structures to the growth of proletariats and political forces whose shape was determined by forces outside the individual city.

The argument here is that industrial urbanization restructured social relationships, generally by eroding older, multiple social roles and systems of authority and by creating large, relatively autonomous subcultures. Here again, however, the process was not confined to the cities, nor did it typically begin with the move from county to town. Under the influence of agricultural transformation and protoindustrial growth, large rural proletariats were being created or expanded. For them, and also for many in densely populated peasant areas, the structures of traditional society were either severely threatened or lacking altogether. However hard and unfamiliar the urban environment might be, it offered the chance to construct new lives with new webs of relationships, and multitudes grasped at that chance.

As the scale of social life increased, so necessarily did specialization. Already complex urban societies became more fragmented and highly differentiated, while simpler ones evolved in the same direction. Individuals were unlikely, therefore, to develop multiple, congruent contacts with a given set of neighbors and social elites. Whereas an apprentice in medieval Cologne probably had the same person as employer, landlord, elder of the craft guild, and perhaps town councillor, the worker in late nineteenth-century Cologne would not even know many of the people who separately filled these roles. Although the importance of economic divisions within cities grew over time, so too did distinctions of ethnicity, sex, education, and political allegiance. However, nationality, religion, and neighborhood—to name only a few—also served as integrating forces. Depending upon the extent of cultural sharing and the degree of overlapping among the multiple allegiances acquired by individuals, urban populations in the nineteenth century demonstrated very different amounts of social and political integration. Compare the look of Paris in June 1848, when the haves battled the have-nots over the desired shape of the government, to the temper of Blackburn in the 1850s and 1860s, when crowds of workers and their employers marched together to the polls to vote for the same candidates (Tilly and Lees 1974; Joyce 1980). Class divisions existed in both places, to be sure, but their effect on the propensity for conflict at the level of both city and neighborhood varied widely. To some extent, this was again an effect of scale (L. Lees 1982a), but it also derived from the internal structure of the urban population and its cultural coherence.

As these variations in class, community, and culture were played out amid massive increases in city scale and density, we need to look first at the basic demographic processes that produced the distinctive urban milieu. First migration and then natural increase will occupy the center of the stage.

Waves of Newcomers

Like magnets, cities drew thousands of outsiders into their territories. In Hungary, Germany, Austria, and Sweden well over half
the urban growth in the second half of the nineteenth century came
from migration rather than from natural increase. Places like Naples, Rome, Odessa, Prague, and St. Petersburg would actually
have declined in size during the 1860s and 1870s if migrants had
not regularly moved into the city. French cities, too, depended
upon migration to maintain their numbers. Over half of Parisian
growth between 1820 and 1890 came from migration, and the proportion was even higher for French cities as a whole. Comparing
the major European countries, A. Weber (1899) concluded that
immigration was most important for urban growth in Italy and in
France and least critical in England, where high rates of natural
increase meant that cities sustained and increased their own size.
The countries of central and northern Europe were intermediate
cases. Yet the never-ceasing accretion of city dwellers is only one
aspect of the explosion in mobility. Many left cities, too, most often
to try their luck in a larger place or overseas, but sometimes to
return to the village. Europe's cities housed a population on the
move.

The intensity of migration, however, fluctuated greatly over time.
Intermittent catastrophes forced individuals and households to relocate. During famines, pogroms, land clearings, and depressions,
people left their homes en masse. The Irish in the later 1840s and
the Jews from eastern Europe in the 1890s fled by the thousands
to western cities. Millions were dispossessed, particularly in central
and eastern Europe, during the world wars of this century. While
much of this forced migration eventually led overseas, many thousands remained at the large ports and capital cities along the way.
Yet despite the gigantic scale and pathos of these forced movements,
they are dwarfed by the steady flow into the city of short-distance
migrants who chose both the time and place of their resettlement.
This undramatic relocation also fluctuated with the business cycle.
Highest during times of depression and in periods of peak economic
growth, levels of migration decreased with the return of better times
and again with sagging levels of opportunity.

How did people choose where to migrate? Certainly the presence
of kin and friends in a particular place was a powerful incentive to

migrants to join them. And some regions had long-standing links with towns where a recruiting employer or perhaps chance had directed the first migrants in what would become a long chain. But the typical migrant moved only a short distance, and then perhaps moved again and again in a step-by-step pattern from village to town. Short-distance migration roughly follows the levels of a regional urban hierarchy, because people move after accustoming themselves to environments of increasing complexity and distance from their original homes (Ravenstein 1885). Within a Central Place System migration is primarily intraregional—unless the national capital is the destination—and generally does not involve major breaks with kin or with the culture of one's homeland. Indeed, census tallies of birthplaces show that in France, the Netherlands, Switzerland, Norway, and Hungary, at least half the resettlement in the later nineteenth century took place within the county of birth (A. Weber 1899).

Cities of the Network System draw people from a much wider hinterland, however. Just as they drain natural resources from distant places, cities with international connections attract human capital from regions far away, and long-distance migration came to be of great importance during the nineteenth and early twentieth centuries. Transportation routes, particularly steamboats and railways, moved people directly to the top ranks of urban hierarchies. Only the biggest cities, heavy industrial conurbations, and ports had large numbers of foreign residents. Poles flocked into the Ruhr and the Lorraine, and the Irish into Lancashire. Germans moved west into London and Paris. Marseille and Genoa housed migrants from all over the Mediterranean. In general, a city's zone of attraction increased with its size and complexity of function. More long-distance migrants lived in Milan than in Ravenna or Pisa, and more in Berlin than in Stuttgart or Augsburg. Paris drew newcomers from many backward areas of France, people who overleaped local urban hierarchies to reach the capital (Hohenberg 1974). Often, these long-distance migrants were inexperienced in urban ways and had few skills to sell in urban labor markets. Most of the Irish who flooded London and Glasgow as unskilled laborers held only insecure and low-paying jobs. Michael Piore (1979) argues that the dual structure of modern economies produces intensive long-distance migration of low-skilled workers from rural areas to industrial cities. Capitalist production and service trades need not only relatively skilled labor but also varying numbers of unskilled, low-paid workers. Since the better-educated and better-organized native worker can usually avoid these insecure, undesirable positions, outsiders from rural areas generally fill them.

Rural-to-urban migration remained high in Europe throughout much of the nineteenth century, accelerating with industrial development. Over time it changed in character. Much movement by rural migrants into cities was initially temporary, essentially circular in nature. Underemployed people left their farms or villages to earn extra money during the winter and then returned home. Each year thousands of men from the Limousin went to Paris and other French cities for the spring and summer to work on construction sites. Abel Chatelain (1976) has traced this sort of movement in France and found that it increased during the first half of the

Figure 8.1. Shantytown on the outskirts of Berlin, c. 1880. Fast-growing towns found it hard to house the streams of in-migrating workers and their families, and hastily built settlements often sprang up outside the city. These makeshift houses will soon be replaced with enormous barracks-style apartments. (From *Leipziger Illustrierte,* 1875.)

nineteenth century until it involved perhaps half a million people yearly. These temporary migrants were increasingly drawn into the larger cities, into jobs as servants and as street workers or construction laborers. They came from the mountains down to the plains and from the edges of the Paris basin into the capital. Over time they stayed longer and longer, bringing their families once the construction of railways eased long-distance travel by women and children. In Germany the level of internal migration increased dramatically during the later nineteenth and early twentieth centuries, but much of this movement remained temporary and probably circular. Of all the people who moved into Düsseldorf in the later nineteenth century, over half left within two years (Hochstadt 1981), and about half the single migrants entering the Ruhr city of Duisburg during the later 1860s and in 1890 left within a year of arrival (Jackson 1979). In Graz, Austria, which was growing at only moderate rates during the 1880s and 1890s, the population turnover every year amounted to fully 10 percent of the city's residents (Hubbard 1972).

As the rural population stabilized or fell, the amount of European rural-to-urban migration lessened in relative terms, and the exchange among urban areas intensified. In Duisburg the proportion of immigrants coming from urban residences rose from 15 percent to 30 percent of the total between 1867 and 1890 (Jackson 1979). Zelinsky (1971) has noted that as demographic changes lower both birth and death rates and cap the rural population, the shift of people among cities becomes increasingly strong. This mobility transition might well have taken place in England as early as 1870. In any case, surveys of France and England today show that most moves take place among industrialized, urbanized areas. Even in the less economically advanced countries of Eastern Europe, interurban migration is growing in scale. During the later 1960s in Poland and Bulgaria, moves among cities accounted for over 20 percent of all migration (Salt and Clout 1976).

Who were the newcomers to the European cities? Males and females of all ages made the trek into the towns, but most migrants were young, single adults moving in the years before they married. Where impartible inheritance was practiced, children who did not receive land or a share in a family business had to go elsewhere. In any case, adolescent children were expected to work, and if there was no family business or land to employ them, they had to look for a job, perhaps in another place. Girls worked to earn dowries, flocking into the towns to become servants. Laborers with only seasonal prospects in the countryside could find casual employment on city streets. Journeymen artisans in the early nineteenth century tramped from city to city to earn money in a series of urban workshops. Migration was a regular part of the life cycle for many workers, particularly for those whose families had only small amounts of property or land.

But families and older workers migrated, too. The collapse of rural industry could force people to relocate at any point in the life cycle, and whole households would move when threatened with hunger or permanent unemployment. Pogroms, clearings, potato famines, or industrial collapses could literally put everyone in the same boat. During the 1850s a substantial share of the Irish families in London comprised couples who had married in Ireland and had one child or more before moving to England—44 percent of households with children under fourteen in a sample of families drawn from the 1851 census (L. Lees 1979). Also, a substantial proportion of the German migrants to Duisburg in the later nineteenth century were married household heads who brought kin with them (Jackson 1979).

Even when a family could not afford to move together, they often migrated sequentially. Chain migrations were common among many ethnic groups. Kin offered newcomers a place to stay, help in getting a job, and an oasis of conviviality. Those who came early in the chain could finance the trips of later arrivals. Despite the common image of the isolated, rootless migrant, family ties remained very much alive among them. Michael Anderson (1971b) has found that among the industrial workers of Preston, Lancashire, in 1851, migrants were just as likely as nonmigrants to have additional kin living with their nuclear families. About 85 percent of the sampled Irish migrants in mid-nineteenth-century London lived with at least one relative (L. Lees 1979). Not only was considerable contact maintained with relatives in other areas, but urban migrants made real efforts to stay in touch with kin living nearby. Families were active participants in the process of migration. They helped plan and finance moves and they influenced the choice of destination, often adding at least some of their numbers into the migratory stream.

While migrants tended to follow other migrants in well-worked-out patterns, the nature of an urban labor market also affected who went where. Mining towns and ports drew proportionately more males, whereas women were more plentiful in textile towns and in capitals and provincial centers with a large middle-class population. There was also an important movement by white-collar workers and professionals into the bigger towns and cities. Just as a town's physical zone of attraction increases with its size, so too does the social range of its appeal. National and regional capitals offering a range of commercial and administrative services drew a more varied group of migrants than did small market towns. Moreover, since professional training, civil service jobs, and virtually all advanced education were to be found in cities, a large part of the middle class, as well as those aspiring to rise into this group, had to move into the larger towns. Towns also exercised a differential appeal according to their functions. Among a sample of Irish who came to the United States in the 1890s, about half the merchants and white-collar workers had lived in Dublin, Belfast, or London just before emigrating. Most of the rest came from other medium-sized Irish towns such as Cork, Dundalk, or Athlone. Their transatlantic move was a shift from one city to another, a relocation that had probably been preceded by other moves. Over a third of the skilled Irish workers leaving the country had spent time in a manufacturing town such as Bradford, Manchester, or Belfast. In contrast, the emigrating servants and laborers bypassed the urban hierarchies of both England and Ireland, stopping in Liverpool only to catch a ship (L. Lees 1982b). Barbara Anderson (1977) has shown, in a study of migration into Moscow and St. Petersburg in the late nineteenth century, that newcomers were more likely to have come to Russia's major cities from areas with relatively high literacy and a lower dependence on agriculture than from the least modernized regions. Common metaphors for migration—the "drift" into a city or the "flow" of people from place to place—fail to capture the purposeful element in the process. Individual moves were directed by many constraints: stage in the life cycle, kin, occupation, place of origin, the business cycle. Together they created a nexus for choice, one that in the nineteenth and twentieth centuries led inexorably toward the cities of industrializing societies.

Living and Dying

The challenges posed by the city for these new urbanites were many, but none was as fundamental as the threat posed by migration's demographic consequences. As people mobbed into the towns, density rose and with it urban death rates. Rural life expectancy at birth was considerably higher than urban in both Belgium and the Netherlands during the mid-nineteenth century (W. Lee 1979). In England in 1841 males lucky enough to be born in rural Surrey lived on the average until age forty-four, whereas those born in London would reach a mere thirty-five years of age. The unfortunates whose families had settled in Manchester survived only to twenty-four years (Glass 1964). Throughout Europe urban death rates regularly exceeded rural ones during most of the nineteenth century, although A. Weber (1899) found no consistent relationship between mortality and either city size or the proportion of the population in manufacturing jobs. The most lethal places varied in type from country to country, although city dwellers were more at risk everywhere. In Prussia and Denmark during the 1880s and 1890s, the largest cities had the highest death rates (A. Weber 1899), but the unhealthiest English towns were the industrial centers of Lancashire and Staffordshire, not London.

Most of the appalling gap between urban and rural death rates was produced by differences in infant morality, because the vulnerability to infections of children under one year was relatively high. The dirty chaos of industrial urbanism bred just those conditions that permitted many diseases to flourish. Contaminated water carried typhoid and diarrheal infections, and there were few safeguards against adulterated or spoiled foodstuffs. Damp, dark apartments and severe crowding allowed airborne diseases such as tuberculosis, influenza, and pneumonia to spread unchecked, and the young were particularly susceptible. Lacking even sound theories of disease transmission, public health officials were virtually helpless, notably against the epidemics of cholera that periodically swept through European cities during the nineteenth century.

Over time, as improvements in the urban environment and medical knowledge lowered the incidence of communicable disease, urban death rates decreased—first among adults, later among children, and last among infants. Vaccination decreased the incidence of smallpox, while more effective isolation techniques hindered the spread of diphtheria and typhoid. Sewerage and water supply systems lowered the risks of cholera and diarrheal diseases at the same time that better diets improved resistance to contagion. Meanwhile, city officials struggled to improve housing and restrict overcrowding. No one has yet disentangled the varying contributions of technological and environmental changes to the lowered death rates, although McKeown (1976) argues powerfully that improved nutrition saved far more lives than did medical treatment well into the nineteenth century.

Big cities and national capitals in several countries led the way in this reduction in mortality, which took place earlier in northern and western Europe than in the south or east. National governments cared more about their capitals, and money was more easily forthcoming there for the massive investments that proper sanitation required. At a time when Paris had already built new water and sewerage systems, the Marseille population still drank polluted water from the Durance River. In consequence, the Mediterranean port was the site of the last big cholera epidemic in France in 1884, at a time when death rates in Paris had already fallen (W. Lee 1979; Pinkney 1958). Improvement in urban death rates began in central Europe before 1890. Indeed, in Austria and in Bavaria urbanites had a higher life expectancy than did their country cousins by the later 1880s (A. Weber 1899). Even in southern and eastern Europe, where demographic change set in more slowly, the major cities were far less deadly in 1900 than they had been a century before. In the long run improved life expectancy more than equalized risks between the urban and the rural environment. By the later nineteenth century towns shifted from being killers to being net producers of people.

Urban fertility made little contribution to the shift from a negative to a positive vital balance in cities. Both before and after the demographic transition—which we can date from about 1870, France's premature fall in fertility aside—urban fertility was lower than rural in virtually every time and place for which good data are available (Sharlin, in press). In developing the story of urban fertility we need to focus on a number of points. First, its relative weakness is surprising, since the age structure and social conditions of nineteenth-century cities would appear to favor rather than hinder reproduction. Second, the ongoing deficit of births in towns relative to the countryside masks a sizable transition in both. Third, the difference cannot simply be attributed to urban residence as such. Changes in attitude and circumstance stemming from large-scale social and economic transformation stimulated both urbanization and falling fertility. As much as anything, cities were the channels through which attitudes were translated into new norms and these widely diffused. Finally, it need hardly be said that there were exceptions, and that puzzling gaps in historians' understanding remain.

The population growth that fueled urbanization took place principally in the countryside. After 1750 or so, increased opportunities for protoindustrial and agricultural employment led to relaxation of social controls on fertility. People married younger and in larger numbers (Braun 1960; Levine 1977). Where high fertility is observed in urban settings in the nineteenth century, it was associated with particular occupations, notably mining, or with recent settlement. In other words, the protoindustrial pattern could carry over to towns, but only for a time. In the mining towns of the Pas-de-Calais (northern France) studied by Philippe Ariès (1948), legitimate and illegitimate fertility were highest during the phase of initial immigration, when the settlements included few older people and lacked institutions to control behavior. As the inchoate villages matured into towns with a wider range of ages, a variety of associations, and a more settled standard of living, the abundant sexuality of earlier days was restrained. Similarly, the proletarians of suburban Paris rapidly curbed their fertility once settled into their new habitats.

As we have noted, urban migrants tended to be young and new urban milieus were incompletely organized. Why, then, was fertility lower than in rural districts, except in a limited number of mining and textile centers where job opportunities were particularly conducive to early marriage.[1] In Germany, for instance, John Knodel (1977) has shown that both the marriage age and the proportion of single persons were higher in towns than in the countryside. City dwellers married later than rural residents in France, and Parisians married latest of all (A. Weber 1899). Both examples, by the way, refer to the 1880s but reflect older patterns. One element in the answer is that nineteenth-century urban fertility might not have been low in absolute or historical terms, but only relative to the high levels of the protoindustrial countryside. Another point is that the social effects of industrialization did not make themselves felt in many towns until late into the century. The traditional communal controls on fertility continued in place, notably the large numbers of servants and others who typically married late or not at all.

Recent studies of fertility in Belgium, Germany, Switzerland,

Hungary, and Italy show that birth rates began to decline in cities around 1870. But this time the controlling factor was no longer marriage but the fertility of couples. As early as 1871 marital fertility rates in northern and central Italy were significantly lower in cities of over 100,000 than in smaller towns and rural communes (Livi-Bacci 1977). Similar differences have been noted in Switzerland, France, and Russia. However, Knodel's (1977) work on Germany serves as a caution against too sweeping a conclusion. He found that residence alone explains less than 10 percent of the variance in marital fertility, suggesting that cultural norms determining demographic behavior were widely shared within a region, inside as well as outside its central places. Interestingly, J. P. Bardet (1974) found a similar ecological pattern while studying fertility in eighteenth-century France. Still, we cannot escape the conclusion that significant numbers of city dwellers began to limit family size, in the later decades of the nineteenth century, by means other than postponing marriage.

We know too little about past sexual practices to speak with any confidence to the whys and hows of the drop in fertility. Nor is there reason to think that the diverse ethnic, religious, and occupational groups that made up urban Europe were governed by uniform norms for marriage, sexuality, and contraception. Of course, the population could in theory have come from groups with lower natural fertility, just as urban women might have lengthened the time of postpartum amenorrhoea by longer breast feeding, but what we know of migration patterns, wet-nursing, and infant death rates suggests the opposite bias relative to rural areas. So we must take it as given that couples chose to limit the number of their children and were able to implement the decisions. Such behavior was by no means new in European urban history. The Venetian and Genevan upper classes limited their families in the seventeenth century (Henry 1956; J. Davis 1975). In England the upper and middle classes led in the restriction of births, apparently responding to economic conditions. Changes in the social economy of European cities in the later nineteenth century provided economic motivation for large groups to follow the lead of their social betters. Even for workers, children became more costly as school years replaced work years. Residential space was dear, and cities offered tantalizing immediate uses for discretionary income. The push was stronger still in petty bourgeois circles, where dwelling and dress had to reflect aspirations to respectability but only harsh family discipline could preserve the necessary property.

Environmental considerations were not the only ones shaping demographic behavior. Land-owning French peasants were just as careful to limit the number of heirs as any chief clerk or mercer. Also, people no doubt began to think more in terms of completed family size as child and infant mortality declined. Everywhere, laws and institutions responded to changing modes of production by encouraging more intensive investment in the individual child. Perhaps the only prudent conclusion is that social and economic transformation interacted with cultural norms to reshape urban demographic behavior in ways we understand only imperfectly.

The same sort of caution must be used in relating the increased level of illegitimate births to urbanization in nineteenth-century Europe. High rates of illegitimacy were not universal in cities—many large ones, particularly in England, retained the low extramarital fertility characteristic of early modern Europe—nor confined to them. Regional differences remained important, and the rural transformations of the protoindustrial period occasioned sharp increases there as well. As for the cities, the familiar image of the seduced female, abandoned in the metropolis to bear her child alone, is true enough as a vignette, but it will not serve as a summing up. While French and central European cities had many babies born out of wedlock, they also housed large numbers of single women and men. Also, the urban location of foundling homes and lying-in hospitals drew pregnant women to bear, and sometimes to abandon, their babies. Beyond these qualifying points, however, is the larger fact that illegitimacy changed its meaning in early industrial society. One cannot analyze the frequency of births out of wedlock without taking into account the biases and rigidities of institutions and dominant values. A spectacular example is the case of German towns in the early nineteenth century where authorities forbade marriage for large numbers of workers (Shorter 1972). Elsewhere, many workers neglected to get the stamp of church or state approval for their unions, perhaps to save the fee, given that they had no property to bestow on their children in any case (Tilly and Scott 1978). Both Villermé in the 1840s and Bertillon in the 1880s noted large numbers of common-law marriages in major French cities and judged that these unions were stable, differing little from their legally recognized counterparts (Villermé 1840; Duplessis–Le Guélinel 1954). What proportion of urban workers lived without benefit of clergy is not known, although it seems likely that the rate of free unions increased, at least in western and central Europe in the early and mid-nineteenth century. The key is that the meaning of illegitimacy differed in middle- and working-class culture. What brought social disgrace in the one setting was relatively common and accepted in the other. Finally, illegitimacy rates paralleled those of marital fertility. The sharp increase in illegitimacy that took place after 1750 was reversed by the general decline of fertility in the second half of the nineteenth century. Increased illegitimacy was a temporary phenomenon linked to the first and second phases of industrialization (see Chapter 6). It was another indication of the fact that the process of transition to the industrial city, rather than urban life itself, was disruptive.

Life in the City

The idea that cities affect social relationships is a common one, but debate rages over the results and their moral significance. Disgust with urban social problems has prompted countless critics to link cities to crime, disorder, and deviant behavior. Tennyson, in "Locksley Hall Sixty Years After," charged that "There among the glooming alleys, progress halts on palsied feet / Crime and hunger cast out maidens by the thousands on the street" (1911:566). Louis Wuarin, a French economist, deplored the rush into the city by rural laborers because in front of them lay a "thousand traps set for vanity and sensuality . . . that quietly lead the victim into the abyss" (1900:887). Moreover, he thought that cities, replete with "vagabonds and criminals who form a sort of secret society in order to thwart the power of the law," had a polluted moral atmosphere. Sociologists, too, have joined the chorus of those predicting dire results from urban residence. Park (1928) and Wirth (1938) both thought that urban life brought with it mental instability, loneliness, and alienation, as well as an increase in pathological behavior. Chevalier (1958) in his compelling study of nineteenth-century Paris linked crime, suicide, prostitution, and mental illness to the hordes of people crowding into the capital. High density and poverty, he felt, deformed social life and turned respectable workers into dangerous lunatics. The city became sick because of intensive migration.

There is little evidence to support such charges and much to discredit them. Their most obvious flaw is that the rural term of the comparison was almost never based on fact. In castigating the city, the poets and publicists, and even the physicians and social scientists, followed Rousseau and invoked a bucolic past with little real content. Certainly their vision of rural communities bore no relation to the situation of protoindustrial proletarians, share-cropping peasants, or laborers on large estates—in other words, to many millions of rural Europeans. The judgments also erred in re-lation to the urban scene, not least because they gave too much weight to the middle-class concern for outward respectability. While it is impossible now to probe the psyches of a fair sample of nineteenth-century urbanites to discover how or whether they felt alienated, we can look at different types of behavior and ask whether they are more prevalent in urban or rural envi-ronments.

Let crime be the test case. Studies of both Germany and France during the nineteenth century show that there was little or no systematic relationship between urban growth and crime rates (Lodhi and C. Tilly 1973; McHale and Johnson 1977). Moreover, crime rates in Germany between 1885 and 1912 show only weak corre-lation with the incidence of divorce, suicide, and illegitimacy. The notion that moving into a city disorients individuals and so far removes them from social ties that they turn to crime or self-destruction must be rejected. It is also not true that violent crimes against individuals, such as murder or infanticide, have been more prevalent in urban areas. Only theft and other crimes involving property can be linked to cities, and these connections change over time. In Prussia before 1880, for example, the rural districts of the east were the settings for the highest rates of property crime. Not until after 1900 was there a close correlation between levels of urbanization and rates of theft. Perhaps attitudes toward stealing change over time with social mores and the composition of city populations. Perhaps different levels and styles of policing residents affect the propensity to steal, as well as the system of reporting theft. Note that these arguments are less concerned with cities themselves than with other structures that shape social life. Notions that cities per se tempt citizens into lives of crime are naive and untenable.

Industrial urbanism did change society, but in ways not easily labeled either good or evil. As the size of residential units increases, they become more complex. People in small settlements see one another repeatedly in a variety of roles, whereas in large cities they interact in more superficial, partial ways. Their neighbors might not be their co-workers or members of the same church, union, or club. Each person has multiple contacts, who need not know one another. The networks of social life tend to be fragmented rather than congruent (Berreman 1978). As a result, individuals are less visible and accountable. Social control becomes more impersonal and bureaucratized, while chances for individual mobility increase. Also, setting aside systemic differences, the larger a city, the more diverse its populations. Vienna had more Poles and Portuguese, Muslims and Jews, musicians and nerve doctors than did Graz. And there were enough of each to create subcultures based on ethnicity, religion, or occupation. Large cities bring together the critical mass of similar people needed to found communities. While the Irish in small Leicestershire villages were forced to blend in with the native English, those in Glasgow began Catholic churches and clubs, building communities around their ethnic loyalties. In fact, Claude Fischer argues that "the more urban a place, the more intense its subcultures" (1975:1325). Large cities, in his view, produce strongly articulated value systems rather than isolated individuals. They are not melting pots, but mosaics of disparate groups, each of which fights to maintain its own identity. At first glance, this view of cities is puzzling, for how can a place be both impersonal and culturally intense? How can an individual be both anonymous and closely involved in a specific subculture? The answer is that cities contain both large-scale and small-scale environments (Berreman 1978). Although in public places—the stores, offices, streets, and large institutions—contacts are relatively brief and anonymous, there is a separate, private social life to be found on the level of family, neighborhood, club, and ethnic group that operates with different rules. There, social identities are personalized and longer lasting—multiple rather than fragmented. Aside from the occasional fair or election-day ritual, urban social life in recent times is not a mass phenomenon. It rests on the smaller social worlds created by citizens around units that matter to them.

The most fundamental of these units remains the family. Living alone was not a common practice in nineteenth-century cities. Married couples usually had a child within a year of marriage, and most adolescents remained with their parents until their late teens or early twenties (Wall 1978). Where they went next depended upon local employment possibilities and the structure of local housing, but likely destinations were the home of kin, the residence of an employer, or a lodging house. Migrants commonly lived with married children. In fact, the complex family was an important urban phenomenon in the nineteenth century. In England its incidence increased with industrialization. The tiny urban households of the present are the joint products of the demographic transition and of rising standards of living, whose full impact was felt only in the twentieth century.

Households also expanded beyond the bounds of kinship. The upper and middle classes regularly had servants in their homes. Over a quarter of all factory workers and laborers' households in Preston, Lancashire, in 1851 included boarders (M. Anderson 1971b). Young women in French cities, particularly in the garment trades, often boarded with their patroness, and mid-nineteenth-century London workers in sweated trades sometimes lived with their employers (Mayhew 1861–1862). Complex households were therefore common at all ranks of the population.

The kinds of bonding that extended households beyond the ranks of parent and child were expressed in many more subtle ways than coresidence. Married children could live near parents and maintain a close relationship. Kin acted as welfare agencies, supplementing the inadequate help of church, state, and charities in the early phases of industrial capitalism (M. Anderson 1971b). Whether from custom, calculation, or conviction, city dwellers remained attached to the bonds of family. The isolated urban citizen, cut off from family and friends, is a caricature brought to prominence by urban sociologists whose fields of vision were so vast that they overlooked the homely ties of neighborhood and kin. Adult women played particularly important parts in maintaining extended families. Since wives with children, at least in England, France, and Germany, tended to work not in factories but at home, they had the most time to spend with relatives. Wives who kept house made it possible for relatives to board in their household. Older women took care of nieces, nephews, and grandchildren while parents worked, and they provided the extra services needed in times of illness and family emergency. Besides, they were carriers of the tales, news, and gossip that kept memory and concern alive.

Urban work patterns reinforced the nexus of kinship and neighborhood. The need to live within walking distance of one's job, and the lack of public transportation for any but the well-to-do until late in the nineteenth century, produced districts within cities where a high proportion of the families had the same trade or worked at the same factory. The Croix Rousse section of Lyon was dominated by silk workers, and London's silk workers settled in Spitalfields. Most of the file workers of Le Chambon–Feugerolles had homes in one district of the commune (Hanagan 1980). While many of these enclaves of craft workers were destroyed by urban growth and shifts in economic organization, others were created by similar processes of change.

Despite high rates of geographic mobility, local communities developed even in the largest cities. Although workers in London moved frequently, they moved short distances, remaining for the most part within a territory where they were known and where they could get credit at local shops and jobs with local employers (L. Lees 1979). Urban growth brought into municipalities outlying areas with distinctive social and economic networks that did not disappear after incorporation. Some of the larger Lancashire textile towns were congeries of separate factory villages. Ties to a mill went beyond residence to particular clubs and political parties (Joyce 1980). Housing styles reinforced these communal ties. The lack of private supplies of water and individual toilets, combined with the small size of workers' apartments, forced people into public spaces tenanted by neighbors. Children played in the streets and in alleys and courtyards, while adults escaped to local cabarets, pubs, or *Gaststätten*. In high-rise tenements all used communal stairs.

The bonds of work and neighborhood were reinforced by those of ethnicity and sometimes religion. The Irish, after they immigrated into England, lived in streets or courts where other Irish settled (L. Lees 1979). The presence of a Catholic church nearby cemented a parish social life built around church schools and voluntary associations. Central European cities had their Jewish quarters, and Poles moving west into the Ruhr and into France regularly lived near migrants from their own districts (Wehler 1961). In Paris in the first half of the nineteenth century, migrants from the Massif Central clustered around the Hôtel de Ville and Les Halles (Ariès 1948). As late as World War I migrants to Paris from mountainous and semimountainous departments congregated together. Although

Figure 8.2. Workers' neighborhood in central London. Side streets and alleys were among the few neighborhood centers for crowded urban workers. Many Irish migrants lived in Wild Court and Great Wild Street, shown in this drawing from 1854. The inhabitants work, play, and congregate outside whenever possible. (From *The Builder*, November 12, 1854.)

the degree of separation declined as the size of groups increased, migrants from the Massif Central, Brittany, the Pyrenees, and Alpine areas still chose to live near others from their regions, often near the relevant railway terminal (Ogden and Winchester 1975).

But congregation could only be partial. Especially in large cities, so many outsiders arrived that each group had to share its territory, learning coexistence with neighbors. Rather than ghettos, modern cities produced subcultures, groups of similar background and socioeconomic status who remained partly isolated, partly linked to the larger society.[2]

The Contrasts and Complexities of Social Class

Overarching the divisions of subculture and neighborhood were other ties that bound citizens together and separated them from other groups. Most notably, class and culture arranged the social mosaic into recognizable patterns. Over time in Europe, the progress of capitalism created classes by providing separate social and economic roles for those with large amounts of property and those who lived by the labor that they sold in the marketplace. Owners and workers, who had contrasting relationships to the means of production, acquired vastly different amounts of power, wealth, and status. To be sure, the numbers who commanded small amounts of financial or human capital, and so fell between the social poles, helped to bridge the gulf between rich and poor. Also, individuals retained significant roles other than those conferred by the labor market. As a result, class structure was frequently complicated or blurred by the existence of other hierarchies. Moreover, its ideological weight varied depending upon the intensity of class awareness within a community as well as upon conjunctural conditions. Nevertheless, industrial capitalism gave economic divisions added social force. By the mid-nineteenth century, class was an active molder of urban society.

Class structures varied from place to place, depending upon the shape of the local economy and the position of older elites and groups. Table 8.1 provides elements for comparing the class structures of several English manufacturing towns and London. Every-

Table 8.1. Class structure in four English towns, 1851 (percent of employed population).

Occupation	Northampton	South Shields	Oldham	London
Capitalists, professionals	5	3	3	4
Shopkeepers, small masters, clerks	26	18	14	19
Artisans	11	23	19	40
Semiskilled, domestic service	43 ⎫ 57	40 ⎫ 57	51 ⎫ 64	25 ⎫ 36
Unskilled	14 ⎭	17 ⎭	13 ⎭	11 ⎭
Unclassified	—	—	—	2

Sources: Foster (1974:76); L. Lees (1973:424).

where the elite of capitalists and professionals was tiny, but a substantial and varying share of white-collar workers, shopkeepers, and small employers swelled the bourgeois ranks. Moreover, in towns like London and South Shields, many artisans either owned property or had some expectation of doing so. Significant numbers of craft workers in the mid-nineteenth century were still on the fringes of the middle class. While some had fallen into the ranks of sweated wage workers, others rented substantial houses, could vote, and had a fair measure of both independence and security. The group was in a transitional state in mid-nineteenth-century England, some destined to become entrepreneurs and some to move their children into white-collar positions, while others would sink into the proletariat (Crossick 1978). The unskilled and semiskilled, who comprised only about a third of London's work force but nearly two thirds that of Oldham and South Shields, were virtually all propertyless wage workers whose lack of economic power generally went along with political impotence and limited education.

Major differences distinguished the social structure of the metropolis from that of Oldham, a cotton-spinning town in Lancashire. Oldham had a relatively small middle class. Ownership of its textile factories was concentrated in a few hands, and the town did not have a large group of either administrators or professionals. Most people in Oldham were factory workers or laborers (Foster 1974). In contrast, London housed thousands of civil servants, barristers, and rentiers, not to mention the intermittently resident gentry and nobility. Besides the relatively large and diversified elite and petty bourgeoisie, the city had an abnormally large proportion of artisans, who ranged from the prosperous to the poverty-stricken. Domestic servants, wage laborers of a special sort, comprised a large share of the semiskilled. A capital city with much production but few large factories, London maintained an older style of employment well into the nineteenth century. Its proletariat remained divided among several socially distinct categories. Finally, Northampton represents the service center or central place city beginning to industrialize. The proportion of proprietors, rentiers, and professionals was high, that of artisans had sunk very low. The structures of two German manufacturing towns, Barmen and Bochum, demonstrate the social effects of industrial capitalism in relatively clear terms (Table 8.2). At the beginning of the nineteenth century Barmen was part of a protoindustrial textile-producing region, while

Table 8.2. Male social structure in German industrial towns (percent of total male employment).

	Bochum		Barmen	
	1858	1907	1861	1907
Capitalists	1.6	0.3	1.4	1.4
Merchants, manufacturers	5.4	3.1	2.2	5.7
White collar, civil servants	4.7	9.2	2.5	11.0
Artisan masters	3.2	4.1	4.3	6.6
Craft workers, lower-ranking salaried employees	6.5	4.6	11.0	4.3
Proletariat	78.5	78.7	78.5	71.0

Source: Crew (1979:19). Copyright © 1979 by Columbia University Press; reprinted by permission.

Bochum remained a small market town, populated by merchants, farmers, and a few artisans. By the century's end, over 70 percent of the adult males in both cities were wage laborers. Owners constituted only a tiny part of the population. Over time, however, the growth of service jobs and administration produced a substantial group of white-collar workers. In addition, a small proportion of the artisans managed to maintain their status as independent manufacturers. They and the salaried employees formed a lower middle class, bridging the gap between the very rich and the economically insecure. Owing to its regional role and industrial mix, Barmen retained a somewhat more diverse composition with modest growth in the proportion who derived at least some status from their occupation. By contrast, Bochum kept its very high share of proletarians.

Note the direction of change in the urban population. Karlheinz Blaschke (1967) has calculated that in the towns of Saxony in 1843 dependent workers (*Inwohner*) made up 52 percent of the labor force. Clergy and nobles constituted less than 1 percent, while the remainder were full citizens (*Bürger*) who owned property and had some control over the means of production. If Bochum and Barmen represent the effects of industrial capitalism, it dramatically increased the proletariat in German cities. Much of this growth resulted from the migration into towns of rural proletarians, a group that had been exploding in size but went back in the east at least to the later sixteenth century. In the towns themselves, the continued development of large workshops and factories opened up more jobs for wage laborers. C. Tilly (1979) estimates that the number of urban proletarians in Europe increased from approximately 10 million in 1800 to about 75 million in 1900, but he argues persuasively that the gigantic size of this group arose more as a result of natural increase than from progressive expropriation. It is clear, at least for England, that proletarians had relatively high fertility and that they lowered their birth rates later and more slowly than did artisans and the middle classes (Innes 1938). During the course of the nineteenth century, therefore, the European urban proletariat came to dominate many city populations.

Marx predicted a dire future for this group under industrial capitalism. Economies of scale and appropriation of surplus value, he argued, ensured that capital accumulated faster than the need for labor power. As a result, proletarians manned a reserve army of workers that kept down wage levels for all. Only in the longer run would they escape misery by transforming the economic system through revolution. This scenario, which entailed growing class consciousness and class conflict, pictured proletarianization as a one-way process. People moved into wage labor and stayed. Yet recent work on social mobility raises some problems with this interpretation and helps to show why many workers did not see the necessity to fight to overturn the capitalist economy.

Overall, of course, few changed from penniless laborer to captain of industry. The need for capital and advanced education was simply too great to permit those on the bottom to rise to the top. Especially in heavy industry and in textiles after the adoption of expensive machinery, the cost of starting a business limited entry largely to people from propertied families. Industrialization did not automatically permit high rates of upward social mobility, of course. In a few industries, hosiery, for example, skilled workers had regular chances to become small manufacturers and perhaps eventually large ones (Erickson 1959). Yet even though textiles were a relatively unconcentrated industrial group, no more than a minority of workers in any trade attained nonmanual jobs or independence during their lifetimes. Michael Anderson (1971b) found that about 6 percent of Preston textile workers between 1840 and 1850 became self-employed. In Rotterdam between 1850 and 1860, only 7 percent of workers moved into nonmanual jobs (van Dijk 1973). These rates, however, if continued over the thirty or so years of a worker's career, could produce a sizable amount of movement in the absence of backsliding. Just half of Bochum's skilled metal, construction, and wood workers in 1880 remained in the same occupation twenty years later; almost 20 percent of those in metalwork or the building trades and 30 percent of those working with wood or leather took up nonmanual jobs (Crew 1979). In the Siemens firm, foremen and work managers were commonly drawn from skilled employees. A majority of Ruhr mine inspectors came from miners' families (Glovka Spencer 1975). And about one third of the French and English female servants surveyed by McBride (1974) saved enough money for a dowry to be able to marry someone of a higher status than their parents. On the one hand, opportunities for individuals to improve their position *within* the working class were not uncommon. On the other hand, a growing employee class provided alternatives to proletarian status that depended on control of human rather than financial capital.

A pessimistic view of workers' chances for upward mobility must be qualified, therefore, in three major ways. First, skilled workers and those of a "labor aristocracy" had far better prospects for upward mobility than did their unskilled cousins. Not only were they better educated, but they were more likely to accumulate the capital necessary to start a business. Moreover, prospects of becoming a foreman during times of great industrial expansion were not rare, and the chance to find white-collar or technical jobs increased further during the twentieth century. Second, workers' male children were not unlikely in fact to move into nonmanual jobs. Around 20 percent of workers' sons in Copenhagen in 1850, 26 percent in Västeras, Sweden, in 1880, and 45 percent in Esslingen, Germany, in 1870 took up white-collar occupations (Kaelble 1981). While rates of social mobility clearly varied over time and place, the expectations of children were not bounded by their parents' situations. Several studies of European cities reveal higher intergenerational mobility rates than those found for North American towns like Newburyport or Hamilton, Canada (Kaelble 1981). Third, research on social mobility often depends upon incomplete records and uses rather crude measurements. Movement into more secure jobs, the accumulation of savings, a shift into better-paying, more pleasant work are all missed by judgments based upon occupational titles.

All sorts of minor achievements, missed by most mobility studies, could affect status within a community as well as the life chances of children.

The notion that social mobility was possible for oneself, or at least for one's children, took some of the sting out of class divisions. So, too, did the fact of geographic mobility, which allowed people to try again in a different setting. Even Irish street sellers who found in Liverpool some irregular work, schools for their children, and poor relief from the parish could count themselves better off in England than starving at home. Studies of three Swedish cities show that people who moved had twice as much chance to rise socially as did the sedentary. In fact, almost one third of all working-class migrants surveyed in the early twentieth century moved into white-collar jobs, while almost two thirds of migrant unskilled laborers moved up in the working class (Åkerman 1977). Swedish workers were not trapped in a culture of poverty, but through migration had substantial opportunity to change jobs and upgrade their family's social status. There were many sorts of proletarian futures, not all of them bleak.

The Marxian model of increasing capitalist concentration was no less ominous for the traditional middle class of independent producers and traders. Even if they escaped proletarianization, they faced a powerless, dependent future in the service of the great enterprises. Certainly, the pinched shop assistants and sweated "artisans" in nineteenth-century cities were a pale caricature of the merchants, guild masters, and other proud burghers of old. Moreover, the offspring of the bourgeoisie had to compete with property-tied rural migrants and with ambitious working-class youths for the positions that promised status or opportunity. Fortunately, the industrial system proved to have an enormous need for skills and initiative, especially in the third, and most urban, phase of industrialization. We have seen that fast-growing German industrial centers increased not only the number but the proportion of middle-class jobs in the second half of the century. Also, the large towns in which new enterprises and influential positions were concentrated more than held their own in terms of growth. We cannot know, of course, precisely how the competing groups fared in the race for advancement, but established urban families could launch their offspring with appreciable advantages in terms of schooling, connections, savoir-vivre, and capital. We do know that in the late twentieth century old families are still heavily represented in the schools and universities where the supposed meritocracy recruits its cadres (Ringer 1979). Even their less successful offspring manage to find places in the larger bureaucracies—diplomacy and banking, for example—where style counts as much as substance. We shall see that the middle classes gained political voice with a vengeance in the twentieth century. In the meantime, it is clear that the expansion of the middle classes proved strong enough to cushion the decline of many whom capitalism elbowed aside, as well as to take in the clever and ambitious poor.

Class Culture, Mass Culture, and Subculture

Class divisions, however they were perceived and judged, were reinforced by cultural differences. Dress, leisure activities, accent, and sometimes language distinguished elites from the masses in nineteenth-century Europe. P. Burke (1978) has argued that by the nineteenth century the largely unified popular culture of preindustrial times had disintegrated. Elites contracted out of communal rituals and sports, finding threatening and crude the celebrations that they had formerly enjoyed. Even if Burke's assumption of early unity is rejected, the division between the cultural world of the masses and that of the elite was well advanced by 1800 in the regional and national capitals of Europe, and it deepened thereafter. The larger cities were the homes of the European "Great Tradition" (Redfield 1955). Their universities, cathedrals, and libraries, their artists, musicians, and wealthy citizens constituted a milieu that kept alive the high culture of the past and supported its continual enrichment and eventually its renewal. These older cultural forms were quickly adopted in newer manufacturing towns as they grew and developed an upper middle class. The affluent residents of industrial towns imitated citizens of the older, more prestigious cities and founded their own schools, museums, and libraries. If no medieval town hall or cathedral graced a central square, a modern equivalent complete with stone carvings, leaded glass, and oil paintings could easily be commissioned. As Manchester grew from a village to the commercial center of the cotton industry, it acquired an orchestra, a college, a literary and philosophical society, public libraries, and a museum of nineteenth-century art (Briggs 1963). Barmen developed an active musical culture, and after 1850 a theater opened and several literary and scientific discussion groups were established (Köllmann 1960). Nineteenth-century cities nurtured an active middle-class culture. Restaurants and men's clubs multiplied in central districts. Theaters, concert halls, and opera houses drew elaborately dressed audiences to evening performances. Middle-class women found outlets for spare time and energy in lending libraries, charitable societies, and church groups. Museums, zoos, and even botanical gardens offered tastes of the exotic. These pastimes were designed for those with some leisure and extra cash. While workers were rarely excluded formally, standards of dress, costs, and hours of operation in practice excluded most of the urban population. In Zola's L'Assommoir the laundress Gervaise and her friends make their first and only trip to the Louvre on her wedding day.

In contrast, the social world of urban workers revolved around the pub and the street instead of the club and the concert hall. Workers developed alternative cultural forms from the inherited wisdom of the past and the experience of the present. European cities had their own "little tradition" of urban folklore, saints' days, parish feasts, and occupational subcultures. It drew continuing vitality from many sources: surviving communal festivals and fairs, the routines of work, the newly invented rituals of early trade unions, as well as importations from the countryside. For example, manufacturing towns in England had their parish wakes and summer fairs. Guy Fawkes Day brought bonfires and the parading of crude effigies. The pre-Lenten celebration of Carnival continued in many Spanish, Italian, French, and south German towns. Its parades, plays, and masking were the high points of the ritual year. Patron saints' days were still feted by craft workers in France with parades, dances, and fireworks, and May Day still produced decorations of flowers. Lille textile workers continued their yearly festival of le broquelet (Pierrard 1965). The ritual calendar of workers in early industrial society was certainly not as rich as that of their counterparts before the Reformation; yet it included many celebrations other than the Christmas and Easter holidays. In both Protestant and Catholic areas, churches kept alive a round of feasts and public occasions that drew more than the regular worshipers.

Below the level of elite society in the towns there flourished a local sociability that linked people of similar age, sex, occupation, and neighborhood. Workers from a particular craft or street chose

nineteenth century in clubs and societies for virtually any purpose (Lidtke 1974; Meller 1976). While many were joined primarily by members of the middle class, others had a definite popular appeal. The Young Men's Christian Association provided recreation rooms and sports. Most English towns had their sections of Band of Hope, a children's club that offered entertainment in return for a pledge of total abstinence from alcohol. Founded in Leeds in 1847, it counted three million members by 1900 (Roberts 1971a). Churches organized football and cricket clubs or opened recreation rooms. Political parties founded ward clubs in the 1870s and 1880s to attract the support of new voters. The membership of many of these groups crossed class lines by combining skilled workers, shopkeepers, and other elements of the lower middle class. Religious clubs, in particular, softened the social divisions of industrial society.

A new cultural capitalism found in the new mass culture an attractive outlet for entrepreneurial energy, and its success helped blur the distinction between elite and workers' culture. The Crystal Palace exhibition and the succeeding Universal Expositions in major capitals attracted people of all ranks. Large European theaters sold tickets at several prices, thereby including the poor but restricting them to the top balcony. The new dance and music halls drew middle-class as well as working-class patrons, and the appeal of professional sports substituted gender for class lines from the outset. Moreover, as both literacy and workers' incomes increased, those who aspired to social mobility or who valued education for its own sake could use the growing number of public libraries and museums. This mixing narrowed for some the gap between the elite and mass cultures, largely through a linking of the lower middle class and the more highly paid, skilled workers. While the world of the beggar, prostitute, thief, and semiemployed laborer continued its distinctive ways on the fringes of town society, public culture for the respectable expanded around commercial recreation, churches, schools, and city institutions. One result may well have been a dilution of political radicalism. G. S. Jones (1974) notes the success of London music hall managers in excluding songs of serious political and social criticism, and he blames the spread of an innocuous, commercial culture for British workers' retreat from socialist ideals.

While the social changes of the late nineteenth century did not lessen the differences of wealth and income that separated the rich

Figure 8.4. Shopping gallery in Milan. Among the many nineteenth-century innovations in larger towns were department stores and shopping arcades. Cast iron and glass are used here to enclose a large, light area arrayed with tempting goods for the shopper. With its cafes, restaurants, and artificial lighting, the Victor Emmanuel Gallery has become a social center for Milan's middle-class consumers. (Personal collection of P. Hohenberg.)

and the poor, they did dampen many of the cultural differences that threatened to become extreme in the preceding period. Rising incomes along with the mass production of consumer goods helped to standardize life-styles. The great urban department stores on the model of the Bon Marché had their mail order departments and, later, provincial branch stores that spread middle-class styles and furnishings all over the land. In France, the army drafted sons of the poor, often taught them French along with basic skills, and showed them a bit of their country. Once off the farm they found it easy to make the move into towns to become civil servants and other sorts of urban workers (E. Weber 1976). An even stronger impact was created by universal primary education, which spread in Prussia in the eighteenth century, in France after the Guizot laws of 1834 and the Ferry reforms of 1882, and in England after 1870. A literate population spoke the same language, could read the same newspapers, and could be reached by the political propaganda of major parties. Indeed, fascist regimes in Germany and Italy during the 1920s and 1930s used sports, clubs, parades, and mass meetings to solidify loyalties to the government and nation (Mosse 1966; De Grazia 1981).

But those times of flamboyant cultural unity, which temporarily overrode divisions, disintegrated with the regimes that produced them. In complex industrial societies, culture is not homogeneous for all regions and ranks. Much is shared, to be sure, and the unifying effects of language, political loyalties, and consumer goods are considerable. Yet mass and national cultures coexist alongside many subcultures. Within the cities, people are stratified by occupation, sex, age, neighborhood, religion, and place of origin. Urban culture constitutes a mosaic built from the differing values and life-styles of Catholics and Jews, natives and newcomers, prostitutes and pensioners. Class is only one of many dividing lines that separate people into social worlds.

While national cultures contended with smaller-scale affinities, they also interacted with the larger developing system of modern Western ideas. The competitive, sometimes acrimonious, interplay and spread of these traditions brought into play the urban ties we have attempted to model in this study. The dual urban systems have an important cultural role. In the nineteenth-century context each could be seen as the vehicle of progress and the guardian against obscurantist or dangerous trends conveyed by the other. On one level, the Central Place System serves a homogeneous people well settled in its historical lands. The national capital distills and formalizes the common folk culture and reinjects the civilized product back into local life. Thus the urban system helps unify and modernize the society with a minimum of cultural dislocation. The contrast in this picture is with the rootless cosmopolitanism of the Network System, with its sharp cultural discontinuities between city and country and between core and periphery.[3] Colonial rule is the classic case. Core values and techniques are superimposed on a traditional periphery with no attempt at integration or gradual synthesis. Indeed, the small and distant core power must, as a practical matter, rely on controlling the existing social system. Think of the disparity between Holland and the East Indies or England and India.

Yet there is another side to the story. For centuries the European Network System nurtured and propagated the free ideas of humanism, enlightenment, and radical thought. Forbidden books were published, and persecuted thinkers and leaders found refuge, for instance, in Amsterdam and Geneva. Karl Marx wrote in London while Lenin bided his time in Zurich. Cultures have also been enriched by cross-fertilization from the time that Arabic/Jewish science and Tuscan cooking spread northward. In the nineteenth century Paris welcomed German musicians and later Catalan painters, just as London had feted Haydn and Van Dyck earlier. In the economic sphere the Network System cities were home to colonies of Levantines, Jews, and Greeks, who typically worked in the very trades that carry network links: shipping, banking, brokerage.

If network cities have been more than the vehicles of soulless capitalist exploitation, it is also true that the Central Place System has failed to fulfill all the aspirations of territorial communities. The national culture it diffused was often alien to some people and regions, so that the leadership of the capital amounted to suppressing local languages and traditions. Examples are embarrassingly numerous, beginning with the "nationality questions" that agitated political life in nineteenth-century Europe from Ireland to the polyglot Habsburg Empire. Elsewhere, the resistance to cultural centralism has surfaced more recently. The Welsh, Bretons, Basques, and Macedonians, among many others, have forced the world to notice them. Even when linguistic differences are subtle, the national culture can weigh on the identity of Geordies, Saxons, or Gallegos, who serve mainly to people the ethnic jokes at which the capital laughs. Certainly it is no accident that cultural chauvinism has been such a fixture of authoritarian regimes in Europe.

The Location of Protest

Common problems disturbed urban and national polities during the last two centuries. New distributions of political and economic power had to be arranged. But how much would each be shared by its hereditary keepers? As absolute kings and emperors gave way to representative governments, who would actually rule? Who would decide how work was to be organized? How would the material fruits of technology be distributed? While cities were only indirectly the prizes in contests over political and economic power, they were one arena in which organized groups struggled to impose their point of view. Cities had their own political parties, trade unions, and branches of national reform societies. Locally elected mayors, town councillors, and police helped set the rules of the game for demonstrations, elections, meetings, and strikes. Not only did cities group together the raw popular material for protests, but as the sites of industry and government, they housed the symbolic focuses for action. To take over a town hall, people had to march in town. Only there could they find the officials, the journalists, and the employers whom they needed to impress. French workers seeking to force political and economic changes built barricades and marched on city halls in 1831, 1834, 1848, and 1870. English citizens seeking universal suffrage paraded through London streets in 1848 and rioted in Hyde Park in 1886. Protests against food taxes in 1886 and against the arrest of socialists for their political activities in 1898 brought the Milanese outside to demonstrate (L. Tilly 1972b). And one need only recall the urban centers of revolution in Russia in 1905 and 1917, the street battles of Fascists and Socialists in Bologna in 1920, and the clashes of Communists and National Socialists in Berlin in the early 1930s to note that urban spaces have remained a battleground for political differences.[4] Of all areas of France, the big cities had the highest rates of participation in collective violence during both the mid-nineteenth and the mid-twentieth centuries. About 75 percent of the violent incidents in Germany between 1850 and 1913 broke out in cities, even though less than half the population was urban at that time. Strikes are also urban phenomena (Shorter and Tilly 1974; McHale and Johnson 1977). In modern times, mass movements are located in towns.

Not all urban areas mount similar challenges to the status quo. Collective actions vary in strength over time and among regions. The numbers of demonstrations, meetings, and strikes rose in English, French, and German cities during years of intense political conflict and then subsided. But even in times of mass mobilization, not all became equally involved. Compare the parades of Parisian workers in June 1848, which produced several days of bloody street battles, with the relatively placid response of Bordeaux proletarians when faced with the same political challenge. Although thousands of workers struck and Chartists marched in the towns of Lancashire and Yorkshire, those living in the urban East Midlands mounted few demonstrations and almost no strikes in the spring of 1842 (L. Lees 1982a). Collective political action was greater in certain sorts of places.

Scale has clear effects upon the ability of people to mobilize. It brings together a critical mass of those willing to act in common, and it forces them to articulate their aims in the face of competing groups (Fischer 1975). The thousand people who might care to campaign against vivisection in Berlin would form a more powerful and prominent lobby than the ten in Landshut with similar concerns. Cities, because they attract a more diverse and larger population, abound with parties, clubs, and reform groups; and there are more organized interests in Amsterdam than in Breda, in Vienna than in Graz. Organizations set the framework for collective actions in the nineteenth and twentieth centuries (C. Tilly 1972). To effect large-scale protests, people must be mobilized, money must be raised, information must be shared. These are quintessentially urban services. The linkages of the Central Place System and the Network System are ideally suited for the transference of people and ideas. Places at the top of urban hierarchies are therefore particularly important sites for mass movements. In England and in France, major political campaigns commonly began in London or in Paris, then spread to provincial capitals and finally to smaller towns. Revolutions broke out in capital cities like Berlin, Vienna, and St. Petersburg near the seats of power and then were echoed in other cities where only local elites had to be dispossessed. Scale and centrality shaped both the location and the transmission of political movements in recent times.

Urban social structure also exercises a determining influence on the siting of mass movements. Not all populations are equally ready to protest or to organize. Foster (1974) has shown that the English textile town of Oldham developed a radical workers' movement during the early nineteenth century, while the port and mining town of South Shields developed a nonmilitant, nonconfrontational style of politics. His explanation of this difference rests in part on class structure and class consciousness. In Oldham divisions between the bourgeoisie and the lower ranks of society were deep, and workers had little chance for upward mobility. Artisans developed close ties with laborers through intermarriage and residence in mixed neighborhoods, thereby furthering class solidarity. But in South Shields class divisions were far weaker. A multiplicity of occupational groups, each with pride in its own work, developed. Artisans cared for craft more than class, and they had the chance to become small masters by accumulating capital. As a result, artisans and laborers remained socially and politically distinct. In a study of three French industrial towns, Michael Hanagan (1980) has also linked different amounts of worker militancy to the internal structure of the proletariat. Artisans, who were the best organized, mobilized when their skills and their control of the work process were threatened by technological change. Industrial workers, who had fewer unions, were less likely to strike during the mid-to-late nineteenth century. In the Stéphanois region the towns where artisans allied with metalworkers had more strikes than those where the artisan trades had collapsed. Industrial workers, who were not well-organized, needed the stimulus and aid of their craft neighbors to mount effective challenges to the owners. Strong socialist movements in the later nineteenth century relied on the solidarity of craft workers with factory hands and miners.

The combined effects of scale and class structure can be used to distinguish styles of urban social action in England and Germany in the nineteenth century (see Figure 8.5). In many small towns, particularly the market centers of the Central Place System, class lines were weakly drawn. People knew one another in a variety of contexts other than the economic one, and their social identities were compounded from many factors. The strength of a lower middle class, when added to the important role of the clergy and gentry, further masked class divisions. In addition, xenophobia and isolation combined to mute participation in larger political struggles. Mack Walker (1971) has described the social life of German "home towns" where acceptance of the primacy of communal membership, mistrust of wandering strangers, and self-righteous hostility toward the outside bred internal solidarity. Moreover, market towns had too few people to create effective political groups and unions. The handful of individuals in Leicestershire settlements interested in socialism during the 1890s had to travel to the county town to join a chapter of the Independent Labour Party. The best organized unions in the East Midlands had their headquarters in Leicester and Nottingham, not in Ashby de la Zouch or Melton Mowbray (L. Lees 1982a). Where small scale combined with weak

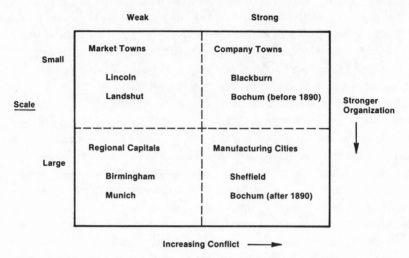

Figure 8.5. Social action in industrial society: an urban typology.

class divisions, the incidence of protest as well as mass mobilization in national causes were likely to be low. Social life was fairly sleepy and organized around activities that cut across class lines. Churches, fairs, schools, and families provided important bases for activity.

A second style of social life could be found in small-scale communities where class divisions were deep but controlled by paternalistic employers. Let us look at factory towns. Joyce (1980) has described a paternalist style of social relationships that could be found in the smaller industrial towns of Lancashire and Yorkshire. The growth of large firms produced deep economic divisions; nevertheless, the presence of resident employers and the close linkages among factory, neighborhood, and social life bred solidarity among owners and workers. Employees were encouraged to think of their firm as a family and to take part in an active cultural life provided by the company. Instead of protesting, workers tended to vote for the boss's candidates and to celebrate his triumphs as their own. Similar examples can be found in Germany where company housing and paternalist social welfare schemes dampened trade unionism and strikes. Within factory neighborhoods people had complex social identities. Face-to-face contacts with employers in churches, clubs, and in the firm blunted the effects of income inequality and made it less likely that an individual would challenge the prevailing order. Protest was both visible and not likely to succeed.

The nature of political life in large cities differed considerably from that of both market towns and company towns. The effect of scale upon the ability to organize has already been discussed. However, cities with large administrative and service sectors, such as regional capitals, offered many white-collar jobs and lower-middle-class positions. Minor amounts of social mobility within families and between generations blurred class lines. When large size is combined with weak class divisions, a complex but often nonviolent style of political life results. People organized, but not along class lines. Many political groups united artisans and lower-middle-class members; cooperation displaced confrontation. Particularly where occupational structure was dominated by crafts, labor consciousness, rather than class consciousness, was found.

In large cities dependent upon heavy industry or textiles, class divisions were deeper than in regional capitals. Where control of the means of production lay in relatively few hands and workers had only limited chances to rise socially, the lines of class were clearly drawn. Compare Sheffield with Birmingham. D. Smith (1982) has shown how the south Yorkshire iron and steel town had in the early nineteenth century a strong working class, which maintained an active neighborhood life cutting across craft lines. Although the increasing scale of the town and growth of new, segregated neighborhoods divided the working class, conflict continued as a small elite of steel producers came to power. Militant artisans and metalworkers engaged in a series of major strikes that periodically paralyzed local industries up through World War I (Pollard 1959). Birmingham, in contrast, had a much less strongly articulated class structure. A wealth of separate occupations and a complex division of labor split workers into tiny categories, while the relatively large number of commercial and service jobs supported a sizable middle class. In addition, professionals and businessmen joined workers in a variety of political and welfare groups. Cooperation in producing social change, rather than conflict, was one result. Here strikes were less frequent and on a smaller scale than in Sheffield. In these West Midland towns, when issues of religion, taxes, and education triggered dissent, divisions cut across social classes.

The Sheffield style of labor militancy can be seen in major German industrial towns. Bochum, which in the mid-nineteenth century operated like a company town run by the Mayer and, later, the Baare families, became too large by the later 1890s for older paternalist styles of social control to be maintained. As the proletariat grew and settled into the city, workers' solidarity increased, too. A series of large and violent miners' strikes broke out as unions formed late in the century (Crew 1979).

National capitals present a mixed record of collective action. They combine great scale with complex divisions of labor. On the other hand, several of them—particularly London, Paris, Berlin, and St. Petersburg—deserve recognition as major manufacturing towns. Where the mode of production gave rise to large firms and concentrated ownership, class divisions were both deep and obvious. The presence of a national government in a city stimulated political activity. Petitions, demonstrations, and speeches could have a more influential audience in Paris than in Lille or Toulouse. Especially when political regimes resisted giving workers and the lower class representation, the result was likely to be collective action in the form of violent conflict. The populations of Paris between 1830 and 1860 and of Berlin between 1850 and 1913 had higher rates of participation in collective violence than did citizens of the major French and German provincial capitals. And the level of political activity in the capitals was great. Therefore, scale coupled with strong class divisions seems conducive to political mobilization, and in the presence of a national government the result can be explosive.

During the 1920s and 1930s, Europe underwent a terrible polarization that was fought out on the streets of many capitals before plunging first Spain and then most of Europe and the world into war. Already by the turn of the century it had become evident that the power of the organized working class was growing. Living in large concentrations, they were able to add substantial political representation to the traditional weapons of direct action and strikes. Yet the interwar conflicts revealed the development of militant right-wing movements, also urban in large measure, that proved fully a match for the proletariat (Mosse 1966). Without trying to untangle the social dimensions of fascism, we need to reconcile the polarization of these urban societies with our earlier argument about the relatively nonconfrontational character of political divisions in large Central Place System cities. Why the violent conflicts in Paris and Vienna, Berlin and Budapest? The answer, we suggest, is to be found in strong threats to the capitalist and national economic order that radicalized the urban petty bourgeoisie. Clearly, they had long been concerned to protect the property and other advantages they had acquired. At the same time, old and new elites were eager to enlist them—along with rural citizens—against the red tide of socialism. In the cultural realm this alliance proved susceptible to currents favoring a turn away from urban, industrial civilization toward older values rooted in nature and folk. However, none of this crystallized into militant action until World War I brought about the breakdown of the international system of trade and finance. Fascist mobilization can be traced directly to economic, and especially, monetary crises. Extraordinary pressures brought about heightened levels of conflict where groups were already well mobilized.

To sum up, the scale of urban settlement strongly conditioned the effects of class relations. By promoting organization, larger places were more likely to see conflicts surface. However, they also furthered alternatives to violent protest in the form of cooperation, bargaining, and political competition. Increases in scale influenced political cultures as well as the forms of social life.

CHAPTER 9

The Evolution and Control
of Urban Space

BY THE END of the nineteenth century citizens could look in awe
at the physical transformation of European settlements. Cities appeared to grow not by the year but by the hour. Massive expanses
of brick and granite engulfed formerly green fields, and miles of
new houses and apartments lined narrow streets. What had capitalism wrought? How ought we evaluate the results for individual
cities of the massive wave of industrial urbanization? Had Blake's
vision of dark satanic mills transforming the landscape come true?
These questions are not only of historical importance but are relevant to our own day when morphological changes are again in full
swing, and we desperately need to know whether market forces
can be relied on, in the main, to guide the process suitably. Although the European past is twice removed from the American
present, it offers evidence even if no simple answers. Could the
economic transformation have proceeded with less or better urbanization? Would more control of land use, or less, have improved
the result or made the process more benign?

These are difficult questions. It will be instructive to approach
them from a theoretical as well as a historical perspective, and to
ask whether the allocation of urban land can be expected to conform
to the general presumption, central to Western economics since
Adam Smith, that the free market guides self-seeking individuals
toward socially efficient decisions. This question has received surprisingly little attention from urban economists who have instead
attempted to model the actual pattern of land use. Yet Koopmans
and Beckmann (1957) have argued that the market system could *not*
be expected to yield an efficient and stable pattern of land use even

under the usual assumptions of ideal functioning that economists make. If they are right, we have an additional explanation for the severity of urban problems in the industrial age. As was true of technology, the economics of capitalism were more effective in promoting urbanization than in coping with it. In this perspective, the various checks to the free market, from archaic ordinances to modern monopoly power, may have been saving graces rather than obstacles to progress, achieving or preserving many valuable but "unprofitable" features to the townscape.

Let us try to outline the issues. In theory, the competitive market works by rewarding the owners of a productive resource according to the value placed by some element of society on the fruits of that resource. The maximizing owner is thus motivated to put the resource (that is, labor or land) to its socially most valued use and to husband its productive capacity. Prices effectively transmit the signals that guide decision making. The model works more or less adequately in the case of agricultural land, regulating the choice of crops and rewarding the preservation or increase of natural fertility. But urban land derives its special value from no intrinsic quality but only from its location. Moreover, the location is purely relative, deriving from the potential interaction of activities carried out there with others taking place elsewhere. Put another way, an urban parcel commands a *site rent* that reflects its accessibility. In modern cities, large yet still relatively monocentric, accessibility means nearness to the center. In a market system, the use of the parcel is auctioned off to the highest bidder, and the value of the land capitalizes this maximum income.

Now for the problems. Whenever a given parcel changes use, presumably in response to profit opportunities in the existing spatial configuration, every element of that configuration is potentially called into question. The effect is probably small in most cases and may reinforce past decisions, but it can also hasten other locational changes and fuel a process of ongoing instability. As Conzen (1978) puts it, there is a perpetual tension between changing needs and the townscape inherited from the past. Many observers have noted that cities never seem finished. In addition to actual construction, there are always both projects for the future and land uses that cry out for change: bottlenecks, blighted areas, land under-, over-, or misused. Although often attributed to growth or external change, this tendency toward instability and disequilibrium is arguably inherent in the workings of the market. It seems to exist even when no overall growth of population drives the processes of "outward extension and internal reorganization" (Smailes 1968:87). It is also easy to see that settlement on the edge of the built-up area decreases the desirability of urban, as compared with suburban, locations by thickening the layer that blocks access to the rural areas. And as the city spreads out, decay at the center is hastened by the increasing traffic mileage that lower density generates. Finally, it cannot be doubted that the shifting nature of locational decisions in the long term reduces the incentive to make major durable investments, since they are subject to locational obsolescence as well as to the other kinds.

The physical problem has a counterpart in value terms. Rewards to the ownership of urban land are unrelated to the activity undertaken there, but totally responsive to what happens elsewhere. All urban land ownership is, in this sense, speculation; every land-value change is a windfall. Moreover, as our discussion of some major efforts to change urban land use will show, public projects are hampered because the need to compensate those whose land is taken or loses value is not matched by the ability to recover fully the private gains from public investments.

The logical failure of the market can be put another way. A given land-use pattern in a city or a large urban district is effective or ineffective for all. The spatial configuration is a system, or a *public good*, whose logic is not congruent with that of the individual elements. But if decentralized decisions coordinated by the market cannot be relied on, will collective action do better? We cannot give the prize to the second contestant after seeing only the first. Certainly, coordinating decisions on a large scale allows many "external" effects to be internalized (Scitovsky 1954). Cities have been most strongly marked by changes that had to be made on a large scale, from extending the walls to removing them, from cutting a new street to developing a large estate. Great decisions mean the opportunity for big mistakes; yet the errors of one generation may be the opportunities of another. To take Paris as an example, the walls built in the 1840s lost their value for defense but allowed circumferential roads to be built later. Grandiose boulevards built to glorify a ruler or preserve his authority serve modern traffic needs. And the market of Les Halles, so long an anachronism in central Paris, outlived the period of mindless infilling to yield some much-needed public space.

The challenge for any system of decision making is to achieve functional, efficient, and visually harmonious spatial design—no mean task in itself—while respecting the legacy of the past and retaining flexibility for the inevitable changes to come (Blumenfeld 1967). For this reason we shall examine the particular decisions that shaped nineteenth-century cities with sympathy and an open mind. To paraphrase Dr. Johnson, it was not always done well but one is amazed to see that it was done at all.

Covering the Land

The spread of cities over the land in nineteenth-century Europe was both a relatively simple and an enormously complex phenomenon. On one level, we can sum it up quickly: endless new streets lined with houses, interspersed by factories. Overlaid on this rather formless "block" structure was the network of rail- and waterways with their junctions and installations (docks, stations, yards). The infrastructure required to service all this—water and sewer lines, later gas and electric conduits—as often as not was added after building, rather than planned beforehand. The dominant idea seemed to be to minimize the "waste" of space for common and unprofitable uses while nevertheless assuring a low, though rising, standard of health and decency.

This capsule description cries out for qualification and nuances, and these will begin to suggest the complexity that is the other face of physical urban expansion. For a start, factories and houses never monopolized the urban "build," even in the districts and neighborhoods they dominated. However minimally, service needs were met: some churches, shops, civic buildings, theaters, bathhouses, and market halls graced all but the most forsaken areas. Drinking establishments, poor men's clubs, came earlier and remained more numerous than any other facility, ranging from a cellar room to a large and showy corner establishment. The "public" house, the cafe, and the beer hall came to be the most characteristic, widespread, and relatively lavish adornment of every European urban setting. On a larger scale, an entirely distinctive type of land use developed in the center of larger towns: the central business district, a beehive by day, a desert by night.

As a result of variations in the layout of streets, the blocks between them also showed great differences. In small or narrow blocks, every house could face the street. Otherwise, internal courts, lanes,

Figure 9.1. Below and above ground in Paris, c. 1850. At mid-century, Paris already boasted an elaborate subterranean infrastructure in central areas. Street drains (A) and manholes (B) lead into the sewers, while underground drain-pipes (D) carry off waste water from houses. Large gas (N,O,P,R) and water (E,H,K,L) pipes provide service to houses whose occupants choose to purchase the service. Note the gas lamp on the left; lighting of the main streets at city expense was provided after the 1820s. (From Texier 1851, II:235.)

or passages were necessary. Sometimes a whole world lay screened from the street, picturesque or sordid, idyllic or menacing.[1] A major distinction, of course, divides the low-rise houses characteristic of England and northern Europe generally (Scottish cities and Berlin excepted) and the high-rise buildings to the south. We shall return to this somewhat puzzling dichotomy. However, building heights were not the only determinants of density. In general, the larger the city, the more densely packed its inhabitants, who were thus doubly deprived of fresh air and accessible space. But the principal variable determining individuals' control over space was increasingly their socioeconomic status. Direct as well as indirect command over space, the amount of light, air, and privacy around the dwelling as well as its actual size, came to constitute an economic good, like cheese or boots, to be "consumed" according to one's means, taste, or station. Here, too, there were nuances: rich and poor households were larger than those of the middle class, because of their propensity to include servants and lodgers, respectively. Some people, perhaps some cultures, attached more importance to the dwelling as an element of one's life-style than did others. The bourgeois apartment of late nineteenth-century Paris shows this factor at work in a complex way. Desiring a relatively favored location as well as a maximum of appearance relative to their means, this class sacrificed everyday comfort. Whereas the "reception" rooms at the front were as grand as could be managed, the bedrooms and service areas huddled darkly at the back of the building.

That the rich should be housed better than the poor was nothing new, of course. It was the careful rationing of space by price that marked a real change. As Vance (1976) points out, the very concept of housing as a service or commodity, unconnected with employment and offered by professional builders or landlords, was itself quite new. Most novel of all, and quite characteristic of the capitalist city, was the social and economic importance that came to be attached to the location of a dwelling, to its setting in a particular district and neighborhood. No longer were the names of urban areas, usually the old parishes or villages, merely aids to orientation. Now they had a clearly normative content. A neighborhood was good or bad or subtle shades in between. It was fashionable or unmentionable, decaying, daring, or solid. The address could almost overshadow the house itself as an index of housing quality.

The class dimension also affected the distinction between planned

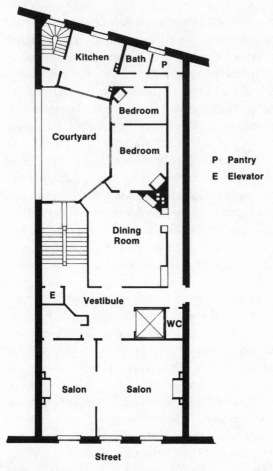

Figure 9.2. Bourgeois apartment in Paris, c. 1895. The design of Parisian apartments for the affluent reveals a preference for style over comfort. Rooms for receiving guests occupy the light, street side and take up most of the space. The kitchen, bath, and bedrooms are compressed at the rear of the dwelling. Servants lodge in the attic. (After Saglio 1896.)

and unplanned extensions of cities. Actually, this dichotomy is somewhat artificial (Blumenfeld 1967; see also Hartog 1962). Plans are almost never realized in full or sustained without change, while totally anarchic siting is impossible with a continuous street network. However, the dwellings of the upper and middle classes required an environment ensuring social homogeneity as well as adequate natural amenity. Therefore, the degree of planning was roughly proportional to the social rank of the area being developed. There was also an evolution over time. Planning of a sort became gradually more democratic. Conzen (1978) points out that the systematic development of large tracts in British towns moved down the social scale from the fashionable squares of London and Edinburgh's Newtown, to middle-class and respectable worker terraces, and to rows of worker houses built right down to bylaw standards. As we shall see, systematic attention to worker housing, except in small or recently urbanized settlements, only became significant relatively late in the century. Until then, their households occupied odd corners, vacant bits of land between and behind existing buildings, or took over subdivided houses once of a better sort.

Thus, cities acquired a social geography. In Paris and London, the west was fashionable and the east plebeian, perhaps because the prevailing wind blew westerly, perhaps because the courts at Versailles and Westminster, respectively, had once pulled fashion westward. English manufacturing towns featured an elevated and somewhat peripheral location for the homes of the dominant industrialists, as noted by John Braine's 1950s novel, *Room at the Top*. By contrast, continental elites retained an interest in more central locations. The Ring in Vienna, suddenly opened to development yet immediately adjacent to the old core, provided a choice opportunity during the heyday of liberal prosperity.

To be sure, most of the population of towns, being neither prosperous nor destitute, located itself more eclectically. They neither congregated according to the dictates of fashion nor were segregated into shameful slums (Vance 1977). A study of Edinburgh at mid-nineteenth century shows clearly that the rich and the poor occupied well-delimited and comparatively small areas, whereas the large middle group spread out more evenly over the city (Gordon 1979). As is usual, most attention has focused on the extremes, while the great in-between stretches, lacking either grandeur or pathos, suffer a historiographic oblivion that mirrors their physical mediocrity. Wealth is not the only way in which social groups are spatially defined. Ethnic distinctions mattered, as did household composition as a function of the life cycle (L. Lees 1979). However, such distinctions never assumed the importance in Europe that they did in the United States.

If market forces were important in generating the social geography of European towns, they also threatened its stability. Increasingly, land use was determined by the market: almost any piece of land could be captured for use by offering a high bid-rent. The solvent power of money accelerated land-use succession, and the forces of economic development overrode the physical legacy of the past. Land prices rose relative to construction costs and the urban price gradient became steeper; so a central location, in particular, was stripped of protection for its current use unless insulated in some way from the market. The principal processes driven by these powerful forces were the displacement of residential by commercial uses and the filtering of housing from higher to lower occupancy status. Looked at in another way, the urban scene was characterized by constant displacement of slums, with the internal clearing offset by spread at the outer margin.

In terms of the competition for highly valued central locations, commercial uses brooked little resistance and none on economic grounds. But the poor as a group could compete quite effectively with their betters for residential land. Their tolerance for crowding and their need to preserve access to diverse sources of potential employment made up for inferiority of means, and this was even more true in transitional areas where houses marked for eventual destruction still yielded their owners rental income with no further upkeep costs. The least favored competitor was the general interest, since taking private property involved full compensation and there was little inclination to approve it except for compellingly utilitarian purposes such as traffic.

Strangely, it was capitalist industry, as much as anything, that began to reverse the almost implosive rise in urban density. Factories sought out large parcels of land near freight transport and far from neighbors with sensitive noses and good access to the authorities. In turn, they drew to them masses of workers, already urban or newly migrated, along with their dwellings. Paris developed its "red belt," while London spread to the north and east. Milan acquired a northern and a southern industrial zone outside the walls. In Lille lower-middle-class speculators rushed in to build two-room houses along the newer, unpaved and undrained streets outside the old line of fortifications (Pierrard 1965). In Vienna, on the other hand, early political fears had relegated industry to an outer ring (the *Gürtel*), well removed from the city walls. This gradually fused with the expanding city into a popular suburban belt somewhat like that of Paris (Czeike 1978). From the start, these extensions were grim: shabby, monotonously alike, surrounded by mud, as much like barracks as the factories themselves. Yet they promised newness and a standard of spaciousness higher than those who moved in were likely to have known.

Land-use succession, filtering, and a movable social geography are characteristic of American as well as of European cities. It is worth dwelling a moment on the differences between the two. In general, these processes proceeded more strongly and freely in the United States, since European cities were comparatively homogeneous in ethnic composition and their elites were more traditional in outlook and behavior. The rich were less apt to move their residence by choice. In the United States, where social distinctions were less openly acknowledged though perhaps not less important than in Europe, locational choices and physical separation developed into crucial elements of the social process. On the other hand, the power of money suffered fewer restraints in the New World. The differences were only of degree perhaps, but the result was a reorganization of social geography: incomes rose with distance from the city center in America, whereas they typically fell in Europe. This generalization must be qualified in at least two ways. Northern Europe, England in particular, evolved more nearly as the United States did, while the larger and older cities of the East Coast and Canada retained a morphological kinship with the European continent.

Changes in the composition of urban economic activity also influenced the evolution of land use. Production grew rapidly overall and trade grew more rapidly still, giving great impetus to central place functions. As we have noted, the common element of the tertiary or service activities of cities is information, an intangible and therefore bulkless commodity that manifests itself mainly in the act of being transferred or exchanged. Town centers were the natural location where those trafficking in knowledge congregated, and they displaced not only residents but also most activities dealing with visible commodities. The business center was taken over by an army of brokers, clerks, bankers, couriers, and other dealers in the quintessentially urban commodity, information. The complement of this great concentration of employment was a massive daily movement of workers from all over the urban realm into the central business district and out again. When the railroads commuted their daily fares into a monthly ticket, these people acquired a name that would stick: commuters.

During these changes, the ideological commitment of the majority to private property and individualism remained dominant. This had a pervasive effect on urban geography, which Daunton (1983) speaks of as the "privatization of space." Public and private places were separated ever more clearly, every activity was to be allocated a specific territory, and individual control over space was to be as great as possible. Thus, shops or stalls in covered markets replaced street vendors; factories centralized work; and the detached villa, enclosed in its garden, became the dream of the city dweller. By contrast, in streets and other public places social custom and community ties gave way to total anonymity governed by formal rules of public order. As Lavedan (1959) points out, traffic pushed aside the role of the street as a meeting place or agora. To bridge

Figure 9.3. Urban transport in central Berlin, c. 1880. Horse-drawn trams bring commuters in from outer and suburban districts. This early postcard shows a convergence of lines in the central business district. Before the turn of the century, electric cars would serve the veritable urban region that imperial Berlin had become. (Personal collection of P. Hohenberg.)

Figure 9.4. The Paris metro. Technological advances in transportation, notably electric traction, helped relieve urban congestion even as large cities grew larger. The Paris network of (mostly) underground lines was begun in 1898 and largely completed by 1914, although it had to be extended to the suburbs in later decades. Used extensively by workers, the metro permitted easy and cheap travel throughout Paris. (Personal collection of P. Hohenberg.)

the gap between the individual household and the faceless collectivity, a whole host of organizations grew up, often with their own space and facilities: clubs, associations, societies, circles for every conceivable purpose. Collective activities, such as entertainment, also became more specialized and confined to particular spaces. Finally, the line between government and the private sector was drawn more sharply. Soldiers lived in barracks rather than being billeted with the citizenry; public offices were no longer farmed to private parties; and only rarely, as in Vienna, would the sovereign still share his park with the public.

The Morphology of Urban Expansion

With this rapid survey of the complexities underlying the changing uses of urban land during a period of industry-driven growth, we have perhaps justified the need to classify the unit processes at work in the "growth" of cities. Conzen (1978) distinguishes two classes of processes, additional and transformational. It takes little effort to grasp the point that cities needed to grow by annexing land at the fringe of the existing built-up area, even though the ways this addition took place are not simple. The reorganization of previously built space is less obvious, less universal, and more problematic, and we shall focus on it first.

Conceivably, the new and the old could coexist. Colonial cities from Algiers to Old and New Delhi or, to retreat in time several centuries, the bastide and citadel of medieval Carcassonne are cases in point. Many European cities, such as Strasbourg, Florence, and Munich, grew substantially without modifying their medieval core to any extent, though note that the examples are towns that remained medium-sized and only weakly industrialized until quite recently. In these cases, a ring around the old town served to distribute vehicles and keep all but local traffic out of the narrow central streets. The ring or circular boulevard replaced the wall or bulwark.

Yet such stability, so prized today, remains the exception, particularly for cities that grew to large size. Before investigating changes in land use more closely, it is important to note that nothing is less plastic by its nature than the urban fabric. The mere widening of a street would seem to require destroying the houses that line it, at least along one side. A residence is poorly suited to serve as a factory or a warehouse, only a little better as a workshop or retail outlet. Perfectly sound buildings are often destroyed for no reason save that they have come to occupy the wrong site: they are locationally obsolete. And visible structures are far from the whole of it. Underground are sewers and conduits, and legal ties and property rights impose an invisible set of fetters on change. Even when bombings have eliminated the urban "build" above ground, planners have had to respect the plan. Thus, Conzen (1978) argues that the urban plan is the most resistant to change, the build less so, and actual functional land use the most changeable, with buildings and activities adapting to each other. We shall return to the forces of resistance later in examining major efforts at morphological transformation such as those of Haussmann in Paris. But Blumenfeld (1967) makes the important point that in the nineteenth century there began a simultaneous reduction in urban plasticity and an acceleration of the incentives to reorganize land use. New processes of construction as well as great advances in public utilities reduced the rate of natural decay of urban artifacts. Fire and flood, in particular, were much better controlled. Yet economic and technological changes continually called the past configuration into question, while the rapid growth of area and population exerted pressure to make more room for traffic near the city center.

In many, perhaps most, European cities the great acceleration in urbanization began with internal changes, namely, the filling in of existing sites. Put more simply, it was only when crowding reached extreme stages that cities proved able to expand spatially. Moreover, this growth by increasing density and vertical accumulation was largely unplanned and made no provision for alleviating the congestion that resulted. In fortified cities, such as Lille, Strasbourg, or Vienna, the reasons for not expanding outward were plain. Elsewhere, the barrier was political or institutional, but there were technical reasons, too. With transportation no faster than walking speed, workers had to live near their workplace, and the interactions that typified urban activities also encouraged agglomeration. Of course, such a degree of concentration was largely self-defeating, because congestion only slowed things down further.[2]

Eventually, the urban fabric had to loosen. The quality of urban life aside, technology required it, particularly the widespread diffusion of steam power. The optimal scale of industrial production increased dramatically. Even more importantly, the railroad demanded substantial and continuous tracts of urban land. Reformers and administrators largely welcomed these technological imperatives, because the dense concentrations of poor people in and near the town center were perceived as sinister nurseries of disease, vice, crime, and rebellion. In rough terms, we can say that the centripetal phase ended around the middle of the nineteenth century, whereas the later 1800s saw the beginning of a loosening up that is not yet at an end. Studies of many towns agree that 1850 represents a peak in urban densities and crowding (Hall 1973).

Thereafter the suburban exodus of the middle classes intensified. The expansion of villages on a town's fringes and ribbon development along major roads were soon followed by speculative development of nearby tracts of land. Rows and rows of new streets dignified as "terraces," "crescents," or "allées" spread out in profusion. The most attractive of these settlements combined villas and winding streets with open fields or woods, but such places were far outnumbered by the monotonous rows of small, identical houses

Figure 9.5. Suburban villas in Vienna. The desire for more space and family privacy led many wealthier citizens to trade central-city apartments for houses on the outskirts of town after tramways had eased travel to offices and shops. These two homes were built around 1890 in the Währing-Döbling cottage estate outside Vienna. (From Kortz 1906:439.)

that could be afforded by the lower middle class. As the lines of brick and mortar multiplied, churches, schools, taverns, and shops were added, as well as railway lines and tram tracks to give commuters daily access to the city center. The development of transportation proceeded in tandem with housing estates. The phrase *streetcar suburb* describes the European as well as the American experience (Warner 1962). In England large estate owners granted leases to contractors, sometimes specifying the type of house and the density with which land could be built. But whatever the intention, in the longer run elegant communities often deteriorated into ordinary collections of modest houses as the upper middle class moved farther out of town and new, smaller dwellings were added to the estate. Where land was held in tiny parcels, no such control was possible even in the initial stages of development. Building societies, small contractors, and private owners produced a hodgepodge of undistinguished homes. Still, the appeal of a separate dwelling with a garden in a socially homogeneous neighborhood was great.

In a sense, the distinction between land-use transformation and the addition of peripheral space to a town is misleading. A town is not confined to the built-up spaces or those used for traffic. At any given time, it has an internal as well as an external margin, where the developed area touches on open land. Although such areas were typically perceived and coveted as only waiting to be developed, this perception was often inaccurate as well as pernicious. Within the town, "unused" spaces afforded a welcome respite from congestion and pollution, serving as oases of peace and vegetation. Even a flood plain, a swamp, or a steep slope would eventually represent a great opportunity to build a park, rail line, or other major project without massive disruption of the existing urban fabric. At the edges of cities, the apparently vacant land served for many humble and noisome tasks; here were the quarries, dumps, slaughterhouses, and noxious industrial plants. In both cases, a change in land use involved big, rather than piecemeal decisions, so that urban expansion tended to take place in waves or cycles.

The fluctuating nature of additive urban expansion was also fueled, of course, by technological and economic forces. Growth quickened and slackened; migrants flooded in and then stopped coming; building cycles emerged, with an apparent life of their own. Because development, like other investments, represents a commitment to the future, it is inherently risky and subject to the swings of collective psychology. Waves of active building were typically followed by pauses or consolidations, although the financial aspect of these fluctuations tended more to wild speculative booms followed by panic, collapse, and depression.

It is difficult to generalize meaningfully about the extensions of cities and towns, since they took every conceivable form. Some were carefully planned, some totally haphazard. The former have tended to leave more complete records and to interest the principal students of physical urban growth, the planners and town planning historians. So they are better known (Dyos 1961; Hartog 1962; F. Thompson 1974). Yet unplanned growth with a tardy minimum of rationalization was more common, and we can make a few general comments about it. Aside from topographical complications and prior suburban activities, the land surrounding a city offered two distinguishing features: roads and villages. The normal pattern was for development to string out along the approaches to the city, with the interstices settled later, if at all. Rail lines also channeled settlement, though with more clustering around the stations. As regards villages or other existing settlements, the picture is somewhat more complicated. They could grow as satellite towns if their activity fitted in with the urban economy.[3] Otherwise, the urban juggernaut simply rolled over them and swallowed them up. Even today, large cities are interspersed with vestiges of earlier small nodes, and the village flavor is preserved in unexpected corners of the metropolis. Finally, a special pattern developed in areas of new urbanization around mines and dispersed factories. Here growth proceeded from isolated centers, from worker colonies next to the job, even from old villages, and urban entities were formed by the coalescing of these settlements. They had little urban identity, either official or otherwise, few central place functions, no real form, and little amenity (Schöller 1978). But they were prosperous, and in many cases they afforded better conditions of housing and lower density than more interesting and better-known places. The coal fields of Europe could almost be traced by these new kinds of towns from the river "sides" of Great Britain to the valleys of the Maas/Meuse and the Ruhr. Eventually, the towns flowed together into conurbations, whole urban regions whose collective motto seemed to be the old English saying: "Where there's muck, there's brass [money]." Of course, conurbations could also result from the spread or coalescence of major centers, such as industrial Lancashire or Randstad, the horseshoe of cities in Holland from Rotterdam to Utrecht (Hall 1966).

Despite the general lack of planning or other formal land-use controls, Europe's cities expanded more continuously and with higher density at the leading edge than their North American counterparts. Even though little systematic work appears to have been done on this question, it is clear that Europe was marked by higher opportunity cost for the agricultural land being lost, coupled with greater construction costs for brick and masonry compared with American lumber. Since the rich stood their central ground, the European urban periphery was settled by poorer people, on the average, again leading to higher density. One consequence today is that planners find more nearby open space in European cities, but that these green areas, naturally coveted also by developers and transportation planners, are more desperately needed there than they would be in America. It remains true that the city dweller in Europe finds much easier access to open space for recreation than is available in the far less densely inhabited cities of the United States. One need only compare the numerous walking trails around a city such as Munich with the American joggers battling suburban traffic for a share of oxygen and pavement.

Finding Shelter

The dominant material issue raised by urbanization was housing, and the "housing question" is a hardy perennial among reformers and students of cities. It must mean more than that large numbers of people are poorly housed, since that plain fact can be subsumed under the larger issue of urban or working-class poverty. Somehow, the squalid dwellings of the poor seem to matter more than their meager access to food, bought objects, or security against the vicissitudes of life. Has housing merely been more visible to observers? Or is it true, as so many have argued, that the quality of the near environment strongly conditions the social and moral, as well as the physical, well-being of people?

In Chapter 8 we considered the experience of living in industrial and other urban slums. We noted that poor housing as such may have had less impact on physical and social welfare than outsiders have thought. The demographic evidence is persuasive, and students of working-class families and society are putting together a less-than-pathetic picture of adaptation and resilience. In this chapter we look at the supply and demand aspects of housing. The economist's approach helps balance accomplishments and insufficiencies, whereas so much of the literature tends to stress one or the other.[4] We focus on housing for the poor and on large cities and industrial conurbations, having already alluded to the interesting case of company towns with their trade-off of comfort for control.

Let us first define the "good" in question. Housing or housing services are provided by or in a fixed structure, which itself is capital, in exchange for rent. This has two implications. First, investment in construction must be complete before any housing can be supplied. Second, urbanization means total reliance on new capital with no contribution from the existing rural stock. The quantity of housing depends on the interaction between the building itself and the environment, which provides amenities such as air and light, access and privacy, clean water and drainage of wastes, and a specific social setting. In a word, there is more to housing than a number of square feet or a certain structural quality. Finally, the standard of housing varies with the occupying household: its numbers, ages, relationships, and activities. For example, the poor took in lodgers or ran a workshop, while the rich reserved parts of their great houses for special occasions and kept numerous servants.

Even though housing is an obvious economic good in that it is costly to produce, its allocation has remained at least partially outside the framework of the market in otherwise market-using societies (Vance 1976, 1977). This was largely true in preindustrial Europe both for the assignment of land and for the occupancy of dwellings. Those who did not own or "hold" a house were reckoned as dependent and could expect to receive shelter from their master. Correspondingly, the household was defined more often by social and economic criteria than by ties of blood alone, whether it occupied one structure or several. New building took place when the household unit expanded or a new one was formed. It scarcely existed as an independent economic sector. The triumph of the market turned housing, that is, the use of particular sites and structures, into a commodity in the same way it did the services of labor (Polanyi 1944). A new housing industry grew up with builders and landlords as entrepreneurs. The ongoing relationship between landlord and tenant differed from that between other buyers and sellers, which was becoming more impersonal and anonymous, but it did resemble the strife-filled capitalistic employment relationship. No wonder then that the poor in particular moved often if not usually far, while urban landlords and their agents were popular figures of fear and hate.

With all the variations owing to place, time, environment, and household circumstance, what can we meaningfully say about the housing of European working-class people in the nineteenth century? How much space did they command or how little? How much did they pay? Had matters improved by the beginning of the twentieth century? Certainly, there is plenty of evidence of miserable housing, not all of it anecdotal. In Liverpool perhaps one person in five lived in a cellar dwelling in 1842, and this was before the big influx of Irish immigrants (Burnett 1978). As late as 1901,

30 percent of the population of Newcastle and 35 percent in the Finsbury district of London were registered as "overcrowded" (Burnett 1978). This statistic takes on added meaning if one notes that a family of two adults and four children (ages one to ten) occupying a two-room back-to-back—one room up and one down, 250 square feet total, and a water tap and privy in the alley—would not qualify. The same family would pay from 2s. 6d. to 5s. a week for this accommodation, depending on location, at a time when 30s. a week constituted a very good laboring wage. Those in rooms, those who shared a tiny house, and the unemployed fared even worse.

No matter how mean the dwelling, in England it almost always had its own door to the street or the court. The Viennese lived in large apartment houses, but otherwise the picture was not so different. Of the 555,000 dwellings registered in 1917, 73 percent were classed as small (Hardy 1934). This meant at the most one largish room, one small sleeping chamber with no outside window, and a kitchen—a maximum of 400 square feet in all. Remember that these lodgings were in large, four-to-six-story buildings covering 70 percent or more of the lot surface. The water tap and the toilets were out in the hall. One third of the Viennese lived more than two to a room and one quarter of the dwellings housed sub-

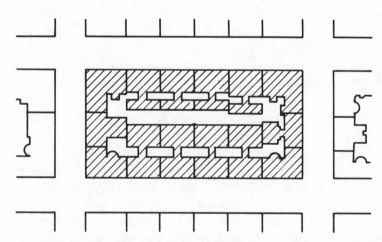

Figure 9.6. Workers' apartment houses in Vienna, c. 1900. Until 1930 Vienna's building regulations permitted developers to cover up to 85 percent of a site with multistory dwellings. A typical apartment opened off a long interior corridor and consisted of one or two rooms and a small kitchen. Many rooms fronted only on small, dank courts. (After Hardy 1934:11).

tenants or lodgers. Rent absorbed about 15 percent of working-class income, perhaps a bit more than the English average but not out of line with other European cities (Gauldie 1974).

It is tempting to conclude that conditions were particularly bad and slow to improve in very large cities and in industrial areas of rapid urbanization. But the evidence suggests caution: there were success stories and mixed pictures as well. In France around 1885, for instance, one-room dwellings could be more common in a sleepy market town such as Fougères than in Bordeaux or Lyon (Lequin 1983). Factory workers and miners often fared better than others. Contrast the employer-built housing estates in Mulhouse and Carmaux with the workshop-slums inhabited by protoindustrial weavers or seamstresses. Back in England some industrial cities made real progress: by 1901 no more than 3 percent of Birmingham or Nottingham's people lived in fewer than three rooms (Burnett 1978). The infamous back-to-back, a triumph of parsimonious land use and construction, was giving way to some form of through-terrace house, open to the air at the back.

As we try to apply simple demand and supply analysis to the task of sorting all this out, let us listen to a poor London tenant resisting a philanthopic landlady's urgings to take a second room. This "silent, strong, uncringing woman, living with her seven children and her husband, [argued that] 'there were many things she could get for the children to eat which would do them more good than another room' " (Hill 1875:21). She was finally persuaded by the landlady who reports the story. Octavia Hill, a Christian Socialist disciple of Ruskin, rehabilitated blighted houses and let them to poor tenants who would obey the rules. The clear implication is that the poor, when left to their own devices, put housing fairly low on their list of spending priorities. Food and fuel needs were pressing and relatively incompressible, while a host of out-of-doors temptations competed for any discretionary income. On the other hand, better housing was crucial to any social improvement. Decency required no less than two rooms to the dwelling (Burnett 1978). And nothing so clearly indicated class differences as the glaring contrasts between slums, middle-class flats or terraces, and opulent villas or town houses. Yet the evidence suggests that the share of housing in total consumption varied little across social strata, indeed that poorer folk might devote more of their income to housing than those better off (Burnett 1978). To put the point more technically, the income elasticity of demand for housing was apparently close to one, whereas intuition suggests that housing should absorb a higher fraction of higher incomes, at least for large income differences. One can only conclude that despite their bad accommodations the poor were overhoused in the sense that they were somehow made to devote income to housing that they would willingly have spent elsewhere.

Why did working-class Europeans spend as much as they did on housing? Alternatively, why did they get so little for their money? Note that this spending kept pace with income as the century progressed. Indeed, Sutcliffe (1981) has argued that housing costs absorbed most or all the purchasing power freed up by the falling prices of other commodities in the last quarter of the century. While accommodations improved, rents were rising too—85 percent in England and Wales from 1845 to 1910, by one estimate (Burnett 1978). Demand played a role, even though few poor people listened to the Octavia Hills or read the pamphlets of reform-minded physicians. We have already mentioned income-producing uses of the home and the need to occupy land near the city center, the docks, or other sources of jobs (G. S. Jones 1971). Living standards did evolve as people adopted urban ways; even modest households moved away from rural practices of casual sharing of rooms and beds and using the kitchen as the common living area. Yet it was not individual demand that made the difference, but rather the mass of people who flocked to towns, particularly large ones.

Demand was growing for other commodities, too, but capitalism responded so strongly that prices of food, fuel, metals, and clothing typically fell. Why was the supply response so much less powerful in the case of housing? Some things changed, notably in the manufacture and transport of bricks, glass, and cement. The development of mechanical systems for houses—lifts, piped water and gas, electricity, sewer lines and water closets, and central heating—made it possible to accommodate quite high density without the squalor and contagion that crowding evokes. Unfortunately, the poor districts and houses were the last to benefit. A 1919 survey of Vienna showed 77 percent of "small" dwellings with neither gas nor electricity and fewer than 5 percent with running water (Hardy 1934). Finally, cheap rail transportation alleviated the constraints of distance on the spread of working-class districts. This helped compensate the losses that resulted from slum clearances and from the expansion of commercial and transportation activities. At least in the short run, eliminating substandard housing worsened the situation for all the poor, whether they were directly displaced or felt the effects indirectly through higher rents. The same may be said of minimum standards for construction as embodied in bylaws or other regulatory measures. In Leeds it was argued—successfully—that back-to-backs should continue to be built, since the poor could afford no better (Gauldie 1974).

Land scarcity aside, the principal reason why supply could not keep up was the building industry. Capitalism very nearly passed it by, whether one looks at financing, organization, technology, or the labor force. Builders, like landlords, were predominantly small businessmen; a Thomas Cubbitt who employed 1,000 men in the late 1820s or an Edward Yates who built some hundreds of houses in Camberwell half a century later stand out from the crowd (Burnett 1978). The financial institutions that grew up—building societies, *Bausparkassen*, Crédit Foncier, or the Metropolitan Association for Improving the Dwellings of the Industrious Classes—had strong cooperative, eleemosynary, or public elements. Everywhere, building appears as a prototypically competitive industry with predictably low profits. The traditional high standards of European building, the result of working with heavy materials such as stone and tile, were threatened in the age of jerry-building, but regulations restored a certain minimum of quality (Bardet 1971). The labor force, with its masters, journeymen, and apprentices and numerous temporary or new rural migrants, harked back to an earlier mode of production. Only land ownership promised large, though noncapitalistic profits, and it was mostly scattered, except in Britain where aristocrats and nonprofit institutions reaped the windfalls.

Thus, construction costs did not fall. The industry was successful in supplying housing for the thriving middle class and for growing numbers of skilled workers, clerks, and technicians. But reconciling what the masses could or would pay with growing costs for land and infrastructure, static construction technology, and rising community standards proved an enduring predicament. It delayed the construction of new worker housing in cities for a long time, and later occasioned one of the first major departures from free enterprise in the form of public housing. Let us briefly look at each of these in turn.

Three short-term solutions were favored before much new housing was actually built for working-class families: crowding, which needs no further comment, vertical social differentiation, and filtering (Vance 1976). The idea of vertical segregation or a vertical social gradient means simply that the poor shared the dwellings of their betters but occupied the highest and lowest floors as well as odd corners. Even today, Italians distinguish the "noble" from the "servile" floors in older urban houses. The poor might also be lodged in subsidiary buildings on the plot, lacking the "gable end on the street" that denotes respectability in French. As urban growth proceeded, many aging structures were vacated by their prosperous owners and so made available for occupancy by people of lesser means. This filtering process never took on the importance in Europe that it has had in the United States, where fashion has so often dictated a new address. But it can be observed, for instance, in town centers when merchants finally decided to separate home and business (Scargill 1979).

By the middle of the nineteenth century these "solutions" had reached their limits in much of Europe. Not only was the pace of urban growth, particularly the in-migration of workers, too rapid, but the growing social specialization of urban space also meant that haphazard changes in occupancy were resisted. An aging building in a "good" area would be pulled down rather than let to unsuitable tenants. It therefore became imperative to provide newly built housing for workers. But as we have seen, no way was found to reconcile workers' wages and the rents necessary to make decent housing profitable. An example: in Marseille in the 1880s it was estimated that a mason with a wife working part-time could earn about 1,800 francs a year, but that the full cost of adequate housing required a rent of 500 to 700 francs, or about one third of their income (Roncayolo 1983). The "housing question" provoked widespread discussion of alternatives beginning in the 1890s, but some limited action only after World War I when inflation, rent controls, and wartime neglect of the housing stock made a mockery of pledges to take care of returning "heroes."

At first, public and publicly assisted housing schemes overcame objections of principle by posing as emergency measures. They were soon followed by larger plans. Municipal governments took the lead, with or without state subsidies. Between 1920 and 1938 public funds contributed to 77,000 of the 320,000 dwellings built in and around Paris (Roncayolo 1983). Vienna's Social Democrats did even more, managing to house one eighth of the city's population in *Gemeindebauten* before the political crisis of 1934 ended the program (Hardy 1934). And the effort of the British local councils was even more ambitious. In twenty years public assistance contributed to one and a half million houses out of four million built, while many slums were demolished or rehabilitated (Burnett 1978).

Even though these public housing programs proved costly and did not solve the problem of housing the masses, they and similar ones in other countries worked reasonably well. It may be noted that they generally followed prevailing norms and tastes: blocs of flats in Vienna and Paris, low houses in England. This raises the question whether simple rent subsidies to private housing might not have worked as well. It also points up the more checkered experience of the radical and ambitious public housing efforts since 1945. Without question, European workers have taken more readily to the earlier than to the later type.

To return to the nineteenth century, it took an enormous volume of building and rebuilding to house the population even poorly. And of course many millions were housed reasonably well or opulently, according to means and tastes. The rhythm of activity varied over time, with some evidence of autonomous building cycles. The volume of construction also varied by city and country, governed by specific factors such as industrial growth or crisis, changes in central place functions, autonomous variations in the rate of immigration, and large-scale projects such as railroad building, destruction of walls, or slum clearance. In conclusion, we must remain impressed by the sheer magnitude of the task and by the efforts that were mobilized, largely by market forces. Overall, the standard of comfort and decency indoors rose slowly, although this was offset for a time by deterioration of conditions on the macro scale. Densities and congestion were high, the amount of open land fell sharply in many places, and uniformity of styles combined with the vastness of urban settlements to produce great drabness. However, we must also consider the possibility that the availability of housing and the lower limits imposed by authorities on poor or casual lodgings served to regulate the pace of urban migration. To the extent this was true, it was inevitable that some would be housed at the limit of human or social tolerance, since any improvement would simply open up places for new arrivals. It is certain that the forces drawing migrants to towns, whatever their nature, were too strong to be deterred by the squalor and meanness of slums or the smoke and noise of the crowded streets.

Managing Cities

The prevalance of congestion and pollution points to a pervasive issue in nineteenth-century cities, and indeed in those of every age.[5] Putting up more houses was the visual expression of urbanization, and it seemed to solve the most pressing problems associated with it. Yet more building only aggravated the "housekeeping" problems that municipalities faced. In looking at these, we focus once again on efforts at solutions.

The mundane matter of urban management illustrates the lag between the technological and institutional forces promoting urbanization and the innovations necessary to control and humanize urban life. Our vivid concern with pollution today may lead us to forget that earlier industrial processes were readily put to work in a far cruder state than would be tolerated or even attempted today, in large part because of poor knowledge and brash laissez-faire ideology. Accidents were frequent, public protection of workers and consumers almost nonexistent, and the links between pollutants and their effects only vaguely perceived. Municipal authorities could and did worry about the more obvious dangers and nuisances, but they lacked the technical means to do much besides try to exclude the offending activity. The history of urban management is thus one of building professional services as well as establishing adequately strong municipal government. The size and complexity of the problems were compounded by all manner of resistance on the part of taxpayers, industrialists, property owners, central governments, and other opponents of change or rival powers. Without question, the reformers, engineers, public health workers, and criminologists are all unsung heroes of industrial urbanization.[6]

The lag between the application of industrial technology in towns and technological progress in the quality of urban life corresponds roughly to the successive waves of innovation sometimes called the first and second industrial revolutions. Different sources and conduits of energy are the key. The cluster of techniques introduced in England in the late eighteenth century—steam, coal, and iron and their applications to mechanized textile production and later railroads—did little for the city as a physical system. Steam power was ineffective in such small-scale applications as street vehicles, lifts, and workshop machinery. Coal could be burned in hearths, stoves, or small furnaces, but at the cost of soot-begrimed facades and killing pea-soup fogs. Transforming the coal into gas was an important step toward supplying flexible and clean energy, but electrification proved decisive. Electricity made possible the street-car and the skyscraper, of course, but it also revivified the pro-toindustrial urban workshop and freed large numbers of married women and household servants for outside work. By contrast, the equally momentous development of internal combustion, widely applied to urban transportation, has acted as a solvent rather than a cement to the urban fabric.

The sheer size and rapid growth of urban concentrations posed severe logistical problems, and many urban activities became increasingly noxious as well. In established towns and districts the prevailing congestion of streets or chronic inadequacy of waste and water systems could quickly turn into crisis as a result of even a minor shock—a runaway horse in one case, a dry spell in the other. Or, demand for services could pass a critical threshold. For instance, "night soil" was habitually removed to suburban gardens during the night, but the journey became too long in expanding urban areas, leaving them with no solution short of massive investment in sewers. The problems were slightly different, though no less serious, in new areas of unplanned urban extensions. Uncontrolled building quickly overran the environmental capacity of the countryside or villages. Neither an administrative nor a physical infrastructure was typically put in place beforehand, and residential locations were constrained by the factories or pitheads. Mining itself, as well as the heavy industries attracted to mines and coal ports, generated particularly intense environmental hazards.

To the effects of high density and substandard housing were added the dangerous consequences of bad sanitation. Insufficient water was a major problem. Street sellers hawked bucketfuls to residents of St. Petersburg until well into the nineteenth century. Inadequate amounts supplied by private companies to the houses only of those who would pay were the norm in British cities in the 1840s and 1850s. The poor had to take what they could get from local wells or outside taps, which ran only a few hours a day.

Similarly, gas lighting was available only where landlords paid for pipes to be installed in their apartments. While courts and streets were commonly lighted in England around 1850, the homes of the poor were not. Nor did cities and towns have adequate sewerage systems until the second half of the nineteenth century. Even places as wealthy as London and Paris dumped raw sewage into, and drew water from, their rivers until cholera epidemics and noxious smells prodded public authorities to redesign and expand underground drainage systems during the later 1850s and 1860s. And other towns lagged behind. Sheffield built an effective drainage system and a sewage treatment plant in the mid-1880s (Pollard 1959). Lille did not have an extensive network of underground sewers until the years of the Third Republic. In any case, drains solved only one part of the sanitation problem. Most houses in nineteenth-century cities had privies and cesspools, rather than water closets connected to town sewers. As long as inadequate commercial systems of waste removal were relied upon, town residents continued to find their water sometimes polluted, cellars flooded, and noses offended by leakage from thousands of privies. Not until the later nineteenth and early twentieth centuries were there massive conversions to modern plumbing.

Against the many obstacles to adequate provision of public services, sheer necessity furnished the strongest positive impetus. Epidemics and fires were the most immediate threats, but long-run forces also furthered a positive approach. This was, after all, an age that believed in progress through science and technology. For their part, conservatives were eager to ensure order and to counter the siren song of radicalism. In time, notably with the extension of suffrage, it became politically profitable to show concern for the welfare of the urban masses. While urban political organization in Europe never achieved the colorful heights of American city "machines," parallel causes produced similar effects. Vienna's mayor of the late years of the century, Carl Lueger, was a worthy forerunner of Chicago's Richard Daley. Joseph Chamberlain built a national political career on the basis of his tenure as lord mayor of Birmingham. And French politicians inaugurated the tradition of the *député-maire*, a member of the National Assembly whose political base rested with his office as mayor of a sizable provincial city. Urban politicians were typically to the left on the conventional political spectrum, but their "municipal socialism" was very different from that of revolutionary socialists or trade union leaders. It was fiscally prudent and entrepreneurial, a tradition that survives in Western Europe in our own time (Ardagh 1979).

For all the urgency, progress was agonizingly slow. Typically, a campaign against a particular abuse, set off by a catastrophe or by a vivid tract from the pen of a reformist doctor or novelist, would eventually triumph with the passage of a law. Yet this was only the first step, since early measures tended to enjoy neither the material means nor the political power to ensure enforcement. Only gradually were inspectors appointed, administrative procedures worked out, and judicial precedents established. Cities of the early industrial age were poorly provided with the two necessary ingredients for effective management: a professional corps of civil servants and adequate fiscal resources. Indeed, they were considerably worse off in these respects than the more nearly sovereign cities of early times. Traditionally, "free" cities had been able to call on the purses as well as the persons of their citizens, invoking the communal tradition. At the same time, the oligarchical reality of urban government provided a source of funds and leadership, complemented by the resources of guilds, religious associations, and the like. This system weakened as cities became more integral parts of modern states, not least because central governments were wary of competing concentrations of power, loyalty, and fiscal authority. Even as wealth was becoming increasingly mobile and production more market-oriented, the abolition of internal trade barriers deprived cities of an effective source of tax revenue. Nonetheless, as late as the 1890s, Paris still derived half its revenues from the *octroi* or municipal customs tariff, while imperial Germany formally abolished it only in 1902 (Bellan 1971).

Of course, national governments were forced to help, particularly in such areas as criminal justice, poor relief, and education. In the first case, it would seem that the rationale lay in affirming the sovereignty of the state, while the latter areas were so open-ended and costly that local resources could never cope. This was particularly true in fast-growing industrial regions, where rapid immigration and the vagaries of the business cycle regularly swamped whatever means and institutions were at hand. It must be remembered that these newly industrial urban areas had no cadre of elites in place. Wealth and authority were represented by factory masters who, in the first couple of generations at least, were too busy seeing the Industrial Revolution through its teething troubles to spare much time for civic responsibility.

To sum up, the priorities were roughly as follows. Immediate problems of health and safety were tackled first, notably fire, water, and waste, although the standard achieved in the first half of the twentieth century was not, of course, reached in one step. Police problems in the wider sense, including the regulation of trade as well as public safety and criminal justice, came next. Large-scale public enterprise, for instance, transportation, came relatively late, as did true planning. Throughout, the problems of education and poor relief remained chronically awkward: the magnitude of the task, the ambivalent attitudes of opinion leaders, and the continuing interplay of public and private efforts as well as local and national ones, were a few of the interweaving strands in a story we are forced to leave almost wholly out of our account.

In order to make concrete some of our too sweeping generalizations about managing cities, let us take a short detour through Milan to see what was done there and who was responsible for change.[7] During the later part of the nineteenth century, Milan became the economic capital of Italy. Long a commercial and financial center as well as a protoindustrial producer of textiles and metal goods, it became a leading force in Italian industrialization. Milan's combination of new, capital-intensive industries, railway links to the north, and aggressive banks allowed the elites to manage much of the new state's economic development. The first wave of Milanese growth expanded industry within the old Spanish walls. Workshops were randomly scattered within the historical district, although the larger mills, chemical plants, and engineering works settled outside the walls or near city gates. Not until late in the century did many plants move out of central Milan to a northern and a southern industrial zone near major railway stations. Workers poured into the city from the countryside, but the demand for housing so exceeded the urban supply that a growing proportion had to live in rather dismal suburban areas.

During most of this time, urban services lagged far behind the need for them. The city was run by men from wealthy landowning families whose political allegiances were to various conservative parties and whose attention was occupied by commercial development. But a few changes were made to improve the functioning of the essentially Renaissance city. A horse-drawn omnibus service began in 1841, gas pipes were laid after 1845, and in the early 1860s slaughterhouses were exiled to a peripheral location. Urban renewal of the city's center began in the 1860s with the creation of an elegant shopping gallery that linked the Duomo and the Piazza della Scala, reviving the appeal of the historical core for the rich and fashionable. New department stores soon moved into this expanding central business district. The aesthetic appeal was restored, a park added, and regulations enacted that prescribed building heights and street plans. Meanwhile, outer districts needed decent housing, paved streets, adequate water supplies, sewers, and schools. Workers lived packed into multistory dwellings that lacked running water, flush toilets, and lighting. Available tax money was funneled into highly visible projects that would benefit the middle class more than the workers.

The direction of municipal planning changed, however, after suffrage expanded in the early 1880s. As more and more radicals were elected to the city council, the pressing issues came to the fore. Town administrators discussed the need for hospitals, better lighting, and new streets in districts beyond the old walls. More money was voted for education and sanitation as the numbers of moderates and liberals on the council increased. A telephone and an electricity company were founded. The council also funded a new network of sewers and a large aqueduct to improve water supplies. Finally, in 1911 the advent of universal suffrage brought in a Socialist mayor, and the pace of urban modernization quickened. The city bought an electric tram system, large wholesale markets were built outside the central area, and more parks were provided. A municipal housing office, founded in 1908, attempted to help would-be renters locate suitable apartments. Much remained to be done, of course, but by World War I the Milanese government had at least accepted the principle that it was responsible for monitoring urban growth and providing a range of services for citizens.

Urban Visions

Many of the aspects of spatial evolution in cities of the industrial age are thinly documented. The case studies are few and largely descriptive, hard to tie in with the great themes of capitalism, nationalism, and technology that concern historians. This disparity between a massive experience of urban growth and a spotty, weakly conceptualized record is very different from the situation regarding urban planning. In this domain the rather minor and scattered realizations—certainly before 1914 and even prior to 1939—are overshadowed by an enormous literature.[8] The brevity of our treatment reflects the little that was done rather than the wealth of commentary, then and since. Yet the discussions and hopes, even the failures and false starts, point up important issues.

As we noted in Chapter 7, the middle third of the nineteenth century witnessed an acceleration of the pace of urban growth throughout western and central Europe, particularly in established large cities. Initially at least, population densities rose, meaning that the area urbanized grew less rapidly than the number of inhabitants. The congestion and crowding that resulted were aggravated by the nature of urban activities and by the increasing scale of the physical city: a given density could be tolerable over one square mile but not twenty. Existing reserves of space and environmental capacity were quickly used up. And this development was largely private, decentralized, and almost anarchic.

We have already surveyed the principal attempts to alleviate congestion: opening up the periphery to building, setting housing standards, and improving public services. But more was needed. Piecemeal building decisions did not mesh with, and could not anticipate, the effects of parallel efforts. In consequence, they often aggravated congestion in the very act of trying to escape it. Coordination was obviously required—in other words, planning. The decongestion of town centers presented the most acute problems, while the prospective outward extensions of the urban fabric offered the best opportunities. Yet both transformational and additive processes were fated to go forward on a massive scale with little guidance from coherent plans.

There was a long tradition in Europe of conscious, large-scale design and comprehensive central control of cities. As recently as the late eighteenth century, after all, such places as Edinburgh and Nancy had received elegant and harmonious additions, while Berlin, St. Petersburg, and Bath developed along formal lines. Indeed, the baroque and neoclassical traditions continued to exert a strong stylistic influence when major projects were undertaken in the nineteenth century. Planners could also draw upon the English tradition of landscape architecture and on the colonial experience of checkerboard cities (Choay 1969). The Netherlands, whose most populous areas are virtually social artifacts, took the lead in passing planning legislation. There were now social as well as aesthetic motives for controlling and improving the city, widely seen as the crucible where all the ills of the new industrial age fused together.

The dual impulses to reform and to control the consequences of industrialism gave rise to a series of urban experiments. In model towns, idealists of various sorts carried out ambitious attempts at social engineering intended to improve people in tandem with their environments. When Robert Owen took over his father-in-law's cotton mill and factory village in Scotland in the 1780s, he promptly built a school, a cooperative store, and an Institute for the Formation of Character. Housing was soon improved and child labor regulated. Owen laid down rules and expectations for conduct intended to build healthy minds and bodies, and then wrote about his ideas and the results. Owen's schemes for model communities were widely noticed and soon imitated by other industrialists in England and abroad. A Quaker, John Richardson, built Bessbrook in the 1840s in Ireland around his linen mill. Workers were rented three- to five-room granite houses lit by gas. Moreover, the town had a park, playing fields, and garden allotments, in addition to schools, churches, cooperative stores, and a dispensary. Thrift and sobriety were encouraged through the exclusion of pubs and pawnshops and the provision of banks. Titus Salt's Yorkshire town, Saltaire, which still thrives today, was similar (G. Burke 1971). In France Jean Baptiste Godin put some of Fourier's ideas of community to work at his iron foundry in Guise. During the 1860s he began work on a model community centered on three large buildings that contained apartments, workshops, and stores and were surrounded by open land. Inhabitants shared the cooperatively run day-care centers, schools, kitchens, laundries, and recreational facilities. By 1880 the workers ran the entire complex, and factory profits were used to support the communal enterprises of the Familistère, as it was called (Benevolo 1971). Socialist ideals inspired few other urban schemes, but a fair number of industrialists grasped the connection between a contented labor force and a well-run factory. By the end of the nineteenth century a series of model towns had been built, both in England and in Germany, that combined a high standard of housing with nicely designed parks and public buildings. Because of the rapidity of German industrialization, employers there were under added pressure to supply housing if they wished to expand. Most

Figure 9.7. Block housing for Krupp workers in Essen. After 1860 the Krupp works built a great deal of model housing for its workers in and near Essen. The apartments in Friedrichshof, the settlement shown here, offer much lower density than in the central city, as well as parks, recreational grounds, and other communal facilities. (From Meakin 1905:371.)

notably, the Krupp firm sponsored a series of garden communities near Essen to attract and hold workers in their booming establishments. Both paternalism and good business sense encouraged their foray into town planning.

Technology and its acolyte the engineer were important to planning, offering practical solutions and a sustaining faith that urban problems, too, are tractable. Although England was the acknowledged technical leader, the country retained strongly rural values typified by the art of landscaping. Foreigners were also impressed by British *Wohnkultur,* the care given the "home" inside the house (Sutcliffe 1981). The unparalleled exterior drabness of industrial and petty bourgeois residential areas was all the more shocking, encouraging English planning initiatives to reunite urban habitats with the life-giving countryside for all classes of people. Although they did not turn out so, both Hampstead Garden suburb and Letchworth were intended to include a broad social spectrum. Finally, Britain shared with the United States a tradition of private association, philanthropy, and civic-mindedness responsible for many improvements. Indeed, such legislation as was passed to improve urban conditions and regulate growth was typically permissive, aimed at giving scope to private as well as to public local efforts.

Before World War I British achievements in planned urban growth were limited. The opening up of new streets for center-city traffic fell far short of needs even then, and every urban node in the road network represented an incipient bottleneck as Britain entered the motor age. Some of the worst early slums were cleared, notably in Scottish cities, although this must as always have put greater pressure on adjoining areas of low-cost housing. A few well-publicized estates were built by owners of large works situated outside existing towns and by railway companies. Port Sunlight, Saltaire, and Bournville are examples of the first; Crewe represents the second (Bell and Bell 1969). But the finest efforts were reserved for the urban extensions housing the well-to-do. However significant in the development of planning as a discipline and a profession, the "garden" projects of Unwin did not differ much from other villa suburbs (Purdom 1913).

France lagged in the urban planning movement, even though we shall later focus on Haussmann's Paris as an outstanding example of large-scale intervention in the urban build and plan. Yet the French administrative institutions, refined and exported by Napoleon from their roots in the ancien régime and Revolution, helped develop the modern state and in that sense were basic to the management of urban development. France was also the home of the dominant aesthetic visions of the late nineteenth and early twentieth centuries. To be sure, the major examples of planned development, the remodeling of Paris and a few other cities, obeyed a technocratic impulse. Haussmann's aesthetic amounted to no more than a rough-and-ready predilection for scale, symmetry, and ornamentation along neobaroque or neoclassical lines. France also illustrates another limitation on planning. If the pace of urbanization could be so rapid as to swamp any hope of control through planning, it could also be too slow to generate a sense of urgency and to override the forces of inertia and resistance.

It was on German soil that French precepts and practices were most extensively used. The authorities at all levels of government benefited from the relatively low degree of political development to achieve some insulation from the claims of competing interest groups. They were thus able to indulge their sense of order and their reverence for expertise. Urban administration became professional sooner here than elsewhere and has remained conspicuously so (Ardagh 1979). Sutcliffe (1981) notes a few further features specific to the German situation. Nowhere else did the initial stage of industrial urbanization fill up existing urban spaces more. Combined with a strong sense of tradition on the part of planners, the resultant crowding put the focus squarely on town extensions, the cores remaining largely untouched. German cities achieved a degree of control and an overall level of design in enlarging cities that far surpassed the standard in the other major countries. Nonn (1965) contrasts the careful development of Strasbourg under German rule after annexation from France in 1871 with the experience of Lille. However, although both cities were able to grow physically only after bursting out of their fortified straitjacket, the rate of urban growth also made a difference. It was easier to control expansion in Strasbourg because industry developed slowly, quite unlike Lille's Manchesterlike growth as industrial center and regional capital.

Yet, as in England, the fine German examples of urban design served mainly the middle and upper-middle classes. Their villas were set amid trees along tastefully curved streets free of excess traffic. Meanwhile, the laboring masses were offered little relief from the expanses of *Mietskasernen* (rental barracks). Even though Berlin was the political and intellectual capital of the empire, all its power and expertise failed to improve on the 1862 plan for enlarging the city. The large, densely built blocks of flats marched outward as a booming industry drew new migrants to the city (Hegemann 1930).

Why was more not done? It was clear to many that continued haphazard growth posed great dangers, while planning not only could temper the ills but held out the promise of fulfilling the human and social possibilities inherent in the advance of knowledge. The aspirations of planners were squeezed between power and property (Benevolo 1975). On the one hand, the struggle for municipal autonomy limited their opportunities for large-scale redevelopment; on the other, tenacious resistance from middle-class owners of urban land and buildings blocked change.

The nineteenth century witnessed great advances in individual rights. Alongside the political liberties to which the masses aspired and the opportunities for large-scale capitalist enterprise and accumulation, contemporaries particularly cherished the right to acquire, enjoy, and dispose of property freely. Any state interference must be minimal and closely circumscribed by due process. By property, the nineteenth-century European meant first and foremost *real* property: the peasant's field, the townsman's dwelling, the suburban estate or in-town block on which families like Galsworthy's Forsytes based their fortunes. It was recognized that public purposes might require forced purchase of land, for example, for roads, and that building heights needed to be limited. But only such land as would actually be used could be appropriated by the collectivity, and any regulations imposed on landowners must be the same for all, whatever their location in the city. Thus, large-scale public projects could not recoup their costs by capturing the gains in land value they generated. Nor could the systemic nature of the city be given its due. High density here needs—and makes possible—low density there or even totally unbuilt adjoining space. Yet the first owner cannot be compelled to share rents with the second.[9] Where necessities of traffic and dangerous urban blight dictated, property gave way, but opportunities to build in a far-sighted or imaginative way did not usually prove compelling. It must be stressed that the bourgeois forces that fought large-scale urban schemes were not primarily great industrialists, speculators, or financiers. The latter stood to gain rather than lose from change. The resisters were an older breed of capitalist, men and women of limited means whose very respectability might depend on a freehold or on the rental income from one or two buildings. The prudent bourgeois remained attached to real estate—"safe as houses," the British said.

Haussmann's Transformation of Paris

When Napoleon III assumed full power along with the imperial title in 1852, he was eager to implement his plans for quickening the pace of material progress in France, plans compounded of Saint-Simonian technocracy, Manchester-style free enterprise, and banking innovations with a racily speculative strain. All would be called on toward making Paris reflect and embody the achievements of the new regime.[10] But necessity loomed as large in the plan entrusted to Préfet Georges-Eugène Haussmann as the search for glory. Much has been made of Napoleon's military objectives: providing wide avenues along which troops could maneuver freely, cleaning out rabbit-warren slums beyond the reach of public health or public order. But critical logistical problems had also been piling up. In the fifty years before 1851 Paris had almost doubled its population to over one million, and it just missed doubling again during the twenty-year Second Empire (in the enlarged boundaries of 1860). Surprisingly, the post-1815 period had seen almost no significant changes in the street plan, not even during the eighteen generally placid years of the Bourgeois Monarchy (1830–1848). An east-west axis, begun under Napoleon I, had been slowly carried forward, but the center of Paris remained a medieval tangle of narrow streets. By mid-century a series of new rail terminals were funneling heavy additional traffic to the edge of the city core, while the outer districts were sprouting haphazardly outward from the gates and from their village nuclei.

Haussmann's plan involved three main elements: (1) decongesting the center, essentially by clearing the Ile de la Cité and its bridge-heads; (2) linking the center to the inner ring of boulevards and the nearby rail terminals; and (3) laying out main thoroughfares and

Figure 9.8. Haussmann's Paris, c. 1890. The rebuilding of Paris relied on baroque principles of design. Major buildings or monuments served as focal points for wide, straight streets. The Avenue de l'Opéra is lined with opulent apartment houses and elegant shops. Building heights and designs were regulated by the city. (Personal collection of P. Hohenberg.)

intersections in the outer districts within the 1840s ring of fortifications. In part because of legal limitations imposed on land purchases, the work required large government subsidies. It began rapidly and continued past the 1870–1875 transition to a republic. But the pace slowed from about 1860 and virtually stopped in the depressed 1880s.

Much has been written about the results, from the start more often critically than in admiration. Errors of both omission and commission are easy enough to point out, although time has softened many of the harsh junctions between old and new. The key decision to cut through the prior street plan saved money because the middle of blocks were cheap compared with street facades. Fewer important buildings were destroyed, and the objective of slum clearance was furthered directly, the worst conditions obtaining well back from the street in the alleys and courtyards. Ironically, the worst failure was the timid scope of the plan. The newly incorporated outer *arrondissements* were left to develop with minimal provision for open space and with little design guidance, particularly in the north and east. As for the suburban zone beyond the fortifications, it was simply ignored. The consequences of neglect became serious after rapid growth in the periphery began in the 1890s. Haussmann's failure here is ironic because most critics accused him of grandiose excess, and because the plan's great merit was to treat the great city as a whole, considering the relationships among the parts as well as each separately. As to the basic conflict between preservation of the past and coping with current and anticipated needs, we still search for answers to the dilemma.[11]

It is instructive to look at the opposition to Haussmann. In addition to the predictable objections of the political opposition, of taxpayers, and of preservationists, the transformation of Paris brought to light a panoply of resentments and rivalries. The popular east of the city complained about the attention showered on the high-status west. The center sought renewal while the periphery wanted more stress on development. The city council felt that the imperial government was usurping municipal power. Provincial France grumbled at the sums being lavished on the capital, though Lyon, Marseille, and other towns were also partly "Haussmannized." Finally, even though many property owners felt coerced, it was widely argued that the whole operation represented a coup for the bourgeoisie and against the working class. Collectively, these objections eventually broke the momentum for transformation, for better or for worse. Certainly, they all had a measure of validity, and the later stages of the project were in any case less useful than the earlier. It remains true, however, that the failure to include the area up to and beyond the walls in the plan looms larger in any negative assessment than anything actually done.

In trying to understand why Europe's post-Haussmann planners made little impact on the physical processes involved in mass urbanization, it is worth contrasting his stress on what was with theirs on what should be. Many projects ignored the problematic neighborhoods and towns in favor of making a fresh start. Yet the remarkable fact is that *no* new cities were built in Europe in the century before World War II, if one ignores a few modest satellite suburbs. The new industrial conurbations were the antithesis of planned solutions to the problems posed by rapid urbanization, although they did witness belated efforts to impose a modicum of structural and functional order on urban settlements that "just growed." The men who controlled power and capital were not looking to discard the city, but merely to overcome the frictions and excesses associated with its growth. And now that we can compare examples of both Haussmann's and Le Corbusier's visions for Paris, it is far from clear that the philistine capitalists and technocrats were less capable of providing a livable environment in the large cities than their idealistic critics. Certainly, Paris could have profited from more open space, London from a measure of clustering, and Berlin from more closely spaced streets. But it is difficult to picture alternatives that would have provided a greater measure of stimulation and comfort, at comparable cost and on so vast a scale, than the diverse cities that Europe's industrial age in fact built.

Capitalism did not fully rise to the challenge of building urban Europe as we have posed it, but it did prove capable of mustering the enormous energies necessary to construct the capital-rich cities of the modern age. Because of its deficiencies, it was not allowed to work unchecked; and clearly the results would have been much worse and the process no less brutal if tradition, reform, and authority had not tried to control the driving economic force. As to the result itself, it offers examples to support any judgment from the harshest to the most laudatory. But it is not irrelevant to note that the stock of ideas that animate contemporary planners came primarily from men of the late nineteenth and early twentieth centuries who were trying to make capitalist cities livable. Ebenezer Howard's "garden cities" are the ancestors of the sleek "new towns" in Scandinavia that reflect such harmonious designs of community and natural environment. The Social Democrats in the last thirty years have produced high-rise *Mietskasernen* or garden suburbs rather than true cities. The framework for postwar city reconstruction has been the urban network of the past. In Eastern Europe the centrally planned towns of postwar urbanization are often flawed structurally and deficient aesthetically. The towns that Socialists planned for the masses offer little more than their bourgeois counterparts. In Europe, as elsewhere, where planners' imaginations in the twentieth century have overleaped the past, the results have been disappointing. The grand urban designs of Le Corbusier, Neimeyer, and Costa when translated into reality have produced structures unsuited to their environment and citizenry. Twentieth-century answers to the dilemma of how to build "the good city" have failed when they have gone beyond the reformist traditions of the past.

EPILOGUE

Urban Europe in Our Time

BY THE OUTBREAK of World War I, urban Europe had acquired a
shape that would remain almost unchanged until 1939. Deadly as
it was, the 1914–1918 war spared most major cities, and the economic troubles of the interwar period meant that the pace of urban
growth slowed dramatically. Beyond the reconstruction of cities
involved in the fighting, such as Lille and Liège, only public housing
in large cities, notably in England and Austria, and some new
industrial towns in Soviet Russia stand out against a general record
of limited building. World War II, on the other hand, seemed to
concentrate on cities. Air power terrified and fascinated the public.
Despite the terrible memories evoked by Guernica, Coventry,
Dresden, and the London blitz, however, the bombing of European
cities had less impact on the course of the war than was thought
at the time and often less on the city populations as well. Sieges
and systematic destructions, as well as direct fighting, proved far
more deadly and destructive. Warsaw, Leningrad, Rotterdam, and
Berlin are cases in point.

When the war ended, the sufferings and losses of the population
were reflected in piles of rubble and a general air of decay and
neglect in cities. Even where bombs had not actually fallen, almost
no improvements had been undertaken. It was hard to imagine that
the next three decades would be marked by an unprecedented surge
of prosperity and that the gravest urban problems would soon em-
anate from the side effects of affluence. Not only was economic
growth rapid and virtually uninterrupted, but its fruits were spread
more widely than ever before, thanks in part to social policies of
extraordinary scope and size. Like private affluence, the welfare

state would engender unwanted and unanticipated costs, and eventually a measure of disillusionment. In the meantime, however, the two contributed to reducing the isolation of many whom industrial urbanization had left behind or tossed aside. It can be argued that the dominant feature of European life in the postwar period is generalized urbanization, encompassing in the urban way of life not only the many newly moved to town but also those who remain physically in the countryside.

It is not our purpose in this brief concluding section to deal with urban Europe in the postwar years, a subject that has perhaps stimulated more writing than the whole of the urbanization story for the nine centuries preceding. We want only to follow up some of the themes of earlier chapters and to note some historical roots of current developments.

Styles of Urbanization

Most notable in recent decades is what many call the urbanization of the countryside or the generalization of urban living beyond towns. One can distinguish a figurative dimension, in which the ideas and artifacts of urban living become accessible to rural people, as well as a literal form in which households partake of urban life while retaining rural domiciles. In economic and cultural terms, many rural people, including farmers, bear the full weight of twentieth-century mass culture. Their children see the same films, hear the same rock music, and wear the same blue jeans as those of urban dockworkers or bankers, and it makes little difference here whether one is talking of Croatia, Calvados, or Connaught, only that in the socialist bloc the new consumer goods are rather more coveted than enjoyed. What the postwar boom in agriculture began, mass communications have completed. The cultural homogenization of Europe has proceeded along the lines of the Network System, with such centers as Liverpool, Hamburg, and Munich, along with London, Paris, and Rome, serving as gateways to American influence. Then the paths of the Central Place System came into play, allowing commercial culture to flow down the urban hierarchy to the small market centers and rural habitats. Access to education, medical care, and other services has not quite kept pace, but rural areas have made great strides there, too.

Actual mixing of rural and urban location has become important.

The idea of living in town and working in the fields is both a very old and a new idea. Large agro-villages are common in Sicily, places of 20,000 or more with an almost exclusively agricultural population, while it is a tenet of socialist planning that farm operatives should live in agro-towns. Much more important is the opposite: rural residence with an urban workplace. By the mid-twentieth century the availability of good rail and road transport had established a new type of temporary rural-to-urban migratory movement. Commuters flooded into the cities and the factories daily from bedroom suburbs and farm villages. Today, however, these migrants cover the whole spectrum of occupations and socioeconomic levels; no longer are temporary migrants the least favored, most expendable of workers. Many professionals, bureaucrats, and businesspeople prefer to commute once a week rather than five times. They live in town but maintain a secondary residence, nearby for weekends or farther away for holidays only. In many mountainous areas as well as along the seashores, new settlements have been built and crumbling villages have found a whole new identity. Local people can now choose to remain and provide services to the countrified urbanites instead of leaving as their elders were forced to do.

In part because the countryside and its villages have gained new prosperity, the postwar period has been especially favorable to cities of the Central Place System, which had been rather left behind by industrial urbanization. Regional capitals and lesser central places have largely shed their sleepy "provincialism." They, too, enjoy the benefits of fast and flexible road transport. In addition, the determinants of industrial location have been profoundly transformed by technological change, especially by the kinds of advances that have also helped make large cities manageable. Internal combustion and the harnessing of electricity to provide power and communication make it possible to control activities at a distance as well as to subdivide industrial processes in space. Most new plants are small, clean, and do not need to be part of an industrial complex. Yet these possibilities would not suffice to draw employment to smaller cities if it were not for their positive features, which are largely the result of prior retardation. Many towns that escaped the blighting consequences of earlier industrial growth reap present-day economic and social advantages. They are at least able to retain native sons and daughters, if not to attract many newcomers from outside the region. No longer are these towns mere way stations in a selective, step-by-step migratory drain to the metropolis.

However, the great cities of Europe have not given up any of their dynamic attraction to the invigorated provincial towns. Although their place in the national urban system may have stabilized, the capitals derive enormous stimulation from their role in the supranational system. Indeed, the single most striking and visible dimension of change in Geneva, Milan, and Frankfurt, as well as Paris and London, is their cosmopolitan character. The Network System of long-distance urban contacts is alive and well. Whether one looks at the jet-setters in the Inter-Palace hotels, the *Gastarbeiter* on the early-morning underground trains, or the backpacking students around the parks and squares, the attraction of many cities overleaps the boundaries of region and class. In the largest metropolises, this appeal, along with a vastly expanded set of linkages associated with centralized government services, international business, and the ever-growing role of information in production and distribution, have generated enormous pressure for growth. All over Europe, governments strain to limit metropolitan expansion as well as to manage it by spectacular feats of planning, engineering, and investment. As in the baroque era, these latter efforts are in part motivated by a desire to demonstrate one's prowess to the world. Fortunately, the criteria of international prestige are coming to include amenity, fiscal prudence, and human values as well as sheer scale and technical virtuosity.

With more and more people choosing to live in cities, and with congestion aggravated by the spread of private transportation, the need to accommodate people is very great. An obvious solution is to create cities from scratch, and the "new town" has attracted an enormous amount of attention. Despite interesting realizations, notably in the vicinity of the capitals of northern Europe and in areas of new industrialization in the latecomer socialist countries, it is easy to exaggerate the contribution new towns have made. Most do not fulfill the original expectation of providing a balanced mix of residence and employment. Even when the overall numbers are balanced, there is substantial commuter traffic in and out. Also, new towns have not always proved highly popular, certainly not in France. The best that can be said is that they represent a clustered form of development around metropolitan centers, arguably preferable to uncontrolled sprawl but in no sense true cities.

Finally, the older industrial conurbations now present some of the greatest problems, although outsiders have largely ignored these areas except when massive layoffs or protests have drawn in the media, as in the English urban riots of summer 1981. With a dwindling economic base and a low level of amenity, the coal basins have become the dark underside of a growing Europe. Not even the post-1973 energy inflation has sufficed to breathe new life into them. Less visibly than the capital cities, the aging industrial centers have also acquired a large population of the new *Lumpenproletariat* from overseas, who take advantage of vacant lodgings and a decent—if drab—industrial service base.

The Political Economy of Affluence

Urban Europe demonstrates well the complementarities and contradictions of modern economic systems and the hollowness of neat ideological distinctions. In the capitalist West, rapid growth has generated even faster increases in the demand for, and expenditure on, public services. In the socialist East, on the other hand, the best-laid plans of all-powerful bureaucrats cannot reduce the disparities between metropolis and hinterland nor overcome the qualitative insufficiencies in the standard of living. The small private sector contributes disproportionate amounts of food, while people squander their leisure in queuing.

In fact, the principal issue of political economy in postwar urban Europe is proving not to be whether the market is preferable to central planning or vice versa. Rather, it is the degree to which a modern, interdependent society can decentralize. We shall see this when we look at the system of cities and regions, but the problem is a pervasive one. The excesses of militaristic nationalism in the first half of the century are the most dramatic example of excessive centralization, but many other phenomena illustrate it also, including the disillusionment and sometimes violent alienation of youth in the recent decades. From the provos of Amsterdam and the Parisian students of May 1968 to urban terrorist groups here and there, the tide of protest by the very beneficiaries of urban Europe's newest golden age has swept angry citizens into clashes with their central governments.

Prosperity seems to lead to smugness and boredom and to great expectations with low tolerance for sacrifice. It also imposes tangible

costs. Whereas environmental damage was a direct result of industrialization in the nineteenth century, a much greater volume
of material production today generates far less pollution. However,
the consumption of these riches threatens to choke the air, the
water, and the land with fumes, litter, sewage, and noise. Already,
the Mediterranean is gravely endangered, although a part of the
problem results from rapid industrialization by impatient latecom-
ers such as Spain and Greece. There are also more subtle and
intractable problems with mass prosperity. The newly affluent European consumer clings to older, elitist values. Yet, as F. Hirsch
(1976) has pointed out, many kinds of consumption are deemed
desirable because they are rare, which makes it impossible to de-
mocratize them. Not everyone can eat at one of the twenty best
restaurants in France, summer at *the* fashionable beach, or visit
Rome without being troubled by crowds of tourists. Such "posi-
tional goods" are by their nature not for all; yet a vast system of
communications is mobilized to create demand for them.

A pleasant environment for living as well as recreation is highly
valued by Europeans, however much they may demand the goods
whose production despoils nature and whose consumption gobbles
up the traces of the past. In cities, older areas are being set aside
as automobile-free zones or for restoration and gentrification. Many
decry the artificiality of some of this, particularly the construction
of brand-new "old" townscapes, but they prove popular and attract
visitors as well as residents. Long-standing policies of green-belt
development and clustering in suburbs continue to give Europeans
better access to nature on average than North Americans enjoy,
though at the price of more dense living. The American model of
car-centered settlements dominated by freeways and suburban
shopping malls has not been rejected, but it does not seem to be
on the way to conquering urban space. Doubtless, the result will
be neither totally logical nor ever quite finished or harmonious, but
such a vital hodgepodge of old, new, borrowed, and restored has
always been the rule in European cities.

The Enduring Regions of Europe

A map of Europe in 1950 could well have shown only national
boundaries without causing readers to feel that they were missing
much by not knowing how many subdivisions each country con-

tained. Except for passing school examinations and addressing mail, the *départments*, shires, and *Länder* mattered little. Some people still thought of themselves as from Yorkshire, Catalonia, or Silesia, but these were quite unofficial, and sometimes subversive, loyalties whose days were thought to be numbered. Only in quaint Switzerland could one canton allow women to vote and another not. Lingering xenophobia, after several decades of bitter conflict and nationalism, was matched by insistence on central control of administration and culture. Centralism, especially strong in France, was championed by the Left as well as by much of the Right. Britain was not about to repeat the experience of devolution just completed with the major part of Ireland.

Now all this has changed, at least in the West. Linguistic conflicts have almost torn Belgium apart as a nation, and they sputter along many of the interfaces from Finland to the Adige. Even more bitter ethnic or religious divisions split Ireland and northern Spain, while long dormant or repressed cultures assert their identity from Wales to Occitania and Macedonia. In the East, of course, such expressions of autonomism are severely repressed, but few have much illusion that the cause of loyalty to the greater socialist homeland will win the battle for hearts and minds. In these regional struggles cities have been both the sites and symbols of ethnic conflict, as different groups contest the leadership and language of urban institutions of power.

These conflicts and protests, even the cultural and linguistic revivals, represent the most dramatic side, often overplayed, of a profound revival in the importance of regions. Just as the supranational world of easy travel, multinational marketing, and mass culture is eroding the nation-state from above, the region is challenging its hegemony from below. New or revitalized political institutions are putting governments nearer the people, and many of the old provinces, duchies, and baronies prove to be the right size for modern administration, somewhere between the nation and the small units inherited from the preautomotive era. One group of countries has used federalism as a powerful help in establishing democracy; in others, it offers the promise, though as yet only the promise, of offsetting the effects of urban primacy. In all cases, the regional capitals gain high-order central place functions. French planning refers to these cities as *metropoles d'équilibre*. Some have already gone so far as to suggest a "Europe of regions," with national boundaries and sovereignties simply eliminated (Sampson 1968). There are plenty of reasons to doubt such a change happening, but one can applaud the new life of the regions without suggesting that the process go to an extreme. At a minimum, ties across national boundaries have expanded with economic cooperation.

A quick comparison of the regional structure of western Europe today with that of medieval times (see Figures 2.1 and 7.6) reveals substantial continuity. In the areas of Flanders, the Rhineland, and most of West Germany, a series of middle-sized towns still dot the territory, sharing economic, political, and cultural functions. In contrast, modern-day England, France, and Austria each have one dominant city, which serves both as the hub of a vast transportation network and as a supreme political and service center. While the reach and power of London, Paris, and Vienna have expanded, their hegemony was established in medieval times. Only in the English Midlands and in northern Italy have centuries-old patterns been altered. In the former case, industrialization produced relatively dense urban networks grouped around medium-sized towns. In the latter case, Milan emerged from the rich array of independent city-states to become the economic leader of the territory. On the other hand, the peripheral regions of contemporary Europe have remained less densely populated and more weakly urbanized than the lands of the center. In a few areas, relatively large cities such as Naples, Madrid, Dublin, and Glasgow have emerged to organize a region, but they do not offer the array of services and international links provided by the urban giants closer to the European core. Transportation networks, in particular, are less well developed. Although the size of effective regional units has expanded over the centuries and linkages among cities have become tighter, there has been relatively little change in the *type* of urbanization characteristic of the European core and its periphery.

In fact, the medieval core has recovered in recent years a great deal of the leadership it lost during the period of high industrialization. Recall that this core was a dual one with urban concentrations in the Low Countries and northern Italy and a connecting axis that fluctuated according to the fortunes of war. Once again, the strong cities of Europe are concentrated here except that the axis is now broader, reaching from Lyon to Vienna. The south, however, has not recovered the leading place it once enjoyed. Even though the economic centers of today are not always those of yesterday, they are very close indeed. Rotterdam has replaced Bruges, Brussels outgrown Ghent, Düsseldorf taken the place of Cologne, and Munich that of Augsburg. But Antwerp, Geneva, Milan, and Frankfurt have kept their roles, joined by Turin, Zurich, and Stuttgart. All these cities have a place in the multinational network; some, such as Geneva and Brussels, house specifically supranational institutions. Note that some of the urban leaders are former capitals of the Central Place System, others nodes and gateways of the Network System. Not one owes its origin as a major center to nineteenth-century industry.

In addition to the general concentration of activity in the heart of Western Europe, other locational shifts may be noted. The amenities of climate are drawing people and activities away from the north. This aggravates regional imbalances in Britain and Scandinavia, but also has helped industrialize southern France and Germany. In Spain, geography and history combine to make development centrifugal, the pull of the capital being no match for the coastal zones, the more so, perhaps, as Madrid is associated indelibly with the dark figures of Philip II and Franco. Germany's traditional balance has been reinforced by the division into two nations, which removed the threat of primacy posed by Berlin. On the other hand, Italy is torn between the affinity of the north for Europe and the political commitment to developing the backward Mezzogiorno. The same ambivalence threatens the cultural coalition that is Yugoslavia.

Our brief survey is not intended to give a complete picture of the European urban system today. Its point is to show how regions, urban hierarchies, and the relationships inherited from the past continue to condition powerfully the results of change in Europe. While particular technological innovations, political movements, and outside influences—coca-colonization, oil shocks, or Third World immigration—occasion new episodes in the story, the cast of characters remains much the same. Major continuities in economic and political functions mold responses into familiar patterns. The vocabulary of urban action and development has changed only slowly and incompletely. As unlike as the modern metropolis and the medieval walled town appear, their regional roles and sometimes even their international linkages have remained remarkably similar. Even if airplanes and trucks have replaced water coaches and horse convoys, many of the medieval interurban routes still flourish, and new urbanites continue to arrive from centuries-old hinterlands. Paris and Munich, as well as Hamburg, Budapest, Bologna, and Leicester are recognizable descendants of their late medieval counterparts. Their pasts are written in the street names, the lines of the roadways, and the shapes of the roofs and steeples. Differences in scale cannot obliterate deeply ingrained styles and directions of development. Urban Europe, despite its slick overlay of modernistic architecture and industrial technology, was functionally "made" centuries ago. Much of its strength, as well as its charm, derives from this underpinning of the new by the old.

APPENDIXES

NOTES

BIBLIOGRAPHY

INDEX

A Cyclical Model of an Economy

ECONOMIC THEORY can help us analyze some of the relationships linking town and countryside in early modern Europe. Our model of the cyclical fortunes of urban and rural worlds is depicted in Chapter 4, Figures 4.1a and 4.1b. Although both diagrams relate identical variables, cycles in the former have arbitrary, constant lengths. In the latter, cycles are fitted to data on prices, tying the model to historical periods. These are our variables:

p = *the price level.* This series is derived from grain prices, for which good data are available (Phelps-Brown and Hopkins 1956; Braudel and Spooner 1967). Moreover, price movements and population growth are closely correlated, so the price curve also mirrors the shifting size of the population. One additional function of the price curve must be mentioned. The terms of trade, or the relative prices of grain and other farm products and of agricultural and manufactured goods, are also reflected in the price series. Commodities other than grain may be thought of as combinations of grain and labor. Agricultural products such as meat, wine, and raw materials, and finally industrial goods and services contain progressively more labor than does grain production. Since real wages move inversely to prices, low prices indicate that labor-intensive commodities are expensive relative to grain. Conversely, high prices and low real wages signal the relative cheapness of farm products other than grain, of manufactured goods and urban products in general.

w/p = *wages adjusted for prices, or the real wage rate.* Because money wages tend to remain stable, real wages vary almost inversely with prices (Phelps-Brown and Hopkins 1956). The small delayed change of money wages in response to extremes in living costs is depicted by the placing of the wage cycle in relation to that of prices. It varies not in a precise inverse curve but is shifted slightly to the left.

q = *real output.* Production levels vary in response to prices. Rising prices stimulate the growth of manufacturing until diminishing returns and inflation trigger a downturn. We depict the production curve leading the price cycle, since the final price rise is the result of scarcity.

s_w = *the share of wages in total income.*

s_r = *the share of rents in total income.* Variables s_w and s_r move cyclically in a perfect inverse relationship. Together they depict the division of total income among workers and owners. The wage share, which is the product of the wage rate and the level of employment, is closely tied to real wages. As real wages rise and fall, so does the share of total income earned by workers. Because employment levels take time to respond to wage changes, the s_w curve lags behind the w/p curve. The s_r curve, drawn as the exact inverse of s_w, depicts a variety of claims on surplus by landlords, owners, governments, and others. This share varies with but lags behind changes in prices and population. Many payments of surplus are contractual and are only periodically renegotiated to reflect changes in prices and bargaining power. At a given moment rents reflect conditions of a slightly earlier time.

The model ignores short-run economic fluctuations as well as variations in amplitude, showing a mere leveling of growth, for instance, as a downturn. Be forewarned that the data available to support the relationship we describe are slim. Indeed, the model was devised in order to overcome the lack of reliable, broadly based numbers for variables other than prices. Figure 4.1b was constructed by fitting the curves of p to the known peaks and troughs of recorded price series. Price maxima occurred around 1320, 1650, and 1815, while minima can be located in 1460 and 1740. The remaining series were drawn on the basis of unchanging phase relationships to the price series, which we specified in our definitions of terms. The actual construction of Figure 4.1b was done with the aid of mathematics. A polynomial was fitted to the price turning points, and the other series derived by a phase shift. Calculations as well as plotting were carried out by computer.

Size Distributions and the Rank-Size Rule

BECAUSE our primary concern is historical, we have concentrated on urban growth and compared cities according to the vigor of their population increase over the long run. Yet most of the literature concerned with arrays of cities looks at size distributions at a point in time. By far the most common point of departure for the analysis of such size distributions is the rank-size rule, which states that the population of a city tends to approximate a fraction of the size of the largest city in the array, the denominator being the size-rank of the city in question. Thus the tenth largest city is supposed to be about one tenth the size of the biggest city, but also 40 percent as large as the fourth city in size, and so on.

If one plots size against rank on logarithmic scales, the distribution graphs as a straight line with a slope of minus one (45° downward). Putting the rule in the form of a graph or an equation has the advantage of focusing attention on the entire distribution and not just on the size ratio between a given city and the single largest one. A rank-size distribution has three distinct properties: the straight line in logarithmic coordinates, the 45° downward slope, and the vertical intercept corresponding to the population of the largest city. Thus actual urban arrays can fit the rule or depart from it in any or all of these properties. Figure B.1 shows a number of actual distributions illustrating varying degrees of fit.[1]

If an urban array obeys the rank-size rule at a point in time, size-neutral growth following the law of proportionate effect, or Gibrat's law, will preserve the fit. It seems logical to infer that such growth would therefore not generate a pattern conforming to the rank-size

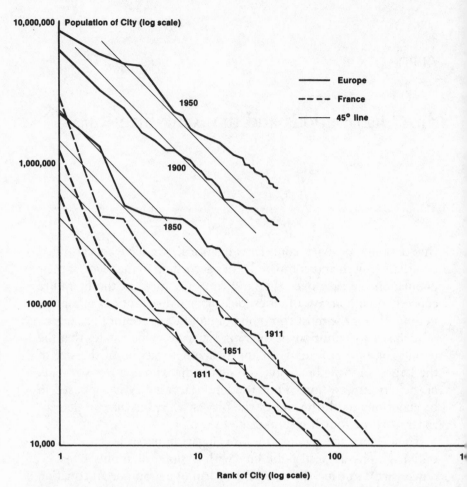

Figure B.1. Changing rank-size distributions of cities in Europe and in France. (Data from Chandler and Fox 1974 and Dupeux 1981.)

rule from a different initial state; yet this could still happen if new towns arise at an appropriate constant rate.

If the rank-size rule is to be more than a mathematical curiosity, it should have some sort of normative properties. For one thing, the rule can serve as a standard against which to describe actual urban size distributions. Robson (1973) calls it an ordering of cities between primacy and oligarchy, in effect defining these two terms with reference to the rank-size rule. The distinctions he draws apply mainly to the upper end of the size distribution: how large the main towns are relative to the first among them, and how quickly size falls off as one descends in rank. When one looks at the whole distribution, the slope becomes useful, including the possibility of curvature or of a kink. Consider the brilliant periodization of early modern urbanization by de Vries (1981). He summarized three stages or subperiods of urban development with rank-size distributions. They showed movement toward the rank-size rule up to 1750 or so and a departure in the century that followed, as first large and then smaller places grew more quickly than average. The findings of Robson (1973) and Dupeux (1981) and our own calculations for the upper reaches of the European hierarchy cast doubt on de Vries's hypothesis that smaller cities were still catching up in the first half of the nineteenth century, but his work effectively uses the rank-size rule to illustrate changes over time in patterns of urban growth.

A more ambitious and uncertain undertaking is to link the rank-size rule to the existence or delimitation of urban systems, as Russell (1972b) did in his work on medieval regions. He assumed that urban systems conformed to the rank-size rule and then defined regional boundaries in such a way as to maximize the fit while preserving a reasonably compact shape (see Chapter 2).

Using a similar criterion, de Vries (1981) argued that European urban systems became more unified by 1600 when actual distributions of city sizes came to resemble the line of the rank-size rule. Others, such as Wallerstein (1974), arrived at similar conclusions based upon economic and political arguments. Let us assume for the moment that rank-size distributions signal functional integration. If we then compare data on city sizes and ranks between 1750 and 1950, we can judge whether industrial urbanization moved the European hierarchy toward systemic unity. Rank-size distributions for different dates are shown in Table 7.2, while Table B.1 gives the ratio between actual size and that predicted by the rank-size rule for cities in different positions in the European urban hierarchy. As can be seen, cities below the top rank were consistently larger than the rule predicts. The urban hierarchy was oligarchic, except for a single case, that of the fifth-ranked city in 1850. The central point, however, is not that the ratios are greater than one but that they increase with falling rank, corresponding to a relatively flat slope for the line. Otherwise, it could be argued that London spoiled the series by being too small! Yet note that the ratios decrease

Table B.1. Rank-size order in the European urban hierarchy, 1750–1950.

| Rank | Ratio of actual city size to size predicted by the rank-size rule | | | | |
	1750	1800	1850	1900	1950
1	—	—	—	—	—
5	1.6	1.4	0.9	1.1	2.1
10	2.0	2.0	1.5	1.5	1.9
15	2.6	2.3	1.6	1.4	2.4
20	2.3	2.4	1.7	1.6	2.6
25	2.5	2.5	1.8	1.9	2.7
30	2.7	2.8	1.8	2.0	2.9
35	2.8	2.9	1.8	2.1	2.9
40	3.0	3.1	1.9	2.2	3.0

Source: Calculated from Chandler and Fox (1974:322-330, 337-338).

toward those of a perfect rank-size pattern between 1800 and 1850, only to move away from it again in the twentieth century. The economic historian may be struck by the way this rhythm corresponds to the rise and fall of free trade, which peaked in the 1860s. Perhaps the removal of tariff barriers, which eased the flow of goods, encouraged proportional amounts of migration to cities of different sizes as it wove closer economic links among cities of several countries. In consequence, an argument might well be made that Europe developed a more unified urban system during the first half of the nineteenth century, but that nationalism slowed the process during the second half and actually reversed it in the twentieth.

There have been attempts to argue that the rank-size rule represents a complete, sophisticated, or efficient form for an urban array or system (Berry 1961). Clearly, an array consisting solely of small towns of like size suggests a lack of interurban ties and little more functional role than servicing the immediate surroundings. But given a range of city sizes, it is unclear why a certain degree of primacy or oligarchy should imply an incomplete or degenerate stage of urbanization. It is not even always true that urban arrays move closer to a rank-size distribution over time. The record is at best mixed. Russia gradually filled the gaps between very large and small centers (Rozman 1976), but other countries continued to exhibit marked primacy (Denmark, England), while still others developed a group of centers to share leading roles (Switzerland and the Netherlands). The French case is somewhat more complex. Although the slope of the rank-size line steepened toward minus one through the nineteenth century, the major provincial cities slipped from a position above the line to one below it, as shown in Figure B.1. The overall distribution became more strongly hierarchical as large centers grew faster than small ones. But the primacy of Paris, undiminished in terms of the distribution as a whole, actually increased relative to the large provincial centers.

By contrast, the five largest cities in neighboring Belgium grew to be much larger than those ranked just below them in 1900. Despite this break in the rank-size distribution, the existence of such a group of major cities argues for rather than against strongly developed links to the outside; indeed, Belgium was an early leader in industrial urbanization.

There is no need to belabor the point. Rank-size distributions are poor indicators of systemic links among towns, at least in modern Europe. Several patterns of relative city size and growth have proved compatible with social and economic development in these highly industrialized societies.

Notes

1. The Structures and Functions of Medieval Towns

1. The major sources for this section are Simmons (1974), Brown (1970), McKinley (1958), and Hoskins (1955).

2. Systems of Early Cities

1. See Christaller (1933), Lösch (1954), and Tinbergen (1968) for the original statement of central place theory and for more recent reformulations. Additional bibliography on this topic can be found in Berry and Pred (1961).

2. Many questions have been raised regarding Russell's work, some concerning the population estimates upon which the analysis is based. Comparison of Russell's figures with those of Chandler and Fox (1974) shows large disparities, and both sets of estimates must be used with caution.

3. Skinner (1977) defines urban systems in China by drawing on the role of the rivers for transportation.

4. The Network System as developed here owes a good deal to James Vance's view of urban systems, best articulated in Vance (1970) and in his critique of Russell (Vance 1975). Edward Fox's *The Other France* (1971) has also stimulated our thinking, notably by suggesting a dual view of urban systems in contrast to Vance's preference for replacing the central place model. See the later discussion in this chapter on alternative views.

5. The staple theory of economic development pioneered by Innis in the context of Canadian economic history attaches importance to the technology and organization of export production (Watkins 1963). Marx's emphasis on the mode and relations of production can also be mentioned.

6. The principal sources for this section are Lane (1973), Diehl (1925), and Luzzatto (1961).

3. The Demography of Preindustrial Cities

1. In addition to specific sources cited, the discussion here draws on Andorka (1978), Helleiner (1967), Wrigley (1969), Guillaume and Poussou (1970), Braudel (1979), Goubert (1965, 1969a), and Wrigley and Schofield (1981).

2. In a premarket society or where peasants own their land outright, they can claim the higher average product of labor. But this also falls as population rises. In the absence of landlords, the equilibrium of misery merely concerns a larger population. Of course, urbanization is quite unlikely in the more egalitarian, but equally dismal, case.

3. Mediterranean Europe had a larger urban population as well as many more major cities than the north. Nevertheless, small places must have contributed a substantial share to the urban total there as well.

4. Henry (1956); Andorka (1978); Wrigley and Schofield (1981); and Coale and Watkins (in press).

5. The material on Nördlingen is from Friedrichs (1979). Population data are estimated from the number of households.

6. In Chapter 5 we examine the special case of large early modern royal capitals.

4. Cities in the Early Modern European Economy

1. For a detailed analysis of the cyclical interplay of population, output, incomes, wages, and farm sizes, see Le Roy Ladurie 1966.

2. A major stimulus to the development of our model has been the view of European development so brilliantly expounded by Fernand Braudel in *Civilisation matérielle, économie et capitalisme, XVe–XVIIIe siècles* (1979). In his magisterial books Braudel pictures a three-leveled structure. As one moves upward, sophistication and the rate of change increase while the constancies of physical and biological necessity and of tradition fade. We hope to have explicated the urban implications of the Braudelian system.

3. Some major recent surveys are Sella (1974), Kellenbenz (1977), and Deyon (1979).

4. See, for example, Strauss (1966), Sella (1979), and DuPlessis and Howell (1982).

5. See Deyon (1967), Goubert (1968), Chandler and Fox (1974), and Sella (1979).

6. See, for example, de Maddalena (1974). While sheep raising is not labor intensive, it supplied the wool industry, which was.

7. The present section draws heavily on van Houtte (1977). See also van der Wee (1975) and Craeybeckx (1976).

8. The low point of the price curve came around 1394 for both Ghent and Bruges (Nicholas 1971).

9. Between varying dates in the later seventeenth century and about 1750, the population decline of major towns was as follows: Antwerp 36 percent, Bruges 26 percent, Ghent 15 percent, and Louvain 9 percent (van Houtte 1977).

10. Nobles, many of whom in fact moved to Brussels or Vienna, owned one quarter of the land in Liège and the Hainault and a tenth of the property in Brabant and Flanders. Bourgeois owners held an additional 23 percent to 38 percent in Liège. Of course, the proportions were higher near the major towns (van Houtte 1977). Remember also that "rent" as used in the model includes claims to surplus by nonlandlords, for example, taxes and tithes.

5. Beyond Baroque Urbanism

1. The principal source for this account is the multivolume Higounet, *Histoire de Bordeaux* (IV,1966; V,1968). See also Mirot (1950), Duby (III,1981), Poussou (1978), Butel (1975), and Cocula (1975).

2. For a marvelous picture of this "enlarged" tertiary sector in eighteenth-century Austria, see the levee scene in act 1 of *Der Rosenkavalier* by Strauss and Hoffmansthal.

3. The effects of income inequality could be muted by social mobility, however, and by access to political power. Rappaport (1982) has shown how in Elizabethan London the majority of male residents became citizens and guild members.

4. Kindleberger (1978) develops the point that a trading system needs and tends toward a single financial center.

5. In any case, we would prefer to characterize the economic organization of the period by a term such as *protoindustrial* or *protocapitalistic*, certainly as it affects urbanization.

6. Modern political economists use the term *rent-seeking* for such fiscal preoccupations. See Buchanan, Tollison, and Tullock (1980).

7. This approach may be compared to the use of the rank-size rule to establish the limits of medieval urban regions (Russell 1972b; see Chapter 2 above). Many English scholars have used the notion of a hierarchical urban array, for example, Hoskins (1955), Everitt (1975), Clark and Slack (1976), and Patten (1978). Rozman's work (1976, 1978) has the merit of distinguishing functional types and of paying explicit attention to process.

6. Industrialization and the Cities

1. On the history of the Ruhr valley and its urbanization, see Pounds (1952), Jäger (1978), and Reulecke (1984).

2. The principal sources for this description of Lancashire are Sharpless (1978), Rodgers (1970), Musson (1978), and Harris (1972).

3. The principal sources for this section are Latreille (1975), Lequin (1977), Léon, Crouzet, and Gascon (1972), and Cayez (1978).

4. An analysis of cities in analogous terms can be found in Tsuru (1963).

5. A good brief discussion is in F. Carter (1975).

6. We return to the issues around urban versus suburban location in Chapter 9. They include nonmarket considerations such as local tariffs and political jurisdiction.

7. Urban Growth and Urban Systems

1. The sources for this section are Thienel (1973), Dickinson (1961), and Matzerath (1981). See also Busch (1971, 1977).

2. The inclusion of Russia narrows the difference between the two components and increases the overall growth of urban population, but neither effect is great.

3. By 1950 the apparent disproportion had lessened, mainly because such agglomerations as Leeds and Manchester were being defined in conurbation terms (data from Chandler and Fox 1974).

4. The sources for this section are Caracciolo (1981), Fedor (1975), Rozman (1976), and Bairoch (1977).

5. Listings for 1800 and 1900 were also compiled.

6. The figure 13.8 represents the mean ratio of 1950 size to 1750 size for the largest city and for all steps in the ranking that are multiples of five (5th, 10th, . . . , 40th). The standard deviation is 1.6.

7. Different closely spaced groups of industrial settlements figure as single conurbations in other sources; examples are Lille-Roubaix-Tourcoing and the pottery towns of Staffordshire.

8. To be sure, Robson's (1973) important study of urban growth in England represents a retreat from the attempt to do a systemic analysis. On the other hand, Russell's exercise (1972b) in fitting medieval European cities into a regional rank-size array comes more under the heading of historical geography than under that of urban history per se. The full synthesis of urban growth and urban systems still belongs on the research agenda.

9. Topographical irregularities aside, equal market areas are best accommodated by having three centers of given order for each higher center. This number, called k-value in the Christaller model (1933), becomes four if small central places are preferentially located on the straight roads joining larger ones. It rises to seven if the territory administered by the larger center is to include the area served by each of its subordinates.

10. Christaller (1933) measured centrality by the number of telephones rather than people, ingeniously stressing the city's outside contacts.

11. The close communication links with the capital and the world give resorts a spuriously high centrality score in the Christaller model (1933).

8. The Human Consequences of Industrial Urbanization

1. For discussions of urban and rural fertility differences, see Knodel (1974), Livi-Bacci (1977), Lesthaeghe (1977), Andorka (1978), and Sharlin (in press).

2. For an American model of this subcultural division of neighborhoods, see Suttles (1968).

3. In this perspective our Central Place and Network Systems recall Redfield and Singer's (1954) orthogenetic and heterogenetic processes.

4. See C. Tilly, L. Tilly, and R. Tilly (1975) for a comprehensive account of the changing forms of collective violence in France, Germany, and Italy during the nineteenth and early twentieth centuries.

9. The Evolution and Control of Urban Space

1. Engels (1845) noted the contrast between the facades and the slums behind them in central Manchester; Cobb and Breach (1980) look behind, as well as at, some of *The Streets of Paris* that have survived from the last century.

2. Economists recognize congestion as a classic case of market failure, akin to pollution. For example, cars will tend to crowd onto a freeway even when the number per hour passing a given point is declining.

3. See Leheu (1954) for the Parisian suburb of Argenteuil.

4. Contrast Gauldie (1974) and Burnett (1978) for the case of England.

5. Boileau's *Embarras de Paris* laments urban disamenity in the 1660s.

6. Bellan (1971) is an important source for this section.

7. On nineteenth-century Milan, see Dalmasso (1971), L. Tilly (1973), and Hunecke (1978).

8. The most recent sources for this section are Benevolo (1975) and Sutcliffe (1981). See also Johnson-Marshall (1966) and Choay (1969). A word about terminology: the English *town planning* corresponds to the French neologism *urbanisme* and to the positive German word *Städtebau* ("city building"), as noted by Sutcliffe (1981).

9. There are two qualifications to the argument. Zoning regulations act to restrict land uses that impose nuisances on adjoining parcels, although they have been used almost exclusively to protect established patterns. Also, real-property taxes tardily capture some of the private gains from public initiatives.

10. Some sources are Réau and Lavedan (1954), Pinkney (1958), Saalman (1970), Sutcliffe (1970), and Gaillard (1977).

11. See Evenson (1979) for a thorough and critical examination of change in Paris after Haussmann.

Appendix B. Size Distributions and the Rank-Size Rule

1. In probability terms the rank-size rule is akin to a Pareto distribution, and similar, though not formally identical, to a lognormal distribution. Robson (1973) and Pumain (1982) summarize a vast literature.

Bibliography

Abrams, P., and E. A. Wrigley, eds. 1978. *Towns in Societies*. Cambridge: Cambridge University Press.

Ackerman, E. B. 1978. *Village on the Seine: Tradition and Change in Bonnières, 1815–1914*. Ithaca, N.Y.: Cornell University Press.

Adams, I. I. 1978. *The Making of Urban Scotland*. London and Montreal: Croom Helm.

Agulhon, M. 1969. "La Fin des petites villes dans le Var intérieur au XIXe siècle." In *Villes de l'Europe méditerranéenne*. Annales de la Faculté des Lettres et Sciences Humaines de Nice, 9–10, pp. 323–326. Nice: Centre de la Méditerranée Moderne et Contemporaine.

Agus, I. A. 1965. *Urban Civilization in Pre-Crusade Europe: A Study of Organized Town Life in Northwestern Europe during the Tenth and Eleventh Centuries based on the Responsa Literature*. 2 vols. Leiden: E. Brill.

Åkerman, S. 1975. "Internal Migration, Industrialization, and Urbanization, 1895–1930." *Scandinavian Economic History Review* 23(2):149–158.

——— 1977. "Swedish Migration and Social Mobility: The Tale of Three Cities." *Social Science History* 1(3):178–209.

Alonso, W. 1964. "The Historic and the Structural Theories of Urban Form: Their Implications for Urban Reveval." *Land Economics* 40:227–231.

Altick, R. 1957. *The English Common Reader: A Social History of the Mass Reading Public, 1800–1900*. Chicago: University of Chicago Press.

Anderson, B. A. 1977. "Who Chose the Cities? Migrants to Moscow and St. Petersburg Cities in the Late Nineteenth Century." In *Population Patterns in the Past*, ed. R. D. Lee, pp. 277–296. New York: Academic Press.

Anderson, M. 1971a. "Urban Migration in Nineteenth-Century Lancashire: Some Insights into Two Competing Hypotheses." *Annales de Démographie Historique* 1971:13–26.

——— 1971b. *Family Structure in 19th Century Lancashire*. Cambridge: Cambridge University Press.

Andorka, R. 1978. *Determinants of Fertility in Advanced Societies*. New York: Free Press.

Arberry, A. J. 1967. "Muslim Cordoba." In *Cities of Destiny*, ed. A. Toynbee, pp. 166–177. New York: McGraw-Hill.

Ardagh, J. 1979. *A Tale of Five Cities*. New York: Harper and Row.

Argan, G. C. 1969. *The Renaissance City*. New York: Braziller.

Ariès, P. 1948. *Histoire des populations françaises et de leurs attitudes devant la vie depuis le XVIIIe siècle*. Reprint. Paris: Seuil, 1971.

Armengaud, A. 1972. "Industrialisation et démographie dans la France du XIXe siècle." In *L'Industrialisation en Europe au XIXe siècle*, ed. P. Léon, F. Crouzet, and R. Gascon, pp. 187–200. Paris: Editions du CNRS.

Arrow, K. 1962. "Economic Welfare and the Allocation of Resources for Invention." In *The Rate and Direction of Inventive Activity*, pp. 609–626. Princeton: Princeton University Press.

Aydalot, P., L. Bergeron, and M. Roncayolo. 1981. *Industrialisation et croissance urbaine dans la France du XIXe siècle*. Paris: Université de Paris I Panthéon Sorbonne.

Babelon, J. P. 1969. "L'Urbanisme d'Henri IV et de Sully à Paris." In *L'Urbanisme de Paris et l'Europe, 1600–1800*, ed. P. Francastel, pp. 47–60. Paris: Editions Klincksieck.

Bacon, E. N. 1974. *The Design of Cities*. Rev. ed. New York: Viking Press.

Bairoch, P. 1977. "Population urbaine et taille des villes en Europe de 1600 à 1970: Présentation de séries statistiques." In *Démographie urbaine, XVe–XXe siècle*, pp. 1–42. Lyon: Centre d'Histoire Economique et Sociale de la Région Lyonnaise.

——— 1981. "Urbanization and Economic Development in the Western World: Some Provisional Conclusions of an Empirical Study." In *Patterns of European Urbanization since 1500*, ed. H. Schmal, pp. 61–75. London: Croom Helm.

Bardet, J. P., ed. 1971. *Le Bâtiment: Enquête d'histoire économique XIVe–XIXe siècles*. Paris and The Hague: Mouton.

——— 1973. "Review of M. Térisse, La Population de Marseille et de son terroir de 1694 à 1830." *Annales de Démographie Historique* 1973:353–375.

——— 1974. "La Démographie des villes de la modernité, XVIe–XVIIIe siècles: Mythes et réalités." *Annales de Démographie Historique* 1974:101–126.

Bardet, J. P., et al. 1977. "Une Nouvelle histoire des villes (Note critique)." *Annales (ESC)* 32(6):1237–46.

Barel, Y. 1977. *La Ville médiévale: Système social, système urbain*. Grenoble: Presses Universitaires de Grenoble.

Baron, H. 1966. *The Crisis of the Early Italian Renaissance: Civic Humanism and Republican Liberty in an Age of Classicism and Tyranny*. Rev. ed. Princeton: Princeton University Press.

Barraclough, G., ed. 1979. *The Times Atlas of World History*. London: Times Books Ltd.

Bater, J. H. 1976. *St. Petersburg: Industrialization and Change*. London: Edward Arnold.

——— 1977. "Urban Networks in Russia, 1750–1800, and Premodern Periodization." (Review of Rozman 1976.) *Economic History Review* 30(1):211–212.

Beckmann, M. J. 1958. "City Hierarchies and the Distribution of City Sizes." *Economic Development and Cultural Change* 6:243–248.

—— 1970. "City Size Distributions in a Central Place Hierarchy: An Alternative Approach." *Journal of Regional Science* 10:25–33.

Bédarida, F. 1970. "Cities: Population and the Urban Explosion." In *The Nineteenth Century*, ed. A. Briggs, pp. 99–130. New York: McGraw-Hill.

Bell, C., and R. Bell. 1969. *City Fathers: Town Planning in Britain from Roman Times to 1900*. New York: Praeger.

Bellan, R. C. 1971. *The Evolving City*. Vancouver: Copp Clark.

Beloch, K. J. 1937. *Bevölkerungsgeschichte Italiens*. 3 vols. Reprint. Berlin and Leipzig: De Gruyter, 1961.

Benevolo, L. 1971. *The Origins of Modern Town Planning*. Cambridge, Mass.: MIT Press.

—— 1975. *History of the City*. Reprint in English trans. Cambridge, Mass.: MIT Press, 1980.

Bennassar, B. 1967. *Valladolid au siècle d'or: Une Ville de Castille et sa campagne au XVIe siècle*. Paris: Mouton.

Beresford, M. W., and H. P. R. Finberg. 1973. *English Medieval Boroughs: A Handlist*. Newton Abbot, England: David and Charles.

Bernard, J. 1972. "Trade and Finance in the Middle Ages, 900–1500." In *The Fontana Economic History of Europe*. Vol. 1, *The Middle Ages*, ed. C. Cipolla, pp. 274–338. London: Collins.

Bernard, L. 1970. *The Emerging City: Paris in the Age of Louis XIV*. Durham, N.C.: Duke University Press.

Berreman, G. D. 1978. "Scale and Social Relations." *Current Anthropology* 19(2):225–245.

Berry, B. J. L. 1961. "City Size Distribution and Economic Development." *Economic Development and Cultural Change* 9:573–588.

—— 1964. "Cities as Systems within Systems of Cities." *Papers and Proceedings of the Regional Science Association* 13:147–163.

—— 1967. *Geography of Market Centers and Retail Distribution*. Englewood Cliffs, N.J.: Prentice-Hall.

—— 1972. "Hierarchical Diffusion: The Basis of Development. Filtering and Spread in a System of Growth Centers." In *Man, Space, and Environment: Concepts in Contemporary Human Geography*, ed. P. W. English and R. C. Mayfield, pp. 340–359. New York: Oxford University Press.

—— 1973. *The Human Consequences of Urbanisation: Divergent Paths in the Urban Experience of the Twentieth Century*. London: Macmillan.

Berry, B. J. L., and W. L. Garrison. 1958. "Functional Bases of Central Place Hierarchy." *Economic Geography* 34:145–154.

Berry, B. J. L., and F. E. Horton. 1970. *Geographic Perspectives on Urban Systems*. Englewood Cliffs, N.J.: Prentice-Hall.

Berry, B. J. L., and A. Pred. 1961. *Central Place Studies: A Bibliography of Theory and Application*. Philadelphia: University of Pennsylvania Regional Science Research Institute.

Bertaux, P. 1971. *La Civilisation urbaine en Allemagne*. Paris: A. Colin.

Bezucha, R. 1975. "Masks of Revolution." In *Revolution and Reaction: 1848 and the Second French Republic*, ed. R. Price, pp. 236–253. London: Croom Helm.

Biddle, M. 1976. "Towns." In *The Archeology of Anglo-Saxon England*, ed. D. Wilson, pp. 99–150. Cambridge: Cambridge University Press.

Bird, J. H. 1977. *Centrality and Cities*. London: Routledge and Kegan Paul.

Blaschke, K. 1967. *Bevölkerungsgeschichte von Sachsen bis zur industriellen Revolution*. Weimar: Boehlau.

Blom, G. A., ed. 1977. *Urbaniseringsprocessen i Norden*. 3 vols. Oslo: Universitetsforl.

Blumenfeld, H. 1967. *The Modern Metropolis*. Cambridge, Mass.: MIT Press.

Boal, F. W. 1971. "Territoriality and Class: A Study of Two Residential Areas in Belfast." *Irish Geography* 6:229–248.

Bora, G. 1976. "Regional Development Structure and the Development of Urban Systems in Hungary." *Papers of the Regional Science Association* 36:133–145.

Bortolotti, L. 1979. *Storia, Città e Territorio*. Milan: F. Angeli.

Boulding, K. 1956. "General Systems Theory: The Skeleton of Science." *Management Science* 2:197–207.

Bourne, L. S., and J. W. Simmons, eds. 1978. *Systems of Cities: Readings on Structure, Growth and Policy*. New York: Oxford University Press.

Boutruche, R. 1966. *Bordeaux de 1453 à 1715*. Vol 4 of *Histoire de Bordeaux*, ed. C. Higounet. Bordeaux: Fédération Historique du Sud-Ouest.

Bouvier, J. 1961. *Le Crédit Lyonnais de 1863 à 1882*. Paris: SEVPEN.

Braudel, F. 1967. *Civilisation matérielle et capitalisme*. Paris: A. Colin. Rev. as vol. 1 of Braudel (1979).

——— 1966. *The Mediterranean and the Mediterranean World in the Age of Philip II*. 2 vols. 2nd rev. ed. Reprint in English trans. New York: Harper and Row, 1975.

——— 1979. *Civilisation matérielle, économie et capitalisme*. 3 vols. Paris: A. Colin.

Braudel, F., and F. Spooner. 1967. "Prices in Europe from 1450 to 1750." In *Cambridge Economic History of Europe*, vol. 4, ed. E. E. Rich and C. H. Wilson, pp. 378–486. Cambridge: Cambridge University Press.

Braun, R. 1960. *Industrialisierung und Volksleben: Die Veränderung der Lebensformen in einem ländlichen Industriegebiet vor 1800*. Zurich: E. Rentsch.

Briggs, A. 1963. *Victorian Cities*. New York: Harper and Row.

Brown, A. A., and E. Neuberger. 1977. *Internal Migration: A Comparative Perspective*. New York: Academic Press.

Brown, A. E., ed. 1970. *The Growth of Leicester*. Leicester: Leicester University Press.

Brown, A. J. 1972. *The Framework of Regional Economics in Great Britain*. Cambridge: Cambridge University Press.

Brucker, G. A. 1968. "The Ciompi Revolution." In *Florentine Studies*, ed. N. Rubenstein, pp. 314–356. Evanston, Ill.: Northwestern University Press.

Brüggemeier, F. J., and L. Niethammer. 1978. "Schlafgänger, Schnapskasinos und schwerindustrielle Kolonie." In *Fabrik-Familie-Feierabend*, ed. J. Reulecke and W. Weber, pp. 135–175. Wuppertal: Hammer.

Brugmans, H., and C. H. Peters. 1909. *Oud-Nederlandsche Steden*, vol. 1. Leiden: Sijthoff.

Buchanan, J. M., R. D. Tollison, and G. Tullock. 1980. *Toward a Theory of the*

Rent-Seeking Society. College Station, Tex.: Texas A&M University Press.

Bur, M. 1972. "Remarques sur les plus anciens documents concernant les foires de Champagne." In *Les Villes: Contributions à l'étude de leur développement en fonction de l'évolution économique*, pp. 45–62. Reims: Faculté de Lettres et de Sciences Humaines.

Burghardt, A. F. 1971. "A Hypothesis about Gateway Cities." *Annals of the Association of American Geographers* 61(2):269–285.

Burke, G. L. 1956. *The Making of Dutch Towns: A Study in Urban Development from the Tenth to the Seventeenth Centuries*. London: Cleaver-Hume.

———— 1971. *Towns in the Making*. London: Edward Arnold.

Burke, P. 1974. *Venice and Amsterdam: A Study of 17th Century Elites*. London: T. Smith.

———— 1975. "Some Reflections on the Pre-industrial City." In *Urban History Yearbook*, pp. 14–20. Leicester: Leicester University Press.

———— 1978. *Popular Culture in Early Modern Europe*. London: T. Smith.

Burnett, J. 1978. *A Social History of Housing*. Newton Abbott, England: David and Charles.

Busch, O. 1971, 1977. *Industrialisierung und Gewerbe im Raum Berlin/Brandenburg*. Band 1, *1800–1850*. Band 2, *1800–1875*. Berlin: Colloquium.

Butel, M. 1975. "Les Aires commerciales européennes et coloniales de Bordeaux au XVIIIe siècle." In *Aires et structures du commerce français au XVIIIe siècle*, ed. P. Léon, pp. 107–134. Lyon: Centre d'Histoire Economique et Sociale du Sud-Ouest.

Butlin, R. A., ed. 1977. *The Development of the Irish Town*. London: Croom Helm.

Cairncross, A. K. 1949. "Internal Migration in Victorian England." *Manchester School of Economics and Social Studies* 1949(17):67–81.

Cameron, R. 1961. *France and the Economic Development of Europe, 1800–1914*. Princeton: Princeton University Press.

————, ed. 1967. *Banking in the Early Stages of Industrialization*. New York: Oxford University Press.

Caracciolo, A. 1981. "Some Examples of Analyzing the Process of Urbanization: Northern Italy, Eighteenth to Twentieth Centuries." In *Patterns of European Urbanization since 1500*, ed. H. Schmal, pp. 131–141. London: Croom Helm.

Carrière, F., and P. Pinchemel. 1963. *Le Fait urbain en France*. Paris: A. Colin.

Carter, F. W. 1975. "Č-K-D Employees, Prague, 1871–1920: Some Aspects of Their Geographical Distribution." *Journal of Historical Geography* 1(1):61–97.

————, ed. 1977. *An Historical Geography of the Balkans*. New York and London: Academic Press.

Carter, H. 1966. *The Towns of Wales: A Study in Urban Geography*. Cardiff: University of Wales Press.

———— 1969. *The Growth of the Welsh City System*. Cardiff: University of Wales.

———— 1970. "The Urban Hierarchy and Historical Geography: A Reconsideration with Reference to Northeast Wales." In *Geographical Interpretations of Historical Sources*, ed. A. R. H. Baker, J. D. Hamshere, and J. Langton, pp. 269–290. London: David and Charles.

———— 1976. *The Study of Urban Geography*. 2nd ed. London: Edward Arnold.

——— 1978. "Towns and Urban Systems, 1730–1900." In *An Historical Geography of England and Wales*, ed. R. A. Dodgshon and R. A. Butlin, pp. 367–400. London and New York: Academic Press.

Carter, H., and W. K. D. Davies. 1970. *Urban Essays: Studies in the Geography of Wales*. Harlow, England: Longman.

Castells, M. 1977. *The Urban Question: A Marxist Approach*. London: Edward Arnold.

Cayez, P. 1978. *Métiers jacquard et hauts fourneaux*. Lyon: Presses Universitaires de Lyon.

——— 1981. "Une Proto-industrialisation décalée: La Ruralisation de la soierie lyonnaise dans la première moitié du XIXe siècle." *Revue du Nord* 63(248):95–104. Numéro spécial: Aux Origines de la révolution industrielle, 2nd fasc.

Chalkin, C. W. 1974a. *The Provincial Towns of Georgian England*. London: Edward Arnold.

——— 1974b. "The Making of Some New Towns, 1600–1720." In *Rural Change and Urban Growth, 1500–1800*, ed. C. W. Chalkin and M. A. Havinden, pp. 229–252. London: Longman.

Chandler, T., and G. Fox. 1974. *3000 Years of Urban Growth*. New York: Academic Press.

Charanis, P. 1972. *Studies on the Demography of the Byzantine Empire: Collected Studies*. London: Variorum Reprints.

Charrier, J. B. 1970. *Citadins et ruraux*. Paris: Presses Universitaires de France.

Chartier, R., and H. Neveux. 1981. "La Ville dominante et soumise." In *Histoire de la France urbaine*. Vol. 3, *La Ville classique*, ed. G. Duby, pp. 16–285. Paris: Seuil.

Chassagne, S. 1981. "Aspects des phénomènes d'industrialisation dans les campagnes françaises au XIXe siècle." *Revue du Nord* 63(248):35–58. Numéro spécial: Aux Origines de la révolution industrielle, 2nd fasc.

Chastel, A. 1964. "Du Paris de Haussmann au Paris d'aujourd'hui." In *Paris: Présent et avenir d'une capitale*, pp. 1–28. Paris: Institut Pédagogique National.

Chatelain, A. 1969. "Migrations et domesticité féminine urbaine en France, XVIIIe–XXe siècles." *Revue d'Histoire Economique et Sociale* 1969(4):506–528.

——— 1976. *Les Migrants temporaires en France de 1800 à 1914*. 2 vols. Lille: Publications de l'Université de Lille III.

Chaunu, P. 1966. *La Civilisation de l'Europe classique*. Paris: Arthaud.

Chaussinand-Nogaret, G. 1981. "La Ville jacobine et balzacienne." In *Histoire de la France urbaine*. Vol. 3, *La Ville classique*, ed. G. Duby, pp. 539–631. Paris: Seuil.

Chevalier, L. 1958. *Classes laborieuses et classes dangereuses à Paris pendant la première moitié du XIXe siècle*. Paris: Plon.

Childe, V. G. 1936. *Man Makes Himself*. London: Watts.

Chinitz, B. 1961. "Contrasts in Agglomeration: New York and Pittsburgh." *American Economic Review* 51:279–289.

Chisholm, G. G. 1897. "On the Distribution of Towns and Villages in England. Pt. 2, Historical Aspects." *Geographical Journal* 10:511–530.

Choay, F. 1969. *The Modern City: Planning in the Nineteenth Century*. New York: Braziller.

Christaller, W. 1933. *Central Places in Southern Germany*, trans. C. W. Baskin. Reprint. Englewood Cliffs, N.J.: Prentice-Hall, 1966.

Cipolla, C. M. 1967. *Clocks and Culture*. London: Collins.

———, ed. 1972, 1974. *The Fontana Economic History of Europe*. 6 vols. Vol. 1, *The Middle Ages*. Vol. 2, *The Sixteenth and Seventeenth Centuries*. Glasgow: Collins.

——— 1976. *Before the Industrial Revolution: European Society and Economy, 1000–1700*. New York: Norton.

The City as an Economic System. 1973. Bletchley, England: The Open University Press.

Clark, B. D., and M. B. Gleave, eds. 1973. *Social Patterns in Cities*. London: Institute of British Geographers, special pub., 5.

Clark, C. 1945. "The Economic Functions of a City in Relation to Its Size." *Econometrica* 13(2):97–113.

——— 1951. "Urban Population Densities." *Journal of the Royal Statistical Society*, ser. A, 114:490–496.

Clark, P., ed. 1976. *The Early Modern Town*. London: Longman.

——— 1979. "Migration in England during the Late Seventeenth and Early Eighteenth Centuries." *Past and Present* 1979(83):57–90.

Clark, P., and P. Slack. 1976. *English Towns in Transition, 1500–1700*. New York: Oxford University Press.

Clarke, M. V. 1926. *The Medieval City-State: An Essay in Tyranny and Federation in the Later Middle Ages*. London: Methuen.

Claval, P. 1981. *La Logique des villes*. Paris: litec.

Cliff, A. D., and B. T. Robson. "Changes in the Size Distribution of Settlements in England and Wales, 1801–1968." *Environment and Planning* 10:163–171.

Clout, H. D., ed. 1977. *Themes in the Historical Geography of France*. London and New York: Academic Press.

Coale, A., and S. C. Watkins, eds. In press. *The Decline of Fertility in Europe*. Princeton: Princeton University Press.

Cobb, R., and N. Breach. 1980. *The Streets of Paris*. New York: Pantheon Books.

Cochrane, E. W. 1973. *Florence in the Forgotten Centuries, 1527–1800*. Chicago: University of Chicago Press.

Cocula, A. M. 1975. "Pour une définition de l'espace aquitain au XVIIIe siècle." In *Aires et structures du commerce français au XVIIIe siècle*, ed. P. Léon, pp. 301–330. Lyon: Centre d'Histoire Economique et Sociale du Sud-Ouest.

Codaccioni, F. P. 1976. *De l'Inégalité sociale dans une grande ville industrielle: Le Drame de Lille de 1850 à 1914*. Lille: Université de Lille III, Editions Universitaires.

Cohn, S. K., Jr. 1980. *The Laboring Classes in Renaissance Florence*. New York: Academic Press.

Conzen, M. 1978. "Zur Morphologie der englischen Stadt im Industriezeitalter." In *Probleme des Städtewesens im industriellen Zeitalter*, ed. H. Jäger, pp. 1–48. Köln: Boehlau.

Corfield, P. J. 1976a. "Urban Development in England and Wales in the Sixteenth and Seventeenth Centuries." In *Trade, Government, and Economy in Pre-Industrial England: Essays Presented to F. J. Fisher*, ed. D. C. Coleman and A. H. John, pp. 214–247. London: Weidenfeld and Nicolson.

——— 1976b. "A Provincial Capital in the Late Seventeenth Century: The Case of Norwich." In *The Early Modern Town*, ed. P. Clark, pp. 233–272. London: Longman.

────── 1982. *The Impact of English Towns, 1700–1800*. Oxford: Oxford University Press.

Couturier, M. 1969. *Recherches sur les structures sociales de Chateaudun, 1525–1789*. Paris: SEVPEN.

Craeybeckx, J. 1976. "L'Industrie de la laine dans les anciens Pays-Bas méridionaux de la fin du XVIe au début du XVIIIe siècle." In *Produzione Commerzio e Consumo dei Panni di Lana*, ed. M. Spallanzani, pp. 21–43. Florence: Leo Olschki.

Crew, D. F. 1979. *Town in the Ruhr: A Social History of Bochum, 1860–1914*. New York: Columbia University Press.

Croix, A. 1974. *Nantes et le pays nantaix au XVIe siècle*. Paris: SEVPEN.

Cronin, J. E., and J. Schneer, eds. 1982. *Social Conflict and the Political Order in Modern Britain*. London: Croom Helm.

Crossick, G. 1978. *An Artisan Elite in Victorian Society: Kentish London, 1840–1880*. London: Croom Helm.

Crouch, D. P., D. J. Garr, and A. I. Mundigo. 1982. *Spanish City Planning in North America*. Cambridge, Mass.: MIT Press.

Crouzet, F. 1972. "Conclusions du colloque." In *L'Industrialisation en Europe au XIXe siècle*, ed. P. Léon, F. Crouzet, and R. Gascon, pp. 599–603. Paris: Editions du CNRS.

Curl, J. S. 1970. *European Cities and Society*. London: L. Hill.

Curson, P. H., and T. G. Bester. 1972. "Urbanism as a Way of Life: Reality or Myth?" *International Journal of Contemporary Sociology* 9(1):15–26.

Czeike, F. 1978. "Wachstumsprobleme in Wien im 19. Jahrhundert." In *Probleme des Städtewesens im industriellen Zeitalter*, ed. H. Jäger, pp. 229–272. Köln: Boehlau.

Dalmasso, E. 1971. "Milan: Capitale économique de l'Italie." Ph.D. diss., Université d'Aix-Marseille.

Daumas, M., ed. 1976. *Evolution de la géographie industrielle de Paris et sa proche banlieue au XIXe siècle*. Paris: Centre de Documentation d'Histoire des Techniques.

Daunton, M. J. 1978. "Towns and Economic Growth in Eighteenth Century England." In *Towns in Societies*, ed. P. Abrams and E. A. Wrigley, pp. 245–277. Cambridge: Cambridge University Press.

────── 1983. "Public Place and Private Space: The Victorian City and the Working-Class Household." In *The Pursuit of Urban History*, ed. D. Fraser and A. Sutcliffe, pp. 212–233. London: Edward Arnold.

Daunton, M. J., and J. W. R. Whitehead. 1978. "The Building Cycle and the Urban Fringe in Victorian Cities: Comment and Reply." *Journal of Historical Geography* 4(2):175–191.

Davis, J. C. 1975. *A Venetian Family and Its Fortune, 1500–1900: The Donà and the Conservation of Their Wealth*. Philadelphia: Memoirs of the American Philosophical Society, 106.

Davis, N. Z. 1975. *Society and Culture in Early Modern France*. Stanford: Stanford University Press.

Davis, R. 1973. *The Rise of the Atlantic Economies*. Ithaca, N.Y.: Cornell University Press.

——— 1976. "The Rise of Antwerp and Its English Connection, 1406–1510." In *Trade, Government, and Economy in Pre-Industrial England: Essays Presented to F. J. Fisher*, ed. D. C. Coleman and A. H. John, pp. 2–20. London: Weidenfeld and Nicolson.

De Grazia, V. 1981. *The Culture of Consent: Mass Organization of Leisure in Fascist Italy*. New York: Cambridge University Press.

Delumeau, J. 1975. *Rome au XVIe siècle*. Paris: Hachette.

de Maddalena, A. 1974. "Rural Europe, 1500–1700." In *The Fontana Economic History of Europe*. Vol. 2, *The Sixteenth and Seventeenth Centuries*, ed. C. M. Cipolla, pp. 273–353. Glasgow: Collins.

de Roover, R. A. 1963a. "The Organization of Trade." In *Cambridge Economic History of Europe*. Vol. 3, ed. M. M. Postan, E. E. Rich, and E. Miller, pp. 42–118. Cambridge: Cambridge University Press.

——— 1963b. *The Rise and Decline of the Medici Bank, 1397–1494*. Cambridge, Mass.: Harvard University Press.

Désert, G. 1976. "Centres urbains et courants migratoires." *Annales de Démographie Historique* 1976:261–278.

de Seta, C. 1973. *Storia della città di Napoli*. Rome and Bari: Laterza.

———, ed. 1982. *Industrial Archeology in Eighteenth Century Naples*. Paris: Maison des Sciences de l'Homme (exposition).

de Vries, J. 1976. *Economy of Europe in an Age of Crisis*. Cambridge: Cambridge University Press.

——— 1981. "Patterns of Urbanization in Preindustrial Europe, 1500–1800." In *Patterns of European Urbanization since 1500*, ed. H. Schmal, pp. 77–109. London: Croom Helm.

Deyon, P. 1967. *Amiens, capitale provinciale*. Paris and The Hague: Mouton.

——— 1978. "Entreprise mercantiliste et dynamisme urbain." In *Histoire économique et sociale du monde*. Vol. 2, *Les Hésitations de la croissance, 1580–1740*, ed. P. Léon, pp. 197–343. Paris: A. Colin.

——— 1979. "L'Enjeu des discussions autour du concept de 'proto-industrialisation.'" *Revue du Nord* 61(240):9–15. Numéro spécial: Aux Origines de la révolution industrielle, industrie rurale et fabriques.

——— 1981. "Un Modèle à l'épreuve: Le Développement industriel de Roubaix de 1762 à la fin du XIXe siècle." *Revue du Nord* 63(248):59–66. Numéro spécial: Aux Origines de la révolution industrielle, 2nd fasc.

Deyon, P., and A. Lottin. 1967. "Evolution de la production textile à Lille aux XVIe et XVIIe siècles." *Revue du Nord* 44:23–33.

Dickens, C. 1854. *Hard Times*. Reprint. New York: New American Library, 1961.

Dickinson, R. E. 1961. *The West European City: A Geographical Interpretation*. 2nd rev. ed. London: Routledge and Kegan Paul.

Diehl, C. 1915. *Une République patricienne: Venise*. Paris: Flammarion.

Dodgshon, R. A., and R. A. Butlin. 1978. *An Historical Geography of England and Wales*. London: Academic Press.

Dollinger, P., and P. Wolff. 1967. *Bibliographie des villes de France*. Paris: Klincksieck.

Duby, G. 1973. "L'Urbanisation dans l'histoire." *Etudes Rurales* 1973(49–50):10–13.

—— 1973. *Guerriers et paysans, VIIe–XIIe siècle.* Paris: Gallimard.

—— 1980. *The Three Orders: Feudal Society Imagined.* Chicago: University of Chicago Press.

——, ed. 1980–1985. *Histoire de la France urbaine.* 5 vols. Vol. 1, *La Ville antique.* Vol. 2, *La Ville médiévale.* Vol. 3, *La Ville classique.* Vol. 4, *La Ville de l'âge industriel.* Vol. 5, *La Ville d'aujourdhui.* Paris: Seuil.

Dupeux, G. 1981. *Atlas historique de l'urbanisation de la France, 1811–1975.* Paris: Editions du CNRS.

DuPlessis, R. S., and M. Howell. 1982. "Reconsidering the Early Modern Urban Economy: The Cases of Leiden and Lille." *Past and Present* 1982(94): 49–84.

Duplessis–Le Guélinel, G. 1954. *Les Mariages en France.* Paris: Colin.

Dyos, H. J. 1961. *Victorian Suburb: A Study of the Growth of Camberwell.* Leicester: Leicester University Press.

——, ed. 1968. *The Study of Urban History.* New York: St. Martin's Press.

Dyos, H. J., and M. Wolff, eds. 1973. *The Victorian City: Images and Realities.* 2 vols. London and Boston: Routledge and Kegan Paul.

Dziewonski, K. 1964. "Urbanization in Contemporary Poland." *Geographia Polonica* 3(1):37–56.

Earle, P., ed. 1974. *Essays in European Economic History, 1500–1800.* Oxford: Clarendon Press.

Einaudi, G., ed. 1978. *Storia d'Italia.* 11 vols. Turin: G. Einaudi.

Ellis, C. D. B. 1948. *History in Leicester, 55 B.C.–A.D. 1900.* Leicester: City of Leicester Information Bureau.

Engels, F. 1845. *The Condition of the Working Class in England.* Reprint. Stanford, Calif.: Stanford University Press, 1968.

English Urban History, 1500–1780. 1977. Milton Keynes, England: The Open University Press.

Engrand, C. 1979. "Concurrences et complémentarités des villes et des campagnes: Les Manufactures picardes de 1780 à 1815." *Revue du Nord* 61(240):61–77. Numéro spécial: Aux Origines de la révolution industrielle, industrie rurale et fabriques.

Ennen, E. 1967. "The Different Types of Formation of European Towns." In *Early Medieval Society,* ed. S. C. Thrupp, pp. 174–182. New York: Appleton-Century-Crofts.

—— 1979. *The Medieval Town.* Amsterdam and New York: North-Holland.

Erickson, C. 1959. *British Industrialists: Steel and Hosiery, 1850–1950.* Cambridge: Cambridge University Press.

Evenson, N. 1969. *Paris: A Century of Change, 1878–1978.* New Haven: Yale University Press.

Everitt, A. 1973a. "Town and Country in Victorian Leicestershire: The Role of the Village Carrier." In *Perspectives in English Urban History,* ed. A. Everitt, pp. 213–240. London: Macmillan.

——, ed. 1973b. *Perspectives in English Urban History.* London: Macmillan.

—— 1975. "The Primary Towns of England." *The Local Historian* 11(5):263–277.

————1976. "The Market Towns." In *The Early Modern Town*, ed. P. Clark, pp. 168–204. London: Longman.

Ewig, E. 1963. "Résidence et capitale pendant le haut moyen âge." *Revue Historique* 1963(230):25–72.

Fales, R. L., and L. N. Moses. 1972. "Land-Use Theory and the Spatial Structure of the Nineteenth Century City." *Papers of the Regional Science Association* 28:49–80.

Fedor, T. S. 1975. *Patterns of Urban Growth in the Russian Empire during the Nineteenth Century*. Chicago: University of Chicago, Department of Geography, research paper, 163.

Feldbauer, P. 1980. "Le Marché du logement à Vienne, 1848–1934." *URBI* 1980(4):36–59.

Fischer, C. S. 1975. "Toward a Subcultural Theory of Urbanism." *American Journal of Sociology* 80(6):1319–41.

Fisher, F. J. 1976. "London as an 'Engine of Economic Growth.' " In *The Early Modern Town*, ed. P. Clark, pp. 204–215. London: Longman.

Fontanon, C. 1982. "Mobilité citadine et transports en commun: Paris, 1855–1914." *Les Annales de la Recherche Urbaine* 1982(14):99–117.

Fortier, B., and B. Vaissière. 1980. "L'Architecture des villes: Espaces, cartes et territoires." *URBI* 1980(3):53–62.

Foster, J. 1974. *Class Struggle and the Industrial Revolution: Early Industrial Capitalism in Three English Towns*. London: Weidenfeld and Nicolson.

Fox, E. W. 1971. *History in Geographic Perspective: The Other France*. New York: Norton.

Fox, R. G. 1977. *Urban Anthropology: Cities in their Cultural Setting*. Englewood Cliffs, N.J.: Prentice-Hall.

François, E. 1975. "La Population de Coblence au XVIIIe siècle: Déficit démographique et immigration dans une ville de résidence." *Annales de Démographie Historique* 1975:291–339.

———— 1978. "Des Républiques marchandes aux capitales politiques: Remarques sur la hiérarchie urbaine du Saint-Empire à l'époque moderne." *Revue d'Histoire Moderne et Contemporaine* 25:587–603.

Fraser, D., and A. Sutcliffe, eds. 1983. *The Pursuit of Urban History*. London: Edward Arnold.

Freeman, T. W. 1957. *Pre-Famine Ireland*. Manchester: Manchester University Press.

Freudenberger, H. 1977. *The Industrialization of a Central European City: Brno and the Fine Woollen Industry in the Eighteenth Century*. Edington, England: Pasold Research Fund.

Fried, R., and P. M. Hohenberg, eds. 1974. *The Quality of Life in European Cities*. Pittsburgh, Pa.: Council for European Studies.

Friedlander, D. 1970. "The Spread of Urbanization in England and Wales, 1851–1951." *Population Studies* 24:423–443.

———— 1974. "London's Urban Transition, 1851–1951." *Urban Studies (Great Britain)* 2(2):127–142.

Friedlander, D., and R. J. Roshier. 1966. "A Study of Internal Migration in

England and Wales. Pt. 1, Geographic Patterns of Internal Migration, 1851–1951." *Population Studies* 19(3):239–279.

Friedmann, G., ed. 1953. *Villes et campagnes: Civilisation urbaine et civilisation rurale en France.* Paris: A. Colin.

Friedrichs, C. R. 1978. "Capitalism, Mobility and Class Formation in the Early Modern German City." In *Towns in Societies*, ed. P. Abrams, and E. A. Wrigley, pp. 187–213. Cambridge: Cambridge University Press.

——— 1979. *Urban Society in an Age of War: Nördlingen, 1580–1720.* Princeton: Princeton University Press.

Fustel de Coulanges, N. D. 1864. *The Ancient City.* Reprint. Garden City, N.Y.: Doubleday, 1956.

Gaillard, J. 1977. *Paris la ville, 1852–1870.* Paris: Champion.

Ganshof, F. L. 1943. *Etude sur le développement des villes entre Loire et Rhin au moyen âge.* Paris: Presses Universitaires de France.

Garcia-Barbancho, A. 1967. *Las Migraciones interiores españolas: Estudio cuantitativo desde 1900.* Madrid: Escuela Nacionál de Administración Pública.

Garden, M. 1970. *Lyon et les lyonnais au XVIIIe siècle.* Paris: Société d'Edition "Les Belles Lettres."

——— 1977. "La Démographie des villes françaises du XVIIIe siècle: Quelques approches." In *Démographie urbaine, XVe–XXe siècle*, pp. 43–86. Lyon: Université Lyon II.

Garrier, G. 1978. "Les Faits démographiques." In *Histoire économique et sociale du monde.* Vol. 4, *La Domination du capitalisme, 1840–1914*, ed. P. Léon, pp. 20–67. Paris: A. Colin.

Gascon, R. 1971. *Grand commerce et vie urbaine au XVIe siècle: Lyon et ses marchands.* 2 vols. Paris: SEVPEN.

——— 1977. "La France du mouvement: Les Commerces et les villes." In *Histoire économique et sociale de la France*, vol. 1, pt. 2, ed. P. Chaunu and R. Gascon, pp. 231–467. Paris: Presses Universitaires de France.

Gauldie, E. 1974. *Cruel Habitations: A History of Working-Class Housing, 1780–1918.* London: Allen and Unwin.

Gay, C. 1971. *Au Fil des trams.* Lille: Amitram.

Geddes, P. 1915. *Cities in Evolution.* Reprint. New York: Oxford University Press, 1950.

Gerneke, C., and F. Siravo. 1980. "Early Industrialization in Gand." *Storia della Città* 17:57–78.

Gerschenkron, A. 1962. *Economic Backwardness in Historial Perspective.* Cambridge, Mass.: Harvard University Press.

Giddens, A. 1973. *The Class Structure of Advanced Societies.* London: Hutchinson.

Gieysztor, A. 1960. "Position du problème." In *Les Origines des villes polonaises*, ed. P. Francastel, pp. 15–26. Paris: Mouton.

Gille, B. 1962. "Fonctions économiques de Paris." In *Paris: Fonctions d'une capitale*, pp. 115–151. Paris: Hachette.

Glass, D. V. 1964. "Some Indicators of Difference between Urban and Rural Mortality in England and Wales and Scotland." *Population Studies* 17–18:263–267.

Glass, D. V., and D. E. C. Eversley, eds. 1965. *Population in History*. London: Edward Arnold.

Glovka Spencer, E. 1975. "Between Capital and Labor: Supervisory Personnel in Ruhr Heavy Industry before 1914." *Journal of Social History* 9:178–192.

Gordon, G. 1979. "The Status Areas of Early to Mid-Victorian Edinburgh." *Transactions of the Institute of British Geographers*, n.s. 4(2):168–191.

Goubert, P. 1965. "Recent Theories and Research in French Population between 1500 and 1700." In *Population in History*, ed. D. V. Glass and D. E. C. Eversley, pp. 457–473. London: Edward Arnold.

——— 1968. *Cent mille provinciaux au XVIIe siècle: Beauvais et le Beauvaisis de 1600 à 1730*. Paris: Flammarion.

——— 1969a. *L'Ancien régime*. Vol. 1, *La Société*. Paris: A. Colin.

——— 1969b. "Economie et urbanisme en France dans la première moitié du XVIIe siècle." In *L'Urbanisme de Paris et l'Europe, 1600–1800*, ed. P. Francastel, pp. 37–45. Paris: Editions Klincksieck.

Gras, N. S. B. 1922. *An Introduction to Economic History*. New York: Harper.

Gravier, J. F. 1972. *Paris et le désert français en 1972*. Paris: Flammarion.

Green, S. G. n.d. *French Pictures Drawn with Pen and Pencil*. London: Religious Tract Society, c. 1878.

Gregory, D. 1978. "The Process of Industrial Change, 1730–1900." In *An Historical Geography of England and Wales*, ed. R. A. Dodgshon and R. A. Butlin, pp. 291–311. London and New York: Academic Press.

Grigg, D. B. 1977. "E. G. Ravenstein and the 'Laws of Migration.' " *Journal of Historical Geography* 3(1):41–54.

Guichonnet, P. 1972. "Vers de nouvelles formes d'industrialisation: Le Type alpin—l'expérience italienne." In *L'Industrialisation en Europe au XIXe siècle*, ed. P. Léon, F. Crouzet, and R. Gascon, pp. 547–556. Paris: Editions du CNRS.

Guignet, P. 1979. "Adaptations, mutations et survivances proto-industrielles dans le textile du Cambrésis et du Valenciennois du XVIIIe au début du XXe siècle." *Revue du Nord* 61(240):27–59. Numéro spécial: Aux Origines de la révolution industrielle, industrie rurale et fabrique.

Guillaume, P. 1972. *La Population de Bordeaux au XIXe siècle*. Paris: A. Colin.

Guillaume, P., and J. P. Poussou. 1970. *Démographie historique*. Paris: A. Colin.

Gutkind, E. A. 1964–1972. *International History of City Development*. 8 vols. Glencoe, Ill.: Free Press.

Haines, M. R. 1979. *Fertility and Occupation: Population Patterns in Industrialization*. New York: Academic Press.

Hall, P. 1966. *The World Cities*. New York: McGraw-Hill.

———, ed. 1973. *The Containment of Urban England*. 2 vols. London: PEP and George Allen and Unwin.

Hamblin, D. J. 1973. *The First Cities*. New York: Time-Life Books.

Hamm, M. F., ed. 1976. *The City in Russian History*. Lexington: University of Kentucky Press.

Hammarström, I. 1978. "Urban History in Scandinavia: A Survey of Recent Trends." In *Urban History Yearbook, 1978*, pp. 46–54. Leicester: Leicester University Press.

Hammond, M. 1972. *The City in the Ancient World*. Cambridge, Mass.: Harvard University Press.

Hanagan, M. P. 1980. *The Logic of Solidarity: Artisans and Industrial Workers in Three French Towns, 1871–1914*. Urbana: University of Illinois Press.

Handlin, O., and J. Burchard, eds. 1963. *The Historian and the City*. Cambridge, Mass.: MIT Press.

Hardy, C. O. 1934. *The Housing Program of the City of Vienna*. Washington, D.C.: Brookings Institution.

Harris, J. R. 1972. "Trends in the Industrialisation of Merseyside, 1750–1850." In *L'Industrialisation en Europe au XIXe siècle*, ed. P. Léon, F. Crouzet, and R. Gascon, pp. 57–69. Paris: Editions du CNRS.

Harrison, B. 1971. *Drink and the Victorians*. London: Faber and Faber.

Hartog, R. 1962. *Stadterweiterungen im 19. Jahrhundert*. Stuttgart: W. Kohlhammer.

Haufe, H. 1936. *Die Bevölkerung Europas*. Berlin: Junker und Dünnhaupt.

Hauser, P. M., ed. 1965. *The Study of Urbanization*. New York: Wiley.

Head, G. 1835. *A Home Tour through the Manufacturing Districts of England in the Summer of 1835*. Reprint of 2nd ed. New York: A. M. Kelley, 1968.

Hechter, M., and W. Brustein. 1980. "Regional Modes of Production and Patterns of State Formation in Western Europe." *American Journal of Sociology* 85:1061–94.

Heers, J. 1977. *Family Clans in the Middle Ages*. Amsterdam and New York: North-Holland.

Hegemann, W. 1930. *Das steinerne Berlin*. Reprint. Berlin: Ullstein, 1963.

Helleiner, K. F. 1967. "The Population of Europe from the Black Death to the Eve of the Vital Revolution." In *Cambridge Economic History of Europe*. Vol. 4, ed. E. E. Rich and C. H. Wilson, pp. 1–95. Cambridge: Cambridge University Press.

Henry, L. 1956. *Anciennes familles genevoises: Etude démographique, XVIe–XXe siècle*. Paris: Presses Universitaires de France.

Herlihy, D. 1965. "Population, Plague and Social Change in Rural Pistoia, 1201–1430." *Economic History Review*, 2nd ser. 18(2):225–244.

—— 1967. *Medieval and Renaissance Pistoia: The Social History of an Italian Town, 1200–1430*. New Haven and London: Yale University Press.

—— 1978a. "Urbanization and Social Change, pt. 1." In *Seventh International Economic History Congress. Four "A" Themes*, ed. M. Flinn, pp. 55–74. Edinburgh: International Economic History Association.

—— 1978b. "The Distribution of Wealth in a Renaissance Community: Florence, 1427." In *Towns in Societies*, ed. P. Abrams and E. A. Wrigley, pp. 131–157. Cambridge: Cambridge University Press.

Herlihy, D., and C. Klapisch. 1978. *Les Toscans et leurs familles*. Paris: Fondation Nationale des Sciences Politiques (Ecole des Hautes Etudes en Sciences Sociales).

Hibbert, A. B. 1978. "The Origins of the Medieval Town Patriciate." In *Towns in Societies*, ed. P. Abrams and E. A. Wrigley, pp. 91–104. Cambridge: Cambridge University Press.

Hibbert, A. B., and R. Oehme. 1955. *Old European Cities*. London: Thames and Hudson. (Reprints of Braun and Hogenberg drawings.)

Higounet, C., ed. 1962–. *Histoire de Bordeaux*. 8 vols. Bordeaux: Fédération Historique du Sud-Ouest.

Hill, O. 1875. *Homes of the London Poor*. Reprint of 2nd ed. London: Frank Cass, 1970.

Hindle, B. P. 1976. "The Road Network of Medieval England and Wales." *Journal of Historical Geography* 2(3):207–222.

Hirsch, F. 1976. *The Social Limits to Growth*. Cambridge, Mass.: Harvard University Press.

Hirsch, W. Z., ed. 1963. *Urban Life and Form*. New York: Holt, Rinehart and Winston.

Hirschman, A. O. 1958. *The Strategy of Economic Development*. New Haven: Yale University Press.

Hittle, J. M. 1979. *The Service City: State and Townsmen in Russia, 1600–1800*. Cambridge, Mass.: Harvard University Press.

Hobsbawm, E. J. 1967. "The Crisis of the Seventeenth Century." In *Crisis in Europe, 1560–1660*, ed. T. Ashton, pp. 5–62. Garden City, N.Y.: Doubleday, Anchor Books.

Hochstadt, S. 1981. "Migration and Industrialization in Germany, 1815–1977." *Social Science History* 5(4):445–468.

Hodges, R. 1982. *Dark Age Economics: The Origins of Towns and Trade A.D. 600–1000*. London: Duckworth.

Hohenberg, P. M. 1967. *Chemicals in Western Europe, 1850–1914*. Chicago: Rand-McNally.

—— 1968. *A Primer in the Economic History of Europe*. New York: Random House.

—— 1974. "Migrations et fluctuations démographiques dans la France rurale, 1836–1901." *Annales(ESC)* 29(2):461–497.

—— 1977. "Maize in French Agriculture." *Journal of European Economic History* 6(1):63–101.

Holzner, L. 1970. "The Role of History and Tradition in the Urban Geography of West Germany." *Annals of the Association of American Geographers* 60(2):315–339.

Holzner, L., E. J. Dommisse, and J. E. Mueller. 1967. "Toward a Theory of Cultural-Genetic City Classification." *Annals of the Association of American Geographers* 57(2):367–381.

Hoselitz, B. 1954. "Generative and Parasitic Cities." *Economic Development and Cultural Change* 3(3):278–294.

Hoskins, W. G. 1955. "An Elizabethan Provincial Town: Leicester." In *Studies in Social History: A Tribute to G. M. Trevelyan*, ed. J. H. Plumb, pp. 33–67. London: Longmans Green.

—— 1976. "English Provincial Towns in the Early Sixteenth Century." In *The Early Modern Town*, ed. P. Clark, pp. 91–105. London: Longman.

Hubbard, W. H. 1970. "Politics and Society in the Central European City: Graz, Austria, 1861–1918." *Canadian Journal of History* 5(1):25–46.

—— 1972. "Der Wachstumsprozess in den Oesterreichischen Gross-Städten, 1869–1910: Eine historische-demographische Untersuchung." In *Soziologie und Sozialgeschichte: Aspekte und Probleme*, ed. P. C. Ludz, pp. 386–418. Opladen:

Westdeutscher. Special issue of the *Köllner Zeitschrift für Soziologie und Sozialpsychologie.*

Hufton, O. H. 1967. *Bayeux in the Late 18th Century: A Social Study.* Oxford: Clarendon Press.

——— 1974. *The Poor of Eighteenth Century France, 1750–1789.* Oxford: Clarendon Press.

Hughes, D. O. 1975. "Urban Growth and Family Structure in Medieval Genoa." *Past and Present* 1975(66):3–28.

Hunecke, V. 1978. *Arbeiterschaft und industrielle Revolution in Mailand, 1859–1892.* Göttingen: Vandenhoeck und Ruprecht.

Illeris, S. 1967. "Funktionelle Regioner i Danmark Omkring, 1960." *Geografisk Tidsskrift* 66:225–251.

Innes, J. W. 1938. *Class Fertility Trends in England and Wales, 1876–1934.* Princeton: Princeton University Press.

Jackson, J. H., Jr. 1979. *Internal Migration and the Problem of Marginality in the Ruhr Valley, 1867–1890.* Paper presented to the American Historical Association conference, Washington, D.C., 1979.

Jacobs, J. 1969. *The Economy of Cities.* New York: Random House.

Jäger, H., ed. 1978. *Probleme des Städtewesens im industriellen Zeitalter.* Cologne: Boehlau.

Jasper, K. 1977. *Der Urbanisierungsprozess dargestellt am Beispiel der Stadt Köln.* Cologne: Rhein-Westphalisches Wirtschaftsarchiv.

Jeannin, P. 1980. "La Protoindustrialisation: Développement ou impasse." *Annales(ESC)* 35(1):52–65.

Johnson, J. H. 1972. *Urban Geography.* 2nd ed. Oxford: Pergamon Press.

Johnson, J. H., and C. G. Pooley, eds. 1982. *The Structure of Nineteenth Century Cities.* London: Croom Helm.

Johnson-Marshall, P. 1966. *Rebuilding Cities.* Chicago: Aldine.

Johnston, R. J. 1977. "Regarding Urban Origins, Urbanization and Urban Patterns." *Geography* 62(1):1–8.

Jones, E. L. 1981. *The European Miracle.* Cambridge and New York: Cambridge University Press.

Jones, G. S. 1971. *Outcast London.* Oxford: Clarendon Press.

——— 1974. "Working-Class Culture and Working-Class Politics in London, 1870–1900: Notes on the Remaking of a Working Class." *Journal of Social History* 8:460–508.

Joyce, P. 1980. *Work, Society and Politics: The Culture of the Factory in Later Victorian Britain.* Brighton, England: Harvester Press.

Juillard, E. 1973. "Urbanisation des campagnes." *Etudes Rurales* 1973(49–50):5–9.

Juillard, E., and H. Nonn. 1976. *Espaces et régions en Europe occidentale.* Paris: Editions du CNRS.

Jutikkala, E. 1968. "Town Planning in Sweden and Finland until the Middle of the Nineteenth Century." *Scandinavian Economic History Review* 16(1):19–46.

Kaelble, H. 1981. *Historical Research on Social Mobility: Western Europe and the USA in the Nineteenth and Twentieth Centuries.* New York: Columbia University Press.

Kahn, A. E. 1966. "The Tyranny of Small Decisions: Market Failures, Imperfections, and the Limits of Economics." *KYKLOS* 19(1):23–45.

Kellenbenz, H. 1972. "Les Industries dans l'Europe moderne." In *L'Industrialisation en Europe au XIXe siècle*, ed. P. Léon, F. Crouzet, and R. Gascon, pp. 75–114. Paris: Editions du CNRS.

——— 1977. "The Organization of Industrial Production." In *The Cambridge Economic History of Europe*. Vol. 5, ed. E. E. Rich and C. H. Wilson, pp. 462–548. Cambridge: Cambridge University Press.

Kindleberger, C. P. 1978. *Economic Response: Comparative Studies in Trade, Finance, and Growth*. Cambridge, Mass.: Harvard University Press.

Knodel, J. E. 1974. *The Decline of Fertility in Germany, 1871–1939*. Princeton: Princeton University Press.

Kocka, J. 1980. "The Study of Social Mobility and the Formation of the Working Class in the Nineteenth Century." *Le Mouvement Social* 1980(111):97–118.

Köllmann, W. 1960. *Sozialgeschichte der Stadt Barmen im 19. Jahrhundert*. Tübingen: Mohr.

——— 1971. "Les Mouvements migratoires pendant la grande période d'industrialisation de la Westphalie-Rhénanie." *Annales de Démographie Historique* 1971:91–120.

——— 1972. "Demographische 'Konsequenzen' der Industrialisierung in Preussen." In *L'Industrialisation en Europe au XIXe siècle*, ed. P. Léon, F. Crouzet, and R. Gascon, pp. 267–284. Paris: Editions du CNRS.

——— 1974. *Bevölkerung in der industriellen Revolution*. Göttingen: Vandenhoeck und Ruprecht.

Konvitz, J. W. 1978. *Cities and the Sea*. Baltimore: Johns Hopkins University Press.

Koopmans, T. C., and M. Beckmann. 1957. "Assignment Problems and the Location of Economic Activities." *Econometrica* 25(1):53–76.

Korn, A. 1953. *History Builds the Town*. London: Humphries.

Kortz, P. 1906. *Wien am Anfang des XX. Jahrhunderts*. Vienna: Österreichischer Ingenieur- und Architekten-Verein.

Kraeling, C. H., and R. M. Adams, eds. 1960. *City Invincible*. Chicago: University of Chicago Press.

Krantz, F., and P. M. Hohenberg, eds. 1975. *Failed Transitions to Modern Industrial Society: Renaissance Italy and Seventeenth Century Holland*. Montreal: Interuniversity Centre for European Studies.

Kriedte, P., H. Medick, and J. Schlumbohm. 1977. *Industrialisierung vor der Industrialisierung*. Göttingen: Vandenhoeck und Ruprecht.

Kriegel, A. 1966. "Histoire ouvrière aux XIXe et XXe siècles." *Revue Historique* 235(2):455–490.

Laferrère, M. 1960. *Lyon ville industrielle*. Paris: Presses Universitaires de France.

Lamfalussy, A. 1961. *Investment and Growth in Mature Economies*. London: Macmillan.

Lampard, E. E. 1954. "The History of Cities in the Economically Advanced Areas." *Economic Development and Cultural Change* 3(3):278–294.

Lampe, J. R. 1979. "Modernization and Social Structure: The Case of the pre-1914 Balkan Capitals." *Southeastern Europe/L'Europe du sud-est* 5(2):11–32.

Landes, D. S. 1969. *The Unbound Prometheus*. Cambridge: Cambridge University Press.

Lane, F. C. 1973. *Venice: A Maritime Republic*. Baltimore: Johns Hopkins University Press.

—— 1976. "Economic Growth in Wallerstein's Social Systems: A Review Article." *Comparative Studies in Society and History* 18(4):517–532.

Langholm, S. 1975. "Short-Distance Migration: Circles and Flows." *Scandinavian Economic History Review* 23(1):37–62.

Larquie, C. 1974. "Quartiers et paroisses urbaines: L'Exemple de Madrid au XVIIe siècle." *Annales de Démographie Historique* 1974:165–195.

Larroque, D. 1982. "Enjeux politiques et financiers autour d'une technique urbaine: Paris et ses transports." *Les Annales de la Recherche Urbaine* 1982(14):70–98.

Laslett, P. 1965. *The World We Have Lost*. London: Methuen.

—— 1977. *Family Life and Illicit Love in Earlier Generations: Essays in Historical Sociology*. Cambridge: Cambridge University Press.

Laslett, P., and R. Wall. 1972. *Household and Family in Past Time*. Cambridge: Cambridge University Press.

Laszlo, E. 1972. *The Systems View of the World*. New York: Braziller.

Latouche, R. 1967. *The Birth of the Western Economy*. London: Methuen.

Latreille, A., ed. 1975. *Histoire de Lyon et du Lyonnais*. Toulouse: Privat.

Lavedan, P. 1959. *Géographie des villes*. Rev. ed. Paris: Gallimard.

Lavedan, P., and J. Hugueney. 1974. *L'Urbanisation au moyen âge*. Paris: Arts et Metiers Graphiques.

Law, C. M. 1967. "The Growth of the Urban Population in England and Wales, 1801–1911." *Transactions of the Institute of British Geographers* 41:125–143.

Lawton, R. 1968a. "Population Changes in England and Wales in the Later Nineteenth Century: An Analysis of Trends by Registration Districts." *Transactions of the Institute of British Geographers* 44:55–74.

—— 1968b. "The Journey to Work in Britain: Some Trends and Problems." *Regional Studies* 2:27–40.

—— 1970. "The Population of Liverpool in the Mid-Nineteenth Century." In *Geographical Interpretations of Historical Sources*, ed. A. R. H. Baker, J. D. Hamshere, and J. Langton, pp. 381–418. London: David and Charles.

—— 1972. "An Age of Great Cities." *Town Planning Review* 43(3):199–224.

—— 1978. "Population and Society, 1730–1900." In *An Historical Geography of England and Wales*, ed. R. A. Dodgshon and R. A. Butlin, pp. 313–366. London and New York: Academic Press.

Lee, E. 1969. "A Theory of Migration." In *Migration*, ed. J. A. Jackson, pp. 282–297. Cambridge: Cambridge University Press.

Lee, J. J. 1978. "Aspects of Urbanization and Economic Development in Germany, 1815–1914." In *Towns in Societies*, ed. P. Abrams and E. A. Wrigley, pp. 279–293. Cambridge: Cambridge University Press.

Lee, R. D., ed. 1977. *Population Patterns in the Past*. New York: Academic Press.

Lee, W. R., ed. 1979. *European Demography and Economic Growth*. New York: St. Martin's Press.

Lees, A. 1985. *Cities Perceived: Urban Society in European and American Thought, 1820–1940.* New York: Columbia University Press.

Lees, L. H. 1973. "Metropolitan Types: London and Paris Compared." In *The Victorian City: Images and Realities*, ed. H. J. Dyos and M. Wolff, vol. 1, pp. 413–428. London and Boston: Routledge and Kegan Paul.

Lees, L. H. 1979. *Exiles of Erin.* Ithaca and Manchester: Cornell University Press.

———— 1982a. "Strikes and the Urban Hierarchy in English Industrial Towns, 1842–1901." In *Social Conflict and the Political Order in Modern Britain*, ed. J. Cronin and J. Schneer, pp. 52–72. London: Croom Helm.

———— 1982b. "The Irish Transatlantic Migration System in the Nineteenth Century." Unpublished.

Lees, L. H., and J. Modell. 1977. "The Irish Countryman Urbanized: A Comparative Perspective on the Famine Migration." *Journal of Urban History* 3(4):391–408.

Le Goff, J. 1972. "The Town As an Agent of Civilisation." In *The Fontana Economic History of Europe*. Vol. 1, *The Middle Ages*, ed. C. Cipolla, pp. 71–106. London: Collins.

———— 1977. *Pour un autre Moyen Age: Temps, travail et culture en Occident.* Paris: Gallimard.

Leheu, P. 1954. "Le Développement d'une banlieue: Argenteuil." *La Vie Urbaine*, n.s. 1954(3–4):195–220.

Léon, P. 1970. *Economies et sociétés préindustrielles.* Vol. 2, *1650–1780.* Paris: A. Colin.

———— 1977. "Les Nouvelles répartitions." In *Histoire économique et sociale de la France.* Vol. 3, pt. 2, ed. F. Braudel and E. Labrousse, pp. 543–580. Paris: Presses Universitaires de France.

Léon, P., F. Crouzet, and R. Gascon, eds. 1972. *L'Industrialisation de l'Europe au XIXe siècle.* Paris: Editions du CNRS.

Lepetit, B. 1977. "Démographie d'une ville en gestation: Versailles sous Louis XIV." *Annales de Démographie Historique* 1977:49–84.

———— 1979. "L'Évolution de la notion de ville d'après les tableaux et descriptions géographiques, 1650–1850." *URBI* 1979(2):99–107. (Followed by a debate, pp. 108–118.)

Lepetit, B., and J.-F. Royer. 1980. "Croissance et taille des villes: Contribution à l'étude de l'urbanisation de la France au début du XIXe siècle." *Annales(ESC)* 35(5):965–986.

Lequin, Y. 1977. *Les Ouvriers de la région lyonnaise, 1848–1914.* 2 vols. Lyon: Presses Universitaires de Lyon.

———— 1978. "Les Débats et les tensions de la société industrielle." In *Histoire économique et sociale du monde.* Vol. 4, *La Domination du capitalisme, 1840–1914*, ed. P. Léon, pp. 355–395. Paris: A. Colin.

———— 1983. "Les Citadins et leur vie quotidienne." In *Histoire de la France urbaine.* Vol. 4, *La Ville de l'âge industriel*, ed. G. Duby, pp. 275–355. Paris: Seuil.

Le Roy Ladurie, E. 1966. *Les Paysans de Languedoc.* Paris: SEVPEN.

———— 1967. *Histoire du climat depuis l'an mil.* Paris: Flammarion.

———— 1981. "Baroque et Lumières." In *Histoire de la France urbaine.* Vol. 3, *La Ville classique*, ed. G. Duby, pp. 288–535. Paris: Seuil.

Lescure, M. 1980. *Les Sociétés immobilières en France au XIXe siècle*. Paris: Publications de la Sorbonne.

Lesthaeghe, R. J. 1977. *The Decline of Belgian Fertility, 1800–1970*. Princeton: Princeton University Press.

Lestocquoy, J. 1952. *Aux Origines de la bourgeoisie: Les Villes de Flandre et d'Italie*. Paris: Presses Universitaires de France.

Levi, G. 1974. "Sviluppo urbano e flussi migratori nel Piemonte del 1600." In *Les Migrations dans les pays méditerranéens au XVIIIe et au début du XIXe*, pp. 26–52. Nice: Université de Nice.

Levine, D. 1977. *Family Formation in an Age of Nascent Capitalism*. New York: Academic Press.

Lewis, R. A., and R. H. Rowland. 1969. "Urbanization in Russia and the USSR, 1897–1966." *Annals of the Association of American Geographers* 59:776–796.

Lewis, W. A. 1954. "Economic Development with Unlimited Supplies of Labor." *Manchester School* 1954:131–191.

Lidtke, V. 1974. "Social Democratic Cultural Organizations in Imperial Germany." Paper presented at the American Historical Association conference, Chicago, 1974.

Livi-Bacci, M. 1977. *A History of Italian Fertility during the Last Two Centuries*. Princeton: Princeton University Press.

Lodhi, A. Q., and C. Tilly. 1973. "Urbanization, Crime and Collective Violence in Nineteenth-Century France." *American Journal of Sociology* 1973(79):296–318.

Lombard, M. 1972. *Espaces et réseaux du haut moyen âge*. Paris: Mouton.

Lopes, A. S. 1972. "The Economic Functions of Small Towns and Rural Centers." Ph.D. diss., Oxford University.

Lopez, R. S. 1963. "The Crossroad within the Wall." In *The Historian and the City*, ed. O. Handlin and J. Burchard, pp. 27–43. Cambridge, Mass.: MIT Press.

Lösch, A. 1954. *The Economics of Location*. New Haven: Yale University Press.

Luzzatto, G. 1961. *Storia Economica di Venezia*. Venice: Centro Internazionale delle Arti e del Costume.

Lynch, K. 1960. *The Image of the City*. Cambridge, Mass.: MIT Press.

Malcolmson, R. W. 1973. *Popular Recreations in English Society, 1700–1850*. Cambridge: Cambridge University Press.

Malthus, T. R. 1798. *An Essay on the Principle of Population*. Reprint. New York: Norton, 1976.

Marshall, J. U. 1969. *The Location of Service Towns: An Approach to the Analysis of Central Place Systems*. Toronto: University of Toronto Press.

Martines, L., ed. 1972. *Violence and Civil Disorder in Italian Cities, 1200–1500*. Berkeley and London: University of California Press.

——— 1980. *Power and Imagination: City States in Renaissance Italy*. New York: Vintage Books.

Marx, K. 1867. *Das Kapital*. Reprint, 3 vols. New York: International Publishers, 1967.

Marx, K., and F. Engels. 1848. *The Communist Manifesto*. New York: New York Labor News Co., 1964.

Matzerath, H. 1981. "The Influence of Industrialization on Urban Growth in Prussia, 1815–1914." In *Patterns of European Urbanization since 1500*, ed. H. Schmal, pp. 143–179. London: Croom Helm.

Mauco, G. 1932. *Les Migrations ouvrières en France au début du XIXe siècle.* Paris: A. Lescot.

Mauersberg, H. 1960. *Wirtschafts- und Sozialgeschichte zentraleuropäischer Städte in neuerer Zeit.* Göttingen: Vandenhoeck und Ruprecht.

Mayer, J. 1974. "Quelques vues sur l'histoire des villes à l'époque moderne." *Annales(ESC)* 29(6):1551–68.

Mayer, K. B. 1952. *The Population of Switzerland.* New York: Columbia University Press.

Mayhew, H. 1861–1862. *London Labour and the London Poor.* Reprint. New York: Dover, 1968.

McBride, T. 1974. "Social Mobility for the Lower Class: Domestic Servants in France." *Journal of Social History* 8:63–78.

McClure, P. 1979. "Patterns of Migration in the Late Middle Ages: The Evidence of English Place-Name Surnames." *Economic History Review*, 2nd ser. 32(2):167–182.

McHale, V. E., and E. A. Johnson. 1977. "Urbanization, Industrialization and Crime in Imperial Germany, pt. 2." *Social Science History* 1(2):210–247.

McKay, J. P. 1976. *Tramways and Trolleys: The Rise of Urban Mass Transit in Europe.* Princeton: Princeton University Press.

McKeown, T. 1976. *The Modern Rise of Population.* London: Edward Arnold.

McKeown, T., and R. G. Record. 1962. "Reasons for the Decline in Mortality in England and Wales During the Nineteenth Century." *Population Studies* 1962(16):94–122.

McKinley, R. A. 1958. *Victoria History of the County of Leicester.* Vol. 4, *The City of Leicester.* London: Oxford University Press.

Meakin, J. B. 1905. *Model Factories and Villages.* London: T. F. Unwin.

Meller, H. E. 1976. *Leisure and the Changing City, 1870–1914.* London: Routledge and Kegan Paul.

Mendels, F. 1972. "Proto-industrialization: The First Phase of the Industrialization Process." *Journal of Economic History* 32(1):241–261.

Merian, M. 1638. *Neuwe archontologia cosmica,* ed. J. L. Gottfried. Frankfurt: Wolffgang Hoffman.

Miller, D. A. 1969. *Imperial Constantinople.* New York: Wiley.

Miller, M. B. 1981. *The Bon Marché: Bourgeois Culture and the Department Store, 1869–1920.* Princeton: Princeton University Press.

Millward, R. 1974. "The Cumbrian Town between 1600 and 1800." In *Rural Change and Urban Growth, 1500–1800*, ed. C. W. Chalkin and M. A. Havinden, pp. 202–228. London: Longman.

Milward, A. S., and S. B. Saul. 1973. *The Economic Development of Continental Europe, 1780–1870.* Totowa, N.J.: Rowman and Littlefield.

——— 1977. *The Development of the Economies of Continental Europe, 1850–1914.* Cambridge, Mass.: Harvard University Press.

Mirot, A. 1950. *Manuel de géographie historique de la France.* Vol. 2, *Les Divisions religieuses et administratives de la France.* 2nd ed. Paris: A. and J. Picard.

Miskimin, H. A. 1975. *The Economy of Early Renaissance Europe, 1300–1460*. Cambridge: Cambridge University Press.

——— 1977. *The Economy of Later Renaissance Europe, 1460–1600*. Cambridge: Cambridge University Press.

Miskimin, H. A., D. Herlihy, and A. L. Udovitch, eds. 1977. *The Medieval City*. New Haven and London: Yale University Press.

Mitchell, B. R. 1975. *European Historical Statistics, 1750–1950*. New York: Columbia University Press.

Mitchell, B., and P. Deane. 1962. *Abstract of British Historical Statistics*. Cambridge: Cambridge University Press.

Moch, L. P. 1983. *Paths to the City*. New York: Sage.

Mokyr, J. 1976. *Industrialization in the Low Countries, 1795–1850*. New Haven: Yale University Press.

Molmenti, P. 1927–1929. *La Storia di Venezia*. 7th ed. 2 vols. Bergamo: Instituto Italiano d'Arti Grafiche.

Mols, R. 1954–1956. *Introduction à la démographie historique des villes d'Europe du XIVe au XVIIIe siècle*. 3 vols. Gembloux, Belgium: Duculot.

——— 1974. "Population in Europe, 1500–1700." In *The Fontana Economic History of Europe*. Vol. 2, *The Sixteenth and Seventeenth Centuries*, ed. C. Cipolla, pp. 15–82. London: Collins.

Morrill, R. L. 1964. "The Development of Spatial Distributions of Towns in Sweden: An Historical-Predictive Approach." In *Regional Development and Planning*, ed. J. Friedmann and W. Alonso, pp. 173–186. Cambridge, Mass.: MIT Press.

——— 1970. *The Spatial Organization of Society*. Belmont, Calif.: Wadsworth.

Morris, A. E. J. 1981. *History of Urban Form*. 2 vols. 2nd ed. New York: Wiley.

Morris, A. S. 1971. "The Medieval Emergence of the Volga-Oka Region." *Annals of the Association of American Geographers* 61(4):697–710.

Mosse, G. L., ed. 1966. *Nazi Culture: Intellectual, Cultural and Social Life in the Third Reich*. New York: Grosset and Dunlap.

Muller, E. K. 1977. "Regional Urbanization and the Selective Growth of Towns in North American Regions." *Journal of Historical Geography* 3(1):21–39.

Mumford, L. 1938. *The Culture of Cities*. London: Harcourt Brace.

———1961. *The City in History*. New York: Harcourt Brace and World.

Munro, W. B. 1909. *The Government of European Cities*. New York: Macmillan.

Musson, A. E. 1978. *The Growth of British Industry*. New York: Holmes and Meier.

Myint, H. 1971. *Economic Theory and the Underdeveloped Countries*. New York: Oxford University Press.

Myrdal, G. 1956. *The International Economy*. New York: Harper and Brothers.

Nadal, J. 1972. "Industrialisation et desindustrialisation du Sud-Est espagnol, 1820–1890." In *L'Industrialisation en Europe au XIXe siècle*, ed. P. Léon, F. Crouzet, and R. Gascon, pp. 201–212. Paris: Editions du CNRS.

Nadal, J., and E. Giralt. 1960. *La Population catalane de 1553 à 1717: L'Immigration française et les autres facteurs de son développement*. Paris: SEVPEN.

Nicholas, D. 1971. *Town and Countryside: Social, Economic and Political Tensions in Fourteenth-Century Flanders*. Bruges: De Tempel.

——— 1978. "Le Développement urbain dans la Flandre médiévale." *Annales(ESC)* 33(3):501–527.

Nonn, H. 1965. *Strasbourg: Des Densités aux structures urbaines.* Paris: Les Belles Lettres.

North, D. C., and R. P. Thomas. 1973. *The Rise of the Western World: A New Economic History.* Cambridge: Cambridge University Press.

Oberle, R. 1972. "Industrialisation et urbanisme à Mulhouse au XIXe siècle." In *Les Villes: Contributions à l'étude de leur développement en fonction de l'évolution économique,* pp. 269–288. Reims: Faculté de Lettres et de Sciences Humaines.

Obermann, K. 1971. "Du rôle et du caractère des migrations internes vers Berlin de 1815 à 1875." *Annales de Démographie Historique* 1971:133–159.

Odell, P. R. 1954. "A Study of the Development of Urban Spheres of Influence in Leicestershire." Ph.D. diss., Birmingham University.

Ogden, P. E. 1977. *Foreigners in Paris: Residential Segregation in the Nineteenth and Twentieth Centuries.* London: Queen Mary College. (University of London, Department of Geography, Occasional Paper Series.)

Ogden, P. E., and S. W. C. Winchester. 1975. "The Residential Segregation of Provincial Migrants in Paris in 1911." *Transactions of the Institute of British Geographers* 1975(65):29–44.

Ohngren, B. 1978. "Urbanization and Social Change, pt. 2." In *Seventh International Economic History Congress. Four 'A' Themes,* ed. M. Flinn, pp. 75–82. Edinburgh: International Economic History Association.

——— 1981. "Urbanization in Sweden, 1840–1920." In *Patterns of European Urbanization since 1500,* ed. H. Schmal, pp. 181–227. London: Croom Helm.

Ormrod, D. 1975. "Dutch Commercial and Industrial Decline and British Growth in the Late Seventeenth and Early Eighteenth Centuries." In *Failed Transitions to Modern Industrial Society: Renaissance Italy and Seventeenth Century Holland,* ed. F. Krantz and P. M. Hohenberg, pp. 36–43. Montreal: Interuniversity Centre for European Studies.

Ozment, S. E. 1975. *The Reformation in the Cities: The Appeal of Protestantism to Sixteenth Century Germany and Switzerland.* New Haven: Yale University Press.

Palliser, D. M. 1978. "A Crisis in English Towns? The Case of York, 1460–1640." *Northern History* 14:108–125.

Palmer, R. R. 1964. *The Age of the Democratic Revolution.* Vol. 2, *The Struggle.* Princeton: Princeton University Press.

Pariset, F.-G. 1968. *Bordeaux au XVIIIe siècle.* Vol. 5 of *Histoire de Bordeaux,* ed. C. Higounet. Bordeaux: Fédération Historique du Sud-Ouest.

Park, R. 1928. "Human Migration and the Marginal Man." *American Journal of Sociology* 33:881–893.

Parker, W. H. 1968. *An Historical Geography of Russia.* London: University of London Press.

Paroisses et communes de France: Dictionnaire d'histoire administrative et démographique. Pas-de-Calais. 1975. Lille and Paris: Université de Lille III and Editions Universitaires.

——— *Région parisienne.* 1974. Paris: Editions du CNRS.

Parr, J. B. 1969. "City Hierarchies and the Distribution of City Sizes: A Reassessment of Beckmann's Contribution." *Journal of Regional Science* 9:239–254.

—— 1980. "Frequency Distributions of Central Places in Southern Germany: A Further Analysis." *Economic Geography* 56(2):141–154.

Parrish, W. L. 1973. "Internal Migration and Modernization: The European Case." *Economic Development and Cultural Change* 21:591–609.

Partner, P. 1976. *Renaissance Rome, 1500–1559: A Portrait of a Society.* Berkeley: University of California Press.

Patten, J. 1976. "Patterns of Migration and Movement of Labour to Three Pre-industrial East Anglian Towns." *Journal of Historical Geography* 2(2):111–129.

—— 1978. *English Towns, 1500–1700.* Folkestone, England: Dawson.

Pawson, E. 1978. "The Framework of Industrial Change, 1730–1900." In *An Historical Geography of England and Wales,* ed. R. A. Dodgshon and R. A. Butlin, pp. 267–289. London and New York: Academic Press.

Perrenoud, A. 1979. *La Population de Genève, XVIe–XIXe siècle.* Geneva: SHAG.

Perrot, J. C. 1975. *Genèse d'une ville moderne: Caen au XVIIIe siècle.* 2 vols. Paris and The Hague: Mouton.

Petraccone, C. 1979. *Le Città italiane dal 1860 a oggi.* Turin: Loescher Editore.

Le Peuplement urbain français: Aspects historiques. 1973. Travaux de Recherche de Prospective, 43. Paris: La Documentation Française.

Phelps-Brown, E. H., and S. V. Hopkins. 1956. "Seven Centuries of the Price of Consumables, Compared with Builders' Wage Rates." *Economica,* n.s. 23(92):296–314.

Phythian-Adams, C. 1978. "Urban Decay in Late Medieval England." In *Towns in Societies,* ed. P. Abrams and E. A. Wrigley, pp. 159–185. Cambridge: Cambridge University Press.

—— 1979. *Desolation of a City: Coventry and the Urban Crisis of the late Middle Ages.* Cambridge: Cambridge University Press.

Pierrard, P. 1965. *La Vie ouvrière à Lille sous le Second Empire.* Paris: Bloud et Gay.

Pinkney, D. H. 1958. *Napoleon III and the Rebuilding of Paris.* Princeton: Princeton University Press.

Piore, M. J. 1979. *Birds of Passage: Migrant Labor and Industrial Societies.* Cambridge: Cambridge University Press.

Pirenne, H. 1925. *Medieval Cities.* Reprint. Princeton: Princeton University Press, 1952.

Platt, C. 1976. *The English Medieval Town.* London: Granada.

Plumb, J. H. 1955. *Studies in Social History: A Tribute to G. M. Trevelyan.* London: Longmans Green.

Polanyi, K. 1944. *The Great Transformation.* New York: Rinehart.

Pollard, S. 1959. *A History of Labour in Sheffield.* Liverpool: Liverpool University Press.

Poni, C. 1980. "A Proto-industrial City: Bologna, XVI–XVIIIth Century." Paper presented at the Social Science History Association conference, Rochester, N.Y., 1980.

Pons, V. 1978. "Contemporary Interpretations of Manchester in the 1830s and 1840s." In *Manchester and São Paulo: Problems of Rapid Urban Growth,* ed. J. D. Wirth and R. L. Jones, pp. 51–76. Stanford, Calif.: Stanford University Press.

Popenoe, D. 1965. "On the Meaning of 'Urban' in Urban Studies." *Urban Affairs* 1:17–34.

Pounds, N. J. G. 1952. *The Ruhr: A Study in Historical and Economic Geography.* Bloomington: Indiana University Press.

———— 1971. "The Urbanization of East-Central and Southeastern Europe: An Historical Perspective." In *Eastern Europe: Essays in Geographical Problems*, ed. G. W. Hoffman, pp. 45–78. London: Methuen.

———— 1973. *An Historical Geography of Europe, 450 B.C.–A.D. 1330.* Cambridge: Cambridge University Press.

———— 1974. *An Economic History of Medieval Europe.* London: Longman.

———— 1979. *An Historical Geography of Europe, 1500–1840.* Cambridge: Cambridge University Press.

Pounds, N. J. G., and S. S. Ball. 1964. "Core Areas and the Development of the European States System." *Annals of the Association of American Geographers* 54:24–40.

Pounds, N. J. G., and W. N. Parker. 1957. *Coal and Steel in Western Europe.* London: Faber and Faber.

Pourcher, G. 1964. *Le Peuplement de Paris.* Paris: Presses Universitaires de France.

Poussou, J. P. 1970. "Les Mouvements migratoires en France et à partir de la France de la fin du XVe siècle au début du XIXe siècle: Approches pour une synthèse." *Annales de Démographie Historique* 1970:11–78.

———— 1974. "Introduction à l'étude des mouvements migratoires en Espagne, Italie et France méditerranéenne au XVIIIe siècle." In *Les Migrations dans les pays méditerranéens au XVIIIe et au début du XIXe*, pp. 4–24. Nice: Université de Nice.

———— 1977. "Les Relations villes-campagnes en Aquitaine dans la deuxième moitié du XVIIIe siècle." In *Démographie urbaine, XVe–XXe siècle*, pp. 185–206. Lyon: Université Lyon II.

———— 1978. "L'Immigration bordelaise, 1737–1791." 6 vols. Ph.D. diss., University of Paris.

———— 1980. "Les Crises démographiques en milieu urbain: L'Exemple de Bordeaux, fin XVIIe–fin XVIIIe siècle." *Annales(ESC)* 35(2):235–252.

Pred, A. R. 1977. *City-Systems in Advanced Economies.* New York: Wiley.

———— 1980. *Urban Growth and City-Systems in the United States.* Cambridge, Mass.: Harvard University Press.

Preston, R. E. 1971. "The Structure of Central Place Systems." *Economic Geography* 47(2):136–155.

Pritchard, R. M. 1976. *Housing and the Spatial Structure of the City.* Cambridge: Cambridge University Press.

Prost, M. A. 1965. *La Hiérarchie des villes en fonction de leurs activités de commerce et de service.* Paris: Gauthier-Villars.

Pumain, D. 1982. *La Dynamique des villes.* Paris: Economica.

Purdom, C. B. 1913. *The Garden City.* Letchworth, England: Temple Press.

Rabinbach, A. 1980. "Politique et pédagogie: Le Mouvement autrichien de la jeunesse social démocrate, 1931–32." *URBI* 1980(4):30–45.

Rappaport, S. 1982. "Social Stability in Sixteenth-Century London." Paper presented at the Social Science History Association conference, Bloomington, Ind., 1982.

Ravenstein, E. G. 1885. "The Laws of Migration." *Journal of the Statistical Society* 48:167–227.

Réau, L., and P. Lavedan. 1954. *L'Oeuvre du Baron Haussmann*. Paris: Presses Universitaires de France.

Redfield, R. 1955. *Peasant Society and Culture*. Chicago: University of Chicago Press.

Redfield, R., and M. B. Singer, 1954. "The Cultural Role of the Cities." *Economic Development and Cultural Change* 3(1):52–73.

Reissman, L. 1964. *The Urban Process: Cities in Industrial Societies*. New York: Free Press.

Reulecke, J. 1984. "The Ruhr: Centralization versus Decentralization in a Region of Cities." In *The Metropolis, 1890–1940*, ed. A. Sutcliffe, pp. 403–430. London: Mansell.

"Review Symposium: The Modern World System by Immanuel Wallerstein." 1977. *Peasant Studies* 6(1):2–40.

Rich, E. E., and C. H. Wilson, eds. 1977. *Cambridge Economic History of Europe*. Vol. 5, *The Economic Organization of Early Modern Europe*. Cambridge: Cambridge University Press.

Richardson, H. W., J. Vipond, and R. Furbey. 1975. *Housing and Urban Spatial Structure: A Case Study*. Farnborough, England: Saxon House.

Ringer, F. K. 1979. *Education and Society in Modern Europe*. Bloomington: Indiana University Press.

Ringrose, D. 1973. "Madrid and Spain, 1560–1860: Patterns of Social and Economic Change." In *City and Society in the Eighteenth Century*, ed. P. Fritz and D. Williams, pp. 59–75. Toronto: Hakkert.

Roberts, B. 1978. "Agrarian Organization and Urban Development." In *Manchester and São Paulo: Problems of Rapid Urban Growth*, ed. J. D. Wirth and R. L. Jones, pp. 77–108. Stanford, Calif.: Stanford University Press.

Roberts, R. 1971a. *The Classic Slum*. Manchester: Manchester University Press.

——— 1971b. *A Ragged Schooling*. Manchester: Manchester University Press.

Robson, B. T. 1973. *Urban Growth: An Approach*. London: Methuen.

——— 1981. "The Impact of Functional Differentiation within Systems of Industrialised Cities." In *Patterns of European Urbanization since 1500*, ed. H. Schmal, pp. 111–129. London: Croom Helm.

Rodgers, H. B. 1970. "The Lancashire Cotton Industry in 1840." In *Geographical Interpretations of Historical Sources*, ed. A. R. H. Baker, J. D. Hamshere, and J. Langton, pp. 337–358. London: David and Charles.

Rokkan, S. 1975. "Dimensions of State Formation and Nation-Building: A Possible Paradigm for Research on Variations within Europe." In *The Formation of National States in Western Europe*, ed. C. Tilly, pp. 601–638. Princeton: Princeton University Press.

Roncayolo, M. 1983. "Logiques urbaines: Production de la ville." In *Histoire de la France urbaine*. Vol. 4, *La Ville de l'âge industriel*, ed. G. Duby, pp. 25–125. Paris: Seuil.

Rörig, F. 1967. *The Medieval Town*. Berkeley and Los Angeles: University of California Press.

Rostow, W. W. 1960. *The Stages of Economic Growth*. Cambridge: Cambridge University Press.

Roupnel, G. 1922. *La Ville et la campagne au XVIIe siècle: Etude sur les populations du pays dijonnais*. Reprint. Paris: A. Colin, 1955.

Rouvière, R. 1928. *Le Problème de la désertion des campagnes*. Nîmes: Imprimerie Nouvelle.

Rozman, G. 1976. *Urban Networks in Russia, 1750–1800, and Premodern Periodization*. Princeton: Princeton University Press.

——— 1978. "Urban Networks and Historical Stages." *Journal of Interdisciplinary History* 9(1):65–93.

Rugg, D. S. 1972. *Spatial Foundations of Urbanism*. Dubuque, Iowa: William C. Brown.

Russell, J. C. 1972a. "Population in Europe, 500–1500." In *The Fontana Economic History of Europe*. Vol. 1, *The Middle Ages*, ed. C. Cipolla, pp. 25–70. London: Collins.

——— 1972b. *Medieval Regions and their Cities*. Bloomington: University of Indiana Press.

Saalman, H. 1970. *Paris Transformed*. New York: Braziller.

Saglio, M. 1896. "City Apartment Houses in Paris." *Architectural Record* 5:347–361.

Salt, J., and H. Clout. 1976. *Migration in Post-War Europe: Geographical Essays*. Oxford: Oxford University Press.

Sampson, A. 1968. *Anatomy of Europe*. Paperback reprint. New York: Harper and Row, 1970.

Samuelson, P. A. 1980. *Economics*. 11th ed. New York: McGraw-Hill.

Sarfalvi, B., ed. 1975. *Urbanization in Europe: Selected Papers in English, German and French*. Budapest: Akademiai Kiado.

Scargill, D. I. 1979. *The Form of Cities*. New York: St. Martin's Press.

Schmal, H., ed. 1981. *Patterns of European Urbanization since 1500*. London: Croom Helm.

Schöller, P. 1978. "Grundsätze der Städtebildung in Industriegebieten." In *Probleme des Städtewesens im industriellen Zeitalter*, ed. H. Jäger, pp. 99–107. Cologne and Vienna: Boehlau.

Scitovsky, T. 1954. "Two Concepts of External Economies." *Journal of Political Economy* 62:143–151.

Sekon, G. A. 1938. *Locomotion in Victorian London*. London: Oxford University Press. (Pseudonym of G. A. Nokes.)

Sella, D. 1974. "European Industries, 1500–1700." In *The Fontana Economic History of Europe*. Vol. 2, *The Sixteenth and Seventeenth Centuries*, ed. C. Cipolla, pp. 354–426. London: Collins.

——— 1979. *Crisis and Continuity: The Economy of Spanish Lombardy in the 17th Century*. Cambridge, Mass.: Harvard University Press.

Sewell, W. H. 1976. "Social Mobility in a Nineteenth Century European City: Some Findings and Implications." *Journal of Interdisciplinary History* 7:217–234.

Sharlin, A. 1978. "Natural Decrease in Early Modern Cities: A Reconsideration." *Past and Present* 1978(79):126–138.

——— In press. "Urban-Rural Differences in Fertility in Europe during the Demographic Transition." In *The Decline of Fertility in Europe*, ed. A. Coale and S. C. Watkins. Princeton: Princeton University Press.

Sharpless, J. B. 1976. "The Economic Structure of Port Cities in the Mid Nineteenth Century: Boston and Liverpool, 1840–1860." *Journal of Historical Geography* 2(2):131–143.

———— 1978. "Intercity Development and Dependency: Liverpool and Manchester." In *Manchester and São Paulo: Problems of Rapid Urban Growth*, ed. J. D. Wirth and R. L. Jones, pp. 131–156. Stanford, Calif.: Stanford University Press.

Shaw, D. J. B. 1977. "Urbanism and Economic Development in a Pre-industrial Context: The Case of Southern Russia." *Journal of Historical Geography* 3(2):107–122.

Shorter, E. 1972. "Sexual Change and Illegitimacy: The European Experience." In *Modern European Social History*, ed. R. J. Bezucha, pp. 231–269. Lexington, Mass.: D. C. Heath.

Shorter, E., and C. Tilly. 1974. *Strikes in France, 1830–1968*. Cambridge: Cambridge University Press.

Simmons, J. 1974. *Leicester Past and Present*. Vol. 1, *Ancient Borough to 1860*. London: Methuen.

Sismondi, J. C. L. 1807–1815. *History of the Italian Republics in the Middle Ages*. Reprint. London: Longmans, Green, 1906.

Sjoberg, G. 1960. *The Preindustrial City*. New York: Free Press.

Skinner, G. W., ed. 1977. *The City in Late Imperial China*. Stanford, Calif.: Stanford University Press.

Slicher van Bath, B. H. 1963. *The Agrarian History of Western Europe*, A.D. 500–1850. London: Edward Arnold.

———— 1977. "Agriculture in the Vital Revolution." In *The Cambridge Economic History of Europe*. Vol. 5, ed. E. E. Rich and C. H. Wilson, pp. 42–132. Cambridge: Cambridge University Press.

Smailes, A. E. 1944. "The Urban Hierarchy in England and Wales." *Geography* 29:41–51.

———— 1947. "The Analysis and Delimitation of Urban Fields." *Geography* 32:151–161.

———— 1968. *The Geography of Towns*. Chicago: Aldine

Smith, C. T. 1951. "The Movements of Population in England and Wales in 1851 and 1861." *Geographical Journal* 117:200–210.

———— 1967. *An Historical Geography of Europe Before 1800*. New York: Praeger. (Reprinted by Longman, London, in 1978.)

Smith, D. 1982. *Conflict and Compromise: Class Formation in English Society, 1830–1914: A Comparative Study of Birmingham and Sheffield*. London: Routledge and Kegan Paul.

Smith, D. M. 1970. "The British Hosiery Industry at the Middle of the Nineteenth Century." In *Geographical Interpretations of Historical Sources*, ed. A. R. H. Baker, J. D. Hamshere, and J. Langton, pp. 359–380. London: David and Charles.

Smith, J. G. 1979. *The Origins and Development of the Heavy Chemical Industry of France*. Oxford: Clarendon Press.

Soliday, A. 1974. *A Community in Conflict: Frankfurt Society in the 17th and Early 18th Centuries.* Hanover, N.H.: University Press of New England.

Soly, H. 1977. *Urbanisme en kapitalisme te Antwerpen in de 16de eeuw: De stedebouw-kundige en industriele ondernemingen van Gilbert van Schoonbeke.* Brussels: Gemeentekrediet van België.

Spengler, J. J. 1938. *France Faces Depopulation.* Reprint of postlude ed. Durham, N.C.: Duke University Press, 1979.

Steinberg, H. G. 1967. *Sozialräumliche Entwicklung und Gliederung des Ruhrgebietes.* Bad Godesberg: Bundesanstalt für Landeskunde und Raumforschung.

Storch, R. D. 1976. "The Policeman as Domestic Missionary: Urban Discipline and Popular Culture in Northern England, 1850–1880." *Journal of Social History* 9:481–509.

Strauss, G. 1966. *Nuremberg in the Sixteenth Century.* New York: Wiley.

Sturdy, D. 1972. "Correlation of Evidence of Medieval Urban Communities." In *Man, Settlement and Urbanism,* ed. P. J. Ucko, R. Tringham, and G. W. Dimbleby, pp. 863–865. Cambridge, Mass.: Schenkman.

Sutcliffe, A. 1970. *The Autumn of Central Paris.* London: Edward Arnold.

———— 1981. *Towards the Planned City: Germany, Britain, the United States and France, 1780–1914.* Oxford: Blackwell.

————, ed. 1984. *The Metropolis, 1890–1940.* London: Mansell.

Suttles, G. D. 1968. *The Social Order of the Slum: Ethnicity and Territory in the Inner City.* Chicago: University of Chicago Press.

Teisseyre-Sallmann, L. 1980. "Urbanisme et société: L'Exemple de Nîmes aux XVIIe et XVIIIe siècles." *Annales(ESC)* 35(5):965–986.

Tennyson, A. 1911. *The Works of Alfred Lord Tennyson.* London: Macmillan.

Texier, E. 1851. *Tableau de Paris.* 2 vols. Paris: Paulin et Le Chevalier.

Thienel, I. 1973. *Städtewachstum im Industrialisierungsprozess des 19. Jahrhunderts.* Berlin: de Gruyter.

Thomas, B. 1972. *Migration and Urban Development.* London: Methuen.

Thomas, D. S. 1941. *Social and Economic Aspects of Swedish Population Movements, 1750–1933.* New York: Macmillan.

Thompson, E. P. 1963. *The Making of the English Working Class.* New York: Pantheon Books.

Thompson, F. M. L. 1974. *Hampstead: Building a Borough, 1650–1964.* London: Routledge and Kegan Paul.

Thompson, I. B. 1965. "A Review of Problems of Economic and Urban Development in the Northern Coalfields of France." *Southampton Research Series in Geography* 1965:31–60.

Thrupp, S. 1961–1962. "The Creativity of Cities: A Review Article." *Comparative Studies in Society and History* 4:53–64.

Tikhomirov, M. N. 1959. *The Towns of Ancient Russia.* Moscow: Foreign Language Publishing House.

Tilly, C. 1972. "How Protest Modernized France." In *The Dimensions of Quantitative Research in History,* ed. W. Aydelotte, A. Bogue, and R. Fogel, pp. 192–255. Princeton: Princeton University Press.

————, ed. 1975. *The Formation of National States in Western Europe.* Princeton: Princeton University Press.

—— 1976. "Migration in Modern European History." Ann Arbor, Mich.: Center for the Study of Social Organization.

——, ed. 1978. *Historical Studies of Changing Fertility*. Princeton: Princeton University Press.

—— 1979. "The Demographic Origins of the European Proletariat." Ann Arbor, Mich.: Center for the Study of Social Organization.

Tilly, C., and L. H. Lees. 1974. "Le Peuple de juin 1848." *Annales(ESC)* 29(5):1061–91.

Tilly, C., L. Tilly, and R. Tilly. 1975. *The Rebellious Century, 1830–1930*. Cambridge, Mass.: Harvard University Press.

Tilly, L. A. 1972a. "La Révolte frumentaire: Forme de conflit politique en France." *Annales(ESC)* 27(3):731–757.

—— 1972b. "I Fatti di Maggio: The Working Class of Milan and the Rebellion of 1898." In *Modern European Social History*, ed. R. J. Bezucha, pp. 124–158. Lexington, Mass.: D. C. Heath.

—— 1973. "The Working Class of Milan, 1881–1911." Ph.D. diss., Toronto University.

Tilly, L. A., and J. W. Scott. 1978. *Women, Work and the Family*. New York: Holt, Rinehart and Winston.

Tinbergen, J. 1968. "The Hierarchy Model of the Size Distribution of Centres." *Papers and Proceedings of the Regional Science Association* 20:65–68.

Tipton, F. B., Jr. 1976. *Regional Variations in the Economic Development of Germany during the Nineteenth Century*. Middletown, Conn.: Wesleyan University Press.

Toynbee, A., ed. 1967. *Cities of Destiny*. London: Thames and Hudson.

Trenard, L. 1970. *Histoire de Lille*. Vol. 1, *Des Origines à l'avènement de Charles Quint*. Lille: Giard.

Troedsson, C. B. 1959. *The Growth of the Western City during the Middle Ages*. Göteborg, Sweden: Transactions of the Chalmers University of Technology, 217.

Tsuru, S. 1963. "The Economic Significance of Cities." In *The Historian and the City*, ed. O. Handlin and J. Burchard, pp. 44–55. Cambridge, Mass.: MIT Press.

Tugault, Y. 1975. *Fécondité et urbanisation*. Paris: Presses Universitaires de France.

Tunnard, C. 1953. *The City of Man*. New York: Scribners.

Vance, J. E., Jr. 1970. *The Merchant's World: The Geography of Wholesaling*. Englewood Cliffs, N.J.: Prentice-Hall.

—— 1971. "Land Assignment in the Precapitalist, Capitalist, and Postcapitalist City." *Economic Geography* 47:101–120.

—— 1975. "Cities of External Trade in a Feudal Countryside." *Journal of Urban History* 1:484–488. (Review of Russell, 1972b.)

—— 1976. "Institutional Forces that Shape the City." In *Social Areas in Cities*. Vol. 1, *Spatial Processes and Forms*, ed. D. T. Herbert, and R. J. Johnson, pp. 81–109. New York: Wiley.

—— 1977. *This Scene of Man*. New York: Harper and Row.

van der Wee, H. 1975. "Structural Changes and Specialization in the Industry of the Southern Netherlands, 1100–1600." *Economic History Review*, 2nd ser. 28(2):203–221.

——— 1975–1976. "Reflections on the Development of the Urban Economy in Western Europe during the Late Middle Ages and Early Modern Times." *Urbanism Past and Present* 1:9–14.

van Dijk, H. 1973. "De Beroepsmobiliteit in Rotterdam in de negentiende eeuw." In *Lof der historie*, ed. J. van Herwaarden. Rotterdam: Universitaire Pers.

van Engelsdorp Gastelaars, R., and M. Wagenaar. 1981. "The Rise of the 'Randstad,' 1815–1930." In *Patterns of European Urbanization since 1500*, ed. H. Schmal, pp. 229–246. London: Croom Helm.

van Houtte, J. A. 1977. *An Economic History of the Low Countries, 800–1800*. New York: St. Martin's Press.

van Werveke, H. 1963. "The Rise of Towns." In *Cambridge Economic History of Europe*. Vol. 3, ed. M. M. Postan, E. E. Rich, and E. Miller, pp. 3–41. Cambridge: Cambridge University Press.

Vercauteren, F. 1969. "Un Exemple de peuplement urbain au XIIe siècle: Le Cas d'Arras." In *Villes de l'Europe méditerranéenne*, pp. 15–27. Nice: Centre de la Méditerranée Moderne et Contemporaine.

Veyrassat-Herren, B. 1972. "Les Centres de gravité de l'industrialisation en Suisse au XIXe siècle (aspects géographiques et sectoriels): Le Rôle du coton." In *L'Industrialisation en Europe au XIXe siècle*, ed. P. Léon, F. Crouzet, and R. Gascon, pp. 481–496. Paris: Editions du CNRS.

La Ville. Pt. 2, *Institutions économiques et sociales*. 1955. Bruxelles: Recueils de la Société Jean Bodin.

La Ville balkanique, XVe–XIXe siècles. 1970. Sofia: Académie Bulgare des Sciences, Institut d'Etudes Balkaniques.

Villermé, L. R. 1840. *Tableau de l'état physique et moral des ouvriers employés dans les manufactures de coton, de laine, et de soie*. Paris: J. Renouard.

Vine, J. R. 1879. *English Municipal Institutions: Their Growth and Development from 1835–1879*. London: Waterlow and Sons.

Violich, F. 1972. "An Urban Development Policy for Dalmatia," pts. 1 and 2. *Town Planning Review* 43(2, 3):151–165, 243–253.

Waley, D. 1969. *The Italian City Republics*. New York: McGraw-Hill.

Walker, M. 1971. *German Home Towns: Community, State and General Estate, 1648–1871*. Ithaca, N.Y.: Cornell University Press.

Wall, R. 1978. "The Age at Leaving Home." *Journal of Family History* 3:181–202.

Wallerstein, I. M. 1974. *The Modern World-System: Capitalist Agriculture and the Origins of the European World-Economy in the Sixteenth Century*. New York and London: Academic Press.

——— 1980. *The Modern World-System*. Vol. 2, *Mercantilism and the Consolidation of the European World-Economy, 1600–1750*. New York: Academic Press.

Ward, B. 1963. "City Structure and Interdependence." *Papers of the Regional Science Association* 10:207–221.

Ward, D. 1969. "The Internal Spatial Structure of Immigrant Residential Districts in the Late Nineteenth Century." *Geographical Analysis* 1:337–353.

——— 1975. "Victorian Cities: How Modern?" *Journal of Historical Geography* 1(2):135–151.

Warner, S. B. 1962. *Streetcar Suburbs: The Process of Growth in Boston, 1870–1900*. Cambridge, Mass.: Harvard University Press.

Warren, K. 1980. *Chemical Foundations: The Alkali Industry in Britain to 1926*. Oxford: Clarendon Press.

Watkins, M. H. 1963. "A Staple Theory of Economic Growth." *Canadian Journal of Economics and Political Science* 29(2):141–158.

Watkins, S. C., and J. Menken. 1982. "A Quantitative Perspective on Famine and Population Growth." Unpublished.

Weber, A. F. 1899. *The Growth of Cities in the Nineteenth Century*. Reprint. Ithaca, N.Y.: Cornell University Press, 1963.

Weber, E. 1976. *Peasants into Frenchmen: The Modernization of Rural France*. Stanford, Calif.: Stanford University Press.

Weber, M. 1958. *The City*. Ed. D. Martindale and G. Neuwirth. New York: Free Press.

Wehler, H.-U. 1961. "Die Polen im Ruhrgebiet bis 1918." *Vierteljahrsheft für Sozial- und Wirtschaftsgeschichte* 48:203–235.

Wheaton, W. C., and H. Shishido. 1981. "Urban Concentration, Agglomeration Economies, and the Level of Economic Development." *Economic Development and Cultural Change* 30(1):17–30.

Whebbell, C. F. 1969. "Corridors: A Theory of Urban Systems." *Annals of the Association of American Geographers* 59(1):1–26.

White, L., Jr. 1972. "The Expansion of Technology, 500–1500." In *The Fontana Economic History of Europe*. Vol. 1, *The Middle Ages*, ed. C. Cipolla, pp. 143–174. Glasgow: Collins.

Whitehead, J. W. R. 1974. "The Changing Nature of the Urban Fringe: A Time Perspective." In *Suburban Growth*, ed. J. H. Johnson, pp. 31–52. New York: Wiley.

Wild, M. T., and G. Shaw. 1975. "Population Distribution and Retail Provision: The Case of the Halifax Calder Valley Area of West Yorkshire during the Second Half of the Nineteenth Century." *Journal of Historical Geography* 1(2):193–211.

Winchester, H. P. M. 1977. *Changing Patterns of French Internal Migration, 1891–1968*. Oxford: University of Oxford.

Wirth, L. 1938. "Urbanism as a Way of Life." Reprinted in *On Cities and Social Life*, ed. A. J. Reiss, Jr., pp. 60–83. Chicago: University of Chicago Press, 1964.

Wolpert, J. 1965. "Behavioral Aspects of the Decision to Migrate." *Papers of the Regional Science Association* 15:159–169.

Wrigley, E. A. 1969. *Population and History*. New York: McGraw-Hill.

———— 1972. "The Process of Modernization and the Industrial Revolution in England." *Journal of Interdisciplinary History* 3(2):225–260.

———— 1978a. "Parasite or Stimulus: The Town in a Pre-Industrial Economy." In *Towns in Societies*, ed. P. Abrams and E. A. Wrigley, pp. 295–309. Cambridge: Cambridge University Press.

———— 1978b. "A Simple Model of London's Importance in Changing English Society and Economy, 1650–1750." In *Towns in Societies*, ed. P. Abrams and E. A. Wrigley, pp. 215–243. Cambridge: Cambridge University Press.

Wrigley, E. A., and R. S. Schofield. 1981. *The Population History of England, 1541–1871: A Reconstruction*. Cambridge, Mass.: Harvard University Press.

Wuarin, L. 1900. "La Crise des campagnes et des villes." *Revue des Deux Mondes* 154:859–889.

Wyrobisz, A. 1976. "Small Towns in Sixteenth and Seventeenth Century Poland." *Acta Poloniae Historica* (34):153–164.

Zelinski, W. 1971. "The Hypothesis of the Mobility Transition." *Geographical Review* 61:219–249.

Index

HARVARD STUDIES IN URBAN HISTORY

	DATE DUE		